THE OLYMPICS
AT THE MILLENNIUM

The Olympics

at the Millennium

POWER

POLITICS

AND THE GAMES

EDITED BY
KAY SCHAFFER and
SIDONIE SMITH

RUTGERS UNIVERSITY PRESS
New Brunswick, New Jersey, and London

To David

Library of Congress Cataloging-in-Publication Data

The Olympics at the millennium : power, politics, and the games / edited by Kay
Schaffer and Sidonie Smith.
     p.   cm.
   Includes bibliographical references and index.
   ISBN 0-8135-2819-4 (cloth : alk. paper) — ISBN 0-8135-2820-8 (pbk. : alk.
paper)
   1. Olympics—Social aspects. 2. Olympics—History. I. Schaffer, Kay, 1945–
II. Smith, Sidonie.
GV721.5.O425 2000
796.48—dc21
                                        99-056801

British Cataloging-in-Publication data for this book
is available from the British Library

Manufactured in the United States of America

CONTENTS

ILLUSTRATIONS

TABLES

ACKNOWLEDGMENTS

The editors wish to thank the University of Adelaide for providing a brief period of special leave for Kay Schaffer to work with Sidonie Smith at the University of Michigan in the early phase of the project, and ARCHSS, the Adelaide Research Centre for the Humanities and Social Sciences, for granting her a six-month period of teaching release. We express our continued appreciation of Leslie Mitchner, our editor at Rutgers University Press. She recognized and supported our vision of this collaborative project bringing scholars from Australia, the United States, and Great Britain together to consider the cultural politics of the Olympic Games. We are also grateful to several people who offered invaluable support over the course of the project. These include research assistance of Agapi Amanatidis and Melissa Iocca at the University of Adelaide and Deborah Dunk at the University of Michigan. Their interest in the project as well as their steady and reliable assistance is warmly acknowledged. Thanks as well to Caroline Guerin, who provided excellent editorial support in the final phases of compilation of the anthology. We also wish to thank Sherri Joyner for her help with the preparation of the manuscript and Suzanne Sherman Aboulfadl for her preparation of the index. And finally, to our partners, Robert Iseman and Greg Grieco, for their bemused but unfailing interest and advice from the bleachers.

THE OLYMPICS
AT THE MILLENNIUM

The Games at the Millennium

KAY SCHAFFER

SIDONIE SMITH

The 2000 Olympic Games in Sydney announce the twenty-first century as the first modern Olympics in 1896 announced the beginning of the twentieth century. Its symbolic significance as a marker for the millennium had not been missed by the five cities keen to host the games: Istanbul, Berlin, Manchester, Beijing, and Sydney. Lobbying had been fierce, with Beijing and Sydney the front-runners after three rounds of balloting. Juan Antonio Samaranch, chairman of the International Olympics Committee (IOC), announced the winner of the host city for the 2000 millennial games to a packed press conference in Monaco and a television audience that numbered in the billions. Would it be Beijing or Sydney?

The tense atmosphere was palpable at a glance as cameras panned the taut, nervous faces of the Chinese and Australian delegations. Samaranch solemnly approached the microphone, removing the heavily contested ballot results

> [T]he solemn and periodic exaltation of male athleticism, with internationalism as a base, loyalty as a means, arts for its setting, and female applause as a reward.
>
> —*Pierre de Coubertin,
> first International Olympic
> Committee president*

> *Citius, Altius, Fortius*
> (Faster, Higher, Stronger)
> —*The Olympic motto*

> The most important thing in the Olympic Games is not to win but to take part. Just as the most important thing in life is not the triumph but the struggle.
>
> —*Pierre de Coubertin*

1

from his suit pocket. Silence fell upon the crowd of intense listeners. Addressing the camera, Samaranch haltingly announced the words the audience longed to hear: "And the winner is . . . Syd-e-ney." John Fahey, premier of the state of New South Wales, jumped four feet out of his seat in jubilation. Members of the Sydney Olympic bid committee shouted, danced, cried, and hugged each other as the news of their win hit them. Their joy in victory was shared by millions of Australians who took to the streets in raucous celebration. Australian prime minister Paul Keating announced that the decision had put Australia "in the swim with the big boys" (Booth and Tatz 1993–94, 7). And SOCOG (Sydney Organising Committee for the Olympic Games) chair Christopher Finn commented, in the overblown rhetoric popular with the press at the time, "[W]e'll show the world what freedom really means at the dawn of the 21st century" (Booth and Tatz 1993–94, 7).

"Sydney 2000"—the catchy slogan of the twenty-fourth summer games—has become a marker of the Australian nation's future. As Ian Jobling's essay demonstrates, with this, Australia's second successful Olympics bid, the country is "in the swim with the big boys." Major cities across Australia prominently display calendars that count down the days and minutes until the opening of the games on September 15, 2000. In Sydney itself a huge clock tower looms over Darling Harbor, Sydney's most prominent tourist attraction. There it has stood since it announced the opening of the grand celebration that was broadcast throughout the country. Every minute of public time across the country is a minute marked by the games. In Sydney the future is on its way.

The Olympic Games have reached the third millennium!

The modern Olympic Games were born at the turn of the last century: Athens, 1896. After a hiatus of some fifteen hundred years, the French baron Pierre de Coubertin revived the games and with them his dream of uniting humankind through an international festival dedicated to athletic greatness. For Coubertin the modern games would become a semireligious festival of order, nobility, and taste, a periodic testament to humanity's loftiest ideals. In keeping with his sense of ritual, he accorded the winning athletes titles of nobility and charged them with the sacred duty of uniting the world into one international community of mutual respect. Yet beneath the lofty ideals that he espoused lay anxious motives rooted in his French nationalism and a desire for renewed international leadership, military prowess, and masculine fitness. On an international level then, as Allen Guttmann (1992) reminds us, the games have been a cauldron of political intrigue, international conflict, and less than noble competition—from the outset.

Still there is no other event to match the drama, spectacle, and pageantry of the games or the moments of elation when the world unites to cheer on the victorious Olympians. We forget the sordid intrigue as we gear up for the marathon hours of television coverage over seventeen days every four years (and now every two years). Images from the games remain etched in our collective memories. We carry the dramatic moments with us as intimate aspects of our own experience. Olympic images, powerfully etched on our collective memories, include the following:

— The photo of Jim Thorpe returning his gold medals after the 1912 Stockholm games

— Photos of the flying Fin Paavo Nurmi checking his watch as he paced himself during the 5,000-meter run at the 1924 Paris games

— Sonja Henie twirling her best to win Olympic gold in 1928, 1932, and 1936

— Jessie Owens rising to the winner's platform in Leni Riefenstahl's documentary on the 1936 Berlin games, *Triumph of the Will*

— The news photos of Czech Emil Zátopek, the greatest runner of all time, crossing the finish lines of the 10,000-meter and 5,000-meter races and the marathon at the 1952 Helsinki games

— Cassius Clay dancing to the light heavyweight gold medal at the 1960 Rome games

— Haile Selassie's bodyguard, Abebe Kikila of Ethiopia, winning the demanding marathon in successive games (1960 and 1964)

— The clenched fists of Tommie Smith and John Carlos raised in a Black Power salute in the 1968 games in Mexico City

— The masked faces of Palestinian gunman holding the Israeli team hostage at Munich in 1972

— The breathtaking gold-winning performance of the diminutive Olga Korbut, first of the prepubescent gymnasts, at the 1972 games

— The glitter of the seven gold medals draped across the lithe body of swimmer Mark Spitz at the Munich games

— The repeated trips of the East German women to the winner's stand in the 1976 games as they donned eleven swimming and nine track-and-field gold medals

— Hans Klammer's awkward body flying recklessly down the Alps in the 1980 downhill race

— The graceful body of Greg Louganis falling as if weightless through the air into the pools in the 1984 Los Angeles games and the 1988 Seoul games

— The tasteless *Time* magazine–fed spats of Tonya Harding and Nancy Kerrigan, playing their appointed roles as tough, working-class athlete and elegant, middle-class skater and heightening interest in the 1992 Winter Olympics

— The dramatic entry of the United States' "Dream Team" onto the basketball court at the 1992 Barcelona games

— Louganis's courageous revelation in 1995 of his HIV status in his autobiography, *Breaking the Surface*

— The torturous gait of a torch-bearing Muhammad Ali as he climbed the steps at the 1996 Atlanta games

— Cari Shrug nailing her last vault in great pain at Atlanta

— Gentlemanly Carl Lewis returning to the gold-medal platform in his fourth consecutive Olympic Games (1984, 1988, 1992, 1996)

The games look radically different now than they did at their tentative beginnings in 1896. Over time the scope of events and the number of athletes and countries sending athletes have all expanded, as table 1 illustrates.

Gaps in the four-year intervals reveal the intrusion of world wars upon the Olympic ideal. The Berlin games of 1916 were canceled. Winter and summer games were suspended during World War II. Dips in the number of athletes and countries participating highlight in other ways the politicized nature of the games. Participation dropped in 1932 (Los Angeles)—the Great Depression games. It dropped again in years of the boycotts: in the 1956 (Melbourne) boycott over the Soviet Union's invasion of Hungary and United States' involvement in the Suez crisis; in 1976 (Montreal) with the African nations' boycott after the New Zealand rugby

TABLE I.1

Statistical history of the Olympic Games

Year	City	No. of athletes	Countries	Events	Male	Female	% Female
1896	Athens	245	14	43	245	0	0
1900	Paris	1,216	26	87	1,206	10	0.82
1904	St. Louis	687	13	94	681	6	0.87
1908	London	2,035	22	109	1,999	36	1.7
1912	Stockholm	2,547	28	102	2,490	57	2.2
1920	Antwerp	2,669	29	154	2,591	78	2.9
1924	Paris	3,092	44	126	2,956	136	4.3
1928	Amsterdam	3,014	46	109	2,724	290	9.6
1932	Los Angeles	1,408	37	116	1,281	127	9
1936	Berlin	4,066	49	129	3,738	328	8
1948	London	4,099	59	136	3,714	59	1.4
1952	Helsinki	5,025	69	149	4,407	618	12
1956	Melbourne	3,342	72	151	2,958	384	11
1960	Rome	5,348	83	150	4,738	610	11
1964	Tokyo	5,140	93	163	4,457	683	13
1968	Mexico City	5,531	112	172	4,750	781	14
1972	Munich	7,123	121	195	6,065	1,058	14
1976	Montreal	6,028	92	198	4,781	1,247	20
1980	Moscow	5,217	80	203	4,092	1,125	21
1984	Los Angeles	6,797	140	221	5,230	1,567	23
1988	Seoul	8,465	159	237	6,279	2,186	25
1992	Barcelona	9,367	169	257	6,659	2,708	29
1996	Atlanta	10,332	197	271	7,060	3,684	35

Source: Adapted from Wallechensky (1996).

team toured apartheid South Africa; in 1980 (Moscow) with the U.S.-led boycott against the Soviet invasion of Afghanistan; and in 1984 (Los Angeles) with the Soviet bloc's boycott in obligatory retaliation.

In almost every Olympic year, one country or another has refused to send athletes or has been refused entry into the games. In 1948 neither Germany nor Japan could participate in the London games. China exited the Olympic movement in 1958 and was only reinstated by the IOC in 1971. South Africa was banned from competition after the Rome games in 1960. Numbers rise with the inclusion of women's events (from 1900 with the inclusion of women's tennis and golf in the roster of events) and the introduction of new sports events. It was only in 1992, some ninety-six years after the first modern Olympics, that every country in the world participated, to the delight of IOC chairman Juan Antonio Samaranch, whose desire for a Nobel peace prize based on this achievement is widely known (see *The Australian,* September 21, 1993).

Even as the games rehearse a set of rituals that sustain an Olympic ideal that is twenty-five hundred years old, they are a site of continual change, of radical transformation. The roster of events changes. Sports policies change. International politics changes. And the bodies of the games change.

The World of Elite Sports and Politics

In the race toward the games, governmental or quasi-governmental agencies lay out plans to train elite athletes, those figures who will be expected to represent the country itself. Of course, there are differing commitments to the games in general and to particular sports in the nations across the globe. The Norwegians imagine themselves as synonymous with ski jumping and its culture of radical risk. The Kenyans train for the endurance of long-distance runs. The Australians expect their swimmers to bring home the gold. The Bulgarians expect the same of their weight lifters. The Austrians expect their teams to bring home medals in the Alpine events of the winter games. The Chinese watch their gymnasts of summer and their skaters of winter compete against the Russian and American teams. The Cubans, isolated through years of exclusion from the games, cheer on their boxers and their baseball teams.

In many countries the debates around national sports policy lead to major changes in the status of amateur athletics. For instance, in the United States radical changes in the number of, participation in, and funding for women's athletics followed the passage of Title IX legislation, releasing increased funding for women's sports in colleges and universities around the country. Lynn Embrey's essay "Sports for All?" calls our attention to how decisions of legislators or of ministries affect which athletic organizations get the public money and which sports get organized support. Of course, there are as many structures of support for amateur athletics as there are countries participating in the games. But whatever the structure and the extent of support, the games get embroiled in the politics of funding and participation.

Just think of the way in which the intersection of local and global sports policies is played out in decisions to boycott or not to boycott. Such decisions focus international attention on human rights issues, whether in South Africa or in Mexico or in the 2000 Sydney games. In the case of the refusal to welcome athletes from South Africa to the games during the late years of the apartheid regime, the "united nations" of the world recognized the opportunity to put one more kind of international pressure on the apartheid regime in South Africa by refusing to recognize the rights of its athletes to participate in this spectacle of progress and modernity. The united nations announced that hosting South African athletes, products of a racist regime, violated the ethos of "fair play" so much a part of the foundational mythology of the Olympic Games. In this way the Olympic Games became one very visible site of political pressure through an international event. Conversely, when, with the end of the apartheid era in South Africa, its athletes were admitted back into the games in 1992 and 1996, the overwhelming crowd support signaled not only the change in political regime in South Africa but also the importance of the Olympics as a site for bringing about international change. When the South Africans entered the field, the crowd in Atlanta went crazy, cheering a victory over racism in which they imagined themselves as symbolic participants.

But, as Allen Guttmann, Heather Kestner, and George Eisen remind us in their essay, "Jewish Athletes and the 'Nazi Olympics,'" calls for a boycott create dilemmas for the athletes themselves as they ask themselves that profound question: "To go or not to go?" And as they also remind us, elite German athletes, earlier celebrated as heroic representatives of the nation, were not immune from the Nazi's "final solution," or program of genocide. Alfred Flatow, an Olympian who represented Germany in the first games of 1896, was one of the world-class athletes to perish in the Holocaust.

Boycott decisions also focus attention on the precarious reach of geopolitics. In the case of the boycott of the United States in 1980 and the Soviet retaliation in 1984, the decision was made by the governments not to participate. Locked in the deadly conflict of the cold war, the United States and the Soviet Union used the refusal to participate in the games as a tactic on the big board game of geopolitics. During the cold war, for instance, tensions between competitors from East and West were played out amongst the athletes in Olympic pools and basketball courts as well as in the Olympic Village. Few who were watching will forget the water polo match between Hungary and the Soviet Union at the 1956 Melbourne games when battles between opposing sides brought bloodshed to the pool. Police quelled the riot. But the upshot was that half of the Hungarian team defected to Australia. Many will also remember the basketball game between the Soviet Union and the United States at the 1972 Munich games. There the Soviet team beat the U.S. team on its third try at the final field goal. The United States lodged an unsuccessful protest. Then the U.S. winners failed to appear for the ceremonies. They left their silver medals behind.

The Olympic Games offer opportunities to bring nations together—through the ideals of athletic excellence, shared experiences, codes of engagement—and to divide and exacerbate divisions among nations—through competition, aggression, and the projection of an "enemy" to be defeated. Cultural chauvinism gets imported into the stadiums and onto the playing fields, ski slopes, swimming pools, and ice arenas. Cynthia Nadalin provides a painful firsthand account of her experiences at the 1960 Rome games where she unsuccessfully represented Australia in the kayaking events. Her essay graphically demonstrates how Olympians themselves inevitably get drawn into national and international politics in an international context.

In these instances an athlete's national affiliation and national identity is absolutely clear. One is a member of the team that decides whether to boycott or not. Either one is a Soviet citizen or one is not. But with increased global mobility, the relationship of an athlete and his or her "nation" is becoming precarious. Olympic athletes now train in countries other than their "mother" country. Russian skaters train at the ice arena in Lake Placid, New York. African athletes train to compete in winter sports in northern Europe. Some athletes compete for a country other than their mother country, as the French Canadian ice-dancing couple (the Duchenevs) skating for France. Such crossings of national boundaries, such blurring of national identities, raise fascinating questions about the relationship of the colors one wears and the place one lives. What is the thing called a "country" that claims the athlete? And what might become of Olympic Games where group identity no longer determines the colors one wears and the anthems one sings on the winner's stand?

And always this politics of nationalism and pan-nationalism gets played out in the elaborate spectacles created for the consumer public. In his essay, "Carrying the Torch for Whom?" Alan Tomlinson explores how a selective cultural politics, replete with nationalist agendas and idealist internationalist themes, has always been at work in the spectacles through which the Olympic Games are represented to the world, whether in *The Olympiad* of Leni Riefenstahl or in the torch-bearing run of Muhammad Ali up the stairs in Atlanta.

As the world turns its attention toward Sydney in the buildup to the 2000 games, Australians self-consciously ponder their identity in the eyes of the world. In Australia, two significant national issues feed into and fuse with preparations for the games. One is the question of if and when Australia will become a republic, independent of its colonial ties to Britain. The other, related question concerns the nation's ability to recognize the rights of indigenous people and accept responsibility for past and lasting injustices. Several of the essays in this anthology highlight these issues. Darren Godwell, himself an indigenous Australian, juxtaposes the unabashed promotion of Aboriginal Australia in Olympic publicity with the blatant lack of concern for indigenous political issues and the all but token presence of indigenous people in Olympic decision-making circles. When Aboriginal involvement has taken place, however, as in the evocative spectacle of the "awakening" ceremony which opened the 1997 Olympics' cultural Festival of the Dreaming, it has been on distinctly indigenous terms. Lisa Meekison details the merging and management of separate and competing indigenous and non-indigenous interests in her incisive essay, "Whose Ceremony Is It Anyway?" Her essay also reminds us of the important role cultural festivals have played in Olympic history. Harking back to the ancient games, Coubertin's vision was to conjoin art and athletic performances to "show beauty and inspire reverence." Today host nations claim that the cultural festivals promote the goals of Olympism: the "brotherhood of man" and the pursuit of world friendship and peace. They also allow host nations to show off their excellence in the arts to the world. The Sydney Olympic Arts program, offering a festival each year for the four years leading up to the games, will reputedly be the biggest since Berlin. In this forum, at least, indigenous actors have utilized local agency to transform the internationalist agendas of the Sydney Olympic Committee.

Elite Sports and the Life of Athletic Identity

> [Coubertin] thought and frequently said that the distortions
> caused by exertions made women hideous, that athletics
> might impair the capacity for childbearing, that
> competition was masculinizing, and that public exhibition
> by females was vulgar.
> —Ellen Phillips, *The VIII Olympiad*

> Perhaps no single institution in American culture has
> influenced our sense of masculinity more than sport.
> —Nick Trujillo, "Hegemonic Masculinity on the Mound"

Even as the games rehearse a set of rituals that sustain the Olympic ideal every two years, they are a site of continual change and transformation. And that change can be read off the changing features of the bodies in the Olympic arenas.

The early modern Olympics brought to the fields of competition the toned body of the amateur athlete—the elite athlete of good breeding and good manners. This was one of its purposes—to display before large and enthralled crowds the rituals of manliness and modernity. The early Olympians were primarily, if not exclusively, white men, many of whom were well-educated, well-bred, and well-off. The most brutally physical of the early competitions was wrestling. But this brute encounter was carefully controlled through "gentlemanly" rules of engagement. When in later Olympics the sport of boxing was included in the list of competitions, new bodies entered the playing field—at least new bodies from countries such as the United States. Boxers were more likely to be imagined as a modern kind of gladiator, a different figure of masculinity from the figure of the wrestler. The men with these new bodies often came from the working classes and, in the United States, from the African American community. As the games incorporate new events, the notion of the "elite" athlete has had to become more and more flexible.

With diverse masculinities come diverse styles of flesh. There are the lean machines of the runners, the compact and stocky bodies of the discus throwers, the aerodynamic bodies of the swimmers, the durable bodies of the long-distance runners, the flexible and springy bodies of the downhill racers. But no matter the style of the flesh, for spectators the bodies are exemplary of the "fit body" necessary to a healthy body politic: a fit body means a fit nation. It is also a normatively heterosexual body indicating the efficient reproduction of the body politic. Spectators assume the normative heterosexuality of the hypermasculine bodies arrayed in the fields and arenas of the games. But as Toby Miller suggests in his essay, "Men of the Game," the ambiguity of the manliness of certain events, in particular swimming events, generates compensatory strategies for asserting manliness—on the part of swimmers themselves and on the part of the media representing the swimmers. Becoming and remaining "a man of the game" requires constant attention.

There are, of course, those moments when the ethnic and racial difference of bodies becomes palpably visible. Two of the first three blacks to compete in the modern games were Zulus imported to the games from the 1900 Paris World's Fair to run the marathon. On the field with all those white men, the two Zulu runners added, as it was expected that they would, an exotic element to the games. The strangeness of their difference contributed to the spectacle of the uncanny. By 1936 and the Berlin games, the black American body on the field had become a far more common body in the games. But Hitler's pique at the failure of the Germans to best Jessie Owens suggests the stakes involved in the victory of the black body over the white Aryan body. Owens's triumphant rise to the winner's podium threatened Nazi ideology. Some thirty years later, two African American runners rose to the winner's platform at the 1968 Mexico City games. Raising their clenched fists in the sign of solidarity with the Black Power Movement, Tommie Smith and John Carlos registered their protest against the degrading climate of racial discrimination in American society. As resisting icons of elite athleticism, they also called attention to the complex positioning of the African American athlete who, as C. Keith Harrison suggests in his essay, "Racing with Race at the Olympics," was recognized for his athletic abilities on the field (though subject to the persistent stereotype of the "natural" athlete) and yet off the field was still treated as a second-class citizen.

By the summer Barcelona games when every country of the world sent its Olympic "team," the many hues of the bodies on the fields and in the arenas testified to an elite athleticism that was no longer so invested in a racial hierarchy of superiority and inferiority. But it is important to remember that the playing field is not yet "level," in the sense of its being available to everyone. Aboriginal sprinters have regularly been excluded from participating in the Olympic Games on the Australian team—despite winning regional races and beating top times in track and field for one hundred years (Tatz 1987). (As an aside, Aboriginal sprinters are credited with the "invention" of the crouch start.) And we might think back to the tragic fate of Jim Thorpe, "the world's greatest athlete," who was stripped of the medals he won in the 1912 Stockholm Olympics because he had played baseball for money during the summers of his college years. As Trace DeMeyer reminds us in her essay on Thorpe and his medals, the United States Olympic Committee (USOC) decided to make an example of Thorpe as a way of diverting criticism from its failure to police the line between amateur and professional athlete. But why Thorpe? Why humiliate this young man who came from a poor family and supported himself in the way that was available to him? And why humiliate this paragon of excellence who had refused to conceal his identity or the fact that he had earned a small pittance from baseball? Not until the 1980s did Thorpe's descendants receive the medals back from the USOC.

The bodies of the summer and winter games still display their differences. Almost as soon as the modern games were reinvented, so too were the Nordic Games. Being confined to Sweden, Norway, and Denmark, however, the Nordic Games were labeled regional games. But complex cultural forces have always influenced the emergence of new competitions, as the case of the Nordic Games exemplifies. According to E. John B. Allen, in his essay on "the Nordic way" of *ski-idraet,* a demand for the skiing competitions had to build in order to justify the transformation of the Nordic Games, games requiring snow and ice, into the Winter Olympics. It didn't take the Scandinavians long to press their cause of winter games that could showcase the skill of the Nordic skiers and jumpers, "real" athletes exhibiting Nordic masculinity, as opposed to the suspect Alpine skiing attributed to peasants and "frivolous amusement seekers" further south in Europe. The Winter Olympics began formally in 1924 at Chamonix, France; but it took another six years before the Norwegians would join the Winter Olympics and accept Alpine skiing as part of the program of events.

The bodies of winter are predominantly white bodies, hailing from Scandinavia, Austria, Germany, Switzerland, Canada, and the United States, although now the bodies are those of the Chinese and Japanese as well. Among the crowds at the winter games, the understanding that the bodies of winter will be certain colors may explain the fascination with and popular appeal of the Jamaican bobsledders who competed in the 1988 Calgary Winter Olympics (and of the film version of their odyssey, *Cool Running*). The dark bodies of the Jamaican bobsledders were presented as adding a touch of "exoticism" to the event. That exoticism had to do with the spectacle of those bodies, more used to sun and sand than snow and frigid temperatures, sluicing down the slick ice tunnel.

And what of the movement of female bodies onto the courts and into the arenas of the Olympic Games? Of course, it did not take women long to make a lie of Coubertin's early pronouncement that the appropriate spectator for the rituals of athletic masculinity would be the women who could offer up "female applause as a reward." In 1900 Charlotte Cooper of Great Britain became the first female Olympic champion in tennis. The 1904 games in St. Louis featured women's archery and, surprisingly, women's boxing as a demonstration event. Women early on competed in tennis, golf, and pairs sailing, but overall the number of events open to them was very limited. Then in 1920, after the continued exclusion of women from the official games, the French rower Alice Milliat organized the Women's Olympics.

Milliat also founded the first international federation of women athletes. Sixty-five women from five nations came together to compete in eleven events in Paris in 1922 before twenty thousand spectators (Phillips 1996, 121). Not surprisingly, given the exhibition of female athleticism in Paris, women were allowed to compete in the 1928 Amsterdam games in five events—including the eight-hundred-meter race. In the 1932 games in Los Angeles, Babe Diedrickson became the first celebrity female Olympian (and one of the greatest female athletes of all time). In Los Angeles the games included women's gymnastics, swimming, ice skating, fencing, and, after heated debate, track and field. By then the national committees of the IOC had decided that these were appropriate and proper sports for women. During the 1930s women would compete in tennis, golf, archery, ice skating, fencing, swimming, and "tasteful" exhibitions of gymnastics.

In the early years of the games, women athletes had to pressure the IOC to let them compete. In arguing for the right to a place on the fields, they were fighting against the cultural assumption that the proper female body (the body of the white woman of the middling and upper classes) was a body too delicate, enervated, and pliable to achieve the kind of strength and agility necessary for the "elite" athlete. But since the '20s, when women broke into the Olympic stadiums in more than token competitions and demonstrations, they have had to contend with the identification of the muscular, fit female bodies of elite athletes as "lesbian" bodies. Accusations linking female fitness and muscularity with lesbianism surfaced in the 1930s (in the United States at least) as "female athleticism" became culturally coded as "contrary to heterosexual appeal, which appeared to rest on women's difference from and deference to men" (Cahn 1998, 71).

Women athletes have confronted the power of this label—which implicitly assumes the identification of sports with masculinity (Cahn 1998, 78)—well into the 1990s. Of course some of the events present normatively femininized styles of the flesh before the crowds. Pairs figure skating presents the spectacle of normative heterosexuality, "pairing" a masculine male with a feminine female in routinized rituals of romance. The event itself ensures the world that gender relations remain intact. Events such as synchronized swimming and gymnastic ribbon routines, however, recall the Busby Berkeley movies of the 1930s and lock women and their spectators into bizarre, anachronistic spectacles of femininity.

Well into the 1990s the labeling of girls good at sports as "lesbian" has persisted, affecting the ways in which straight and lesbian athletes negotiate the pressures within sports culture to conform to and "perform" traditional notions of femininity (see Krane 1999). Take the figure of Florence Griffith Joyner. This celebrity track star sported a signature self-presentation of overtly sexual femininity. Griffith Joyner made an excessive heterosexual femininity visible even in the midst of grueling competition. Her particular self-fashioning suggests how the coding of the body as heterosexual determines the cultural positioning of particular athletes and the popularity of particular sporting events. That normative coding also ensures more lucrative endorsement contracts for elite women athletes and greater media coverage, as the case of the differential treatment of Chris Evert and Martina Navratilova makes clear. Or take the more recent case of the French tennis star, Amelie Mauresmo, an openly gay star athlete. When Lindsay Davenport lost to Mauresmo in the 1999 Australian Open, she took a swipe at her by saying that she was "playing like a guy," a comment that was picked up and exploited by the media. Davenport later regretted the outburst and offered apologies to her devastated opponent. On the other side of the world, however, the French tabloids pictured their newest champion in a cartoon displaying Mauresmo's head on the body of Arnold Schwarzenegger with the caption: "It's the first time in the history of French sport that a man says he's a lesbian." Mauresmo's athletic ability faded into the background. Her "manly" body became her identity.

Another aspect of proper and improper bodies on the tracks and in the arenas concerns the use of performance-enhancing drugs and body-altering steroids. Helen Yeates and Andrea Mitchell study the drug controversy in their essay, "Who's Sorry Now?" which details the crisis in the Olympic Games around the pumped-up bodies of the women from the former East Germany and China. These women, filled with performance-enhancing drugs, made visible a hypermasculinized female body—a body that blurred the boundary between masculinity and femininity. Of course the use of drugs violated Olympic rules about performance-enhancing substances and was an affront to the gentlemanly ethos of fair play. But these women's bodies also became a scandal and a deceit in part because the sight of these women's bodies violated the rules of normative female embodiment. The threat of the "masculine" female body led, as Cheryl Cole explores in her essay, "One Chromosome Too Many?," to mandatory sex testing, initiated at the 1966 Budapest European Track-and-Field Championships. Since then, the verification methods to authenticate an athlete's gender have gone through various permutations. And they have been justified, as Cole notes, through a variety of rhetorical strategies. Rumors of "female masculinity" continue to spread through the games; and in the name of equality of opportunity on the playing fields, medical experts and Olympic officials seek ways to fix the fluidity of biological sex.

The addition of more and more competitions for women has brought different bodies and different femininities to the playing fields: the sleek and only apparently muscle-less bodies of the figure skaters, the flexible and daring bodies of the downhill skiers, the compact bodies of many of the softball players. Since the wins of Olga Korbut at the 1972 Munich games, fourteen-year-old Nadia Comaneci at the 1976 Montreal games, and petite Mary Lou Retton at the 1984 Los Angeles games, the world has adjusted to the sight of the prepubescent bodies of the gymnasts.

But now new adjustments have become mandatory. The opportunities for women's participation in the Olympics expanded significantly by the time of the Atlanta games in 1996. In part, this had to do with intense lobbying by sportswomen and their supporters and with changes in women's legal status; but it also had to do with rising TV ratings confirming the worldwide audience's interest in women's sports as spectacle. And as Donna A. Lopiano catalogs in her essay on the coming of age of women's sports, it had to do with a variety of other factors, including a more activist and organized global feminist sports movement and the coming of age of social justice as a global value. By 1996 women's team sports—not only gymnastics but also softball and basketball—drew large crowds. And so at the end of the millennium, multiple athletic identities are much more available to young women because of the increase in the number of sports open to women and the diversity of those sports. But Leslie Heywood cautions in her essay, "The Girls of Summer," that the cultural trends in support of athletic women can become too easily equated with the cure-alls for the social problems confronting women and can thus obscure the continuing sexism still so much a part of the environment of women's sports.

That women have entered the sporting fields and the games in greater and greater numbers cannot be denied. And that women's sports are attracting more and more coverage in the media cannot be denied. After all, women's sports now garner 30 percent of the coverage of the Olympics, although this is not surprising given that the majority of the viewers of the Olympics are now women. But, it is still the case that twenty-three (mainly Muslim) countries send no women to compete in the games. Muslim women cannot participate in public games such as the Olympics because of the religious customs and dress codes in predominantly Islamic countries (although they have staged an alternative Muslim Women's Games). And some games are more glamorous for women than others. Gymnastics and swimming draw far larger viewing audiences than hockey and archery, thus attracting more funding and sponsorship. In Europe, the United States, New Zealand, Australia, and Canada, women may be multiplying on the playing fields, but they are still underrepresented as coaches and sports administrators and in the media as reporters. Moreover, women's sports get far less coverage in the press, and far less sponsorship. Not only are women grossly underrepresented in sports administration; when they are represented they tend to take up positions related to affirmative action, youth sports, disabilities, women's events, human resources, and public relations. They are not visible in the fields of sports finance, marketing, policy, talent identification, or scientific research. Sports culture has its core and periphery. Men occupy the core occupations and positions of authority while women remain marginalized (McKay 1997, 22).

Prime Minister Paul Keating's response to the Samaranch announcement that Sydney would host the 2000 games, detailed earlier, is a telling instance of this: the decision had put Australia "in the swim with the big boys." The nation's newspapers also announced that the search had begun for "Mr. Right"—the man to head the Australian Olympic Committee. In the search for Mr. Right, a committee of fourteen selectors was announced. Only one of those selected was a woman; and she was appointed only at the last minute, with considerable embarrassment, when it was brought to the Sidney Organising Committee for the Olympic Games' attention that the committee was composed solely of men. This was 1996. And, as Darren Godwell points out, although the games purport to showcase Aboriginal culture, there is no Aboriginal representation on the committee. Godwell also examines the ways Olympic promoters have exploited indigenous cultures by adopting and beaming to the world static and long-abandoned images of Aboriginal and Torres Strait Islander peoples. Are we that much further along in recognizing and affirming ability regardless of racial or gendered differences than we were in 1896 when 285 men, and no women, participated in the first of the modern Olympic Games? The games change continually, but the direction of change is unpredictable and the pace of change is slow to the point of exasperation. The games at the millennium continue to preserve normative, Western identities even as the games themselves blur the boundaries between gendered and racialized identities as more and more women and athletes of color move onto the fields and into the arenas.

There is yet another manifestation of the Olympics as a marker of cultural changes in identities and bodies. This has to do with the ways in which the Olympic Games spawn ancillary games. In the last decades of the century we've seen the proliferation of "Olympic" events—Special Olympics, the Gay Games, the Paralympics, and so on. But this is not a new phenomenon. As early as 1925 alternative Olympic events have been held around the world. In the early decades of the century, as the world was responding to the political revolution in Russia and to the promises of socialism, progressives and radicals organized a workers' sports festival that would mime with telling differences the sports culture of the Olympic Games. At its peak in 1931, the Workers' Sports Festival drew approximately eighty thousand athletes from twenty-three nations to Vienna. In the excitement of early 1930s Vienna, 250,000 spectators gathered to watch two hundred different events, artistic displays, mass choirs, human pyramids, fireworks, a parade, and group exercises. Teams waved the red banners of socialism during the impressive opening ceremony, which promoted sports for the masses rather than the elite athleticism of singular representatives of a nation (Phillips 1996, 121).

Today the Paralympics and the Gay Games challenge prejudice, promote inclusiveness, and enable athletes to strive for excellence on their own terms, as Vikki Krane and Jennifer Waldron argue in their essay on how the Gay Games create an alternative sports culture, one inclusive of the radical differences of sexuality.

WE CONCEIVED this collection of essays as an opportunity to explore various moments in the history of the Olympic Games and through these moments to ponder the larger and profoundly complex struggles over the shifting meanings of masculinity, femininity, ethnicity, race, and embodiedness associated with the spectacle of athletic nationalism and the everyday life of the Olympics. In the pages that follow we will be reminded of particular moments. The moment before the 1936 Olympics when Jewish athletes and their Olympic committees had to decide whether to boycott the games or not. The lingering effects of that moment when the Israelis were murdered in the Olympic Village at the 1972 games. The moment of outrage created by claims that East German and Chinese women athletes had taken performance-enhancing drugs. The moment an Australian rower refused to respond to the friendship proffered by a Japanese Olympian in the 1960 games in Rome. The moment when two men glided onto the ice for their pairs routine in borrowed skates at the 1998 Gay Games in Amsterdam. But we'll be looking at these moments because all of them dramatize conflicts on a personal, national, and global scale and thereby highlight the ways in which the games intersect with larger social and cultural issues confronting the modern world.

Thus *The Olympics at the Millennium* is not a book about sports per se or about remarkable athletes and their performances. Rather, the essays here blur the boundaries between sports and other forms of public culture. Although the collection does not intend to explore all the themes in depth, the essays touch upon a number of significant and contested cultural issues as they intersect with the Olympic movement. On an international level they consider the clean and dirty sides of the Olympic ideal and, in particular, the intersection of national agendas and international politics. On the national level they take up the issues of cultural diversity and national identity. On the local level they explore the diverse ways in which everyday life becomes inflected with the culture, economics, and politics of all those processes involved in bidding for, planning, and staging the games, inflections that Kay Schaffer and Sidonie Smith trace out in their essay, "The Olympics of the Everyday." On a personal level they consider the relationship of the athletic ideal to the pragmatic needs of training before the games and to the lure of celebrity after the games. Throughout they explore the interpenetration of sports and realms of everyday life: the media, fashion, big business and advertising, and art. And they tease out the play of identity as variously embodied athletes take to the fields, the courts, and the arenas.

John Tulloch's essay focuses specifically on the intersections between the Olympics, everyday life, and the media. His piece considers the effects of media coverage of terrorism at the games. As part of a Sydney-based research team he interviewed some two hundred people to study the impact of television coverage of terrorist activities on their everyday lives. For many Australians, memories of Munich fuel fears for Sydney 2000. The essay maps out what he calls their "landscapes of fear." Excerpts from interviews reveal a fascinating spectrum of different perceptions of terror, perceptions which draw on different aspects of the social, environmental, and biographic identities of people interviewed.

Issues raised in the media attach themselves to the Olympics in ways that spark, fuse, and meld with larger cultural currents, discussions of national ideals

and international competition, the concept of "fair play," drug use and its regulation, the management of terror and the lure of spectacle, proper and improper
behavior and dress, the recognition of racial, ethnic, sexual, and gendered differences and their effects, as well as the imprint of transglobal media and the flow
of forces beyond local geographies and spaces. Each of these themes reaches far
beyond the call of the games to sportsmen and women and their fans. And each
deserves a book in itself. By asking contributors to address the cultural issues which
reverberate around the phenomenon of the games, we hope to offer readers a more
complex sense of why and how the Olympic Games matter to all of us—not only,
or even primarily, sports fans—at the beginning of the new millennium.

PART ONE

CULTURAL

DIFFERENCE AND

"ELITE" SPORTS

CHAPTER 1

The Olympics

in Retrospect:

Winners, Losers,

Racism, and the

Olympic Ideal

CYNTHIA NADALIN

The many strands of this, my Olympic story, came together for me beside Lake Albano one sweltering Saturday in August 1960. The lake, about thirty miles from Rome, was the venue for the canoeing and rowing events during those games. My canoeing partner, Heidi Sager, and I traveled out from Rome to watch the events, especially the final of the Women's Kayak Double. We deeply believed that we should have been out there on the water, a part of it all. The truth was we were not; we had failed. I was wracked with shame and humiliated into silence and still-ness by that reality. The manner of our elimination the previous day had so seared my mind that I had actually forgotten to bring a hat with me from the Olympic Village. Nor did I have my purse. But that was no big deal. There was no money in it anyway. I had used my last two shillings three days before. I would have to wait another four days before the team members received their allowances from the team's office staff. I thought at the time that money was unimportant com-pared to what had happened to us the day before. I was never more wrong about anything.

The Italians had erected a bamboo awning along the edge of the lake to cre-ate some shade for the athletes and officials. They had also placed metal chairs in the shallow water, allowing people to remove their footwear and dabble their feet and lower legs in the cool water. It was a consideration and kindness for which I still bless the Italians. It was there in the shade of the awning, on the outer edge

FIGURE 1.1

Front, Heidi Sager and, rear, Cynthia Nadalin training on Albert Park
Lake in preparation for the ladies kayak doubles event in Rome 1960.

Courtesy of the *Age* (Melbourne).

of the joking, laughing crowd, that I allowed the words of our coach to filter through my mind. It was there where I experienced the incident which would haunt my Olympic memories for the next thirty years.

Although Rome was our first international competition, our coach, a defector from a top canoeing nation in eastern Europe, had prepared us well. A recent world champion and Olympic competitor himself, he was the reason that we two young women, seemingly isolated in Australia, had access to the most recent training methods, information, and psychological techniques then available to women in Australia. We had been superbly conditioned and knew that our Olympic qualifying trial time, done in early 1960, had placed us fifth among the nations entered in our event in Rome. It was a time well inside the qualifying standard set by the IOC.

Our coach, well attuned to what the Europeans and Americans were doing in our event, had really made us believe in ourselves, not only because of our qualifying time in the trial but because we turned in such times constantly. We had every reason to believe that, with a little luck, we might get beyond a fifth place at Rome. A mere position in the Olympic final was a worst-case scenario. He had us train with and against male paddlers all the time. From that training we knew that we had a blinding fast start and had mastered the skill of controlling our stamina and minds during the demanding middle section of a race. We had also learned how to fight out a finish, I mean *really* fight a finish, right down to tooth and claw if necessary. Yet it had all gone wrong. We had to wear the responsibility for that, or so we believed.

Before leaving Melbourne for the games our trainer reminded us of our strengths. However, he could not take his mind off the fact that we would not have our own kayak double to train or race in at the games. Financial pressures, especially for me, meant that we could not afford to transport our boat to Rome. The Australian Olympic Federation refused to pay for such items, stating that transport costs of such essential equipment had to be borne by the sports federations or the competitors themselves. The Olympic Federation justified such tight-fistedness by reminding competitors they were amateurs and, as such, could not receive such help from anywhere. The canoeing team manager, based in Sydney, informed us that he had arranged with some male paddlers from that city to allow us to use their training boat, but, naturally, only when and if they did not want it. It was the best that could be done for us. We accepted that offer rather than forgo competition at the games altogether.

These matters drifted through my mind as I sat in the shade of the bamboo awning beside Lake Albano. Deep in thought, I initially failed to notice some soft drink and gelato vendors coming toward us. If I had noticed them earlier, I would have moved away to the nearby water fountains, thus covering the fact I had no money. But situated on the edge of the crowd, further out in the water than most, I could not pass through those gathered without upsetting everyone there. Consequently, I sat quietly as I watched the males buy either a drink or a gelato for every young woman present but me. On the part of some it was perhaps accidental, but not all. At one point a male stood in front of me, drink in hand, looked directly at me, then passed a drink right past my cheek to an extremely attractive girl behind me. He knew I had nothing and made no attempt to get anything for me. A moment later another Olympian (not an Australian as the first young man had been) looked at my empty hands from his position a few paces away. His eyes flicked from me, then out over the lake, back to me again, and then at the unopened can in his hand. He hesitated, glanced once more at me, then turned and splashed away through the shallows. Every female there received either a drink or a gelato. I was passed over. In the coolness of the present I am not angered by the actual selective behavior as such. I am angry that even now I still come across males who seem to believe, through their attitudes and speech, that males have some sort of right to treat plain women in such a way.

I pretended I hadn't noticed what had happened and momentarily pretended none of it had taken place. But I did know what had happened and why. I was not the tall, slim, long-legged, blonde Australian Olympic ideal. I was average height, dark like my Cornish Celtic forebears and had limbs too powerfully developed to be accepted as pleasantly female. I knew I was not the idealized beauty of Australian magazines and I lived well enough with that.

However, after years of strain just to get to the games, the terrible canoe team in-fighting in the weeks prior to the start of competition, and the dreadful event which led to our elimination from competition the day before, the last thing I needed to be reminded of, in any way, was my plainness—not then, not that way. I knew I had been passed by in the general hustle and bustle of buying and impressing. Suddenly, everyone else seemed to know it too, all at the same time. Worst of all they, like me, probably understood why I had been missed. For all of us there the embarrassment was awful and the silence deafening. To ease my own and their strain I turned around and concentrated on looking out over the lake.

It was then that I felt a light tap on my right shoulder. I turned and saw a young rower from Japan holding out a can of soft drink toward me. I shook my head, declining his offer. Heavens, I thought, imagine taking anything from anyone from Japan. He insisted. Again I declined. He then pointed over his shoulder to indicate that the offer was not from him but from a slightly older man sitting behind him. I understood immediately, decided to take the drink just to end the whole scene, smiled my thanks, and immediately turned back to look at the lake.

As I looked over the water tears welled in my eyes and my hands shook. I could not have spoken if my life had depended on it. How could an older male, from another culture, comprehend what had happened to me, what I was feeling, what I needed then. He was, after all, a "Jap" and one from the war generation at that. Years of training, ending in humiliating defeat, and it had all led to this—my first contact with the Japs. Even worse was my inner knowledge—the war-generation Jap held the moral high ground but he did not know it. However, I did. In that instant I felt I was close to emotionally unraveling.

Although I had smiled my thanks to the Japanese official, I felt I should make a genuine effort to thank him properly. I looked for him in their team kitchen but gave that up: they all looked the same to me. In the following days I returned to Lake Albano to collect the last of my things. I failed to see him anywhere there. I told myself that I would repay his kindness later, sometime later. Later never came. That unpaid debt worried me for the next thirty years.

No Whining: The Aussie Code of Silence

Looking back, I believe that the incident was a sharp and dramatic end to the first phase of my life. It was also the beginning—a framework, scholars would say—of my survival as a losing Olympian in a society which loves and remembers only winners, male or female. At the time I had reacted to defeat as Australian society and the Olympic stereotype (or the Australian version of it) decreed I should—I had remained silent and subdued. Years before I went to Rome, I had read a dictum on a rowing-shed wall at Ballarat. Cut deeply into the wood were the words, "If you win, say nothing. If you lose, say even less." It was a lesson I had learned well and one I began rigidly putting into action that day beside the lake.

I told myself that being an Olympian meant nothing. Years of effort and strain and the Rome experience itself were a waste. It was like ash in my mouth. Penniless, I knew I would have to start life again in a workplace where unequal wage rates had been set. Consequently, female wages, for all age groups in all jobs, were basically half that of male wages, even for the same office work. Unskilled, single females like myself received appallingly low wages. The only national group with worse wage rates were the Aborigines. I knew exactly what I would return to. I would be back where I had been as a fifteen-year-old clerk. My wage had been lifted from five to eleven pounds a week, but it was, even with the raises, a wage on which it was almost impossible to survive. Living away from home during the two years prior to the Rome games had shown me that. I was acutely conscious of an even harsher reality when I returned to Australia from Rome.

At the same time that I would be faced with rebuilding my finances, I would also have to concentrate hard on being a "nice" woman, a proper and respectable loser. The Australian Olympic stereotype did not include "whining" as acceptable behavior. Whining would mean blaming everyone and everything else for my loss. If asked about Rome and my loss, I would have to take the blame. Heidi and I were not good enough—on the hour, on the day, on the week—just not good enough at all. We knew otherwise. Our Olympic qualifying times in Australia had proved that. We understood that this stoic submission was going to hurt the most.

Five weeks after returning from Rome I walked away from canoeing and never returned. In all that time, not one person asked me what had happened, not my family, not my boyfriend, not my workmates who had helped me raise the fare to Rome. A very insightful woman I worked with, Mrs. Burke, understood there was a story. She said that she could see something terrible had happened by the strain on my face and the sadness in my eyes. I did not take the hook to speak, and she died without ever knowing the full story.

I now believe that the silence of our friends and families was based on their own understanding of how Australian losers were expected to behave. They wanted us to be seen by one and all as "good losers," a code phrase for nice women. To help losing Olympians to achieve this, it was essential that no opportunity should be allowed to emerge whereby we could whine. Hence, if no questions were asked about the loss and no comments were made, the matter would soon die. In its own way our society was, psychologically, a complex little world. At the time I was terribly hurt, but in hindsight I believe that their silence was an act of kindness, not indifference. Roy Mullins, a longtime neighbor of one set of my grandparents, helped me understand that the stiff-upper-lip-in-defeat phenomenon, as it worked in Australia, was a British, middle-class concept. It had been designed to cover cruelty, stupidity, and often the raw misuse of power. He advised me to pay it no heed. But of course I couldn't ignore it.

Before Rome, I had believed that the image of winners' and losers' behavior was just the Australian way, the normal and natural state of being. After Rome, I began to question if there was not something wrong with what I had accepted as normal sports behavior in the past. At Rome, the Americans seemed to handle things differently. They seemed to speak out and not be ridiculed automatically for it, not even if threatened with court action, or so it seemed to me. I recalled that American swimmer Lance Larson and the Australian swimmer John Devitt had clocked the same time for the finish of the one-hundred-meter freestyle. First place was awarded to Devitt. Uproar followed. Larson was given the silver medal. The Americans spoke out loud and long—for six years after the incident—and seemed to feel confident in that act. I found it electrifying stuff. After Rome, Roy explained to me that the Americans had a Bill of Rights behind their free speech; we didn't and that was the real difference. They were able to grow up feeling confident about their ability and right to speak freely. I learned fast after Rome.

At her club, Heidi made the mistake of twice trying to raise the issue of Rome and the poisonous relationships in the canoeing squad. She was quickly and quietly told to stop "whining." She never spoke publicly of Rome, and our experiences there, again. Although a migrant from Germany and a youngster who had lived through the firebombing of Hamburg, she quickly learned the Australian Olympic stereotype and how to behave. She acted accordingly.

As Roy noted, Heidi and I were not the only ones fitting in with the image of the proper loser. He had read the papers every day during the games and no one else seemed to be speaking out about Rome either. As the weight-lifting team's results had come through, he had noted that half of our weight lifters seemed to have been disqualified by one judge. "Some fella who was judging the press section. What was going on there?" he asked. I went quiet. I remembered the boiling anger of the weight lifters as they had come back to the team kitchen. These were men who had lifted at international level for years and who had taken medals at the Commonwealth Games. They spoke of the same judge, the same problems. They were helpless with rage. I told Roy that I knew there had been something wrong there but would take it no further. To this day I have never repeated the suspicions which the weight lifters shared with me. Unlike the American swimmer, they did not speak out, behaving instead as good Australian losers.

Neither Heidi nor I, nor perhaps the weight lifters, understood fully the effects of our silence. In a roundabout way, it hurt younger athletes who came after us, both males and females in any number of Olympic sports. However, to expect athletes in mid-career to speak out about serious wrongs in administration and sportsmanship assumes that they would foolishly or willingly jeopardize their careers.

Likewise, there are other assumptions aligned with the expectation that athletes in mid-career would or could speak out. Firstly, there is the assumption that each athlete who knows of or experiences injustice in sports has access to a journalist willing to write about such contentious issues. Secondly, even if a writer does compile an exposé, there is no guarantee that an editor will allow the article to be published. The print media in Australia has long boosted its sales through its close connection with sports. Publication of such material could kill the goose laying the golden egg. Thirdly, there is the assumption that Australia's harsh libel laws would not be used against an athlete speaking out. Athlete's challenges would be touching upon reputations. Australia's libel laws, formulated last century, have operated to protect reputations of the powerful rather than those trying to bring truth forward. In Australia, those laws work well for big organizations and for people with spare cash to fight cases in the courts. Few Olympians have such resources in their competitive years.

Even if we had spoken out about what was crippling Olympic sports for Australians, it might not have made much difference. The men who controlled Olympic selection, especially at the state Olympic council level, were still staunch proponents of the Amateur Code, which defined an amateur as one who has never competed for a money prize, staked bet, or declared wager, or who has not knowingly, and without protest, competed with or against a professional for a prize of any description, or for public exhibition, or who has never taught, pursued, or assisted in the practice of any athletic exercise as a means of livelihood or for pecuniary gain. The rigid enforcement of bans on business advertising, or public displays giving credit to any sponsors, or even a gift of money for travel (which the councils themselves could not control) was deemed by the state Olympic council to be a breach of the Amateur Code. Consequently, as an independent canoeist, I had to pay to enter each race at each regatta, contribute toward petrol for transport to races at the local, state, and national level, and bear the cost of all repairs to my kayak. I could accept no financial help at all. Everything had to be paid for personally—a terrible burden for poor women in such an expensive sport. As long as the financially comfortable, middle-class males who formed the councils remained in power and were untouched by the reality of the monetary stress on poorer athletes, nothing changed.

Controlling Elite Sports: Splitting and Ranking

In the months immediately after Rome, our neighbor Roy said that he believed the day would come when the Olympic movement, overseas and in Australia, would unravel enough to allow journalists and scholars to shed light on its dark heart. He was right, as usual. However, it was not until Montreal in 1976 that the show unraveled, and that unraveling resulted in the establishment of the Australian Insti-tute of Sports (AIS) in the early 1980s. At Montreal Australian Olympians won no gold medals. The tally was one silver and four bronze medals. Sports-mad Aus-tralia was in an uproar. The establishment of the AIS gave hope, encouragement, and fairer distribution of money to all, especially to female athletes. Unfortunately, the astute, powerful sports administrators were still able to find their way into or remain connected with key structures, the structures which really control elite sports in this country.

The selection or grading committee has always been one of these key struc-tures, more so before the development of the AIS. These committees in each sport have always presented themselves to the public as objective and rational. The State Olympic Councils, in their heyday before 1970, also fostered a similar image of themselves. I believe that the role of the selection committees has remained fun-damentally the same as when I was a competitor. The selection committee first selected those eligible for Olympic competition based on performances in Olympic-qualifying trials. Second, they did the actual rankings of these perfor-mances. Theoretically, the lower the rank (numbered one to ten) the better the performance and thus the better the opportunity to be included in the team for the games. After selection and ranking, the names of the athletes from all the sports were submitted to the Australian Olympic Federation (AOF, or Committee, AOC, as it renamed itself) for possible inclusion in the team.

Ostensibly, the selections and rankings were compared objectively with, or based upon, world records, times, distances, weights, or world championship placements. Unfortunately, the rankings were more complex than that. Part of that complexity arose when a specific comparison with overseas performances proved to be difficult. It was one thing to compare weight-lifting or swimming records, quite another to compare yachting, equestrian events, wrestling, or boxing. It was at this point that the officials' subjective assessment came into play.

If competitors within elite sports had believed that the committee in their particular sport did nothing more than compare performances, their groups would not have become the site of dispute that they did. Two words still ring in my ears about the problems of ranking—compromise and payback. Many careers ended on the vagary of ranking. Selection and ranking, done as they were behind closed doors, with all aware of the reality of compromise and payback, became the very point in the system where athletes and their families developed memories like elephants. Those who missed out on a place on the team developed the keenest memories, closely followed by those ranked, often unjustly, far down the list when their performance indicated that a high ranking was deserved.

In sports where females and males were competing for the limited paid places, whether on ships in the early days or on airplanes in my own time, the situation could be explosive. As each Olympic team was announced the same dreary news came through—women were invariably ranked lower than men, or so it seemed to those of us avidly following the Olympic world. Perhaps the classic situation concerning ranking, paid fares, and women was the case of swimmer Nancy Lyons.

Speaking on radio a few years back, Nancy recalled her world-breaking performances prior to the 1948 games in London. Month after month she shattered breaststroke records, including the world record. Yet when the Queensland Olympic Council rankings were passed to the AOF, she was ranked thirty-seventh on the Queensland list. Thankfully, her friends and family helped her get to London where she won a silver medal. To this day, I still wonder who the other thirty-six Queensland world-record holders were.

There was another hurdle in becoming an Australian Olympian in the pre-AIS days, apart from poor wages, transport problems, food costs, the Amateur Code, subjectivity, and ranking. It was the practice known as "splitting" and it went hand in hand with ranking. It was a practice which hurt me rather than Heidi. But we both came to believe that much of what went wrong for us, even before we got on the airplane for Rome, could be attributed to ranking and splitting. Many athletes knew these practices as "the evil twins."

The Australian Olympic Federation's use of splitting meant that teams would have some members ranked higher than others. The fares of those ranked higher on the list would be paid. The rest had to raise their own fares. It was a system which often financially crippled poorer athletes, broke friendships, and weakened team harmony. The whole system was justified by the imposition of the pitiless dictates of the Amateur Code. Athletes' lives were deeply affected by the code, yet few of the athletes had ever seen the code when they joined a sports organization, sometimes as juniors. Some went right through their careers without ever reading it. Finding a copy was not always easy, either.

In theory, the sports federations were supposed to raise the fares, but the onerous task usually fell on the athlete and his or her friends or family. Sometimes a community would help. The system worked well for the AOF because it spread cash further. But it was a system remembered with terrible bitterness by those who competed under it.

How could splitting be justified? The team as a whole had attained Olympic standards, not an individual member within the combination. How could four hockey players have their way paid and the rest be left to fend for themselves? The same could be said for rowing eights, fours, or double-sculls, athletic or swimming relay teams, or water-polo squads. Splitting was a system that was harsh, hurtful, and arbitrary, a system that caused immeasurable heartache to some and financial stress for many. Women especially bore the burden of the system.

Women were already disadvantaged by their weak wage-earning place in the Australian workforce. If a female missed out on Olympic selection, her low wages meant that it was always going to be harder for her to find or save the fare to get overseas to a world championship for experience and thus lift her ranking chances in the next Olympic selections. Likewise, the gendered nature of the Australian workforce meant that she would be going overseas to work to support herself while training, often without a profession or apprenticed skill behind her. The ranking system, the divided workforce, and low wages put women athletes in a no-win situation.

Of the two of us, Heidi became the stronger and faster individual paddler. Based on her Olympic qualifying trial results in 1960, she got the fourth paid place to Rome allocated to canoeists. My workmates, friends, and I found my fare; but the added stress, on top of general survival pressures and training, tore into my emotional reserves. Having to put all my own money into getting to the games meant that I could not afford to pay to transport my club's double kayak to Rome. We had to rely on the offer from the Sydney men to use their old training boat when they did not want it. That meant we trained in the blistering sun of a Roman heat wave after everyone else was resting from the one-hundred-degree-plus, energy-sapping weather. They would not allow us to alter the seating lengths in the boat; they were taller than us, which meant we had trouble reaching the footboards from where much of the leg and low-back drive comes from. This old trainer, complete with willfully imposed restrictions, was what we used in actual competition. At Rome I felt the full force of the ranking and splitting system. There, too, I truly began to understand how lack of money can cripple a person's chances at crucial moments in life.

It was only with the emergence of the women's movement in the 1970s that I could put a name to what had taken place: "sexism." However, to me it was a harsh extension of Australian society, a society which, for women like me, was and remains decidedly unegalitarian.

In hindsight, I do wonder if I would have changed my mind about wanting to be an Olympian if I could have foreseen what lay ahead. Even now, I remain undecided about that decision, taken years before I found myself beside Lake Albano with a can of Coca Cola offered to me from the hand of a member of a hated race.

Childhood Scars: Racism and Female Silence

The story of my time at the Rome Olympics began long before I landed in the Eternal City. I was eight when I first read of Pheidippideas the Runner and, indeed, the Olympic Games themselves in a primary school history lesson. Was it true? Could a person be like him, simply run hard and run long and become famous?

It couldn't be so easy. I decided I would be a runner like Pheidippideas. However, young girls in 1940s Australia knew better than to say such things out loud. Unmerciful ridicule would have been the punishment, as well as isolation in the playground.

I started to run alone along the beach where I lived. I didn't run for pleasure, or to fill in time, or to please anyone by getting out of their way. I ran to emulate Pheidippideas. In today's world I would be classified as an escapist, but in postwar Australia there was still much for the laboring poor and their children to escape from. Not least of these were the demons of the 1930s Great Depression. My parents, their siblings, and both sets of my grandparents lived the rest of their days carrying the invisible scars of the depression. Three words seemed to rule their lives—hunger, despair, and waste, especially waste. The terror of the depression was perhaps the reason I knew that they were always going to be lukewarm to my Olympic aspirations when I finally revealed them. They would always see it as a "waste." If I learned the lessons of the depression at home and understood in some vague way that my dream might be waste, at school I learned to make a place for myself as an outsider by hating the Japanese more fiercely than anyone else.

I believe that my racism came out of terrible childhood hurt and isolation. At the various schools I attended during the war years everyone except me seemed to have a close family member at war. Somehow my father had avoided military call-up; I was regarded as the "coward's kid" but was never allowed to ask questions about it at home. In the very early years at school I used to be hit and hit hard, including punches in the stomach. I had to take what was handed out in taunts, pain, and marginalizing behavior at school, and take it secretly and quietly. I remember, most clearly, that women also treated me very badly. My father was a tall, heavy, strong, aggressive man, understood by all on our street to use his fists on men and women if need be. The women, unable or unwilling to call him names or publicly humiliate him in any way, found his kid an easier target. I can now understand their frustration. I still can't understand why I remained silent about what was happening to me.

Because of what was happening at school I really took notice of all the war news, trying to understand it all, make sense of it. I was an adult before I realized that I had been exposed to too much of the dreadful carnage for my own good. I also came to believe that my absorption with the war's details—coming to me as it did from all forms of media—equated in real measure to the depth of the bullying at school.

As a reaction to these things, and to boost my self-esteem and my low standing with my peers, I felt that I had to be the best Jap hater in the school, and it worked. I had never heard a shot fired in anger. Nor was I at the Japanese bombing of Darwin. Yet my vilification of the Japanese was the best in the school. I was tolerated for that at least. It was really the only defensive weapon I had, that and my mental world of the Olympics. I was good at physical activity;

I was even better at being a racist. Never, in all those years, would I have believed that there was a kind Japanese. Our own propaganda machinery would not allow for such a person either, certainly not for a long time after the war, anyway.

The incident beside Lake Albano was the first time I had to face the issue within myself. Being an Olympian and hating the Japanese, especially for what had happened to two uncles on the Kokoda Trail and the Burma Railway, had been the two givens of my imaginative life. In the following years, after I had left the Melbourne seaside suburb of Edithvale, it took the long, steady influence of two disabled numbers runners, a European Jew, a tea lady, and a Japanese Olympic official to modify my thinking. However, my racism lasted longer than my Olympic career.

Managing Class and Gender at the Games

During the London games in 1948 and the Helsinki games in 1952, our media had people like me believing that Australians were winning anything and every-thing—well, anything that mattered. It was years before I realized how many sports were left out of our press coverage. Either Australia was weak in those areas or we had no representatives. Until the Melbourne games, I really believed that the only sports worth following in the Olympics were swimming and track and field. Those were the sports in which Australian women won their medals. It was only after I entered an expensive sport (for me) that I realized women had entered swim-ming and athletics because they were comparatively inexpensive sports. They were the only sports in which Australian women seemed able to compete, even though Olympic rules also allowed for women's participation in gymnastics, equestrian events, yachting, and canoeing. In a real sense the pittance that women earned in the Australian workplace was often directly linked to which sports they could join and in which they could excel. It held true for poor men as well but to a far lesser degree than for females.

When I finally did see gymnastics, wrestling, and weight lifting at the Mel-bourne games, I was thunderstruck. It was fantastic. However, when I told a wealthy, local dairy owner what I thought about these wonderful, European-dominated sports, he flashed at me, "Why would any decent Australian be interested in such stuff. It's only foreign, Commo rubbish." They were common sentiments in my small, narrow world. When my neighbors in the area realized that I had taken up canoeing, another European-dominated sport, they were disgusted and let me know it. When many came to realize that the sport had entered the Olympics at the Nazi games in 1936, they didn't want to know anything about me, my progress, or lack of it. People told me bluntly, when I was trying to raise my fare to Rome, that they would not support me to continue in such a Nazi sport.

After Helsinki, I noticed how the media stressed the behavior of our Olympians. Most importantly, my attention was drawn to their status as amateurs. I asked the local off-course bookmaker, a Mr. Nagle (a man disabled by polio as a child), what an amateur was. He said an amateur got no money for performing and could not obtain or receive money from anyone but a family member. He also told me about the Amateur Code: "It's a set of rules made up by the rich to keep the poor out of their sports." He believed that the code was the main reason why very few really poor Australians were Olympians.

I read everything I could about Olympians, especially Australian Olympians. The image presented was of a person who was an amateur, a competitor who did not whine, cheat, or hinder fair competition. If beaten, a true Olympian always smiled. However, there seemed to be more rules for women, or so I thought. They were feminine, soft-spoken, modestly dressed in and out of competition, uncomplaining about loss or injury, and slim, very slim. No bulk in our women!

It was intoxicating reading for a lumpy, isolated tomboy. The subtle point made in all this image-making was this: Olympians were the best sort of people a young person could choose to be like. I believed that I would learn all these important things and fulfill the image, if I just set my mind on becoming an Olympian. So I ran harder and longer. I had to, as there was nothing else in my life except Sunday school. In the immediate postwar years at Edithvale, I was aware of no organized sports for girls. I knew of no organized sports at all until I went to Mordialloc High School in 1950.

The financial pressures were terrible. By fourteen I had moved out of home and was living with my grandparents. At fifteen I had started work. I tried to find a sports club to join but soon realized that, financially, it was going to be beyond me. I tried to stretch the five pounds I was paid (half of which went on board and ten shillings for tax) but it was never enough. Without a boyfriend with a car, or even a bike to call my own, I could barely move out of the semi-industrial suburb in which I lived. Besides, the family's silent censure about waste and wasting money on something as silly as women's sports finally drove me away from sports and into the sewing room.

The great blessing for me during those years was yet another disabled off-course bookmaker, Roy Mullins, my grandparents' neighbor, who had been a jockey and was crippled by a racing fall. He was the first to awaken me to all the things that the Olympic stereotype failed to include or that "were givens," things taken for granted.

I began to reread the articles and scrapbooks I had collected. As usual, Roy was right. Underlying the ideal were employed fathers and stay-at-home mothers. They were givens—no doubt about it. The ideal rested on employment and family support. A good diet was also a given. Olympians didn't live and train on bread and drippings, a roast on Sundays, fish and chips each Friday night, and rabbit and vegetables the rest of the week. Never were these exalted beings reported as having had contact with or concerns about family violence or prolonged or constant debt. No journalists writing about Olympians ever seemed to meet athletes who lived in boarding houses, shacks, or caravans. Such things were not part of the image. I could not understand where such people lived. It was in some magic place far removed from the world I knew. In one memorable discussion Roy had said, "Show me an Olympic sheila or bloke who comes from a broke and nutty family." Of course I couldn't.

Roy also helped me to see the patterns in the images, the ideal of the budding athletic star. First, a child showed promise. Second, the family or friends always knew a coach or club able to bring the youngster along. Third, fees, sports clothes, and cars were givens or at least access to them was. Last, injuries, when they occurred, always seemed to be paid for. Medical costs never seemed a problem. Medical bills never went unpaid. Olympians ran for clubs called Harriers or Old Grammarians or came from rich suburbs with swimming pools. Finally, I had to agree with Roy. Aussies who became Olympians seemed to have started life with lots of givens. Or perhaps, I began to think, there were Olympians who didn't have these supports, and the image makers and journalists simply ignored them. When Roy suggested that the Olympics had, for far too long, been a class-based phenomenon, I really panicked. Where did that leave hopefuls like me?

The thrill, color, and excitement of the 1956 Melbourne games rekindled my seemingly insane desire to be an Olympian. Roy and his wife, Lal, continued to steady my thinking even after I found and started canoeing immediately after those games finished. They were still helping me to see the flaws in the image right up to my approaching adulthood. They made me think about officials: Who were they? Where did they come from? Which ones were sent overseas with the teams? And which ones weren't? They made me think about the possibility that perhaps many officials might not be as competent as they should be by international standards. They went after me for my racism even after I left home in 1958, three weeks after my twenty-first birthday.

I was lucky to find some Saturday evening work with Max Rosenberg, a European Jew who had the catering concession at Melbourne's harness-racing fixture, "the trots" to most Australians. From 1958 until well after my return from Rome, Max, like Roy and Lal, discussed, disputed, and used reverse psychology on me to see the image's flaws in my idealized world of the Olympics. Max was really the person who helped me understand that the image was an external one: "An outside persons, dahlinks, an outside persons. Sports peoples are like other peoples, Sin-tee-a, not so perfect good on the inside persons, nu?"

When I discussed this with my workmate, Mrs. Burke, she agreed with Max's assessment of human nature. Mrs. Burke was an Australian of Irish descent, a working-class woman, a Mass-every-day-type Catholic, and the tea lady. She also possessed deep insight into a great range of matters. I admired and respected her as I did my grandmothers. Not long before the Olympic trials she said, "Cynthia, if you win selection and go to the games, do you think you can stop hating the Japanese the way you do, overnight, just because your name could appear in the paper or you start wearing an Olympic uniform?" Her comment was the saving grace which helped me understand that I might one day be an imperfect Olympian but I was probably not going to be alone.

My Olympic Journey

Australia's Olympic canoeing trials for Rome were held in February 1960. Heidi performed outstandingly well. I was quite good. Together we turned in times, in the women's kayak singles and kayak doubles, which were well inside Olympic qualifying standards. I had believed that meeting those standards meant we would be on our way to Rome. A week or so later, the bombshell and compromise of the selection, ranking, and splitting system almost totally crushed me. Either I or the canoeing association—who claimed to have no funds—would have to find my fare. I had given my all for years and in the end it came down to subjective assessment, compromise, and money.

Max refused to allow me to give up hope. He made telephone calls to all his suppliers, raised the issue with the Royal Showgrounds social club, and let the women I worked with each Saturday night know, and they kicked in. "Dahlinks, don't worry. We will get you there!" They did. However, neither Heidi nor I could get from anywhere copies of the International Canoe Federation rules and regulations, rights, and responsibilities. The men who had run canoeing at the Melbourne games expected us to believe that there were no copies of the rules anywhere, or anywhere they knew of. The team manager in Sydney told us to ask officials in Melbourne. Melbourne officials referred us back to Sydney. To this day neither of us have been able to read a copy of those rules.

By the time we left for Rome, I was well under top racing weight, dispirited with the fund-raising effort, and deeply worried by the cold-shoulder treatment that Heidi appeared to be receiving, in Sydney, for being so good as to have gained one of the four paid places. It had been expected and desired, especially by some paddlers in Sydney, that the men's kayak relay team would get the four paid places. It hadn't happened. Heidi's performance had put an end to that expectation. The omens felt terrible. I constantly recalled Max's insight that "sports peoples were like other peoples . . . not so perfect good on the inside persons." He had that right. Consequently, I had ceased to think of or believe in an Olympic ideal by the time I reached Rome.

As the days in Rome passed, I remembered the way everyone had taught me to think and I asked myself about the silence—what the ideal left out about a whole range of things. The host city's organizing committee was not supposed to lose equipment, or even misplace it. That happened in Rome and not only to the Australian team. Then there were the poisonous cold war politics of Olympic Village life. These took the form of constant snide remarks (generally from teams from English-speaking backgrounds) about the size or shape of the Iron Curtain women, rumors about pills and dirty tricks in their training methods. Finally, blue jokes about Soviet males' lack of virility, mental capacity, or plain ugliness. It was constant, cruel talk and quite unwarranted.

The ideal never mentioned airplanes grounded (as in our case in Darwin), our athletes sleeping in parks, on benches, in jail, heat, travel exhaustion, or time zones. The problem of dozens and dozens of languages was stressful beyond belief. Standing in queues in the heat, just waiting for a short turn with an interpreter, was physically draining. Never were personal undercurrents between athletes, in the same team, mentioned. In hindsight, that was the most shattering part of the Olympic experience for me. By the time actual competition began, the last, very last, thing in the world I wanted to be was an Olympian.

More unexpected trouble lay ahead. In the heats of the women's kayak double, the starting instructions were given in English. We didn't ask questions about it, as this seemed normal to us. We did not see the canoe team manager after the race but knew we would take part in the repechage. To have gone directly to the final, we had to have finished in the first three places in the heat. We finished fourth. The next day, Friday, we were lined up at the start when the starter seemed to talk at great length in Italian. Heidi had her hands in the water ready to place them on the paddle. Placed in the back of the double, I saw the other competitors raise their paddles and swing into action. I yelled at Heidi, she instantly saw what had happened, and madness seemed to prevail for what seemed ages. We had been left at the start. The team manager, Max Hill, had not informed us that the starting instructions for the repechage events were to be given in Italian, not English, as had been the case in the heats.

We paddled like mad and made up some ground. Again, we came fourth, missing out on the final by one placing. When we got to the finishing pontoon, Max Hill was ashen faced. He had seen what had happened through his binoculars. Heidi yelled at him, demanding to know why he had not warned us that the starting instructions were to be given in Italian? She was ready to explode; I was totally broken. He said, "It's all right; it's all right. I'll protest. I'll protest." Heidi then noticed my silence and asked me what I wanted to do. I said we could not beat the Russians, we should forget the whole thing. The manager immediately saw his opening and said, "That's right. It wouldn't have legs. It wouldn't win." He was probably right. However, a protest would have brought the whole area of managerial incompetence to the fore. Something would have appeared in the papers back home or been on record with the International Canoe Federation. I backed off, shattered and subdued. In that instant we were really defeated. It was a decision I have regretted ever since. Both Heidi and I needed the facts of such incompetence to be raised publicly. We needed "a fair go."

Aftermath: Guilt and Restitution

When I returned to Australia I told the whole story to Max, my Saturday night boss whose encouragement helped get me to the games. I spoke of the sexist behavior to which so many females in the Olympics were, and I believe still are, subjected. I never once cried from the pain. It was Max who said that I should leave Australia for a while, to travel or study. That chance did not come for another two years. When it did, it was not to Europe or Great Britain I went, but to America.

In California I met other foreign students like myself, some of them "Japs."

I also met a few Americans of Japanese descent. For months I tried to convince myself that the students from Japan were somehow less Japanese because they were outside Japan. The gentle and gracious young people I was in contact with at Los Angeles City College were not the real Japs I knew from wartime media. For months I pulled and twisted the racism in my head this way and that. However, I could feel the change taking place. Perhaps, just perhaps, there was something amiss with my thinking, and not with the Japs I was meeting. It was a hard learning, slow, too, but learning and change for all that. Thus, at a junior college in multiracial California the final pieces of my mental racist jigsaw fell apart. Three decades passed before I could find a way to thank the Japanese official who on the shores of Lake Albano had offered me a drink which I accepted reluctantly against the whisperings of my racist heart. But when that opportunity finally came, nothing, but nothing, stood in my way.

Much later, in the late 1980s, while cleaning the houses of some of Melbourne's wealthy families, I met a ninety-year-old Australian woman, a Mrs. Brown. She told me that she had been an accomplished needlewoman all her life and at seventy years of age had made a hexagon quilt. It was spread out on her double bed when I first saw it. I knew, I just knew, as I looked at that quilt, how I could repay the old debt. I asked her if she would show me how to do hexagon patchwork and she agreed, giving me a quick ten-minute lesson. I joined a patchwork class soon after that. Standing there in front of Mrs. Brown's quilt, I had decided I would make a quilt and send it to Japan. I would repay the official with a handmade quilt. I did not know if he was still alive, didn't know his name, didn't know where he lived. My family were outraged with my plan, my husband in particular. Like the older members of my family, he believed no Australian had any need to say "Thank you" to any Jap for anything. But I knew I had to repay the man's kindness.

As I prepared the quilt, my hairdresser at Northland, a nearby shopping center, asked me how the quilt was going for my "Chinaman." I said he was not a Chinaman, he was a Jap. Hearing myself say Jap like that made me sit stock-still, as if it was the first time I had ever heard the word. Then slowly I corrected myself and said, "No, it's not for a Jap, it's for a Japanese." The hairdresser said, "What's the difference?" I looked at myself in the salon mirror, right into my own eyes. I hesitated, and said, "Thirty years." And it was the truth.

It took me five months to make the quilt, during which time I asked a former Japanese history tutor at La Trobe University, David Huish, to advise me as to what I should and should not include in a letter which I planned to send, with the quilt, to the president of the Japanese Olympic Committee. I planned to ask for the president's help to find the official. Dr. Huish advised me to explain what had happened and not to worry about racism and prejudice. Intelligent Japanese, like intelligent Australians, were aware of the evils of racism and how hard they are to overcome, even in just one case. The gift and its meaning would be enough; I would not have to say anything else. So I just explained what had taken place at the games and how the unpaid debt had worried me all these years. When more than two months passed and there was no word from Japan, not even a letter saying the quilt had arrived, my family felt vindicated in their opposition.

Nearly three months later I received a letter from the president of the Japanese Olympic Committee explaining why it had taken so long to find the official concerned. His letter explained the man's long career in Japanese rowing and the high regard in which the official was held in that sport. The president thanked me very much for what I had done. Within a week the official himself sent me a letter of thanks, complete with a photo of himself with the quilt. Amazingly, after thirty years he, like me, clearly remembered the incident. Finally, some of the pain of the defeat, and the manner in which it had taken place, eased. The shame of not thanking the man properly at the time finally fitted into a context, or so I have come to believe.

Throughout all the years of guilt, I remembered Mrs. Burke's words as I prepared to go to Rome. As the worst of the stress built up, including fear of failure, she looked me straight in the eyes one day and said, "Cynthia, remember, you may be going to Rome for reasons other than to win a medal." "No, Mrs. Burke, no! Medals are what the games are all about." My only defense in failing to understand Mrs. Burke's insight is to admit that, at the time, I was not only quick-tongued but also as thick as a brick. Nor do I have any answers as to why my racism was played out against the backdrop of the Olympic Games.

Have the social factors which drove me into the fantasy world of the Olympics altered? I don't believe they have. Certainly, there is no world war. That particular social evil which allowed adults and older children to take their frustrations out on me no longer prevails. However, frustration is still frustration, whatever its cause. One can only despair at the position of children and teenagers of the long-term unemployed. Recent scholarship in Queensland has clearly shown that competitive sports are increasingly a wealthy or middle-class preserve. I have yet to see research which shows a heavy loading of rural or urban poor or first-generation migrant children in elite sports. I don't believe, nor did Roy or Max, that a child fails to inherit superb athletic ability because a parent's wallet is thin. However, financially comfortable, middle-class males still control sports structures, the AIS scholarship system, and sports medicine. They still retain the power to write the rules of their sports. There are still many Olympic sports which have a less than democratic constitution for a start.

There are certainly more financial rewards for women in elite sports, but that glitter really hides just how few very, very poor Australian women are in top competitive Olympic sports. The basic building blocks for present elite competition are not always there for the desperately poor or marginalized—a balanced diet, personal sleeping space, fee money, and a mentor who doesn't charge for service. Then there is the hurdle of competitive paraphernalia. Few of the truly poor make it past the balanced diet stage. What these privations and frustrations may be doing to the athletically talented young is anyone's guess.

Maybe the media has changed. There has certainly been an opening of the Olympic movement's dark heart through television as Roy predicted. But the print media retains a romantic ideal of the games. What is promising is that younger scholars within universities now view sports as a legitimate area of study. That can be nothing but a force for good, especially for women.

If there is a real weakness in Australia's Olympic ideal, it lies in the fact that its nineteenth-century core has passed its use-by date. It is impossible to expect young athletes to shed, literally overnight, lifelong attitudes about nationalism, sexism, or racism. Besides, the ideal still portrays "an outside persons." A more creditable ideal would allow for cracks, imperfections, bumps, and inner scratches. A future Australian Olympic ideal could stress that overcoming such demons is what should be striven for through contact with others at the games, rather than the dribble which suggests, at present, that Olympians have no such flaws.

Then there is the thorny issue of how Australia's present ideal is, or is not, applied to officials. Far too little is mentioned about officials' behavior, attitudes, networks (which too often cut out new blood in official ranks), and their record on gender issues. In the whole matter of Australia's Olympic ideal and our sports officials, the vast bulk of the media remains deaf, dumb, and stupid—for any number of reasons.

There is no doubt that times have changed. As a sixty-one year old I realize that today's athletes have to face greater challenges to their ideals than those which beset me in 1960. For women, gender issues remain a problem. For both males and females there is the dross now attached to the Olympic Games and competitive life—sponsorship, marketing, tourism, promotions, money, steroids. I would like to think that a new Australian Olympic ideal could stress ideals for life, rather than merely the competitive moment. I do wonder what Mr. Nagle, Max, Roy, Lal, and wonderful, insightful Mrs. Burke would have to say about how Olympic ideals have changed.

?

CHAPTER 2

Honor Restored:

Jim Thorpe's

Olympic Medals

TRACE A. DeMEYER

Honors Denied

The child, born to the Thunder clan of the Sauk and Fox tribe, weighed nine and one-half pounds. His mother named him Wathahuck, which means Bright Path. To the world, however, he became known as Jim Thorpe, the gold-medal winner in both the decathlon and the pentathlon at the 1912 Olympics in Sweden, a feat that has never been duplicated. Thorpe was the first Native American to win gold.[1]

After earning his medals, U.S. President Taft congratulated the Olympic gold medalist in a letter dated July 29, 1912: "Your performance is one of which you may well be proud. You have set a high standard of physical development which is only attained by right living and right thinking, and your victory will serve as an incentive to all to improve these qualities which characterize the best type of American citizens" (Wheeler 1979, 115). But one year later, the medals were gone.

Before the turn of the century, a star rose into prominence with so much splendor that nothing was able to eclipse it. In the spring of 1887, the star was born, not in heaven, but in a one room cabin made of cottonwood and hickory, in the plains country of the Oklahoma territory. The time was 6:30, the morning of May 28.

—Robert Wheeler,
Jim Thorpe,
World's Greatest Athlete

His family blames ugly politics for the Amateur Athletic Union's decision to strip Jim Thorpe of his medals. Some surmise that the decision was racially motivated. It was reported that Thorpe had played semiprofessional baseball in the summers of 1909 and 1910 while a student at Carlisle Indian School. He earned about two dollars per day during the seasons. Thorpe had used his own name, unlike his teammates, who used aliases. He later told newspapers that several northern college players, non–American Indians on the same teams, were regarded as amateurs and that he did not realize that playing for money was wrong. Thorpe biographer Robert Wheeler said in a 1997 interview, "Getting paid to play sports in the summer was a common practice in those days and he was acting on his coach's advice. They used him as an example to try and correct the professionalism that was rampant in the collegiate ranks." Family members and others believe that the Amateur Athletic Union (AAU) created a new rule to punish Thorpe because he would not go on an AAU national tour after his Olympic victory. Why did the AAU choose this man, the American Indian who changed Olympic history, to be an example?

interesting

Thorpe was astonished and humiliated when the bombshell exploded: "Olympic Prizes Lost, Thorpe No Amateur . . ." The news story first broke in the Massachusetts *Worchester Telegram* on January 23, 1913. It hit the *New York Times* headlines five days later. On January 26, 1913, the acting commissioner of the Olympic Games, James E. Sullivan; AAU president Gustavus T. Kirby; and Judge Barton S. Weeks asked Thorpe for a statement. In his letter to Sullivan, Thorpe admitted playing baseball at Rocky Mount and at Fayetteville, North Carolina, in the summers of 1909 and 1910. Thorpe wrote: "I did not play for the money because my property brings me in enough money to live on, but because I liked to play ball. I was not wise in the ways of the world and did not realise this was wrong, and that it would make me a professional in track sports . . . I always liked sports or run races for the fun of things and never to earn money. I received offers amounting to thousands of dollars since my victories last summer, but I have turned them all down because I did not care to make money from my athletic skill. I am very sorry, Mr. Sullivan, to have it all spoiled in this way and I hope the Amateur Athletic Union and the people will not be too hard in judging me." The letter was postmarked Carlisle, Pennsylvania, January 26, 1913 (Wheeler 1979, 144–45).

Judged he was, by Sullivan, Kirby, and Weeks. They ruled that "Ignorance of the definition of professionalism is no excuse." These same men knew that only three weeks prior, Thorpe had refused to sign Pittsburgh or Washington baseball contracts so that he could keep his amateur standing. An excerpt from the AAU statement follows:

> The American Olympic Committee and the AAU selected Thorpe without the least suspicion as to there having been any act of professionalism. Thorpe's standing as an amateur had never been questioned, nor was any protest ever made against him, nor any statement made as to his even having practiced with professionals,

let alone having played with or as one of them. . . . The widest publicity was given
the team members selected . . . and it seems strange that men having knowledge
of Thorpe's professional conduct, did not come forward. Minor league games
were not reported in the important papers of the country. . . . The AOC and
the AAU feel that while Thorpe is deserving the severest condemnation for concealing the facts . . . those who knew of his professional acts are deserving of
still greater censure for their silence.   (Wheeler 1979, 145–46)

According to Wheeler, Charley Clancy, Thorpe's manager at Fayetteville, North
Carolina, was inadvertently responsible. A Pawtucket reporter in search of a hot
story was in Clancy's office, saw the hunting photo of Thorpe, made the connection, and broke the story. It was Clancy who had talked Thorpe into quit-
ting a farm job to play baseball in 1909. Clancy made a sincere effort to deny
that Thorpe was guilty of playing baseball semipro, but it was too late. Medals
and statuettes would soon be taken away by the AAU and the American Olympic
Committee.

Sports writers and editors threw a different light on the scandal. Many criti-
cized the AAU for double standards and for disgracing Thorpe "to purify athletics." The *Philadelphia Times* showed no mercy for the AAU decision: "There
is reason to believe that the AAU knew of many instances [of professionalism]
but winked at them." The *Buffalo Enquirer* in New York wrote, "Thorpe, amateur or no amateur, is the greatest athlete in the world. AAU officials think nothing of taking money for their services. The fact is becoming more evident
every day that the people of this country refuse to accept the judgment of this
[AAU] clique" (qtd. in Wheeler 1979, 148–49).

Perhaps even more strange, prior to the Olympic Games, on the steamship
to Sweden and the 1912 Olympic Games, James Sullivan and his friend Pop Warner,
Thorpe's coach, met daily to discuss training and strategy for the American Olympic
team. Surely they discussed Thorpe's athletic achievements and activities. Earlier,
newspapers had quoted Sullivan praising Thorpe for being "a splendid baseball
player." Later Sullivan claimed he didn't know that Thorpe played sports.

Although Thorpe continued to win acclaim for his athletic prowess, he never
fully recovered from the loss of his Olympic medals.

Honors Restored

Some seventy years later in the early 1980s, armed with biographical information
and research from the Library of Congress, the Jim Thorpe Foundation uncovered
evidence that proved Thorpe's disqualification, for many "the greatest injustice
in sports history," was illegal and invalid. Thorpe's amateur status was reinstated
after efforts by the Oklahoma legislature, Carlisle, Pennsylvania, residents and former New York Yankee pitcher Allie Reynolds.

In 1983, International Olympic Committee president Juan Samaranch of Spain
apologized and returned Thorpe's gold medals. Thorpe's children accepted the return

of two gold medals at a ceremony during the 1984 Olympics in Los Angeles. They are now displayed under a portrait of Thorpe that hangs in the rotunda of the state capitol in Oklahoma City.

But his family had overlooked the gold medals that Thorpe had won in Boston at the 1912 AAU national championships, which at the time served as a qualifying meet for the Olympics. The AAU had restored Thorpe's amateur standing in 1973 but had not returned the qualifying medals. "It was just a total oversight," said Keith Noll, president of the Wisconsin AAU. Noll was instrumental in correcting the matter. "Our organization did this guy a huge injustice," Noll said in an interview on March 1, 1997.

While working on a history project on American legends, six students from Colfax High School in Wisconsin learned about Thorpe's achievements and discovered the AAU oversight. A high school girl approached Keith Noll at a sports event in Colfax, wanting to know why Thorpe's medals had never been returned. "I told her I'd find out. I was stunned," Noll remembers. The coincidence was that Noll, from Colfax, was the Wisconsin AAU president and was just about to leave for an AAU presidents' meeting.

When Noll brought the matter up, the National Youth Sports Council members were also surprised but agreed unanimously to correct the situation. The National Youth Sports chairman, Colonel Tooke, who served on the council some seventy years and was the first vice president of AAU, told Noll that no one had even thought about returning the medals. "It was never brought up," Tooke admitted to Noll. Noll believes Thorpe returned those medals to Carlisle School's football coach Glen Warner, who kept or disposed of them, though no one knows for sure.

On Saturday, March 1, 1997, Thorpe's national championship track and field medals were returned to Thorpe's children in a ceremony at the Lac Courte Oreilles Reservation Casino and Convention Center in Hayward, Wisconsin. The event, sponsored by twelve tribes from Wisconsin and Michigan, drew the attention of national and state news media, including news crews from ESPN and FOX channels. In a brief speech, AAU president Bobby Dodd said he regretted the fact that it took the AAU so long to return the qualifying medals.

Running Strong for American Indian Youth national chairman Billy Mills, a member of the Lakota Nation, from Pine Ridge, South Dakota, gave the keynote address at the ceremony. Mills had won the one-kilometer gold medal at the 1964 Summer Olympics in Tokyo, Japan. "Perhaps the greatest struggle of all is to have accomplished the dream and then to have it all taken away," Mills emphasized. "That was Jim Thorpe's experience." Then he added, "It warms my heart and my spirit to know that the dream of Jim Thorpe is being returned" (interview).

About three hundred people attended the March awards ceremony and banquet to watch the Thorpe family accept replicas of the AAU gold medals encased in crystal. Thorpe's son Richard, now sixty-five years old, presented gold medallions to the six Colfax students in appreciation of their research. "It's absolutely amazing that children of today are remembering my dad," an emotional Gail Thorpe said to the students. Gail, eighty, of Yale, Oklahoma, made the trip with her brothers: Richard, of Oklahoma City; Bill, sixty-nine, of Arlington, Texas; and Jack, sixty, of Shawnee, Oklahoma. Thorpe's daughters Charlotte and Grace and second wife, Freeda, were unable to attend because of health reasons.

"Dad was quite hurt but after a while, he kind of adjusted to it," recalled Jack Thorpe after the ceremony. "Everyone asked him over and over how he felt. Dad used to say to us, 'You can take material items and you can replace material items. One thing you can never take away from someone is what they have in their heart and in their mind.' Dad told us, 'Everybody knows I won it. I know I won it. So what, it doesn't matter.' Now everything is coming back. I think Dad knew it would. He knew eventually it would come around."

Not everything was restored in this occasion, however. When King Gustav V of Sweden proclaimed Thorpe "The Greatest Athlete in the World" in 1912, he awarded Thorpe some very impressive medals and trophies. Also in the royal box at the Olympics in Stockholm were His Royal Highness, Crown Prince Gustav Adolph and Grand Duke Dmitri of Russia. King Gustav presented the new Olympic winner with the laurel wreath, a gold medal, and a life-size bronze bust in the king's likeness for the pentathlon victory. For the decathlon triumph, Gustav gave him a gold medal and a jeweled, thirty-pound silver chalice lined in gold, in the shape of a Viking ship—a gift from the Czar of Russia.

Late one evening on the road, Thorpe had tearfully confided to his roommate Chief Meyers, Giants star catcher and a Mission Indian from California, "The King of Sweden gave me those trophies; he gave them to me." Meyers said Thorpe was heartbroken. Thorpe told him, "I won them fair and square" (Wheeler 1979, 158). A more philosophical Thorpe later told his sons that, even without the medals, he knew his victory would not be forgotten.

In 1998, the jeweled ship, which Grace Thorpe claims was a gift, not a prize, was reportedly on display in a private museum in Switzerland. Efforts are still underway to reclaim the ship for Thorpe's family.

The Consummate Athlete

Glen Warner was building a sports dynasty when he recruited the sixteen-year-old Thorpe on May 12, 1904. Hiram Thorpe, Thorpe's father, was in favor of Thorpe going to the Carlisle Indian School in Pennsylvania, telling his son, "You're an Indian. I want you to show other races what an Indian can do" (Wheeler 1979, 20). One of eleven children, Jim Thorpe was an enrolled member of the Sauk and Fox tribe but was also part Kickapoo, Potawatomi, and Menominee, and also part Irish and French. The Thorpe family had settled in the Sauk and Fox village in Indian Territory, which later became part of Oklahoma.

The school superintendent, Lieutenant Richard Henry Pratt, who opened the Carlisle Indian Industrial School in 1879 in an abandoned army barrack in

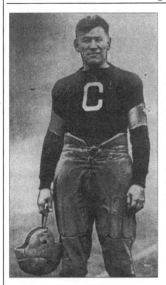

The National Congress of American Indians
Resolution # SFE-97-124
Title: Supporting Jim Thorpe as America's Greatest All-Around Athlete and Greatest Football Player of the Century

Whereas, we, the members of the National Congress of American Indians (NCAI) of the U.S., invoking the divine blessing of the Creator upon our efforts and purposes, in order to preserve for ourselves and our descendants rights secured under Indian treaties and agreements with the U.S., and all other rights and benefits to which we are entitled under the laws and Constitution of the U.S. to enlighten the public toward a better understanding of the Indian people, to preserve Indian cultural values, and otherwise promote the welfare of the Indian people, do hereby establish and submit the following resolution; and

Whereas, the NCAI is the oldest and largest national organization established in 1944 and comprised of representatives of and advocates for national, regional, and local Tribal concerns; and

Whereas, the health, safety, welfare, education, economic and employment opportunity, and preservation of cultural and natural resources are primary goals and objectives of NCAI; and

Whereas, James Francis Thorpe, known as "Jim Thorpe" Wathahuck-Brightpath, Thunder Clan, Sac and Fox Tribe born May 22, 1887 on the Sac and Fox Nation Indian Reservation, South of Prague, Oklahoma, and died March 28, 1953 in Lomita, California; and

Whereas, an amateur in track and field Thorpe won the pentathlon and the decathlon at the Amateur Athletic Union's (AAU's) National Championship Trials held in Boston in May 1912, prior to the Olympics; and

Whereas, Thorpe represented the Sac and Fox Nation and the U.S. at the 1912 Olympic Games held in Stockholm, Sweden. Actually, he did not become a citizen of the U.S. until 1917; and

Whereas, King Gustav V. Of Sweden presenting Thorpe with two gold medals after winning the pentathlon and the decathlon in the grueling track and field events said, "You 'Sir' are the greatest athlete in the world"; and

Whereas, Thorpe was the first U.S. athlete to win the decathlon and the only athlete in the world, to date, to win both the decathlon and the pentathlon during one Olympic year. These athletic feats and the subsequent world wide publicity helped establish the viability of the Olympics that were just getting started in 1912; and

Whereas, Thorpe was stripped of his Olympic medals and awards in 1913, stating that he was a professional since he had played semi-pro baseball in the summers of 1909 and 1910. However, in 1983 he was exonerated, his status was returned as an amateur, his honors were restored and his family received his gold medals, for these extraordinary accomplishments he received as gifts, a life sized bust of King Gustave V of Sweden and a Viking Ship encrusted with semiprecious jewels from Nicholas II, the last Czar of Russia. These priceless trophies have yet to be returned to the Thorpe family. They are currently at the International Olympic Committee Museum, a private museum in Lausanne, Switzerland; and

Whereas, Thorpe's amateur football record was established when he was a student at the Carlisle Indian School in Pennsylvania and was chosen to Walter Camp's First Team All American Half-Back in 1911 and 1912; and

Whereas, Thorpe was a founding father of professional football being the first elected president of the American Professional Football Association now the National Football League. He was a drawing card which caused the growth and development of professional football in its infancy and gave the sport credibility; and

Whereas, Thorpe played major league baseball with the New Your Giants, the Cincinnati Reds and Boston Braves ending the 1919 season with a .327 average; and

Whereas, Thorpe is the only American athlete, to date, to excel, as an amateur and as a professional, in three major sports: Track and Field, Football, and Baseball; and

Whereas, Thorpe was voted America's Greatest All-Around Male Athlete and also chosen as the greatest football player of half-century in 1950 by an Associated Press Poll of sports writers; and

Whereas, Thorpe was named the "Greatest American Football player in History," in a 1977 national poll conducted by Sport Magazine; and

Whereas, Thorpe was enshrined in the National Indian Hall of Fame, the Helms Professional Football Hall of Fame, the Professional Football Hall of Fame in Canton, Ohio, the National Track and Field Hall of Fame, the Pennsylvania and the Oklahoma Halls' of Fame; and

Whereas, Thorpe because of his unsurpassed sports achievements has long been an inspiration to America's youth and America's sports conscious people.

Now therefore be it Resolved, that NCAI does hereby support proclaiming Jim Thorpe America's Greatest All-Around Male Athlete and America's Greatest Football Player of the Century in the year 2000.

CERTIFICATION

The foregoing resolution was adopted at the 54th Annual Session of the National Congress of American Indians, held at the Sweeney Convention Center in Santa Fe, New Mexico on November 16-21, 1997 with a quorum present.

W. Ron Allen, President

Adopted by the General Assembly during the 54th Annual Session held at the Sweeney Convention Center, Santa Fe, New Mexico on November 16-21, 1997.

FIGURE 2.1

Resolution #SFE-97-124, "Supporting Jim Thorpe as America's Greatest All-Around Athlete and Greatest Football Player of the Century."

Sac and Fox News, December 1997. Author's collection.

Pennsylvania, had set up strict conditions for the football players after one student had broken a leg: "If you can set an example, by playing fair and if other fellows slug, you do not return it, then you will make a record for your race. Very soon you'll be the most famous football team in the country, and will do work in the highest interests of your people" (Wheeler 1979, 35). The players agreed to Pratt's conditions.

In April 1907, Thorpe, aged nineteen, 5 feet, 9½ inches tall, weighing 144 pounds, held his first football. His first try at the high jump, set at 5 feet 9 inches, the school record, was broken by an untrained Thorpe wearing overalls and someone's discarded gym shoes. He told Warner, "I could do better in a track suit" (Wheeler 1979, 52). Warner ordered a rigorous training schedule, involving track and football practice.

Glen Scooby "Pop" Warner made football a big-time sport at Carlisle and became one of football's greatest innovators. He was not only the football coach, but the athletic director and track coach. Warner told *Collier's* periodical in 1931, "On the athletic field, where the struggle was man to man, they felt that the Indian had his first even break, and the record [at Carlisle] proves the players took full advantage of it. For fifteen years, little Carlisle took the measure of almost every big university. To this day, Jim Thorpe, Beamus Pierce, Frank Hudson, Jimmie Johnson, Mount Pleasant, Exendine, Lone Star and Pete Hauser still rank among the all-time stars of football" (Wheeler 1979, 36).

Warner admitted that he had all of the prejudices of the average "white." "But," he admitted, "after fourteen years of intimate association, I came to hold a deep admiration for the Indian and a very high regard for his character and capacities." Warner was able to work out a new football idea, the "Indian block," as it came to be called. It required that a player leave the ground entirely, half turning as he leaped, so as to hit an opponent just above the knees with his hip, and following through with a roll, thus using his entire length. The American Indians, Warner said, took to it like ducks to water: "When they blocked a man, he stayed blocked" (Wheeler 1979, 38–39).

Thorpe's biographer, Robert Wheeler, wrote, "Hiram P. Thorpe, Jim's father, had defeated all comers, Indian or white, in contests of strength, speed, coordination and endurance." Apparently, Thorpe, Hiram's son, inherited those abilities. At Carlisle, Jim Thorpe led the football team to victory over some of the nation's best college teams: Army, Navy, Pittsburgh, Syracuse, Pennsylvania, and Nebraska. A tough West Point Military Academy starting right halfback named Dwight D. Eisenhower was severely injured trying to tackle Thorpe in an event that ended Eisenhower's football career. Eisenhower is quoted in Wheeler's biography: "Except for [Thorpe], Carlisle would have been an easy team to beat. On the football field, there was no one like him in the world" (Wheeler 1979, 133).

Robert Wheeler, author of *Jim Thorpe, World's Greatest Athlete,* who attended the March ceremonies in Wisconsin, claims that no athlete has ever surpassed Thorpe's genius for versatility:

Besides being the mightiest all-around football and track competitor in history, and a Major League [base]ball player, he was the captain of the Carlisle Indian basketball team, playing all positions. He was a member of the school's lacrosse team and was a superior tennis and handball player. He could bowl scores in the 200s and shoot golf in the 70s, though he rarely played. He was a fine swimmer and a standout in billiards. Gymnastics, rowing, hockey, and figure skating round out the impressive list of sports in which he excelled. Because of his early environment, he was well versed in marksmanship, hunting, fishing and general forest lore. Jim was not only a great cook but a dance champion. (Interview)

"Dad had a killer instinct," Jack Thorpe said about his father's athletic superiority. "So you don't mind hurting somebody. And you don't mind taking any pain either. And then if you have the combination of that agility, coordination, and thinking, the way Dad did, you get one hell of an athlete."

Jim Thorpe, just under six foot, weighed 179 pounds when he went to the 1912 Olympics. Hiram Thorpe, a direct descendent of the famous war chief Black Hawk, was a great athlete. Thorpe once told a reporter, "My father was the undisputed champion in sprinting, wrestling, swimming, high jumping, and horseback riding." Thorpe resembled his father and Black Hawk, the war chief, in physical appearance and athletic ability. Thorpe's father was a horse breeder and trainer. Thorpe used to run down horses on their ranch on the banks of the North Canadian River, near Old Shawnee, Oklahoma, an activity that helped build his stamina and strength.

Thorpe's dominance over his intercollegiate rivals in football was paralleled by his records as a member of the Carlisle track team. He ran sprints, he ran hurdles, and he ran distance races. He high jumped and broad jumped. He threw the javelin, the discus, and the shot put. And he would perform all these feats at single meets, averaging first place finishes every time out, according to Wheeler.

In the Olympic pentathlon competition, Thorpe faced a test of skill in five events: long jump, javelin, 200-meter dash, discus, and a 1,500-meter race. In the decathlon, he participated in a series of ten events: the 100-meter dash, long jump, shot put, high jump, 400-meter run, 110-meter hurdles, discus, pole vault, javelin, and a 1,500-meter race. "Jim Thorpe finished first in both events. He tripled the score of the runner-up in the pentathlon and finished 688 points ahead of the nearest competitor in the decathlon. After the 1924 Olympics, the pentathlon was dropped from the official program. Thorpe's score in the decathlon will never be matched," Grace Thorpe writes (1996, 627). After the Olympics, Thorpe never quit training and stayed physically strong.

Life after Scandal

Even after he lost the gold, vaudeville managers, theatrical agents, and motion-picture moguls all tried to outbid one another, offering Thorpe $1,000 a week to perform feats of strength on stage. He declined in favor of a more difficult endeavor. In 1913, Thorpe, under the watchful eye of Giants manager John J. "Mugsy"

McGraw, signed a three-year, $6,000 per year contract with the New York Giants Baseball Club. It was one of the largest amounts ever paid to an untried prospect. Offers came from National Baseball League clubs in Pittsburgh, Cincinnati, and New York; and clubs in Chicago, St. Louis, and New York of the American Circuit. Thorpe wanted to go with the best, and at the time it was the Giants. "I would have remained an amateur athlete but that is all over now," Thorpe told reporters (Wheeler 1979, 156).

The same year he signed with the Giants, Thorpe signed a contract for $250 per game with the soon-to-be world champion Canton Bulldogs football team. He managed to lead the Bulldogs team to unofficial world championships in 1916, 1917, and 1919.

Thorpe wasn't as successful in baseball as in football because of his jovial good nature, and because he rubbed McGraw the wrong way, according to Al Schact, Giants pitcher. "His nickname was 'Libbling,' which meant horsing around," Schact said in an interview with Wheeler. "By 1917, Thorpe was loaned out to Cincinnati" (Wheeler 1979, 163). But when he eventually finished in 1928 with the Chicago Cardinals, Thorpe had become an athletic attraction that crowds flocked to see. Thorpe's last official baseball game was in 1928, at the age of forty. Out of sixty games and 156 times at bat, he had fifty-one hits, an impressive .327 batting average in the National League. When Thorpe hung up his spikes and cleats for the last time in 1929, he had played professional baseball and football, concurrently, for seventeen consecutive years. He was forty-two years old.

Thrust into the maelstrom of modern living, and after his request to the AAU for reinstatement as an amateur was denied, Thorpe headed to Hollywood. Unaccustomed to studio dealings and job hunting, Thorpe sold the valuable rights to his life story to MGM for a meager $3,000. The proposed film, *Red Son of Carlisle,* was never made.

In February 1930, he found a job as a painter with a Los Angeles oil firm. By October, he went to Universal Studios and succeeded in landing a bit part, playing Chief Black Crow. Then MGM hired him for a baseball film and later a football picture with his old coach, Pop Warner.

With the country hit by the Great Depression, Thorpe worked as a laborer in an excavation crew for fifty cents an hour. He was too broke to buy a ticket to the 1932 Olympics being held in Los Angeles. When the story reached the newspapers, Charles Curtis, (a Native American) vice president of the United States, said, "Jim Thorpe will sit with me" (Wheeler 1979, 155). The capacity crowd of 105,000 gave Thorpe a standing ovation.

In 1932, *Jim Thorpe's History of the Olympics,* a book written by T. F. Collison, sold few copies. Thorpe went back to his minor roles in Western B movies. In August 1933, he worked for Warner-First National Studios in *Telegraph Trail.* In 1934, he began doing speaking engagements at schools or clubs, but since he didn't have the heart to ask people for money, he had to work even harder to pay for all the traveling expenses. But soon, the motion-picture industry showed promise, as did the roles Thorpe was offered. He even began to recruit other American Indians for movie work. By the spring of 1935, he was playing a major part in *She* opposite Helen Gahagen. The next year, he was offered a good role in an Errol Flynn movie, *The Green Light*. He worked for RKO Studios in *You Can't Take It with You*.

By the end of 1937, Thorpe had returned to Oklahoma and was urging the Sauk and Fox tribe to vote to abolish the Bureau of Indian Affairs and repeal legislation granting the government control over American Indian property. Thorpe said, "Indians should begin management of their own businesses. The Indian should be permitted to shed his inferiority complex and live like a normal American citizen." In place of the Thomas Rogers Act, Thorpe pushed the Wheeler Bill, but it lost by an Oklahoma House of Representatives vote of 202 to 120.

In 1938, Thorpe was offered a role in *Northwest Passage* by MGM, filmed in Idaho. When the picture was complete, he returned to his small cottage in Inglewood, California, to his four growing boys, then thirteen, eleven, seven, and two, and his second wife, Freeda. At fifty-two, Thorpe was lecturing and accepting offers from the movie studios. His school lectures involved four topics: an analysis of the current sports season, the story of his career, an inspirational talk on the significance of sports in modern life, and a commentary on American Indian culture and traditions. He appeared before school assemblies, driving hundreds of miles with his two hunting dogs for company. In order to earn enough for his travels, he usually accepted four scheduled stops per week, sometimes more. At times, he averaged three lectures a day.

Unexpectedly, on April 4, 1941, Thorpe received word that his wife, Freeda, was suing for divorce. Grace Thorpe remembered, "Dad used to take off for weeks; he did the same thing with my mother. It goes back to the old days when men used to do that, that was just the Indian way."

The next four years would be the darkest of Jim Thorpe's entire life, according to his daughter Grace. Thorpe was about to face a new challenge, failing health.

Thorpe was in demand for speaking engagements but he decided to stay in one place awhile and accepted Harry Bennett's offer of work in the security department at the Henry Ford Rouge River plant in Dearborn, Michigan. During the previous year he had covered sixty-seven thousand miles on his lecture tour. He began work on March 20, 1942. Eleven months later, Jim Thorpe suffered his first heart attack.

Thorpe did not give up. He gradually recovered and formally resigned from the plant in November 1943. Thorpe went to Oklahoma for a vacation; while there, he decided to put his four boys in American Indian schools. Phil and Bill went to Chilocco and the younger boys went to Pawnee. At about this time, two American Indian legislators tried to get Thorpe's Olympic medals back, to no avail.

Just when the dream of actively serving his country had vanished, because it was now late in World War II, Thorpe was accepted for duty by the Merchant Marines, where he served anonymously as the ship's carpenter on the

USS *Southwest Victory,* carrying ammunition to the troops in India. By special request, Thorpe entertained the troops with personal appearances in hospital wards, athletic installments, and officers' clubs. Now Thorpe was back in the game and he seemed happier than ever. According to biographer Wheeler, he was the happiest he'd been in two decades: "Jim said in an interview after the war, 'We had some rough weather and some rough times but we had teamwork. Cooperation is important in everything you do and that is what made us winners'" (Wheeler 1979, 210).

Thorpe returned to America on September 7, 1945. He was greeted by Jersey City mayor Frank Hague and Thorpe's new bride, Patricia Gladys Askew, from Louisville, Kentucky. That year, doubling as his manager, she would accompany him on many more appearances in states across the country: California, Illinois, Ohio. A businesswoman, she began by suggesting that Thorpe charge five hundred dollars for his engagements, plus expenses.

Sportswriters across the country, the International Rotary Clubs, and his wife, Patricia, were all attempting to regain Thorpe's Olympic trophies, but without success.

By January 1947, Thorpe embarked on a campaign to bring the 1952 Olympics to Soldier's Field in Chicago. He also championed the cause of a national junior Olympics, writing a letter to Attorney General Tom Clark expressing his concerns about juvenile delinquency. By 1948, Thorpe was a man with a new mission, working as a member of the recreation staff at Chicago Park District, promoting junior Olympics and teaching youngsters the fundamentals of track events.

On July 21, 1948, in Chicago, Jim Burchard of the *New York Telegram* asked Thorpe if he would like his Olympic awards restored. Thorpe quickly answered: "Sure! I played baseball in 1909 and 1910 in the Carolina League but I had no idea I was a pro. I got $60 a month for expenses and that's all. I wouldn't even have tried for the Olympics Team had I thought I was a pro. If [Pop] Warner had backed me up, I wouldn't have had to send back the trophies in the first place. [Avery] Brundage [former president of the International Olympic Committee and Thorpe's teammate in the 1912 Olympics] could get those things back for me but so far, he just played shut-mouth. To give him a break, however, I think he's followed his convictions" (Wheeler 1979, 144–45). The Olympic Committee did not respond. Another effort to regain the awards failed.

Prescott Sullivan of the *San Francisco Examiner* did call, inviting Thorpe to be honored in California, along with Pop Warner and Ernie Nevers. Thorpe, now sixty, graciously accepted and put on a field-goal-kicking contest between halves at the 49ers-Colts game. He dressed in a football uniform.

In August 1949, Warner Brothers made the announcement that it would begin work on Thorpe's autobiography. Although he no longer owned the rights to his life story, he was hired as a technical advisor for the film. By 1951, Thorpe was elected to the National Football College Hall of Fame, and in August the film *Jim Thorpe—All American* had its world premier. Thorpe was played by Burt Lancaster, while Phyllis Thaxter played Thorpe's wife. The movie was a box office hit. Thorpe never received royalties or payments from the film, which continues to be shown to this day.

In 1951, Thorpe attended the dedication of a tablet monument in Carlisle, where his career began. It read: "In Recognition of the Athletic Achievements of Jim Thorpe, student of the Carlisle Indian School, Olympic Champion at Stockholm in 1912 and in 1950 voted the Greatest Athlete and Football Player of the First Half of the 20th Century." After all of this recognition, requests for his appearances at dinners and testimonials poured in from every state and many foreign countries. At the Harrisburg Sportswriters Association banquet, the assembly rose and gave him a five-minute standing ovation. At Carlisle School, the tributes were so touching that Thorpe was moved to tears.

In November 1951, while heading up the all–American Indian song and dance troupe in the "The Jim Thorpe Show" in Philadelphia, Thorpe noticed on his lower lip an infection that failed to heal after several days. The doctors found it was cancer and removed the tumor. The newspapers broke the story: Thorpe was destitute and sick. Money poured in from his fans. Less than ten months later, he was back in a hospital in Henderson, Nevada, after suffering a second heart attack. Doctors were shocked when the seriously ill Thorpe got out of bed in less than seventy-two hours and walked out of the building.

Thorpe's third attack occurred on March 28, 1953. His heart faltered for the last time. Thorpe, sixty-six, died at home in Lomita, California, on his birthday. Perhaps the most touching obituary was in Haskell's boarding school newspaper, the *Indian Leader:* "The Great Spirit has taken Jim Thorpe's life. Will He ever replace him?" (Wheeler 1979, 226).

On January 5, 1998, Frank Keating, governor of the State of Oklahoma, proclaimed January 30, 1998 as Jim Thorpe Day, to be celebrated annually in the state of Oklahoma. On January 30, 1998, at the capitol rotunda in Oklahoma City, on Jim Thorpe Day, a new postage stamp featuring Jim Thorpe was unveiled. The stamp is the twenty-sixth of thirty stamps unveiled over thirty days in the Celebrate the Century stamp program by the U.S. Postal Service. The stamp contains a profile of Thorpe's face as he appeared at the Olympic Games in 1912, next to an image of Thorpe leaping over a high-jump bar.

Editor's Note

There's another aspect of the saga of Jim Thorpe's winning and losing the gold medals of the 1912 Olympics. Jim Thorpe made a tremendous impression upon the general American public when he won the gold medals at the Stockholm Olympic Games. Profoundly ignorant of the lives of Native Americans at the time, this general public lionized Thorpe as a kind of mythic hero. He was represented as the "good Indian brave"—strong, skilled, manly, a loyal friend to the white man and his "mission" of bettering the lives of the formerly uncivilized American Indians. He was a figure in the tradition of Chingochgook of Cooper's Leatherstocking Tales. And he was also a "gentleman"—articulate but soft-spoken, deferential, polite. That he went to Carlisle Indian School suggested to his public that he was out to better himself, to become "American" through the education and uplift offered by the mission schools.

Ordinary people expressed outrage when Thorpe's medals were stripped from him. They saw the decision of the American Olympic Committee as mired in bureaucracy and organizational politics, another instance of the little big guy being punished in service to impersonal politics. And all because Thorpe earned a pittance by playing sandlot and semipro baseball to support himself through Carlisle. It was poverty that put him on the playing field, poverty which had to do with the social, political, and economic disadvantages of being American Indian in America. If the decision to strip him of his medals cannot be attributed to a bold-faced and blatant racism, it surely can be attributed to the poverty endemic in American Indian communities at the time and the racist ideology undergirding economic advantage and disadvantage. The "elite" athlete of the middling and upper classes wouldn't have faced the situation that Thorpe did. And he wouldn't have had to be stripped of his medals. If ordinary people remained oblivious to the racial politics of poverty in America, they were not always oblivious to the struggle of the little guy against the odds of success. Here was a "bootstrap" hero emerging out of Native America. Even in the post–World War II era, the new "baby boomer" generation, which has been reared on a diet of Hollywood Westerns, *Lone Ranger* serials, and cowboy comics, continues to revere him. His fate was not deserved.

NOTE

1. This article draws on the following articles in *News from Indian Country,* a twice monthly newspaper in Hayward, Wisconsin: "Medals Returned, Honor Restored," March 1997; "Jim Thorpe Named America's Greatest All-Around Athlete and Greatest Football Player of the Century," January 1998; "Jim Thorpe Stamp Unveiled," February 1998, "Thorpe Family to Receive Medals at LCO," December 1996; "Soaring Eagles Honored," March 1998; "Thorpe's Medals Stolen, Returned," October 1998. It also draws on the following interviews, all conducted in Hayward, Wisconsin: Robert Wheeler, March 1, 1997; Keith Noll, March 1, 1997; Bill Thorpe, March 1, 1997; Jack Thorpe, March 1, 1997. It also draws on personal interviews with Grace Thorpe in 1997, 1998, and 1999 and with Prague major Ted McBride in December 1997. It also cites Gail Thorpe's speech on March 1, 1997. The Jim Thorpe Foundation was founded on February 8, 1982, by Robert W. Wheeler, president, and Dr. Florence Ridlon-Wheeler, vice president. The foundation also has a Jim Thorpe website.

CHAPTER 3

Yes

Jewish Athletes and the

"Nazi Olympics"

ALLEN GUTTMANN

HEATHER KESTNER

GEORGE EISEN

Hitler as Host

The modern Olympic Games were intended to foster international reconciliation, but more often than not they have been the occasion for bitter rivalry and controversy. Without a doubt, the most controversial games of the twentieth century were the 1936 Berlin Olympics.[1] Set against the background of Nazi Germany and the politically repressive and anti-Semitic regime of the National Socialists, the games created alarm and consternation long before the athletes were selected to participate in them.

In early 1933 the National Socialists, led by Adolf Hitler, came to power in Germany. The incompatibility of Hitler's ideology with the ideals of the International Olympic Committee's first president, Pierre de Coubertin, was immediately apparent.[2] The Olympic Charter required that all athletes be allowed to try out for their national teams, but, if the Nazis were to go forward with their well-publicized anti-Semitic program, then German Jews would be excluded from taking part in the games.

In the wider world, many people were appalled at the very thought of Berlin as a venue for the 1936 Olympics. Others, however, took the view that sports and politics were entirely separate and should not be confused. Opinions among the members of the International Olympic Committee (IOC) also varied, but even those who were able to convince themselves that sports and politics were entirely separate spheres were unable to overlook the contradictions between Nazi ideology and the Olympic Charter.

In June 1933, when the IOC met in Vienna, two American members, Charles Sherrill and William May Garland, together with the second president of the IOC, Count Henri Baillet-Latour, challenged two German members of the committee on the threat to the Olympic Charter. In response to this challenge, Theodor Lewald (who was "half-Jewish") and Karl Ritter von Halt secured a written guarantee from the Reichsministerium that: "All the laws regulating the Olympic Games shall be observed. As a principle German Jews shall not be excluded from the German teams at the Games of the XI Olympiad" (International Olympic Committee 1933, 9).

Sherrill confessed his surprise at this unexpected success to Frederick W. Rubien of the Amateur Athletic Union, saying that it had been the hardest fight he had ever fought. The Germans, he said, had been slow to yield and had initially offered merely to publish the Olympic rules, but he had been adamant and the victory was complete (Brundage Collection, box 35).

Sherrill was wrong. While Jewish athletes were still allowed to use public sports facilities, they were expelled from the private clubs that were the hub and mainstay of German sports.

The American Jewish Congress alerted the president of the American Olympic Association (AOA), Avery Brundage, to this fact, pointing out, in a letter from Bernard Deutsch to Brundage in 1933, that it was a violation of the spirit of the Reichsministerium's guarantee (Brundage Collection, box 153). Pressure to take some sort of action increased when other reports of discrimination began to appear in American newspapers. On November 22, 1933, Gustavus T. Kirby, an influential member of the AOA, called for a boycott of the games unless German Jews were allowed, in fact as well as in theory, to "train, prepare for and participate in the Olympic Games of 1936" (Brundage Collection, box 28).[3]

By the time the IOC met in Athens in May 1934, the committee's British members were as worried as their American colleagues about the sincerity of the German guarantee. Lord Aberdare asked "if the pledge given in Vienna last year had been given practical application and if it really was possible for Jews to go into training with the object of participating in the Olympic Games" (International Olympic Committee 1934, 8). Karl Ritter von Halt, who had by this time become a member of the Nazi party, assured him that Jewish sports organizations had been invited to submit the names of potential Olympians to the Deutscher Leichtathletik-Verband (German Track-and-Field Federation) (International Olympic Committee 1934, 8).

The IOC was satisfied but the American Olympic Association was not. It dispatched Avery Brundage to Germany to investigate. Unfortunately, Brundage was not the best person to undertake an objective view of the circumstances. A sports fanatic who believed that the Olympics were "a religion with universal appeal which incorporates all the basic values of other religions" (Brundage 1968, 80), he was later accused of having made up his mind before he sailed to Germany. Brundage unquestioningly accepted the reassurances of von Halt and the organizer of the games, Carl Diem, both of whom were close friends. And in the New York *Post* on September 26, 1934, he said that he received further "positive assurance" from Hans von Tschammer und Osten, the newly appointed Reichssportführer. He returned to America citing a letter from Rudolf Hess to the IOC president, Baillet-Latour. Testing the bounds of credibility, the letter stated that a law passed on August 16, 1934, forbidding all contact between Nazis and Jews, did not apply to sports (Bohlen 1979, 52).

On September 26, 1934, the American Olympic Committee resolved unanimously to accept the invitation to Berlin.[4] The very next day the issue exploded in the *New York Times*. In an open letter in the *Times* on September 27, 1934, Samuel Untermeyer of the Anti-Defamation League listed numerous instances of Nazi persecution of Jewish athletes. A statement from New York Republican representative Emanuel Celler charged Brundage with "having prejudged the situation before he sailed from America. The Reich Sports Commissars have snared and deluded him."

Anger and skepticism grew as each new report of anti-Semitic persecution came to light. By December, members of America's Amateur Athletic Union, the body that controlled track-and-field sports, voted to postpone acceptance of the German invitation. By mid-1935, American opposition to the Berlin Olympics was intensive. A bitter boycott campaign had begun in Canada and western Europe as well as in the United States.

The Boycott Campaign

To no one's surprise, Avery Brundage put forward the case for acceptance of the invitation to Berlin. In a sixteen-page pamphlet entitled *Fair Play for American Athletes* (1935), published by the AOC, he argued that politics and religion should not be allowed to intrude into the domain of sports. American athletes, he stated, should not become needlessly involved in "the present Jew-Nazi altercation." As Brundage saw it, those calling for a boycott were either Communists or Jews, motivated by political or sectarian bias. Brundage wrote to B. Hallbach on March 17, 1936, "[A]ll of the real sports leaders in the United States are unanimously in favor of participation in the Olympic Games[,] which are above all considerations of politics, race, color or creed" (Brundage Collection, box 153). In a letter to Baillet-Latour on September 24, 1935, Brundage also referred to the "Jewish proposal to boycott the Games," as if only Jews had reason to protest against Nazi violations of the Olympic Charter (Brundage Collection, box 42).

In fact, the boycott movement in America attracted a wide range of supporters. Led by the Roman Catholic president of the Amateur Athletic Union, Jeremiah T. Mahoney, and the influential Jewish member of the American Olympic

Committee, Charles Ornstein, it successfully recruited a number of politically prominent Catholic politicians, such as James Curley and David I. Walsh of Massachusetts and Al Smith of New York, to its cause. Both the Catholic journal *Commonweal* and the liberal Protestant publication *Christian Century* announced their support for a boycott, as did the Catholic War Veterans, who appealed to the AOC to reverse its position (Gottlieb 1972, 181–213).

As the controversy reached its American climax, Mahoney offered the most persuasive case for a boycott. In a pamphlet entitled *Germany Has Violated the Olympic Code,* Mahoney cited specific instances of violations (1935). These included the expulsion of Jews from private sports clubs and from public sports facilities; the ban on competition between Jews and other Germans; and the exclusion of world-class athletes from the German team on the grounds of their allegedly inadequate performances. Subsequent scholarship verified every allegation. But while Mahoney had the facts, Brundage had the votes. In December 1935, at the annual convention of the AAU, Mahoney and Ornstein moved that the United States boycott the games. Their motion was defeated by three votes.

In August 1936, Mahoney and Ornstein gave their support to the World Athletic Carnival sponsored by the Jewish Labor Committee. It was intended to be an alternative to the "Nazi Olympics" and took place on New York's Randall's Island. Although nearly five hundred athletes participated, the event attracted little public attention (Shapiro 1985, 255–277).

Avery Brundage had attempted to dismiss the American boycott movement by claiming that the opposition to the games was limited to Communists and Jews. While this accusation proved baseless in the United States, it was a more accurate description of the Canadian movement. There was no broad support for a boycott in Canada. Eva Dawes was one of the few athletes to express opposition to the "Nazi Olympics" in word and action. A star of Canadian track and field, she and five other Canadians traveled to Spain for a Communist-sponsored alternative Olimpiada in Barcelona. Due to the outbreak of the Spanish Civil War, the event never took place (Kidd 1978, 20–40).

In Britain, opposition to the "Nazi Olympics" was undercut by the very vocal stand taken by Britain's most popular and influential athlete, Harold Abrahams. The winner of the one-hundred-meter sprint at the 1924 Olympics, Abrahams favored British participation. In 1936 he attended the Berlin Olympics as a broadcaster (Murray 1992, 29–49).

The situation in France was much more divided. The general public supported French participation in the games, but strong opposition from key sports administrators and a national election in early 1936 combined to create a volatile mix. Among those pleading for a boycott was Louis Rimet, the powerful head of soccer's Fédération Internationale de Football Association, the presidents of swimming's Fédération Internationale de Natation Amateur and ice hockey's Ligue Internationale de Hockey sur Glace, and the head of the prestigious Racing Club de France, Bernard Lévy.

Late in 1935, a socialist deputy, Jean Longuet, asked the Chambre des Députés to terminate the government's training program for Olympic athletes. The motion was lost by a vote of 410 to 151. The chance to reverse this decision came in early 1936, when the socialists and their allies were swept to victory in the national elections. But the government, led by Léon Blum, an assimilated Jew, was reluctant to defy public opinion, which favored participation. Instead, it tried to mollify the quarreling factions by appropriating money for both the "Workers' Olympics" in Spain and the official games in Germany. The compromise satisfied few. The conservative paper *Le Figaro* expressed disgust at government subsidies for French athletes attending the Olimpiada in Barcelona. At the other end of the spectrum, the Communist daily *L'Humanité* lamented a left-wing government subsidizing a team bound for Berlin (Kidd 1980, 1–18; Murray 1987, 203–230).

Dilemmas of the Jewish Athlete

While the boycott controversy raged in Europe and America, the situation in Germany was far from clear. A number of German Jews continued to train for the Olympics in the belief that the Reichsministerium would honor its promise to accept the Olympic Charter. One of these athletes was high-jumper Gretel Bergmann, one of Germany's best track-and-field competitors.

Bergmann was born in 1914 to non-observant Jewish parents. She grew up in southern Germany in the small town of Laupine. She joined the local sports club at the age of six and at fourteen began to compete as a gymnast and runner. After she completed her education at the local *gymnasium,* she applied for and was accepted into a German university. At the time she felt "there was absolutely no difference between the Jewish and gentile people. . . . I never, never felt . . . different"; in early 1933 the university's administration told her that she should not attempt to matriculate (Goldman).

Bergmann left Germany for England, where she studied physical education and competed successfully in British sports. In June 1934, she won the British high-jump title, describing the triumph as being "like a revenge" (Goldman).

She returned to Germany after her family was threatened. There she learned that she was expected to become a member of the German Olympic team. She was both thrilled and "scared stiff." What was she, a Jewish girl, supposed to do if she won her event and had "to stand up there and say 'Heil Hitler' "? As it happened, she need not have worried. Four times during the two years before the games, she was invited to one of Germany's special training camps. She experienced such open hostility from officials who attempted "to teach other girls how to beat me" that she was determined to surpass them all: "I was so full of rage, the madder I got, the better I jumped" (Goldman). In fact, she jumped so well that she equaled the national record of 1.6 meters. Any prospect of Bergmann competing for Germany, however, was snuffed out with a brutally curt letter from officials informing her that her performance was inadequate (Goldman).[5]

One German athlete of partly Jewish descent who did compete in the "Nazi Olympics" was the fencer Helene Mayer, who had won a gold medal in the 1928 games in Amsterdam. Tall, blonde, and blue-eyed, she looked more like an exemplar of Nordic womanhood than a stereotypical Jew. In the early 1930s Mayer went to live in the United States, where she won three national championships, but she was recalled to Germany to take part in the games. She placed second in the foils competition. It is impossible to know what went on in her mind (or in Hitler's) as she stood on the victor's platform with her arm raised in the Nazi salute.

The situation in the United States was very different. Despite endemic anti-Semitism, elite Jewish athletes could win a place on a team through merit and achievement. Once it was clear that an American team would go to the 1936 Olympics, however, they had to consult their consciences.

To Go or Not to Go

One of those who decided not to go was Jewish track-and-field athlete Milton Green. A native of Brookline, Massachusetts, Green received his religious education at Boston's Temple Israel. His secular education and his athletic career took place at Newton High School, Exeter, and Harvard. After a stellar performance at the 1936 Harvard-Yale track meet, he and his friend Norman Cahners both qualified for the Olympic trials at Randall's Island in New York. Shortly after the meet, the two boys were summoned to Temple Israel to see Rabbi Harry Levy and members of the executive board. During this meeting, Levy and the board informed the boys of the Nazi persecution of the Jews and strongly recommended that they boycott the trials. After discussing the matter with his father, Green accepted this recommendation out of "great respect for [Rabbi] Levy" (Goldman).

During the summer of the Olympics, Green followed the track-and-field competition and wondered "whether [he] could have been a medal winner." In retrospect, he hesitated to consider his decision "as a sacrifice, although it was. But I didn't consider it a terrible blow. . . . I never had any doubts about it one way or another. . . . I didn't lose any sleep over that decision" (Goldman).

Herman Neugass, who had tied the one-hundred-yard world record in 1935, was another who refused the chance to compete in Berlin. And, despite a letter from Lawson Robertson, the head coach of the track-and-field team, asking him to reconsider his decision, Neugass remained adamant (Symer 1996).

Among others who decided to boycott as a matter of conscience were discus thrower Lillian Copeland, who had won a gold medal at the 1932 Olympics in Los Angeles; featherweight boxer Louis Gevinson; and four members of the Long Island basketball team, which had been undefeated in the 1935–1936 season. Their Italian-American and Irish-American teammates supported Jules Bender, Benjamin Kramer, Leo Merson, and William Schwartz in their decision.

Around the world other Jewish athletes were coming to the same conclusion. In a letter to the *Toronto Globe* on July 6, 1936, Canadian boxers Sammy

Luftspring and Norman Yack expressed their reluctance to visit a land that threatened all Jews with extermination. The Canadian water-polo team, which had several Jewish members, also decided to boycott the games, as did Australian boxer Harry Cohen and French fencer Albert Wolff.

During the 1920s and 1930s, very few French Jews competed in the cycle of Winter Olympic Games, but two of them—the French bobsled champions Philippe de Rothschild and Jean Rheims—refused to go to Garmisch-Partenkirchen. Three elite swimmers, of the Jewish sports club Hakoah Wien, who qualified for the Austrian team, decided not to compete in Berlin. Judith Deutsch, Ruth Langer, and Lucy Goldner were all suspended by the Austrian Swimming Federation and banned from competition for two years. Their records were erased from the books (Postel et al. 1965, 401–402). In a particularly eloquent statement, Deutsch said, "I refuse to enter a contest in a land that so shamefully persecutes my people" (Symer 1996).

In Denmark's tiny Jewish population, two world-class athletes, wrestler Abraham Kurland and fencer Ivan Osiier, forfeited the chance to go to Berlin. The decision was particularly painful for Kurland, who had won a silver medal at 1932 games after being narrowly defeated in the Greco-Roman competition. Feeling himself to be at the peak of his powers, he was tempted to go to Berlin, but his club ordered him to boycott the 1936 games, which he did (Kristensen 1966, 163–164).[6] For Osiier, the 1912 silver medalist in the saber division and world champion in 1926, the decision not to compete was a matter of principle (Kristensen 1966, 65).

Ironically, the German organizing committee extended an invitation to the Olympic Committee of Palestine. The invitation was refused.

Those Who Chose to Compete

By far the greatest number of Jewish athletes to compete successfully at the Berlin Olympics came from Hungary. There are probably two reasons for this. Firstly, Jewish athletes may well have had no choice about whether they represented their country or not. At the time, Hungary was ruled by a Fascist clique and there was no boycott movement to raise questions about the appropriateness of Jewish participation in the games (Handler 1985, 81–83). Secondly, Hungarian Jews were especially prominent in sports, particularly in fencing, soccer, and water polo (Charron and Terret 1998, 95–99). For decades there had been a disproportionate number of Jewish athletes on the Hungarian Olympic teams. Hungarian athletes of Jewish and mixed Jewish ancestry who succeeded in the Olympics included Endre Kabos of the Hungarian fencing team, who won two gold medals in the saber competition; Gyorgy Brody and Miklos Sarkany, gold medalists in water polo; and Karoly Karpati, who had "his greatest and undoubtedly most satisfying victory" (Handler 1985, 82) when he defeated Germany's champion wrestler, Wolfgang Ehrl, in front of Hitler in the cavernous Deutschlandhalle.

FIGURE 3.1

Olympic medal ceremony for women's fencing in Berlin, 1936.
Left to right: Ellen Preis (Austria, bronze), Iolona Elek-Schacherer
(Hungary, gold), and Helene Meyer (Germany, silver).

Allen Guttmann's collection.

One of the ironies of the 1936 Olympics—and the games were full of them—is that Germany's silver medalist Helene Mayer was defeated by Ilona Schacherer-Elek, another fencer of mixed Jewish and non-Jewish ancestry.

Apart from the Hungarians, a number of European Jews proved their mettle in Berlin. Belgian Gerard Blitz, who had no real ties to the Jewish community, played with the bronze-medal-winning water-polo team. He scored the goal that dropped Germany from first to third place, at which moment Hitler flew into a rage (Hecq 1998, 61–62). An Austrian, Robert Fein, won a gold medal in weight lifting, while his Olympic teammate Ellen Preis took third place in fencing. Both were probably of mixed ancestry. Three Jewish athletes, Roman Kantor, Shepsel Rotholz, and Ilja Szrajbman, represented Poland in fencing, boxing, and swimming, respectively. Of these, Rotholz, was the only one who had no choice in the matter. As an officer of the Polish army, he was ordered to participate in the games. Although he subsequently apologized to the Warsaw Jewish community, he was expelled from his Jewish sports club (Postel et al. 1965, 401–402; Handler 1985, 83–85).

Little is known about the Canadian athlete Irving Maretzky, who played basketball for the silver medalist team at the Berlin Olympics, but American Jewish athletes have given a number of reasons for taking part in the 1936 Olympics. Brooklyn-born Herman Goldberg seized the opportunity to try out for the Olympic baseball team. (The game appeared in the Olympic program as a "demonstration sport.") Goldberg had played baseball at Brooklyn Boys High School and Brooklyn College and was excited about the chance to introduce Germans to the sport he loved. In an interview with Randy Goldman, Goldberg remembered that he was eager to travel and was only vaguely aware of events in Germany at the time he was selected to be part of the twenty-eight member team. If he was indeed a political innocent, then the ethical question is answered by default (Goldman).

Basketball player Sam Balter was familiar with the arguments against participation, but he decided nonetheless to grasp the once-in-a-lifetime opportunity to take part in the games. A Jewish teammate, Frank J. Lubin, writing to Allen Guttmann on January 3, 1998, recalled another motive: Balter wanted to go and "see for himself" if the newspaper accounts of the Nazi regime were accurate. In short, he appears to have had no serious doubts about the ethics of his decision, and, according to his wife, he had no fears for his personal safety. He was, she said, convinced that Hitler would never "show his hand" at the Olympics (Mildred Balter to Allen Guttmann, January 8, 1998).

The most famous of the American Jews to take part in the Nazi Olympics was a runner who didn't run, Marty Glickman. Glickman was born and reared in Brooklyn. Although his family were not especially religious, he recalled, "My grandfather and my father, my uncles, told me about the pogroms in Europe" (Goldman). From the time that Glickman attended Montauk Junior High School, where he ran, swam, and played baseball and basketball, he wanted to prove to the world that "a Jew could do just as well, perhaps better, than anyone else." At Syracuse University, Glickman played freshman football and competed on the track team. "My life," he recalled, "was built around sports" (Goldman).

In the spring of 1936, Glickman qualified for the final Olympic trials at Randall's Island. Almost straightaway he was surrounded by controversy. In the one-hundred-meter trials, Glickman was sure he had run third behind Jesse Owens and Ralph Metcalfe—"a yard ahead of [Foy] Draper and in a virtual dead heat with [Frank] Wykoff" (Levine 1992, 224). But Dean Cromwell, head track coach at the University of Southern California and assistant head coach for the U.S. Olympic team contested the results, saying Glickman had finished in fifth place behind Owens, Metcalfe, Draper, and Wykoff.

Despite the controversy, Glickman qualified as a member of the four-by-one-hundred-meter relay team, along with fellow Jewish athlete Sam Stoller. Glickman and Stoller were the only two Jewish members of the American track-and-field-team. Neither runner had any doubts about joining the team. Glickman has since claimed that he does not remember seeing the boycott controversy "in the newspapers or hearing it on the radio. . . . I was not aware of any athletes who decided not to go" (Levine 1992, 224). "I qualified my desire . . . to be on the Olympic team in Nazi Germany by rationalizing that if a Jew could make the Olympic team and run in Germany and win, then he would help disprove this myth of . . . Aryan supremacy," he explained (Riess 1998, 32).

Glickman and Stoller went to Berlin but they never had the chance to disprove Nazi claims of Aryan supremacy. The day of the trial heats for the four-by-one-hundred-meter relay, head coach Lawson Robertson and assistant coach Dean Cromwell replaced Glickman and Stoller with Owens and Metcalfe. The Germans, they said, had saved their best runners for the relay, and the American team had to meet the challenge with its fastest runners.

Behind the scenes Cromwell told Stoller that he had opposed the last-minute substitution. Stoller believed that this opposition had to do with the fact that Cromwell was prejudiced against African Americans and the inclusion of Owens and not the fact that he was sympathetic to the Jewish cause. According to Stoller, Cromwell said that "he wanted an all-white relay team" (Levine 1992, 226). Some historians believe that Cromwell might have acted for personal reasons. Both Draper and Wykoff had run for him at the University of Southern California. But Glickman was convinced that both Brundage and Cromwell had been motivated by anti-Semitism. He argued that they had intervened because they "did not wish to further embarrass their Nazi friends by having two Jews stand on the winner's podium" (Glickman 1996, 29). Glickman's strongest emotion, expressed in a poem, is bitterness that he and Stoller were deprived of a chance to compete:

PROLOGUE

Rage.
What might have been.
Those dirty sons of bitches
Hitler,
Robertson, Cromwell, and Brundage . . .
Those dirty bastards,
Evil Nazis.
American Nazis.   (Glickman, 1996, 1)

Glickman's rage has not yet, however, led to second thoughts about his decision: "I'm delighted I went" (Goldman).

After the Games

At least thirty Olympians died in the Holocaust. Three of them were veterans of the 1936 games. One of the oldest Olympians to be a victim of the Holocaust, was Alfred Flatow, who died in Theresienstadt on December 28, 1942. Forty-six years earlier, in 1896, he had represented Germany at the first Olympic Games of the modern era, winning two gold medals for gymnastics. In 1944, his cousin Gustav Felix Flatow, who also won a medal at the 1896 games, died in the same concentration camp. The Flatows were not the only German Olympians to die in concentration camps. On June 5, 1941, Julius Hirsh, a member of Germany's 1912 Olympic soccer team, was murdered in Auschwitz.

The Austrian swimmer and fencer Otto Herschmann, who participated in the 1896 and 1912 games, died in Poland's Izbica concentration camp on June 14, 1942. Oskar Heks, who ran the 1932 marathon as a member of the Czechoslovak team, also died during the Holocaust. The date and place of his death are unknown. Three Polish Olympians are known to have died. Leon Sperling, a member of the 1924 soccer squad, died in the Lvov ghetto. Two of the three Jewish athletes who participated in the 1936 Olympic Games, the fencer Roman Kantor and the swimmer Ilja Szrajbman, died in 1943—Kantor in the Warsaw ghetto and Szrajbman in the Maidanek concentration camp.

At least seven of Hungary's Jewish Olympians perished in the Holocaust. Among them were three of the nation's most successful fencers: Oszkár Gerde, who took gold medals in 1908 and 1912; János Garay, who won silver and bronze in 1924 and gold in 1928; and Attila Petschauer, a silver medalist in 1928 and a gold medalist in 1932. Gerde and Garay were murdered at Mauthhausen in 1944 and 1945, respectively. Petschauer died of exhaustion and malnutrition on January 20, 1943, shortly after the Soviet army liberated his Ukranian labor camp. Other Hungarian Olympians who died in forced labor camps included József Braun (soccer, 1924), András Székely (swimming, 1932) and Imre Mandi-Mandl (boxing, 1936). How and where the seventh victim, soccer player Antal Vágo, died is unknown.

The Holocaust claimed sixteen Dutch Olympians between 1942 and 1944—by far the greatest number to die from any one country. Fifteen of these were murdered in the concentration camps of Sobibor and Auschwitz. Four of the five Jewish women in the 1928 gymnastics team died in Auschwitz and Sobibor in 1943: Estelle Agsteribbe, Helena Nordheim, Anna Polak, and Judijke Simons. Their Jewish coach, Gerrit Kleerekoper, was also murdered at Sobibor on July 2, 1943. Three of the men who competed on the 1928 Netherlands team were also among the victims: Mozes Jacob died in Sobibor in July 1943; Elias Melkman and Israel Wijnschenk died in Auschwitz in 1942 and 1943, respectively. Four members of the 1908 gymnastics team—J. Goudeket, Abraham Mok, Abraham de Oliveira, and Jonas Slier—perished between 1942 and 1944. Another 1908 teammate, wrestler Jacob van Moppes, died in Sobibor on March 26, 1943. Two fencers, Simon Okker and Lion van Minden, who also participated in the games that same year, were killed in Auschwitz in 1944. Finally, a boxer from the 1924 team, Heinz Levy, was murdered in Auschwitz on January 31, 1944.

It is probable that other Jewish Olympians were murdered by the Nazis. Surprisingly, however, most of the European Jews who participated in the 1936 games managed to escape the Holocaust. German fencer Helene Mayer returned to Los Angeles immediately after the games. All of Hungary's gold-medal winners successfully evaded the Holocaust, but Endre Kabos was killed when the Germans mined one of the bridges on the River Danube. Three other medalists—Austria's

Robert Fein and Ellen Preis and Belgium's Gerard Blitz—also survived the war, as did the Polish fencing competitor Shepsel Rotholz. In 1937 the German high jumper Gretel Bergmann, whom Hans von Tschammer und Osten had barred from the games, emigrated to the United States, where she won the national high-jump championships in 1937 and 1938.

Conclusion

The 1936 Berlin Olympics were an extraordinary political event. The moral debate raised by Jewish and non-Jewish boycotters throughout the world and the tumultuous emotions and mixed reactions of the athletes themselves are testament to this. None of the many Jews who decided to boycott the games seems to have doubted the rightness of his or her choice. And none of the many Jews who participated in the Nazi Olympics seems in retrospect to have regretted that decision. The survivors have not dwelled upon whatever psychic wounds they suffered. The stories that the others might have told went with them to their deaths.

NOTES

1. The scholarly literature on the Nazi Olympics is enormous. The most important monographs are Richard D. Mandell (1971), *The Nazi Olympics;* Arnd Krüger (1972), *Die Olympischen Spiele 1936 und die Weltmeinung;* Friedrich Bohlen (1979), *Die XI. Olympischen Spiele Berlin 1936;* Duff Hart-Davis (1986), *Hitler's Game;* and Thomas Alkemeyer (1996), *Körper, Kult und Politik.*

2. Of the many books on Coubertin and his ideals, the best are John J. MacAloon (1981), *This Great Symbol;* and Yves-Pierre Boulongne (1975), *La Vie et l'oeuvre pédagogique de Pierre de Coubertin.*

3. It is worth remembering here the special effort made earlier by Robertson to change the mind of Jewish boycotter Herman Neugass.

4. The American Olympic Committee was in effect the executive committee of the American Olympic Association.

5. Another German athlete who might have performed well was the sprinter Werner Schattmann. He was denied a chance to compete in the German trials. See Bernard Postel, Jess Silver, and Roy Silver (1965), *Encyclopaedia of Jews in Sports,* 401–402.

6. Kurland survived the war and competed in the 1948 games.

CHAPTER 4

Yes

Racing with Race

at the Olympics:

From Negro to Black

to African American

Athlete

1968

C. KEITH HARRISON

Scene 1: After the Games, 1968

In responding to hate mail that he received after the 1968 Mexico City games, Tommie Smith made the following statement:

> I have received many letters and phone calls about my decision to support the Olympic Project for Human Rights. I have tried to explain this at a number of speaking engagements. I will do this again here. It is true I want to participate in the Olympics and also in all of the other track meets scheduled for next year. But I also recognize the political and social implications of some Black people participating for a country in which the vast majority of Black people suffer from unthinkable discrimination and racism. I therefore feel that it is my obligation as a Black man to do whatever is necessary, by any means necessary, to aid my people in obtaining the freedom that we all seek. If I can open a single door that might lead in the direction of freedom for my people, then I feel that I must open that door. I am not only willing to give up an opportunity to participate in the Olympics, but I am also willing to give up my life if there is even a chance that it will serve to dramatize, much less solve, the problems faced by my people.
>
> (quoted in Edwards 1980)

Scene 2: 1996

Imagine holding the torch for the 1996 Olympics and the honor that parallels the moment. The entire world is watching and gazing at Muhammad Ali, once known as Cassius Clay. Imagine the thoughts that Ali must be having. Imagine growing up in segregated Louisville, Kentucky. Imagine rising to heavyweight champion of the world. Imagine grabbing the boxing world and society as a whole with your grace, knowledge, and skill as a pugilist. Imagine searching for your identity and declaring yourself a Muslim in a society that is anything but tolerant.

Imagine refusing to go to war in Vietnam and having your boxing belt taken away from you. Imagine being hated and loved at the same time. Imagine fusing together the peace movement and the Civil Rights movement for African Americans and other oppressed groups. Imagine becoming the most celebrated athlete of all time because of your courage and belief in doing the right thing (while the power structure and mass media portray you as a communist). Imagine returning to the boxing ring and displaying your greatness for several years, only to scar that same excellence with a match against Larry Holmes way past your bedtime (since your career was long over). Imagine being embraced all over the world for charities, celebrity appearances, and community outreach programs. Imagine all of this and not being able to articulate a word because you have Parkinson's disease. This was not hard for Muhammad Ali to imagine because it all happened to him.

For the African American athlete, history is pain, pleasure, triumph, tragedy, contradiction, and opportunity. Du Bois calls these tensions for African Americans and for the African American athlete a "double-consciousness": The sense of being "an American, a Negro; two souls, two thoughts, two unreconciled strivings, two warring ideals in one dark body whose dogged strength alone keeps it from being torn asunder ... The history of the American Negro is the history of this strife" (Du Bois 1961, 17). This double-consciousness of being both black and American, pointed out by Du Bois in 1903, has been evident in the experiences of most black athletes since the late nineteenth century (Wiggins 1997, 200).

Scene 3: Before the Game, 1968

In 1968 the level of racial tension in the United States was rising in both sports and society. Because of the profound contradiction of racism in society yet general acceptance of black athletes as performers, opinions in the black community about how black people should handle the situation varied. And those differences were played out around the question of whether black athletes should boycott the Mexico City games. On the eve of one of the most dramatic events in Olympic history, two cultural icons were asked their opinions on the possible boycott of the 1968 Olympics. Jesse Owens spoke against the boycott. Jackie Robinson spoke for it. The classic tale of good African American and bad African American was played out before America's eyes. Why the difference in opinion by two of the more conservative black athletes?

Tommie Smith's insights, Muhammad Ali's imagined reflections, and the conflicting opinions of Jesse Owens and Jackie Robinson all capture for me the com-

FIGURE 4.1

The images of Tommie Smith and John Carlos appear often on various campus posters that announce political agendas. The image of the clenched fists has been powerful since 1968. Photo taken during the fall term of 1998 on the campus of the University of Michigan, Ann Arbor.

Photo courtesy of the Paul Robeson Research Center for Academic and Athletic Prowess.

plex set of issues that the raised hands of John Carlos and Tommie Smith on the gold-medal platform in Mexico City exemplify. I want to use this moment in 1968 to sketch out some of the challenges that face African Americans as they participate in the Olympic Games.

Reflection 1: History Has Its Place and So Does the Stereotype

It is important to remember that in 1936 Jesse Owens and fellow black Olympians were faced with a dilemma similar to that of the 1968 black athletes: Should they boycott the eleventh Olympiad to be held in fascist Germany? The hypocrisy of 1936 was the fact that American Olympic officials demanded that Germany treat Jewish athletes fairly when nothing was being done to curtail the everyday discrimination against black athletes in the United States (Wiggins 1997, 63). Fewer than ten black athletes chose not to participate.

Jesse Owens and the other black athletes competed at the 1936 Olympics. There were twelve track-and-field performers, four boxers, and two weight lifters. These black athletes won six gold medals and accounted for 83 of America's 167 total points. Jesse Owens alone won four gold medals. Yet, ironically, with this level of achievement came something else—a stereotype of the black athlete.

The stereotype that is still heavily debated by the black athlete today is that the black athlete's ability is "natural," not earned. It is something that "God" has given him or her. It doesn't come from intelligence. The myth that African Americans are "gifted" physically and inferior intellectually continues to this day. Even as the name identification of people of African descent may change and may seem to register liberation, the stereotype persists.

Reflection 2: Momentum

Woody Strode, Marion Motley, and Ken Washington broke into the National Football League (NFL) before Jackie Robinson integrated baseball in 1947, but they did not receive the same accolades. Even earlier, two champions excelled in less popular sports. Marshall "Major" Taylor (a cyclist) and Issac Murphy (a jockey) were icons at the turn of the nineteenth century. Their names haven't become a household word like Robinson's. History has presented only a small piece of the picture of African American participation in sports in America.

Public schools became desegregated in 1954, and three years later Althea Gibson became the first black American to win at Wimbledon in tennis in 1957. Arthur Ashe became the first African American male to win at Wimbledon in 1968. Curt Flood in 1968 fought for free agency not just for baseball but for all athletes. These "first" events and others set the stage for one of the most dramatic political protests in sports history (Home Box Office 1996). They provided the momentum for the 1968 protest.

Reflection 3: Where Are the Sisters?
Black Women Athletes and Their Exclusion

In the 1995 movie *Panther* (a documentary drama about the Black Panther party in the late 1960s) there is a powerful scene that contextualizes the theme of gender discrimination within African American sports. During one of the Black Panther meetings, a black woman interrupts Huey P. Newton, the group's leader, by expressing her view that political strategies were being formulated without including the input of black women. The silence of black women in the political protest movement was mirrored in sports and in the 1968 Olympic boycott debate as well.

While African American women are visible in a few high-profile sports in the United States, they are underrepresented in most sports. The participation patterns and experiences of African American female athletes seldom have been studied, so little is known about the intersection of gender and race in sports or society (Coakley 1998, 269). (Michael Eric Dyson and bell hooks warn us in their scholarship on race and culture of the dangers of excluding black women, especially when addressing black masculinity.)

Reflecting on the weaknesses of the 1968 Olympic boycott thirty years later, Harry Edwards (at the time leader of the boycott movements) admitted that he should have paid more attention to the black woman's perspective on sports: "We also didn't do the job we should have done in terms of women. Even with all of those black women athletes in the Olympics, we never really approached them. In today's language that means we were sexist, an indictment that could be extended to the whole civil rights movement" (Edwards quoted in Leonard 1998, 21).

At the Olympics, black women have experienced the same triumph and tragedy as their male counterparts. Alice Coachman achieved success in track and field in the early 1950s but was never brought to the attention of the public. You will find no frontal view of her face in any pictures and representations of her high jumping, as if the photographer hoped to obscure her race (Smith 1997). In essence, she became a faceless jumper! Nonetheless, her contribution laid the foundation for the African American female athlete in Olympic competition.

Wilma Rudolph, another black female athlete, is credited with having changed the style of women in sports. Rudolph was the first female athlete to display grace and prettiness. She brought female athletes, black and white, from the margins of participation to center stage. More pertinent here, she used her athleticism and fame as a *platform* to address other social issues. Rudolph called attention to the paradoxical treatment of the black athlete—criticizing a public that respects you as an athlete but not as an African American citizen.

Following the Olympics in 1960, Rudolph refused to participate in the parade celebrating her medals in her hometown of Clarksville, Tennessee, unless the crowd was integrated (Home Box Office 1996). Rudolph knew that segregation was wrong, and, by manipulating her visibility in track and field, she directly and indirectly participated in a movement that continued to gain momentum. As a result of her courage, Clarksville had its first integrated banquet and parade. The mayor of Clarksville on the day of Rudolph's celebration had a powerful comment for race relations past and present: "On a piano you have white keys and black keys, and in order to have good music and harmony, both need to be played together" (Home Box Office 1996).

Reflection 4: Stereotypes Revisited

As with their male counterparts in sports, African American women have been channeled to areas that are deemed "more physical" (track and field, basketball). Much like Jesse Owens, the impact of Althea Gibson prompted sports authorities to test and evaluate her gender and race, demonstrating the nexus of sexism and racism. In simple terms, Gibson was believed to be a man. Gibson was thought to be different because of her achievements as a woman and as a black person during her era.

Two African American women who broke these stereotypes during college as well as during the Olympics were Anita DeFrantz (in rowing) and Tina Sloan-Green (in lacrosse). Here were African American women performing in unexpected places. What is more impressive about both these women is that they have both gone on to lead very successful lives since competition. Anita DeFrantz heads the Amateur Athletic Foundation, while Tina Sloan-Green is founder and director of the Black Women's Sports Foundation and a faculty member at Temple University.

Following DeFrantz and Sloan-Green would come several others who proved that sports is not just a club for men—Wyomia Tyus, Evelyn Ashford, Flo Hyman, Florence Griffith Joyner, Cheryl Miller, Jackie Joyner-Kersee, Gail Devers, Sheryl Swoopes, to name a few. They provide a window for analysis of how sexism and racism is negotiated in sports and society. In their successes at the Olympic Games, they allied with the struggles of white women and black men. This should not have been overlooked in 1968, nor should it be ignored in future movements for equality, access, and opportunity.

Reflection 5: The Boycott

Curt Flood (free agency in baseball pioneer) framed the atmosphere of 1968 by saying, "The mood of the 1960s was dark and somber and merely because you're a pro athlete does not rid or dismiss you from that reality." Flood was referring to the senseless Vietnam War, social frustration, racial unrest, riots, and the assassinations of Martin Luther King (and his dream) and Bobby Kennedy, which all formed the background for the 1968 games (Home Box Office 1996).

As the larger society struggled with the concept of integration, sports was without question farther ahead in terms of race relations, primarily because team sports integrated black and white players. Time would tell to what degree this integration prevailed at the Olympic Games. Two particular individuals would force the people of the United States to examine their ideals, beliefs, and attitudes about race.

In the months leading up to the Mexico City games, black athletes were asked the following questions. How do you feel about the issues in America? How do you feel about the Civil Rights movement? Most agreed that they grew up with racism, understood racism, and felt that something had to be done about it. Wyomia Tyus, a track star for the United States, had the following to say about the situation of blacks in the United States: "Something has to be done about everything going on. Who's to say where that battlefield is . . . on the athletic field or in politics, somebody has to make a statement and change this" (Home Box Office 1996).

Despite the cultural portrayal of ethnic groups, among them African Americans, as monolithic, predictable, and one-dimensional, and despite the socialization of members of ethnic groups in the belief that they automatically have views and feelings similar to those with the same skin hue, African Americans are as diverse as people come. This is why I would argue that a consensus could not be reached on whether or not black athletes should compete in or boycott the 1968 Olympic Games.

While it was very clear to Edwards, the boycott leader, that sports was much like the rest of society with the same kinds of limitations, constraints, barriers to opportunity, and the same persistent stereotypes, all the blacks involved in the Olympics could not agree on one single position or strategy. Nonetheless, Edwards kept "the powers that be" speculating and waiting at a press conference shortly before the games would start: "We will let you know about the future of your Olympic team when we deem it proper and we feel you can handle that type of information. Right now we just don't feel that you're ready" (Home Box Office 1996).

The black community was as divided as the black athletes. Jesse Owens and Jackie Robinson, for example, had two different views on the boycott debate. And so after a year of strong debate, the decision was announced that there was no decision on a unified response. Ralph Boston, an Olympic track star and member of the boycott leadership, issued the following statement: "There was no master plan. We could not come to a consensus that would unite everybody. Thus, the decision was made that everyone would do his or her own thing" (Home Box Office 1996).

Reflection 6: The Gesture Seen around the World

On the fifth day of the Olympics, as much of the world sat glued to the television sets, one event changed the world forever. After receiving their medals on the victory stand, Tommie Smith and John Carlos took their shoes off while raising their fists in the air. This symbolic moment had deep meaning for the two brave men: "The black socks worn are for the poverty in Black America. The right glove is for the power that exists in Black America" (Home Box Office 1996).

Hypocrisy would soon follow Smith's and Carlos's display of courage and consciousness. The United States Olympic Committee (USOC) gave Smith and Carlos twenty-four hours to leave Mexico City. Ralph Boston (black teammate of Smith and Carlos) asked the following question that interrogated the contradiction and treatment of the two activists: "If you're going to kick them out of the village, are you going to use their medals in the U.S. medal count?" (Home Box Office 1996).

Boston was never given an answer. The next day's events further alienated the remaining black athletes. A Czechoslovakian gymnast won many medals the next day and protested (her country was seized at the time) with her head turned to the side each time she stood on the victory stand. Her action was clearly visible for all to see, but no one made an issue of it. This clearly indicated that *who* made the protest was critical. Black athletes in revolt were unacceptable to the USOC. Would this make Smith and Carlos heroes?

The medals won by Smith and Carlos were included in the final count for the United States, thus making a difference. Overall, black athletes took home nearly half of the medals won by "the land of the free and home of the brave." Without question, black Olympians in Mexico City called attention to America's problems at home. Smith and Carlos would pay a heavier price later for their actions, but the biggest leap they made was in challenging America to deal with racism. The following year *Apollo 11* astronauts would land on the moon while at home the nation still wrestled with the problems of oppression based on skin color and sexual difference.

Reflection 7: The Better It Gets the Worse It Gets: Race Relations and Sports Today

Many positive changes have occurred since the 1968 Olympic fiasco. Women now have the Women's National Basketball Association (WNBA). African American men dominate high-profile sports such as football, basketball, and baseball. Latinos, Asians, and Samoan Americans are integrating sports as each year society opens new doors via integration and diversity. Michael Jordan recently retired, and one commentator noted that he had changed race relations because of his play and his appeal to the mainstream consumer. Yet some things have gotten worse. What does it mean that African American male athletes are now the number one endorser of products in America when young black males between the ages of eighteen to twenty-five are incarcerated and killed in disproportionate numbers?

Michael Jordan without question has helped race relations in this country, but has he helped change the perception of the average African American male walking down the avenue? I would argue, as scholar Jay Coakley does, that Nike-sponsored images of Michael Jordan may be found around the world but that those images present an illusion that black athletes and citizens have achieved equality and that society operates on a level playing field. Nike and other corporations have worked hard to sever the Jordan persona from connections with African American experiences. This allows consumers comfortably to ignore the legacies of colonialism and racism that still affect people's economic, political, and social lives today in the United States (Coakley 1998).

Michael Jordan transgresses race by becoming "an exception to the rule," which is the stereotype of the young, threatening black male. He serves as the good or safe Negro by means of his celebrity, his apolitical approach to social issues, and his role as the epitome of the assimilation paradigm. What would happen to the sports industry if a figure like Curt Flood, Muhammad Ali, or Paul Robeson were in Jordan's shoes?

And are we so far away from the Jesse Owens who raced against a horse when, in October of 1998, Ben Johnson raced against a horse to justify a charitable endeavor? This is very problematic, as there are too many historical and moral implications associated with this kind of action (see the *Toronto Star,* October 8, 1998). In a time when the "Dream Team" earns more in endorsements than they do on the court, we are humbled by the realities of life after sports for black athletes.

As we move toward the next millennium sports confronts many racial problems. Power is the biggest variable in this struggle, even more than skin hue. African Americans represent less than 5 percent of the leadership in collegiate sports and less than 10 percent in professional sports. Outside of football, basketball, and track and field, there continue to be barriers to participation either at the subordinate or leadership level. And now a generation of athletes walks away from the politics of an earlier group of athletes who paved the way for them. Perhaps the 1999 National Basketball Association (NBA) strike offers a slight sign of a renewed sense of commitment to political and social action.

Overall, black masculinity in postmodern society has taken on new meaning. Black male athletes do not perceive sports as a vehicle for addressing political issues like their forefathers Smith and Carlos did. Sports are a means to making large sums of money, accumulating material goods, and attracting women. This contemporary situation is far from the vision that Harry Edwards and all those involved saw back in 1968. Never before or since have athletes sought to engage in such ambitious social activism. Some African American athletes even reject their obvious responsibility as role models. Modern athletes generally avoid involvement in any movement that is even remotely controversial. What these same athletes should remember and honor thirty-two years after 1968 is the courage of Smith and Carlos to use their athletic excellence to stand for something larger than themselves, to strive to make our society a better, fairer place (see *USA Today,* October 1, 1998).

Harry Edwards recently commented, "Thirty years ago I was hated, told to be quiet, and ostracized. Now they call me a consultant and pay me a whole lot of money and I am saying the same thing now as I was then" (Edwards 1998).

CHAPTER 5

"We Showed the World the Nordic Way": Skiing, Norwegians, and the Winter Olympic Games in the 1920s

E. JOHN B. ALLEN

"I have explained to Sweden and Norway that they are not Olympic Games, that the International Olympic Committee has only given itself as patron. . . . It is absolutely essential, as I have already said . . . to the Marquis de Polignac [French member of the IOC] that the winter games do not take on the character of Olympic Games."[1] So said Sweden's Sigfred Edström in 1922. But everyone else thought of them as Winter Olympic Games.

Ski-Idraet

What was the fuss, especially from those northern folks who owned virtually all the records, whether for speed across country, for distance and style in jumping, or for knowledge and history of the sport? Nothing less than a birthright was at stake. Therein lay the heart of many objections which welled up in the years when skiing was being proposed for inclusion in the Olympic canon. But whose birthright was it? The squabbles of the Scandinavians with those promoting winter games were only equaled by the political infighting between Norway and Sweden, infighting which was played out in assemblies and parliaments, in barracks and officers messes, in ski committee meetings, on the valley floors, in the woods, and on the jumping hills.

For nearly one hundred years, Norway had chafed under Swedish rule. In the nineteenth century, Norwegian romantic nationalism found its voice in poet, playwright, folklorist, and skier Fridtjof Nansen. Nansen became the new Viking incarnate when he crossed Greenland on skis in 1888. Nansen, quipped one nationalist, "got cold for Norway, not for Sweden."[2] The great annual competitions held at Holmenkollen jump on the hills above Christiania (Oslo) became national festivals. Norwegians began to believe that they were born on skis.

FIGURE 5.1

"The Jackson-Harmsworth Polar Expedition—'I am awfully glad to see you': The meeting of Mr. Jackson and Dr. Nansen in Franz Josef Land."
The Illustrated London News, September 12, 1896.

This was not skiing as we think of it today. It carried with it the heavy, philosophical baggage of *ski-idraet*. *Idraet* is always translated as "sport," but it does not mean only that. Nansen once wrote to an Austrian admirer, "It is not my fault that *Idraet* is translated into Sport. . . . Sport has taken on the meaning of making records and championships. I can't stand that. *Idraet* should remain very fresh and free and not fall under such amusement."[3] *Ski-idraet* meant the bettering of the individual body and soul through skiing in the great outdoors. This inspiriting carried over to family and community. The sport, wrote Nansen, "is perhaps of far greater national importance than is generally supposed."[4]

These were the ideas, of course, only of the educated elite, an elite determined to get out from under Swedish domination. The chance came in 1905, at a time when the world seemed convulsed in insurrection, revolution, and war. Norway's consular service had long been under Swedish control. Large mercantile interests in Norway had objected for years, and Norwegian national pride was piqued. Forts were built on the frontier but war was averted; Sweden did not force the issue. Norway became free. Nansen, who had spoken out strongly for independence—he was by this time a European, even a world figure—was struck from his honorary membership in the Swedish Ski Association.[5]

During the pre-separation years, Swedish nationalist Colonel Viktor Balck sponsored the Nordiska Spelen (Nordic Games). He hoped to keep Norway in the fold by giving Norwegians something to crow about yet ensuring continued Swedish control. Immediately dubbed "the Northern Winter Olympic Games" by the rest of Europe, the games were first held in 1901 and were planned to take place in Stockholm every four years. (In fact, they took place in 1905, 1909, 1913, 1922, and 1926.) Pierre de Coubertin, founder of the modern Olympic Games, greatly admired the cross-country running and marveled at the ski-joring (skiers being pulled by a horse, used mostly for military dispatch work). By 1903 he saw the games as a "durable institution."[6] This durable institution was, in fact, a fiercely nationalistic festival in which the drama of Swedish peasantry and homage to royalty past and present were just as important as the games and sports.[7] The Norwegians boycotted the 1905 games; they were actually in progress while the consular crisis reached its most critical moments.

The Nordiska Spelen spawned the Nordische Spiele (Nordic Games) in Mürzzuschlag, near Vienna, Austria. Competitors in Austria raced for the Nansen medals in 1904 and again in 1906, dates chosen to alternate with the Nordiska Spelen in Stockholm.[8] These events had their roots in a curious coincidence. The Norwegian baron Wedel von Jarlsberg held a diplomatic position in the Swedish embassy in the Austro-Hungarian capital. When the Viennese discovered skiing, the baron became their mentor, though he was no expert. Since he was also an uncle of Fridtjof Nansen's wife, Eva, and a major supporter of the building of the *Fram,* Nansen's North Pole ship, the Mürzzuschlag leadership was able to capitalize on Nansen's fame. Nansen accepted honorary membership in the club and allowed his name to be associated with the Nansen hut on the local mountain. Hence the duplication in Mürzzuschlag of the skiing sports of the Nordiska Spelen.

Skiing and Military Readiness

Coubertin had been thrilled over the ski-joring. But he was not the only one. The London *Times* at the 1909 games made much of the "military day," when a squad of sixteen horses pulling skijorers raced round the three-hundred-yard oval in fours.[9] These games, still run by Colonel Balck, had strong support from the Swedish military and from the wealthy sectors of society. Balck, "Trumpet of the Fatherland," saw skiing and physical exercise as excellent military preparation that would make Sweden a strong nation. The commercial interests reveled in the economic possibilities of winter tourism. The summer Olympic Games of 1912 had brought enormous prestige to Sweden, and it was hoped that the 1913 Nordiska Spelen would be the winter complement. But Balck could not control the weather. The races had to be transferred to Östersund, 700 kilometers by rail to the north, and snow by the cartloads was brought in to Fiskartorpet—Stockholm's answer to Holmenkollen—for the jumping. The 150-kilometer military race was run under appalling conditions of rain and slush.[10] It was hardly "Olympic."

With war looming, European leaders were worrying more about each other's military plans than about interesting the Scandinavians in holding Winter Olympic Games. Coubertin later claimed that he had tried continually to get winter events included in an Olympic program, but in reality he had not been enthusiastic. There were problems among skaters, speed skaters, ice hockey players, and bobsledders, let alone the arguments over ski jumping and ski races. Skating, particularly, seemed an artificial, urbanized sport, whereas skiing, at least, belonged far from the city. Coubertin appreciated ski-joring for its military application. Cross-country skiing, too, was useful both for military and civilian communications. Yet Coubertin was not wholly in favor of skiing because, first, it seemed to belong to Norwegians only and, second, those few who did practice it in the Alps were peasant mountain boys. When tourists took to skiing as a sport, Coubertin considered them fêtards—frivolous amusement seekers.[11] He was disinclined to include skiing, for it was hardly a sport to uphold his Olympic ideals of international peace and reconciliation shrouded under the auspices of antiquity.

Others had different ideas. Nothing had come of an 1899 Czech proposal to hold skiing events as part of the 1900 Olympic Games.[12] Over the years, there were minor attempts to get a winter Olympic program going, but they always ran up against the adamantly negative Colonel Balck. Finally, in 1910, there were such harsh words for the colonel that he agreed to bring the issue before the IOC meeting the following year. He had to be reminded to do so, and when pressed, replied simply that it was impossible as the Nordiska Spelen were arranged for 1913. The Italian representative, Baron Eugen Brunetta d'Usseaux, then suggested that

Balck's Nordiska Spelen be accepted as part of the Fifth Olympiad. This produced, according to the minutes, a "very animated" discussion which resulted in a decision a few days later that the Nordiska Spelen would not be part of any Olympic program.[13] The Swedes—and the Norwegians—did not like the idea of "their" sport being controlled by an international group that had not been brought up with skiing, nor did they appreciate that it would make the Olympic Games even more of an extravaganza than it was. After the 1913 Nordiska Spelen were over, the IOC finally allowed cross-country skiing and ski jumping (along with rugby, hockey, archery, polo, ice hockey, and speed skating) as demonstration sports.[14] The Scandinavians, it seemed, were ever more protective of their sport, while the IOC sensed a movement to expand winter sports competitions.

Sports, in the years leading up to World War I, were increasingly seen as preparation for military usefulness. Bound up with a nation's fitness, discipline, and nationalism, preparation for the Olympics was "in the best interest of the army itself," wrote the German Carl Diem by way of preparing for the 1916 games, which had been awarded to Berlin, with the winter section to be held in the Black Forest. In a February 1914 Reichstag debate, a Dr. Müller extolled the Olympic Games as an indicator of the strength of a nation and added ominously that all the training of young people would make them "physically ready for other endeavors as well."[15] By this time, von Hindenburg had mobilized ski detachments, Wilhelm Paulcke had gathered a volunteer corps,[16] and soon German troops would find themselves on skis in the Carpathians, the Dolomites, and the Vosges.

Meanwhile the French had become shrill in their call for the regeneration of France. What was needed was "combatants and the mothers of combatants" in or out of the marriage bed.[17] Pouring off the presses were exhortations in books, pamphlets, and postcards to produce children.[18] The trouble was in the high country—from where recruits for skiing units might come—where "one is unhappily impressed by the ricketts of the race. In 5 male births one has trouble . . . to find a man of 20 fit for service."[19]

The Club Alpin Français (CAF) was quick to realize "skiing's patriotic and military reach." Skiing was the means to halt the dissipation of energies and to regenerate the race, to ensure "strong men and strong soldiers."[20] The ski competitions that CAF organized every year, in 1907 at Mont Genèvre, 1908 at Chamonix, 1909 at Morez, 1910 at Eaux Bonnes and Cauterets, 1911 at Lloran, and so on, that is, all over snow-covered France, through to the war, were not merely international meets; they became tests of the race. The military fully supported the meets; they provided the band, teams of soldiers, and any number of ranking officers who spoke of mountain sports being "incomparable in making men valiant and vigorous."[21] Captain Rivas, the third commander of the military ski school at Briançon, sent his men back to their villages as "apostles for skiing"; it was necessary "for national defense to get skis to the montagnards."[22]

Increasingly CAF's meets took on a military cast. The patronage committee for the 1910 competitions, for example, included the minister of war, the under-secretary to the minister of war, the military governor of Lyon, and five generals.[23] In 1913, CAF also instituted the skier-brevet, whereby successful candidates could choose which ski regiment they joined when called to the colors. It also launched "a patriotic appeal" for skis for mountain youth.[24] "L'Oeuvre de la Planche de Salut" had a double meaning, which no one could miss: skis were not just "boards of salvation" for France, they were also "boards of last resort"—as one might throw out to a drowning swimmer.

Nowhere else in Europe was skiing enjoyed with such desperation. Yet, to the Nordic nations, France's annual Winter Sports Weeks—always with Scandinavians in attendance—seemed a peculiarly French occasion, as little "Olympic" as their own Nordiska Spelen. In an extraordinary about face, just before the war, the Norwegians decided to support skiing in an Olympic program.[25] This amazed and horrified the Swedes and so surprised the Germans, who had been given the 1916 games, scheduled for Berlin, that it was the Norwegians who led the discussion in the IOC for the inclusion of skiing. Here was a chance for Norway to get out from under Balck's tutelage. Besides, the weather worked against the continuation of the Nordiska Spelen at Stockholm. The first Winter Olympic events were scheduled to take place on the Feldberg in the Black Forest. But in 1916 the Great War was the "Great Game."

After the War

The eighteenth IOC meeting, held in August of 1920, was much exercised over the issue of winter games. Coubertin penciled in on one protocol, "Les sports d'hiver sont douteux."[26] They had become doubtful because the Norwegians—in yet another extraordinary move—had returned to their old view that the Scandinavians should control skiing.[27] Swedish and Norwegian representatives issued a formal statement: "If the Olympic Congress takes this step against our wishes—we announce to the Congress that they may not count on participation from the Nordic countries."[28]

The French continued to pursue their goal in the IOC meeting of May 1921. The Comte de Clary and Marquis de Polignac were insisting that France—Paris being the chosen venue for the 1924 Olympic Games—be given the right to stage a "Winter Sports Week." Article 53 of the Olympic Charter, however, said that a designated Olympic city could not split its privilege with another. Paris could not hold winter events. But in discussion the position emerged that this hard and fast rule could not apply to winter competitions. It was tacitly accepted that, should there be winter games, they should be in the same host country, if not city. When, therefore, the French IOC members suggested their traditional Winter Sports Week, held from 1907 on with international participation, it was not seen as unreasonable. However, by far the most appealing aspect of this solution was the immediate acceptance of the proposal by Sweden's Sigfred Edström, who assured the IOC that the Scandinavians would have no objection to a Winter Sports Week. De Clary and de Polignac, however, wanted to tie the Winter Sports Week to the Olympic Games. A formula was worked out whereby it was called "an international olympic meet of winter sports," a "secondary annex," a "winter prelude" to the summer games to be held in Paris.[29]

With much misgiving then, the Scandinavians had decided to compete. Their next Nordiska Spelen were set for 1922. Again, they were not a success. When tobogganers received better prizes than skiers, those from Norrland not only lodged a protest but also threatened to resign from the Swedish Ski Association. There was more to it than that. Sledding was sport; skiing remained part of *idrott,* Swedish for *idraet.* Sledding was for the leisure class; skiing was manly. This was not the first time these arguments had been voiced, but in the past there had been criticism of the Nordiska Spelen mainly from the political center and center left, from papers such as *Social-Demokraten.* Now they were joined by the liberal *Stockholms Tidning* and *Dagens Nyheter* while others drew a picture of ephemeral salon sports compared with the "real" sports.[30] Were the Nordiska Spelen going to be a social extravaganza or were they going to hark back to true *idrott?*

Almost immediately after the Nordiska Spelen ended, Edström wrote to Coubertin, "the Northern Games are now finished. They have not been a success. I much more believe in the coming international games at Chamonix and I am doing my best to persuade the northern countries to take part there." But, he warned the baron, the games must not be called Olympic. "If they are called international, then the Norwegians, Swedes and Finns will all come." This may appear to the modern eye as merely semantic. But not so in the early 1920s. Games called "Olympic" were organized, administered, and adjudicated by the IOC, a body which—for Norwegians—had no knowledge of what skiing was all about. When the French National Olympic Committee called for an IOC Congress to regulate the winter games, it appeared to the Scandinavians that the French were turning their international week into Winter Olympics. "It is essential," Edström wrote separately to de Polignac and to de Clary, "that the winter games do not take on the character of Olympic Games."[31]

All this obviously had some effect on the Chamonix insiders. When Frantz-Reichel, secretary of the games, showed the Chamonix installation plans to the IOC in Rome in April 1923, he carefully referred to the contests as a "Winter Sports Week" even though the paper from which he was talking was titled "Exposé sur la préparation, l'organisation et déroulement des épreuves des Premiers Jeux Olympiques d'Hiver à Chamonix du 24 janvier au 5 février 1924"! He confirmed, in reply to Edström's direct question, that this was not an integral part of the Olympic Games, but merely under IOC patronage. At this same meeting, the Dutch, who were to hold the next Olympic Games, pointed out that it would be impossible to hold the second Winter Sports Week in Holland due to climatic factors.[32] Trouble obviously lay ahead.

If there was a degree of care within the IOC not to offend the Norwegians and Swedes, elsewhere the Chamonix Winter Sports Week was being considered the Winter Olympics. Henry Cuënot, president of CAF's Winter Sports Commission, the organization which had run every Winter Sports Week in France from its inception in 1907, blatantly announced in the Executive Committee that "the Olympic Games would be held at Chamonix, 25 January and the following days." The British referred openly to "the Olympic Games." The Americans were thrilled that the Aerial Railway would take them up to the Aiguille du Midi "in time for the Olympics." "Winter Olympics at Chamonix" headlined the *Mirroir des Sports* in December 1923, and *Neige et Glace* ran a cover photo of the Chamonix valley, "the theater of the first Winter Olympics." There were "eliminatoires Olympiques" held at Briançon. The IOC insisted on the visitors' tax, which no participant to the summer games had to pay, to show that this Winter Sports Week was not like the summer Olympic Games. But in the end, participants did not have to pay the tax. And surely it was not by chance that de Clary asked for and obtained the Olympic oath at the opening of the winter games, something featured on the cover of *L'Illustration,* the middle classes' weekly glossy par excellence. The more proletarian *Petit Journal* described how "The Olympic Games of 1924 have just begun."[33] Quite evidently just about everybody thought of the Chamonix games as the first Winter Olympics.

Skiing and the Amateur

The Norwegians had spectacular success: gold, silver, and bronze medals in every skiing event except one, and then they got the gold *and* silver in that: a clean sweep in the fifty kilometer, in the special jump, and in the most nurtured of their *idraet,* the combined event. Thorleif Haug alone won three gold medals. "We Showed the World the Nordic Way," the Norwegian *Sportliv* headlined.[34]

Norway had been showing the world the organizational way for fourteen years as well. The Norwegian Ski Association was founded in 1908 and put out immediate feelers for the control of international skiing by inviting all the skiing nations to a congress in Christiania in 1910.[35] Ten countries were represented (among them Bohemia and Scotland). An International Ski Commission was appointed comprising a Norwegian, a Swede, and a middle European—who could not be found, so his place was taken by a Norwegian. These congresses were held annually until the Great War. Generally, the Norwegians got their way where rules of competition were concerned. One vexing problem was the judging of the jump, always the centerpiece of any competition. Norwegians believed that style was of more importance than distance achieved. Accordingly, points were assigned to reflect this. Yet many nations' representatives—and jumpers, too—were taken by the ever-attracting notion of record breaking. The Americans at the Chamonix week, for example, jumped "with fierce determination that was admirable but their style was atrocious."[36] Yet if the jump was the most important of the competitions, the real hero was the man who won the combined event, in which points were given for both jumping and cross-country running. Inspired by the *idraet* concept of the all-round skier, the winner of the combined represented the ideal ski man.

However, by far the most contentious issue concerned not only who was and was not an amateur, but also whether those deemed professional could or could not race. The debate was really over ski teachers. According to Norwegian writ, skiing was not something to be taught at all; it was something you did from the moment you could walk. The last thing you should do was pay someone else to show you how to ski. When Captain Roll opened the first international congress in 1910 by saying how fortunate the ski sport was to be purely amateur, he added the Norwegian imprimatur to what elites in Europe had been expressing for a decade.

Among those elites, especially among the British, there was no need of hard and fast lines to be drawn in statutes. There was an understanding that no man had to explain: the relationship between mountaineer and guide, athlete and trainer, and on the cricket pitch between "gentlemen" and "players." It was a surprise to most Europeans that the British came to wield such influence in skiing matters when they were hardly a skiing nation, sending no skier to the 1924 winter week (nor, indeed, to St. Moritz in 1928). Yet, through Arnold Lunn, known both as the "enfant terrible" and the "Pope of Skiing," they had a forthright publicist for what came to be called the "alpine disciplines." Once in the Alps (and only for a comparatively short length of holiday time), the elite wished to learn how to ski. Thus it was that the ski teacher came to play a far larger role in the amateur-professional debate than any discussions over mere money payments. Of course he received money for his services, but he might also obtain better conditions at hotel and ski centers because of his ability to attract clientele. Matters, then, were not so clear on the snows of Switzerland as they were in the London clubs.

Whether the teaching of skiing was a line of work at all caused much discussion prior to 1914, and when extended to the military, class became increasingly important since officers often competed. If a bricklayer, whose strength was derived from his manual labor, was not allowed to enter the Henley regatta, should an army officer in a ski regiment be allowed to enter competitions? The Swedish Sports Federation decided quite clearly in 1906 that "military men on active duty are amateurs."[37] That may have been easy enough for the Swedes, but for the British "all through the history of skiing," wrote a Mr. Howell in 1926, "the best instructors have notoriously in every country come from the 'officer class' rather than from among guides or N.C.O.'s."[38] It seemed possible, then, that officers might be dubbed professionals. Since they made up 44 percent of the Ski Club of Great Britain in 1905, this was not to be taken lightly.[39]

The representatives at the 1913 international congress decided that each national ski association could treat teachers how it wished, increasing, or not, "the stringency of rules for its own requirements."[40] This satisfied no one. As was immediately pointed out, a Swiss instructor could compete in Austria, but an Austrian instructor could not compete anywhere! The Scandinavians remained firm in their efforts to keep professionalism of any ilk out of international competitions, and most of the delegates to these conferences agreed.

Further difficulties were emerging: the beginnings of modern downhill and slalom racing. Both were an anathema to Norwegians in spite of the fact that they delighted in speed, and, of course, slalom was derived from the Norwegian *slalaam*. In 1913, Arnold Lunn, who "opened up a new epoch in skiing and it bore his personal stamp," as his friend, Walter Amstutz wrote in appreciation on his death in 1974,[41] began proselytizing for "downhill" racing.[42] Modern downhill and slalom have their origin in ski mountaineering. Once the peak had been reached, the view imbibed, and the pipe smoked, the skier would descend as straight as a die if possible, for the mark of a good skier was the straight track. Early downhill races were often called straight races, and "taking it straight," redolent of the fox hunt, was the mark of a skier with dash and verve. This was all very well above tree line. Once the woods were entered, the skier had to twist and turn his way down, avoiding the trees. Lunn stuck little branches in the snow, then flags, and finally poles, to simulate "tree running." At the end of it all, the object was to ensure that the good skier, after a glorious mountain day, reached the inn on the valley floor in safety. But skiing like this, especially the turning part, needed practice and instruction. Here is why the instructor in the Alps became such a problem in international meets. Still, before the Great War, there were not large numbers of instructors, and the caliber of skiing, let alone racing, was extremely poor.

The 1914 international congress was testy over rules and regulations for the 1916 games. The Swedes felt that they would lead to an ever more prize-winning ethos, something which could only injure the sport. The French request to have the minutes also in their language was refused. And the English, enthusiastic in their realization that skiing was becoming such a sport, also worried that it was becoming a military necessity.[43]

The International Federation of Skiing

The first international congress after the war met in Stockholm in 1922, just the time, it will be remembered, when the Nordiska Spelen had been such a failure, just the time when the Chamonix Winter Sports Week was becoming the first Winter Olympics in the minds of most people. This congress adopted rules and regulations which were identical to those presented by the Norwegians. It was becoming obvious, though, that with the growth of the sport, some new body was needed. The Czechs proposed an International Ski Association, which became reality as the Fédération Internationale de Ski (FIS) at Chamonix on February 2, 1924.[44]

The Fédération Internationale de Ski, in spite of its French title, continued to be dominated by the Scandinavians. Four Norwegians had been secretaries of the international ski congresses held between 1910 and 1924. The FIS elected Sweden's Ivar Holmquist, who spoke excellent French, as president, and two

Norwegians were vice president and secretary; thus the continued leadership kept the Scandinavian views of skiing to the fore. It was, then, with some surprise that this new FIS was confronted with the IOC decision in 1925, confirmed at Lisbon a year later, to turn the Chamonix Winter Sports Week retroactively into the First Winter Olympic Games. At FIS's second meeting in Lahti, the majority voted in favor of Winter Olympics governed by FIS rules. Norway, Sweden, and Finland voted against it, and the Norwegians actually walked out of the conference. Later the Swedes and Finns voted for holding the next Winter Olympics in St. Moritz.[45]

There remained two battles still to be fought. The first was to bring Norway into the Olympic family. How could a country which had won every skiing medal save one at the Chamonix week not be part of such an international winter festival as the Olympics? The second battle was to include what was now being called "the alpine disciplines," downhill and slalom.

Whether Norway should join in the Olympics engendered long and bitter arguments within the Norwegian Ski Association and, more publicly, in the newspapers. The debate turned on the question of perverting the Norwegian way of skiing, on the evils of specialization versus the excellence of all-round sports. The Norwegian Ski Association's aging board wanted to keep *ski-idraet* as pure as they perceived it had always been, but the new generation of skier, especially after the spectacular wins in France, was eager to compete. Leading the argument to join the Olympics were two well-connected military officers, Colonel Östgaard, one-time mentor to Norway's heir to the throne, and Lieutenant Helset, who had dismissed central European record chasing as something which could not harm Norwegian skiing anyhow. The vote in the Norwegian Ski Association to join in the St. Moritz Olympics was twenty-nine for, twenty-seven against. The leadership of the board resigned, and Östgaard and Helset found themselves in charge of Norwegian and—they trusted—international skiing.

The twenty-nine who voted for Norway's participation were amply vindicated.[46] Although the Swedes gained all the medals in the fifty-kilometer race, Norwegians made a clean sweep of the twenty-kilometer run and the combined, and won gold and silver in the special jump. It really did seem that "unless Norway had taken an active part in the Olympic Winter Games, she would not have been able to regain her position in the FIS and its work. . . . Norway . . . can for the future regard itself as the first ski-ing nation of the world."[47] This was high praise coming from Swedish Count Hamilton, a friend of alpine skiing.

Östgaard and Helset may have been riding high on the results of St. Moritz, but now they had to manage the British proposal for the inclusion of downhill and slalom. It is worth reminding ourselves that downhill and slalom were not at all like the polished performances seen on television today. Racing was a test of inventiveness in differing snow and trail conditions. In 1922, for example, a starter of a downhill event in Switzerland advised the candidates to adopt stick-riding (straddling their pole hobby-horse style) because of the poor conditions.[48]

It was the same with slalom—a Norwegian word! Norwegians had a variety of *laam,* or tracks. Oversimplifying, here are a few (there are so many dialect words): *kneikelaam* (run with bumps), *ufselaam* (run off a cliff), *hoplaam* (run with a jump or jumps), *svinglaam* (run with turns), and a daredevil run mixing all the obstacles, the *uvyrdslaam* or *ville lamir*—wild run. The *slalaam* was a descent around natural obstacles, again to prove that the all-round skier was capable of twisting and turning, and it had been included as an event in Norway in 1879. The race had not been popular but was reintroduced in 1906 to counter the emphasis that youth gave to jumping. In spite of the emphasis on speed, the competitor's style while negotiating the obstacles was taken into account by judges placed at the difficult sections of the course.[49]

When Norwegian skiing began to influence Europeans around the turn of the century, various experiments were tried. In the Black Forest of Germany, a *Kunstlauf* (skill race) was run in 1902. The next season it was described as a *Kunst-oder Hindernislauf* (skill or obstacle race). In 1904 there was a *stilgemässes Laufen* (style point race) which required a run down a steep slope with turns and swings. For 1906 this same race required specific swings, poles were not allowed, and speed was not considered.[50] The above descriptions show very well the experimental nature of early slalom. Mathias Zdarsky's eighty-five-gate *torlauf* set in 1905 has received most attention as the beginning of modern slalom. Although it was officially styled a "ski race" (*Ski-Wettfahren*) rather than a "judged alpine run" (*alpines Wertungsfahren*), as Zdarsky had wished, it was designed as a "testing run" (*Prüfungsfahren*), for technique rather than speed.[51] I have found only two other Zdarsky slaloms, in 1906 and 1909. It was from Lunn's experiments—not Zdarsky's—that modern slalom emerged. After the war Lunn tried various types of rules, like assigning points for falling down. It was some time before he received support, first from the Swiss in 1926. When Norwegian captain Kristian Krefting came to observe what was happening, he reported back to Aftenposten: "They had this weird thing, called the Slalom Race. . . . In this they scurried round some small flags as fast as they could, turning hither and thither, breaking flags and falling down, and altogether looking quite comical."[52] Captain Krefting did not realize that this was the early technique of a new sport! No wonder Norwegians believed that alpine events were "a luxurious sort of skiing for rich people." They looked at the "up-by-rail-down-by-ski" crowd with contempt. Even so, the Norwegians voted within their own organization for the downhill and withheld judgment on slalom. Both were on the agenda for the upcoming FIS meeting in the Norwegian capital. But they were not going in with any enthusiasm. Östgaard wrote, "Englishmen do not sufficiently appreciate what we consider one of the best things of the ski running: the self-denial during training. The strengthening of character and will, of endurance and of energy which the training produces, is just as valuable from a sporting and human point of view, as the results obtained in the competitions themselves."[53] It could have been Nansen speaking.

Lunn marshaled support from several well-known and carefully chosen friends of downhill and slalom, friends such as Dr. Rösen, one of the first German supporters of downhill and slalom, and Rudolf Gomperz, an influential member of the Ski Club Arlberg where Hannes Schneider's *Schuss*—already Anglicized by 1930—had ousted the Norwegian Telemark turn from the Alps. From the Tyrol and the Black Forest came calls for the alpine disciplines. Even the Swedes seemed inclined to try the new forms of skiing, and from far away Canada came word from the Empire that slalom was "the fairest test of all-round ski ability, and should be taken up all over the country."[54] Some Swiss were more blunt: "The Norwegian dictatorship must cease."[55]

Thus the 1930 FIS meeting had high potential for misunderstanding and even anger, or compromise and acceptance. It turned out to be something of an anticlimax because the delegates were much preoccupied over the arrangements for the Winter Olympic Games to be held at Lake Placid in 1932. The Scandinavians especially, but others too, had real doubts that the Americans were up to running such a festival. The alpine disciplines were discussed in a loaded committee with Lieutenant Helset as the lone naysayer. On the floor of the full meeting, according to one observer, Östgaard had "seen the handwriting on the wall, and thought he might as well give in graciously as to be outvoted." The "Peace of Oslo" was signed at last, and Lunn raised his little Union Jack.[56] It would take another six years before downhill and slalom made their Olympic debut at Garmisch-Partenkirchen.

It had taken a full eight years from 1922 to 1930 for Norwegians to join the Winter Olympics as well as to sanction alpine disciplines, however unwilling they had been and still were. General societal changes, especially after the Great War, bore heavily on their decisions. *Ski-idraet* was still a strong enough force to garner all but one of the medals at Chamonix and almost as many at St. Moritz, but *ski-idraet* was not strong enough to resist the challenge that the new disciplines of downhill and slalom presented. The skiing world divided over those that remained "Nordic" and those that became "Alpine." This was not a matter of mere technique. The arguments contained a clash of philosophies. Norwegian *ski-idraet* appeared good, true, healthy, and, above all, real, something that was peculiarly Norwegian. Alpine skiing was social, expensive, what detractors called "hotel sport," and so invented that it required teaching. It was also open to anybody in snow-covered mountain lands.

Since the Olympics were also open to anybody, something of the quality of *ski-idraet* gave way. Yet the Norwegian ski fathers did all they could to ensure that their way of skiing did not disappear in the increasingly large extravaganza of the Winter Olympic Games. The Chamonix Winter Sports Week illustrates the various and many strands to the arguments over what constituted true sports and just who should compete in the international arena of the Olympic Games.

NOTES

1. Letter from Sigfred Edström to Baron de Clary, Vesterås, April 26, 1922. TS (typescript) in Musée Olympique, Lausanne, Switzerland. Archives folder: Chamonix 1924, file: Chamonix General 1924 (hereafter cited as MO).

2. Henrik Angell cited by Tor Bomann-Larsen, *Den evige sne.* (Oslo: Cappelens, 1993), 75.

3. Letter from Fridtjof Nansen to Max Kleinoscheg, Lysaker, February 12, 1904. TS in file: Nachlass Mehl no. 19, Wintersportmuseum, Mürzzuschlag, Austria.

4. Thus the English translation by Hubert Gepp, Nansen, *The First Crossing of Greenland* (London: Longmans, Green, 1919), 55. For the original see Nansen, *Paq Ski over Grøn-land* (Oslo: Aschehoug, 1890), 78–79.

5. Jan Lindroth, "The Nordic Games, Swedish-Norwegian Relations and Politics, 1905–1913—a Study of Sport and Politics in Conflict," in *Winter Games Warm Traditions,* ed. Matti Goksøyr et al. (Lillehammer: ISHPES, 1994), 297.

6. Pierre de Coubertin in *Revue Olympique* (April 1901): 17–249, reprinted in *Textes Choisis,* ed. Norbert Müller (Zurich: Weidmann, 1986), 2:311–317; and *Revue Olympique* (February 1903): 13–14, in Müller, *Textes Choisis,* 2:318.

7. Jens Ljunggren, "The Nordic Games, Nationalism, Sports, and Cultural Conflicts," in Goksøyr et al., *Winter Games Warm Traditions,* 35–37.

8. *Allgemeine Sport-Zeitung,* November 15, 1903, January 3, 1904; *Allgemeines Korrespon-denzblatt,* February 16, 1906.

9. *The Times,* February 10, 1909, 10.

10. Ibid. February 10, 1913, 14, February 11, 1913, 13, and February 14, 1913, 15.

11. Pierre de Coubertin in *Revue Olympique* (February 1908), reprinted in Müller, *Textes Choisis,* 3:240.

12. *Czech Olympic Media Team Guide: XVII Olympic Winter Games* (Praha: Czech Olympic Committee, 1994), cited in Ron Edgeworth, "Nordic Games," *Citius, Altius, Fortius 2,* no. 2 (1994): 34.

13. IOC, Luxemburg, June 11–13, 1910; Procès-Verbal, CIO, Budapest, May 23, 1911. TS in MO. Wolf Lyberg, "The IOC Sessions, 1894–1955," 53. TS in MO. See also Frik Bergvall, ed., *The Official Report of the Olympic Games of Stockholm, 1912,* trans. Edward Adams-Ray (Stockholm: Wahlström and Widstrand, 1913), 53, 60.

14. IOC, Paris, June 15–23, 1914, in Lyberg, "IOC Sessions," 83.

15. Carl Diem, "Aufgaben für 1916," *Fussball und Leichtathletik* 14 (1913): 465, in Arnd Krüger, "The History of the Olympic Winter Games: The Invention of Tradition." Paper read to ISHPES conference, Lillehammer, January 25–30, 1994, TS, 10. This has been published, without footnotes, in Goksøyr et al., *Winter Games Warm Traditions,* 101–122. Dr. Müller (Progressive Party), Deutscher Reichstag, Stenographischer Bericht, 214. Sitzung, February 14, 1914 (Berlin: 1914): 7339, in Krüger, TS, 10. For the 1916 winter games, see *Der Winter* 8, no. 16 (February 11, 1914): 382, and 8, no. 18 (February 25, 1914): 453–454. *The Times* (December 20, 1913): 7; Norges Skifor-bund, *Aarsberetning* (1914): 41–43. See also *Deutsche Turn-Zeitung* (1914): 528, cited in Karl Lennartz, *Die VI. Olympischen Spiele 1916* (Köln: Carl-Diem Institut, 1978), 116.

16. For Hindenburg's interest, see letter from von Hindenburg to Ski Club Todtnau, Berlin, February 5, 1893, where he ordered twenty-four pairs of skis; and from Max Schnei-der he obtained thirty-six pairs. HMS, copy, privately held in Todtnau. See also letter from Max Schneider to CIL [Carl Luther], Rostock, July 13, 1930. HMS in Deutsches Skiverband Archiv, Planegg, Germany: Luther Collection. In 1912, the Prussian War Ministry ordered ten thousand pairs of skis. *Der Winter* 7, no. 8 (December 19, 1912): 232. For Paulcke, see Wilhelm Paulcke, "Freiwillige Ski-Corps," *Der Winter* 6, no. 5 (December 2, 1911): 86–88.

17. Camille Maucliar, "La magie de l'amour," 1913 *Essais sur l'amour I* (Paris: Ollendorf, nd.), 129, 132, cited in Priscilla Robertson, *An Experience of Women: Patterns and Change in Nineteenth-Century Europe* (Philadelphia: Temple University Press, 1982), 221.

18. Richard Tomlinson et al., "France in Peril," *History Today* (April 1985): 24–3 1; E. John B. Allen, "French Skiing: The Way to National Health," in *Sport et santé dans l'histoire,* ed. Thierry Teret (Sankt Augustin: Academia, 1999): 319–326.

19. Henri Clerc, "Rapport des experiences de skis éxécuté dans les environs de Briançon par le 159 me. Reg. D'inf au cours des hivers 1900–1901 et 1901–1902." HMS in Musée Dauphinois, Grenoble. A great number of conscripts were shorter than 1.54 m. André Palluel-Guillard, "Problèmes sanitaires et physiologiques de la Savoie au XIXe siècle," *Mosaïques d'Histoire en Savoie* 88 (1983): 71.

20. Henry Cuënot, "Le ski, ses origines en France et le rôle du C.A.F. dans son développement," *La Montagne* 321 (March–April 1931): 98. Cuënot, "Le rôle de la Fédération Française de Ski," Les *Sports de Neige et Glace* 4, no. 59 (January 16, 1926): 53.

21. *La Montagne* (1908): 31.

22. Captain Rivas, *Petit manuel du skieur* (Briançon: Vollair, 1906).

23. *La Montagne* (1910): 122–123.

24. *La Montagne* 9, no. 4 (April 1913): 240. For a critical view, see Georges Rozet, "Les sports. Officiers, et soldats sportifs: le ski," *L'Opinion* (February 10, 1912), in Album Memento AR 1502, CAF Archives, Paris.

25. Norges Skiforbund, *Aarsberetning* (1914): 41–43.

26. CIO, Antwerp, August 17–21, 23–24, 30, 1920. TS in MO.

27. Norges Skiforbund, *Aarsberetning* (1921): 17–18.

28. Procès-Verbal, CIO, Lausanne, June 4, 1921, 8, in MO.

29. Ibid., June 5, 1921, 10, in MO. See also Pierre Arnaud and Thierry Terret, *Le rêve blanc. Olympisme et sport d'hiver en France: Chamonix 1924 Grenoble 1968* (Bordeaux: Presses Universitaires de Bordeaux, 1993), 58, 73.

30. Ljunggren, "Nordic Games," in Goksøyr at al., *Winter Games Warm Traditions,* 37–41.

31. Letter from Edström to Coubertin, Vesterås, February 14, 1922. TS, copy in Coubertin Correspondence: Sigfred Edström, 1908–1923, in MO. Letter from Edström to de Clary, Vesterøs, April 26, 1922. TS in MO, folder: Chamonix 1924, file: Chamonix General/1924.

32. "Exposé sur la préparation, l'organisation et déroulement des épreuves des Premiers Jeux Olympiques d'hiver à Chamonix du 24 janvier au 5 février 1924." TS in MO, folder: Chamonix 1924, file: General. Procès-Verbal, CIO, Rome, April 7–12, 1923; Lyberg, "IOC Sessions," 113.

33. *La Montagne* 19, no. 163 (June 1923): 202; *Ski Notes and Queries* 22 (December 1923): 2; *New York Times,* December 15, 1923, 4; *Mirroir des Sports* 12, no. 128 (December 14, 1922): 370; *Neige et Glace* 1, no. 1 (October 11, 1923): cover; various notes on the visitors' tax in file: 8 M 58, Renouvellement de la taxe de séjour 1916–1934, in Archives départementales d'Haute Savoie, Annecy. "Programme des Eliminatoires olympiques . . ." by the Briançon Syndicatif d'Initiative, in Bibliothèque de Briançon. *L'Illustration* (February 2, 1924): cover; *Le Petit Journal* (February 1924): cover.

34. Cited by Kristen Mo, "Norwegian Participation in the Winter Olympics of the 1920's: The Debate in the Norwegian Ski Association." Paper read to ISHPES conference, Athens, 1989, TS, 4.

35. "Die internationale Conferenz über Skisport in Christiania February 1910." Program in Holmenkollen Skimuseet Archives.

36. H. de Watteville, "The Olympic Winter Games at Chamonix," *British Ski Year Book* 2, no. 5 (1924): 230.

37. P. Mark, "'Den eviga mumien.' Amatöfragans behandling I svensk idrott, 1890–1967," *Svensk idrottshistorika foreningens aarskrift* 9 (1989), cited in Krüger, "History of the Winter Olympics," TS, 14.

38. *Ski Notes and Queries* 29 (April 1926): 96–97.

39. *Year-Book of the Ski Club of Great Britain* 1, no. 1 (1905): 44–46.

40. "International Regulation for Competitive Races, Approved by the Fourth International Ski Congress, Berne, 1913," *Year-Book of the Ski Club of Great Britain* 2, no. 9 (1913):245.

41. *Ski Suvey* 1, no. 7 (1974): 382–383.

42. Arnold Lunn, *Ski-ing* (London: Eveligh Nash, 1913), 188–191; Lunn, *Come What May* (Boston: Little Brown, 1941), 171.

43. W. H. Weedon, "The Fifth International Ski Congress at Christiania," *Year-Book of the Ski Club of Great Britain* 2, no. 10 (1914): 397–401.

44. The most easily accessible "history" of the FIS is in *Neige et Glace* 8, no. 130 (December 1, 1930): 62–64. For facts, such as lists of officers, see Dietmar Hubrich, "Die historische Entwicklung des Internationalen Skiverbandes 'FIS.'" Diplomarbeit an der Deutschen Hochschule für Körperkultur, Leipzig, 1975, no. D 7086, TS.

45. Letter from Svenska Skiförbundet, Stockholm, to President of the International Olympic Committee, June 6, 1924. TS in MO, file: St. Moritz 1928 Photocopies, Invitations 1926–1928. Commission Executive de Comité International Olympique, Paris., March 7, 1926, TS. Procés-Verbal, IOC Prague, 1925, and IOC Lisbon, 1926. HMSs in MO. For the Norwegian vote, see Mo, "Norwegian Participation," 5–6.

46. Mo, "Norwegian Participation, 5-6.

47. C.G.D. Hamilton, "The Swedish and Norwegian Year Books," *British Ski Year Book* 5, no. 10 (1929): 301.

48. Ibid. (1922): 392.

49. Einar Stoltenberg, cited by Olav Bø, in *Skiing Throughout History* (Oslo: Norske Samlaget, 1993), 53–54. Artur Zettersten, 29–31, HMS in Svenska Skidmuseet, Umeå, Sweden. More readily available is John Weinstock, "Sondre Norhemi: Folk Hero to Immigrant," *Norwegian-American Studies* 29 (1983): 347–348. For the 1879 event in Norway, see *Fedrelandet,* no. 20, cited in Jakob Vaage, *Skiennes Verden* (Oslo: Hjemmenes, 1978),132.

50. *Allgemeine Sport-Zeitung* 32, no. 14 (March 19, 1911): 305, and 34, no. 5 (February 2, 1913):114; Willi Romberg, *Mit Ski und Rodel. Taschenbuch für Wintersportlustige,* 2nd ed. (Leipzig: Leiner, 1910 [?]), 97–98; F. Klute, "Kunst-oder Hindernislauf? *Der Winter* 5, no. 22 (April 28, 1911): 342–343. See also, *Der Winter* 5, no. 23 (June 2, 1911): 357.

51. Letter from Mathias Zdarsky to Erwin Mehl, Marktl im Traisentale, February 3, 1932, Zdarsky-Archiv, Lilienfeld, Austria. Erwin Mehl, "Mathias Zdarsky (1856–1940)," in *Lilienfeld-Marktl: Lilienfeld als Wiege der alpinen Schifahrtechnik und des Torlaufes hier erfand Zdarsky sein lebensrettendes Zelt,* in Zdarsky Archive. Letters from Otto Lutter to Theodor Hutenegger, Graz, April 28, 1950, and to Richard Guttmann, Graz, May 1951. TSs in Fach Beiträge Skigeschichte Wertvoll, section L, Wintersportmuseum, Mürzzuschlag. Wolf Kitterle, *75 Jahre Torlauf* (Wien: Kitterle, 1979), has reprinted the original *Wettfahr-Urkunde ausgestellt für die Wettfahrer, Starker, Wegrichter und Zielrichter welche sich an dem Ski Wettfahren in Lilienfeld am 19. März 1905 beteiligten,* 4–23. For Zdarsky's challenge to the Norwegians, see *Alpiner Winter Sport,* 2, no. 11 (January 27, 1905): 153–154. See also C. M. Schwardtner, "Meine Reise nach Christiania," *Allgemeines Korrespondenzblatt* 2 (February 17, 1905): 109–111; Fleischmann und Steinbruchel, *Lilienfelder oder Norweger,* particularly 61–85. There were other challenges, see *Allgemeine Sport-Zeitung* 24 (April 26, 1903): 471, and 20 (February 5 and 12, 1899): 138, 165. There was also a challenge in 1993 at a meeting of museum directors held at the Olympic

Museum, Lausanne, September 30, 1993, when the director of the Swiss Sports Museum, Max Triet, was challenged over his interpretation of the beginning of slalom by Franz Klaus, of the Zdarsky-Archiv. There has been correspondence in various newsletters.

52. *Aftenposten,* translated by Mrs. Krefting and published in the *British Ski Year Book* 5, no. 2 (1930): 539.

53. N. R. Östgaard, "The Norwegians and Slalom and Downhill Races," *British Ski Year Book* 5, no. 11 (1930): 539.

54. *British Ski Year Book* 5, no. 10 (1929): 109–111.

55. *Sport* [Swiss] (May 24, 1929), translated and reprinted in *British Ski Year Book* 5, no. 10 (1929): 113–115.

56. Fred H. Harris "Report of the 11th FIS Congress, Oslo, 24–26 February 1930." TS in Dewey Archives, Lake Placid, NY. See also, E. John B. Allen, "The 1932 Lake Placid Winter Games: Dewey's Olympics," in *Olympic Perspectives,* ed. Robert K. Barney et al. (London, Ontario: Center for Olympic Studies, 1996), 164–165. For the flag raising, see Lunn, "The Bernese Oberland," in TS, 13–14, in box 4, folder 22, Sir Arnold Lunn Papers, Special Collections, Georgetown University, Washington, D. C.

PART TWO

MASCULINITIES/

FEMININITIES/

SEXUALITIES

CHAPTER 6

Sexism Images

Men of the Game

TOBY MILLER

I want to look here at masculinity on television in the Summer Olympic Games—itself perhaps a task of Olympian immodesty! After all, for much of their history, the games were restricted to men, and the International Olympic Committee excluded women until 1981 (Guttmann 1994, 132). Many more medal opportunities are available to men than women, some nations still decline to send female competitors, and international TV coverage excludes women's events from many Arabic eyes (de Moragas Spà et al. 1995, 22). Overall, most nations dedicate less than 5 percent of their sports media coverage to women, and what there is frequently condescends and trivializes (McKay 1997, 118). That means there is all the more need to interrogate mens' cultural premium on who gets to represent the nation. In this essay, I pay particular attention to an Australian

"Does it hurt?"
　　　—Laurie Lawrence,
　　　swimming coach

"Yeah, it bloody hurts."
　　　—Swimmers

"Does it hurt as much as this?"
　　　—Lawrence, running his knuckles
　　　across a brick wall until they bleed

There is something special about Laurie Lawrence. An indefinable quality which sets him apart—a quality of the human spirit which embodies trust and motivates those around him to give of their very best. . . .

His impact on the business community has been quite spectacular. He has proven to be uniquely capable of drawing clear parallels between business success and high sporting achievement.

　　　—Promotion for the 1996 Nation-
　　　wide Realty National Convention

91

swimmer and his coach at the 1988 Seoul Games. Drawing some conclusions based on debates about masculinity, I investigate the tensions between regimentation and excess that characterize the contemporary male sports body.

In their analysis of Australian nationalism and the Olympics, David Rowe and Geoffrey Lawrence explain why the media "break out into a nationalistic sweat" when a new star emerges. First, the appearance of such a star is an opportunity for the "unbounded rather than qualified exultation" that accompanies winning an ultimate prize. Second, it calls up Horatio-Algerish myths about a meritocracy in which all can rise to their deserved level of achievement and reward. And third, "the hero or heroine embodies an abstraction . . . [the spirit of the nation] and so helps to heal concrete rifts . . . between competing social groups" (Rowe and Lawrence 1986, 196–197). Of course, if the hero fails to appear, falls from grace, or is in some way compromised or rendered contradictory, then these "rifts" emerge anew. In a sense, then, Olympic audiences are witnesses to a potential crisis moment in sports, television, and nationhood. Such moments are ideal for critics to spot fissures in the wall of patriotism.

A Man Named Armstrong

Australian men have been spectacularly unsuccessful at the modern Olympics since 1976. [See chapter 18—eds.] As one of the three countries that has been represented at each modern Olympiad, with vast amounts of public money spent on elite athletics and the quest for a national image, this failure matters—not least given an aberrant demographic history that has contributed to the country's culture of masculinity.

Until this century, men far outnumbered women in post-invasion Australia, with the proportion of married people exceptionally low. This was the case because of a unique immigration pattern combined with the devastating global depression of 1890 and World War I mortality. The ratio of men to women was slightly over two to one in 1840. And it took until 1980 for the ratio to fall to just under one to one (Carmichael 1992, 107, 109, 120–121). These figures make for a deficit in equality and everyday cultural norms. From the first period of colonial settlement, sports were ineffably male, linked initially to drinking houses and the public violence of workingmen, and later to a cross-class, biologistic notion of "manliness." This ideology of manliness grew in power and complexity as connections were adduced across the nineteenth century between vitality, rurality, and the whiteness of Australian-born males ("cornstalks"). Local virility was much remarked on in the newspapers, especially with the advent of organized sculling in the 1850s and the popularity of swimming from the 1890s (Cashman 1995, 73, 76–77, 87). This local manliness made sports a key arena for differentiating the white Australian nation from Britain and then from the rest of the world, a differentiation that has been carried forward since by public mythology, governmental programs and propaganda, international image, media attention, and everyday talk. Sports have evidenced manliness, and manliness has made sports crucial to national identity.

What of sports stars? There have been many such Australian "heroes," from animals (mostly racehorses) to boxers, cricketers, and footballers. The human stars have usually been men. Only in tennis and the Summer Olympics have women taken their place, but normally in a subordinate relationship to men in terms of opportunities, rewards, and mythmaking. Yet despite a pattern of allocating attention and resources to male sports, and the vastly greater numbers of men chosen for the Olympics, Australian women have done much better at the games, especially since the Second World War (McKay 1991, 97). Thus the identification of Australian manliness with national sporting identity has been sorely tested.

Let's pursue the case of male swimmers at the Olympics—an ambiguous sport for both gender and nation. There they are, cocks outlined in form-hugging briefs, body hair trimmed for minimal drag, lean and leggy. We see them ducking and diving, turning and speeding, seemingly oblivious to the gaze of others and the actions of fellow competitors. Bug-eyed in goggles, their muscles strain with each eruption from the water. Our vision of them is from a multitude of angles—warming up, swimming (seen from above and below the water), atop the podium in victory, and shivering in interviews.

Swimming is a strangely androgynous sport. Because of gender segregation in swimming holes and pools, swimming has always been considered appropriate for women in Australia. Victorian and Edwardian commentators remarked approvingly that the submerged female body was mostly hidden at the point of exertion and did not produce unsightly sweat. Yet the near nakedness involved in swimming and the languorous connotations of still water have gradually accreted the activity with suspect meanings. The nineteenth-century argument for women swimming was contingent on proving that women were not "animated by unworthy intent," as some municipal officials feared (Cashman 1995, 87; officials quoted in Stoddart 1986, 143). And the fact that water is open to both sexes has led to a certain androgyny, which in turn stimulates compensatory practices by men. When U.S. Olympic swimmer Melvin Stewart was featured by NBC at the 1992 Barcelona games pumping iron, he offered, "[S]wimmers don't really need to do this. I do this purely for aesthetic reasons, to look better so I can pick up chicks" (quoted in Daddario 1997, 107). Ambiguity again, as "wanna-be" philandering, is acknowledged as aesthetic self-styling. Stewart's *macho* bodybuilding is a compensation for the androgyny of his championship sport.

The uncomfortable sense of the male body straining whilst almost naked can lead to some interesting practices of compensation in the media as well. The British Broadcasting Corporation has seen the perils to conventional masculinity incipient here: instructions to its camera operators for the 1976 Montreal games emphasized the need to capture swimmers' "straight lines," to suggest "strength, security, vitality and manliness" as opposed to "grace and sweetness" and "curved lines" (quoted in Peters 1976, 127). NBC commentators at the Barcelona pool in 1992 referred to the "prettiness" of women competitors rather than their speed, called them "girls," and used first names to identify them. The treatment of male swimmers was radically different (Higgs and Weiller 1994, 242–243).

Unstable gender identities are at work here. We can see them in the iden-tification of swimming with homoeroticism. Consider, for example, Duncan Grant's 1911 painting *Bathing,* which shows young men frolicking naked in the waters. Amongst gay sportsmen, swimming occupies an ambiguous place. On the one hand, it is regarded as "masculine" because of its self-sufficiency, fitness, strength, and skill. On the other, the sport's lack of aggressivity and intersubjective violence and the practice of shaving the legs and torso mark it out from body-contact games and can lead to a "faggy" reputation for college swimmers. Gay swim meets play this up, often featuring a "pink flamingo relay." Team members wear plastic flamingo hats and pull each other along, one kicking and the other stroking (Pronger 1990, 31–32, 270). Ambivalence about the manliness of the swim-mer is at play as well in the elite, heteronormative side to swimming, as we shall see in the case of Duncan Armstrong.

Armstrong, now a member of the International Swimming Hall of Fame, won the men's two-hundred-meter freestyle at Seoul; he was Australia's only male gold-medal winner there. He did so in a highly tactical and controversial way—by "surfing." This technique, pioneered at the 1976 games by Brian Goodell, involves swimming just behind and very close to the man in the next lane, using his drag to get a "free ride." The controversy around surfing derives from a sense that this is not a simple swim-off (although "dragging" is of course an accepted method in bike races). Armstrong swam a "smart" race. There was nothing instinctive. This was a carefully planned and executed manipulation of circum-stance. Here the swimmer becomes an industrial object: schooled in the physics of drag, disciplined, and self-controlled.

But TV coverage of the race captured traces of an erotic side to the event in addition to its mechanics. Australian network Channel Ten, which broadcast the games, went into an orgiastic frenzy when an Australian man finally won some-thing. "Oh my God, oh my God, oh my God," shrieked Channel Ten's commentator, as Armstrong touched the wall for the final time. Remind you of anything? The swimmer's body had become an object of desire in this coverage, consumed by the gaze of the announcer and, through him, of the audience.

Armstrong went on to pose for Brisbane's *Sunday Mail* color supplement. In the photo, he lies on his front in rushing water, elbows up, buttocks sloping away to the shallows, costumed in blue trunks (Budd 1989). Anybody for centerfolds? (A decade on, he could be found as one of Stuart Spence's [n.d.] photographic portraits, this time naked to the navel save for epaulettes and dark glasses.) Inside the 1989 supplement, Armstrong posed with his (then) partner and his sports car at the University of Florida—wages of the National Collegiate Athletic Associ-ation's investment in draining brawn from across the globe (Bale 1991). "As long as I'm swimming, I'm marketable," he told the *Mail* reporter. "As long as I'm breaking world records, I'm even more marketable." Armstrong shifts between the unstable position of the body on display, defenseless before the gaze, and the administrative figure of shrewd self-commodification, in control.

Jim McKay says, "[A]ny male Australian athlete will verify . . . [that] the most insulting accusation a coach can make about a player's performance is to say that he 'played like a sheila' or a 'poofter' " (1991, 55). True. But this portrait of Duncan Armstrong reveals fissures in the representation of manliness, occasioned by the pressure to make men visually appealing, to play up their beauty as part of selling their sports maleness. The commodification of this sports maleness leads to the commodification of the male body.

As we shall see in the instance of Armstrong's coach, the graceless antinomies of fey swimmer and tough organization man are crucial to the latter-day work of being a "man of the game." The complex connection of these subjectivities is referenced in Armstrong's slippage between a self submerged in the waters and one mired in managerialism: "We swam such and such a time. . . . Oh, I mean Laurie and I." Who was Laurie?

Sons, Lovers, Lawrence/Dunkin' Laurie

Armstrong's coach, Laurie Lawrence, also a Hall of Famer, drew more attention from the Australian media throughout the Seoul games than did his charge. Lawrence's body and its psyche were depicted, slowed down, speeded up, analyzed, and repeated over and over again on news and sports programs. This was a response to some bizarre conduct. As Armstrong stood on the winner's podium, Lawrence screamed down at him, crying out pathetically for recognition: "Dunc, Dunc, turn around. I know you, Dunc." Then he sprinted poolside (pursued by Australian news crews) and broke through security to dive, fully clothed ("Bermuda" shorts, "Hawaiian" shirt, and slouch hat), into the pool. At other points this histrionic figure shouted, "He did it," "We did it," and "My boy." He was even wont to refer to Armstrong as "the animal" or "the bastard" (used here as terms of endearment).

As replays treated us to the coach's odd conduct in slow motion, commentators endorsed it as wild but also beautifully controlled: "He wanted to swear, but he didn't" was a representative remark. Even the one critical voice, Clive Robertson's, merely inquired what kind of parent would name their child Laurence Lawrence. Here we have a strange paradox. We pay attention to him because he is *out* of control, but we admire him because he is *under* control.

The relationship between Lawrence and Armstrong was presented as that of a great larrikin casually egging on his pseudo-son. This image distorted Lawrence's competence as a successful administrator. The picture of a harmless, gormless eccentric effectively obscured the reality of his skills in scientific management and time discipline, his entrepreneurial power and routinized business acumen—qualities required of the contemporary professional sports coach. Behind the loveable, fallible, hysterical Australian man functioning in a carnivalesque manner stood a clever disciplinarian. Coaches must know about health, dietetics, vitamins, training schedules, promotion, intrasport politics, swimming techniques and rules, and governmental and commercial contingencies—in short, the forms of discipline that produce sports success. Control over the quotidian activities of their charges frequently extends to personal relationships. The older male coach becomes the complete Svengali (Tomlinson and Yorganci 1997, 134). Armstrong himself became a vocal supporter of coaches' independence from the wider sports bureaucracy, referring to their "individual rights to coach in the way they want" (quoted in the *Daily Telegraph* on July 27, 1996). But Lawrence's cool eye found no place for "Dunc" in his mid-'90s list of great swimmers (Murphy n.d.). The loyalty of coach to swimmer is contingent on the former's exercise of his prerogative to forget emotion and engage in a clinical ranking.

It should come as no surprise that Lawrence was named 1988 Australian Achiever of the Year and that he won an Advance Australia Award. Promoted as "Lawrence of Australia" in advertisements, he is described as the "Master Motivator," who inspires audiences with "Aussie parochialism and good humour." Such representations of the swimming coach blend a crass nationalism and narrow-mindedness with optimism and good nature, suggesting that his life is lived in the name of a joke. Again, relations of power are obscured. The modern managerialism of sports, most actively opposed to worker solidarity and welfare, is made to seem as if it is about patriotism and a few laughs with the lads. But such a message reinforces the exclusivity of the clubhouse—women, transsexuals, and gays seem unwelcome.

Commodification

The representations of Armstrong as an object of the gaze and Lawrence as an hysterical male complicate the message of Australian sports masculinity. How might we understand these contradictions? David Rowe believes that the latter-day commodification of sports stars undermines the power of sports masculinity (1997, 124–125). It may also be that the labor of women broadcasters, journalists, and feminist sports scholars, added to the "pink dollar" market, cable TV efforts to expand coverage beyond conventional games, and inquiries into biases against women's sports in the media, have questioned the very "manliness" of sports culture.

The impact of commodification is clear in the case of the Olympics. The games are "event television," in that they draw different viewers and establish different patterns of viewing from routine TV. This is neither television as usual nor sports as usual because it brings together internationalism and immediacy in spectacular fashion. The Olympics attract female spectators in much larger numbers than the ordinary diet of televised sports (Wenner and Gantz 1998, 235; Daddario 1997, 103–104). For the 1992 winter games, for instance, 57 percent of the U.S. TV audience was female (Daddario 1997, 104). This demography prompts particular genres of presentation. U.S. TV executives operate from the assumption that women are attracted to coverage that hones in on biographical and conceptual narratives about stars and their sports, rather than on statistics or quests for success (Sargent et al. 1998, 47). For the 1992 summer games, NBC initiated "a female-inclusive sports subgenre," offering "private-life" histories of selected contestants (Daddario, 1997, 104). In its 1996 coverage, the network targeted women and families to such effect that 50 percent of the audience was adult women and only 35 percent adult men (Remnick 1996).

The trend toward women watching other "event" TV sports is also telling. In 1995, more women than men in Britain watched Wimbledon tennis on television, and the figures were almost equal for boxing (Sport 1995). In the 1998 National Basketball Association play-offs, more women were drawn to game seven of the Bulls-Pacers series than to *Veronica's Closet* or *ER*. Meanwhile, male viewership of TV sports in the United States is in serious decline, as more and more viewers turn to the History and Discovery Channels (Remnick 1996, 27; Demo Derby 1998; Elliott 1998b, C9). It is clear that major commercial and cultural changes are exerting tremendous pressure on the normativity of sports, endangering the seemingly rock-solid maleness at its core.

Along with a change in audience, we are also witnessing a change in what is viewed and the impact of the gaze on viewers, especially men. Sports allow spectators to watch and dissect men's bodies. It provides a legitimate space for gazing at the male form. Admiring individuated body parts gives a scientistic pleasure and an alibi for that otherwise suspect pleasure. To see a man weight lifting is to experience at close proximity physiognomic signs of pleasure akin to facial correlatives of the male orgasm, something otherwise denied to men defining themselves as straight. It amounts to an encounter of coeval power akin to the carnal, with the contestants as "accomplices" in a bizarre combination of struggle and cooperation (Pronger 1990, 181). Now we can see in sharper relief the complexities of Armstrong and Lawrence's relationship, and its climactic welcome by Channel Ten.

The 1980s saw two crucial conventions that led global advertising agencies to shift direction: "reclassifying people" and "classifying people." Before that decade, male consumption was broken down by race and class. Then these categories were supplemented, with market researchers dubbing the 1990s the decade of the "new man" (Fox 1989). Lifestyle profiles and psychographic research became critical tools for marketers seeking to identify both male and female consumers, who were divided between "moralists," "trendies," "the indifferent," "working-class puritans," "sociable spenders," and "pleasure seekers." Men were further subdivided into "pontificators," "self-admirers," "self-exploiters," "token triers," "chameleons," "avant-gardicians," "sleepwalkers," and "passive endurers" (Nixon 1996, 96–99). Such psychological classifications embody forms of understanding men, forms that divide them more subtly and comprehensively than had previous market research. Their advent marks a sea change in ways of targeting men as consumers, toward a more precise delineation of conduct and subjectivity. Commercial pressures have made visible alternative styles to what had been dominant forms of manliness.

Other cultural changes reflect shifts in the objectification of the male body. Male centerfolds have become common in teen magazines and British tabloid newspapers. Male striptease shows performed for female audiences reference not only changes in the direction of power and money, but also a public site where "[w]omen have come to see exposed male genitalia; they have come to treat male bodies as objects only"—*The Full Monty* writ large (Dyer 1992, 104; Harari 1993; Barham 1985, 62). The North American middle-class labor market now sees wage discrimination by beauty as much amongst men as women, and major corporations frequently require male executives to tailor their body shapes to the company ethos (Hamermesh and Biddle 1994; Wells 1994). American Academy of Cosmetic Surgery figures indicate more than sixty-five hundred men had face-lifts in 1996 (Lemon 1997, 30). New designer pharmaceuticals that encourage follicular and erectile renewal are a further manifestation of the trend.

On another front, gay males have become recognized as a key market for advertisers. Gay magazines circulate information to businesses about the spending power of their childless, middle-class readership. *Campaign*'s slogan in advertising circles is "Gay Money Big Market Gay Market Big Money" (quoted in Rawlings 1993). The mid-1990s brought two famous commercials: for Ikea, two men furnishing their apartment, and for Toyota, a car-buying male couple. Hyundai began appointing gay-friendly staff to dealerships, Polygram's classical-music division announced a special gay promotional budget, and Miller beer was a major sponsor of Gay Games '94 (Rawlings 1993). In the late '90s, Sony, Smirnoff, and Telstra sponsored Sydney's Gay and Lesbian Mardi Gras Festival (Cahill 1997, 34). The spring 1997 U.S. TV season saw twenty-two gay characters across the prime-time network schedule—clear signs of niche targeting (O'Connor 1997). Agencies coined the term "cause-related marketing" as they moved in on gay men. Bruce Hayes, an "out" gay man who won a swimming relay gold medal for the United States at the 1984 Los Angeles games, was a key figure in Levi Strauss's 1998–1999 dockers campaign (Elliott 1998a).

Thanks to commodification, today's athletic men are brought out into the bright light of narcissism and purchase, where the costs and benefits are high, the gaze is constant, and disciplined yet seemingly spontaneous conduct are coterminous—all in the name of purchasing power and freedom. Once, the straight sportsman could be promoted as an icon of his country, a proud figure animated by patriotism. Now, he is revealed as a more contradictory figure, animated as much by a polymorphously perverse self-display and the desire for material gain as by anything else. The mythic national male subject—outside the reach of capital, embodying both nature and history, an elemental agent of progress—is revealed to be very much an object, made so by desiring gazes and plastic money. Duncan Armstrong poses, Laurie Lawrence motivates, and Channel Ten salivates. Simmering above and below those actions, we find the odd blend of industrial precision and gay abandon expected of today's man. Men of the game are subject to change without warning. Watch this space.

CHAPTER 7

Yes

of Progress

The Girls of Summer:

Social Contexts for the

"Year of the Women"

at the '96 Olympics

LESLIE HEYWOOD

1996: Atlanta at its high capitalist best, merchandise dripping from every pore. The Centennial Park bombing. Suspects falsely accused. And the athletes: Michael Johnson, Carl Lewis, and, um . . . Gail Devers, Gwen Torrance, Amy Van Dyken, Dominique Moceanu, Mary Ellen Clark, Kerrie Strug. Mia Hamm, Dot Richardson, Jackie Joyner-Kersee, Rebecca Lobo, Lisa Leslie. The women's gymnastics team, the women's basketball team, the women's beach volleyball team, the women's soccer team. Notice anything different here?

1996 was the "year of the women" at the Olympics. The year the cover of the preview issue of *Sports Illustrated* featured women, specifically five African American members of the women's basketball team, and their coach, Tara VanDerveer. The year women athletes were covered in half the features, as well as half of the ads. Hurdler Kim Batten showing up on one page, Michael Johnson the next. The women's gymnastics team and swimmer Amy Van Dyken on the Wheaties boxes. Ads attesting to female power and self-assertion, like the State Farm ad for the basketball team featuring a woman driving toward the basket; it read, "These days little girls don't live down the lane—they drive down it." Emphasis was on women's achievements, not their looks, like the feature on sculler Ruth Davidon head-lining her status as med student and Ph.D. candidate, not her hair (Bamberger 1996).

Structurally, however, it wasn't as clear that "we'd come a long way" as the media made it look. Despite the fact that 36 percent of the athletes in this

Olympics were women, up from 30 percent in 1992, with 6,500 men and 3,700 women competing overall, and with 382 U.S. men and 280 U.S. women competing (up drastically from the 342 men and 96 women who competed in 1972, the year of Title IX), 36 percent still leaves 64 percent of the competitors men. Even worse, there were only 7 women among the 106 members of the International Olympic Committee. Of the 271 athletic events, 165 were for men only as compared to 95 for women only, and only 11 events were mixed (Women in the Olympics 1997). Like the full implementation of Title IX, it was clear that we still have a long way to go in the achievement of full equality for women athletes.

Still, in this Olympics, unlike any of the Olympics that had preceded the Atlanta games, the focus on female athletes was part of a much larger national focus on women in sports. It was the first Olympics in which the legacy of Title IX of the Education Act of 1972 was fully visible: "[T]he first generation of women who've had a lifetime of opportunity to play," noted Donna Lopiano, executive director of the Women's Sports Foundation. For the first time, "what you see is the female athlete as a rule, not the exception" (Feminist Majority Women in the Olympics 1997). That "rule" had profound consequences for the representation of athletes. Unlike the "genderized" coverage of, for instance, the 1984 and 1988 Olympics, analyzed by Margaret Carlisle Duncan—coverage that emphasized female competitors as women first, athletes second, ignoring their skills and focusing on their looks, while male athletes were described as "powerful" or "great"—in 1996 the emphasis was primarily on women's skill and achievements (Duncan 1990).

In an interview with the Feminist Majority before the 1996 games, Olympics expert and former president of the AIAW (Association for Intercollegiate Athletics for Women) Carol Oglesby was asked whether she thought coverage of female athletes would improve from what it had been in earlier Olympics. Oglesby answered, "[T]he media have been put on notice about their coverage of women—the amount of coverage and the characterization of that coverage. We can watch to see whether commentators refer to women athletes by their first names, while calling men Mr. so-and-so. How will women be portrayed in the commentaries and profiles on athletes?" (Feminist Majority Women in the Olympics 1997).

If the media had been "put on notice," clearly there was more sensitivity in 1996 to stereotypical coverage. Women were not referred to by their first names. That male athletes were fathers was discussed almost as often as the fact that female athletes were mothers (and starting a new tradition, many male as well as female track athletes did their victory laps carrying their sons or daughters). In fact, commentators insisted, the women made for the most interesting stories in 1996. "The 1996 Games will be remembered, no doubt," writes Jere Longman in the *New York Times Magazine,* "as the year women took over the Olympics—setting the stage, perhaps, for an assault on the largely male preserve of professional sports. For it is women who are expected to provide many of the memorable accomplishments, the media focus, and even the controversy of the centennial Games" (1996, 25).

While the Atlanta Olympics coverage did feature some of the usual sexist clichés, such as the alleged "catfight" between sprinters Gail Devers and Gwen Torrance, emphasized the women who were mothers as well as athletes, and dwelled unnecessarily on the heroic sacrifice of Kerrie Strug (making it seem as if female athletes did not in fact sacrifice themselves like this every day), on the whole it was a marked improvement. Yes, the gymnasts, long seen as more "traditionally feminine," still got a disproportionate amount of coverage in relation to other female athletes. But women's track, once seen as so "masculine" and taxing that there was a movement to ban it as an Olympic sport for women after the 1928 games when a woman collapsed at the finish of the eight-hundred-meter race, was at the center of national consciousness that summer. After the 1996 Olympics, Jackie Joyner-Kersee, a heptathlete who, despite the fact that her quest for defending her gold medal was lost due to a torn hamstring, was uniformly cited by children and others as the female athlete they admired most; and Devers and Torrance became household names.

Kerrie Strug most captured the media's eye, however, due not to a winning performance (though it was that, too), but to an injury. "Profile in Courage," a huge layout in *Sports Illustrated* magazine proclaimed, the words in bold over a close-up of Strug's agonized face, complete with tears: "[I]n a competition marked by drama, emotion, and, finally, heroism, the American women won their first team gold medal."

Still, in a world where women athletes are almost never featured on the same par with the men, the *Newsweek* (June 10, 1996) and *New York Times Magazine* covers featuring women Olympians were a marked improvement, as were the *Time* profiles of women's teams and individual athletes in their summer 1996 special edition. Photographers, for the first time, used the same kinds of shots and techniques when photographing male and female athletes. Whereas previously the conventions featured athletic action shots of men and sexualizing beauty shots of women, the July 1996 issue of *Life* magazine featured portraits that combined both athleticism and beauty, in men and women: There were naked portraits of power lifter Mark Henry, the torso of sprinter Michael Johnson, long jumper and sprinter Carl Lewis, diver Russ Bertram, and the U.S. men's water-polo team, all shot with the same conventions and lighting techniques as those used in the naked portraits of female fencer Sharon Monplaisir, diver Mary Ellen Clark, sprinters Gwen Torrance and Gail Devers, heptathlete Jackie Joyner-Kersee, volleyball player Holly McPeak, and Margo Thien and Nathalie Schneyder from the synchronized swimming team (*Life* 1996, 50–64). The photographs, by Joe McNally, were gorgeous studies of erotic beauty and athleticism and included both men and women.

Even more explicitly, in terms of improving on sex stereotypes in the representation of athletes, many national newspapers and magazines made the connection between the prominence of women in this Olympics and the women's movement's fight for equality in all areas, including athletics. According to Jere

Longman, "women make for better stories . . . because women have struggled so long and resolutely to overcome cultural, racial, and religious obstacles, their accomplishments carry a resonance particularly associated with the Olympics: sacrifice, struggle, elusive victory gained over great odds" (1996, 25). Much attention was brought to the fact that twenty-seven countries do not send women to the Olympics because of Islamic dress codes, and much attention was given to women whose performances have helped the political cause of women in their respective countries. Rather than being ridiculed, for the first time female athletes were being used to make a mainstream argument for women's political activism.

The American women came through: due to more industry support and the greater allocation of resources, the women's basketball, soccer, softball, synchronized swimming, and gymnastics teams won gold medals. The women's four-by-one-hundred-meter relay team won gold in track. Gail Devers won two medals, and Amy Van Dyken won four medals in swimming. There was a great deal of national interest in the stories of runner Mary Decker Slaney, diver Mary Ellen Clark, and heptathlete Jackie Joyner-Kersee even though these women didn't win gold, giving credence to the long alternative sports tradition that argues that winning isn't everything.[1] The stage was set like never before for women's sports to be implemented as a vehicle for women's advancement.

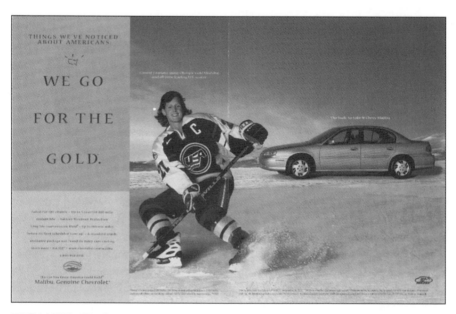

FIGURE 7.1

Corporate support: ice hockey gold medalist Cammi Granato in an ad for Chevrolet.

Sports Illustrated for Women, spring 1999. Author's collection.

But why women, why 1996? What social forces were responsible for this change? Who put the media "on notice"? Why did it respond? Why, after decades of being ignored and/or ridiculed, were female athletes suddenly the focus of national adoration? What was responsible for the sudden interest in and support of athletic women?

Nike Add

The Times, They Are A-Changin'

It started with just a whisper at first, a few hints. As always, on the level of mass public consciousness, we heard it from Nike first, in the spring of 1996: "If you let me play / I will like myself more / I will have more self-confidence / I will suffer less depression / I will be 60 percent less likely to get breast cancer / I will be more likely to leave a man who beats me / I will be less likely to get pregnant before I want to / I will learn what it means to be strong / If you let me play sports." Nike's "if you let me play" advertising campaign in the spring of 1996 was the first nationwide, mass-media spot to call attention to what female athletes, and those who did research on them, had known for more than a century. Sports helps with self-confidence. Playing sports is good for your health.

In the early to mid-nineties, the world began to change in terms of its representation of women in sports due to a number of factors. One was that, facing a stagnant market in men's sports equipment and apparel, the sports industry found a new frontier, a largely untapped consumer market in women, and that market needed a new image to consolidate it. Women, who had been athletes for a long time but largely ignored as such, could both easily supply that image and respond to it with consumer dollars. Indeed, as Donna Lopiano noted in an article discussing Olympics coverage of women, while the sports press dedicated only 10 percent of television hours to women's sports, and more column inches were devoted to horses than women before 1996, since the early nineties "major corporations like State Farm, General Motors, Visa, and Kodak are using female athletes in large-scale advertising and promotional campaigns" (1996, 42). Corporate support, Lopiano argued, would lead to more affirmative coverage of women in the 1996 games, coverage which would have larger social consequences: "[T]hrough the coverage of female athletes in the 1996 Games, we'll see a more balanced picture of women in sports—our achievements, our failures, our joys, and our fears. We'll see great women athletes blow away the mist of prejudice and stereotype with their spirit, skill, persistence, and courage. We'll see the true story of women in sports" (Women in the Olympics 1997). For the most part, Lopiano was right. Although it is de rigueur in academic circles to uniformly criticize corporations and corporate capitalism in all situations at all times, in this case it was corporate America that seemed to have the most positive influence on opportunity for and social acceptance of female athletes.

Due in part to this corporate embrace, by the time of the 1996 Olympics, audiences had already been primed to see female athletes in roughly the same terms as males, and to extend the positive qualities of female athletes to women in general.

In the October 1995 issue of *Outside* magazine, the cover story "The Ubergirl Cometh" proclaimed a new archetype for women: "The age of Gabrielle Reece is upon us. She's big, she's strong, and with thousands more like her out there, she's replicating fast. . . . Reece leads a pack of women who are currently redefining our image of the female athlete, inspiring a generation of young girls to take control of their bodies and pride in their strength. . . . Can you deal with that?"

This image of the female athlete was new. Mass market appeal to the female athlete was new. Offering up athletics as a solution to social problems most often suffered by women was new. A large demographic of women who participate in organized sports was new. The assumption that enough women live in the athlete's world—defined by bravery, competence, and strength—to make up a viable market was new. Female athletes were once oddities, goddesses, or monsters, exceptions to every social rule. Suddenly the female athlete was an institution.

She was the product of circumstances unique to the late twentieth century in the United States: the growth of a consumer economy which meant more women in jobs for the first time, the expansion of the entertainment industry and thereby of sports, a culture marked by progressive movements for change—race rights, gay rights, women's rights—a culture taking notice of girls and the different women they become. Chief among these circumstances was the passage of Title IX, the Education Act of 1972, which mandated equal funding and facilities for women's sports in any institution receiving federal dollars. This one piece of legislation would make millions of women into athletes, changing the shape of the female body forever. The female athlete challenged old ideas of female incompetence and physical weakness, the idea that (white, middle-class) woman's place is decorative and is limited to the home, not the soccer fields.

Reports that heralded the coming of the Übergirl and that played to the issue of girls' self-esteem were to some extent responses to the famous 1991 AAUW study, "Shortchanging Girls, Shortchanging America," the first extensive national survey on gender and self-esteem, which reconfirmed earlier work, such as that of Carol Gilligan. The AAUW study showed that adolescence, for girls, brought a loss of confidence in their abilities to succeed, bitterly critical feelings about their bodies, and a mushrooming sense that they weren't valued by the world around them, with a resulting sense of personal inadequacy.

Since the AAUW study, the question of girls and self-image has been raised as a public health issue of some importance. There is a growing understanding that girls need help with self-esteem; this has led to social initiatives like the Bring Your Daughter to Work Day. Along with these initiatives, one of the most frequently advanced solutions for the esteem problem is sports; and recently the National Girls and Women in Sports Day (February 5) has been coupled with a Take a Girl to the Game program, which is modeled on Bring Your Daughter to Work. Such events show a growing consensus that a lifestyle for girls and women which includes sports or regular physical activity of some kind will "inspir[e] a generation of young girls to take control of their bodies and pride in their strength" (*Outside,* October 1995).

L.A. Sparks star
Jamila Wideman and
her father, author
John Wideman.

Take Our
Daughters To
Work® Day
**Gifts Improve
All Our
Daughters'
Shots.**

Assist our daughters in fully
reaching their potential by
playing a part in 1999's Take
Our Daughters To Work® Day.
By choosing from among 30
unique gifts, you'll be helping
the program stay on target.
Get a free catalog or order
directly by calling 1-800-676-
7780. Or give our website,
www.ms.foundation.org., a shot.

Ms. Foundation for Women • April 22, 1999
TAKE OUR DAUGHTERS TO WORK®

The Ms. Foundation is a not-for-profit public charity. Take Our Daughters To Work is a program
and a registered trademark of the Ms. Foundation. All this merchandise is satisfaction guaranteed.

FIGURE 7.2

Gender activism at play: Bring Our Daughters to Work Day,
National Girls and Women in Sports Day.

Sports Illustrated for Women, spring 1999. Author's collection.

By the time of the 1996 Olympics, there was a new ideal image that matched these social initiatives to value girls. As an article (which ran as a preview to the Atlanta games coverage) in *New York Times Magazine* on June 23, 1996, pointed out, the athletic, muscular woman is an image that has no historical precedent and that, while slow in catching on, has spread like wildfire in the late nineties. In a special Olympics issue, the cover of which featured U.S. women's basketball player Sheryl Swoopes and a headline that proclaimed "Women Muscle In," the *New York Times Magazine* ran an article, by Holly Brubach, which celebrated what she defined as the new "Athletic Esthetic," a "new ideal emerging whose sex appeal is based on strength" (1996, 48–51). Looking at female athletes, at the rapid flowering of ads that show athletic women, Brubach writes, "These women exude competence; they can carry their own suitcases. Their muscles, like the fashion models' slenderness, are hard-earned, but here the means is not abstinence but exertion. Though their bodies have been meticulously cultivated, their bodies aren't the point: the point is their ability to perform. What is most striking, given that it's the other two ideals [anorexic and voluptuous; Kate Moss and Victoria's Secret] that are calculated to please—to win the admiration of women or the affection of men—is the fact that these athletes seem content in a way that the other women don't."

The kind of personal integrity that Brubach alludes to in the athletic image is not a new idea. Advocates of women's sports, from educators to participants, have been articulating the benefits of athletic participation for most of the century, but it isn't until very recently that these ideas have gained widespread cultural currency (Cahn 1994, chap. 1–2). What happened to make arguments which once fell on deaf ears suddenly register so powerfully on the national radar? What made mainstream public perceptions of the female athlete shift so radically from the pejorative female athlete as "mannish lesbian" stereotype to the glorified "women we love who kick ass" of the present moment? (Karbo and Reece 1997, 175).[2] What happened to facilitate—finally—the formation of women's professional leagues, most visibly in basketball?

Part of the cultural shift has a simple demographic explanation. At the time of Title IX, one in nine women participated in organized sports, while now the statistics are one in three, from roughly 250,000 to over 3 million. More bodies, more interest. But what lies behind the increased participation? What cultural ideologies have changed to facilitate such growth? By the early nineties, from growing numbers to a public focus on girl's self-esteem as a public health issue, the elements were all in place to support a widespread acceptance of women's sports and the deconstruction of all the old stigmas. Yet full mainstreaming of the female athlete—the shift from grudging mainstream acceptance to adulation, full iconic status—did not take place until 1996, the "year of the women" at the Olympics. What kick-started public consciousness? How did the female athlete go from near invisibility in the mass media to a ubiquitous presence, hawking everything from Motrin to chewing gum?

FIGURE 7.3

New idols: ad for the WNBA.

Women's Sport and Fitness, June 1998. Author's collection.

Just Sell It

By the early nineties, corporations like Nike began to capitalize on the largely unheard arguments put forth by physical fitness educators, coaches, and athletes themselves about the benefits of sports for women. In 1994, the dollar sales of women's athletic footwear topped men's for the first time, and in 1995 women spent $6 billion compared to men's $5.6 billion (Wallechinsky 1996b, 47). Advertisers responded in kind, taking up the cause of female athletes and the empowerment rhetoric that they imagined would extend sales even further. As Jere Longman noted in the *New York Times Magazine,* "as women have moved out of the home and into the workplace, their purchasing power has grown, and with it the fortune of female athletes" (1996, 24). This capitalization on a newly dollared demographic—and the public response to these advertising campaigns—helped catapult the female athlete into her current iconic status. Nike was the first to sense and then perfectly negotiate the dreams and fears of a continually growing and mostly untapped demographic of women, like myself, for whom athletic participation became central to their lives in the late seventies and after.

Before Nike, the guys got all the attention, and we were the "unsung heroes." We had in the mass media no images of ourselves with which to identify, nothing to let us feel that our experiences were validated and valued by the culture around us. The male athlete was glorified from every corner, but the public silence about female athletes was marked. Recent research has focused on the dearth of images of female athletes before 1996—*Sports Illustrated,* for instance, had only 4 percent of its covers devoted to female competitors between 1954 and 1990 (Nelson 1994, 196). Nike stepped in to fill that void, giving us extremely positive, even heroic images of ourselves, and a way to publicly proclaim our identity as athletes—athleticism as fashion. Of course, because they *had* validated us, we were much more likely to buy their products.

Nike was the start, and many other imitators were soon to follow in the trend of female athlete as the ideal image of female power, imitators who never quite hit Nike's rhetorical or psychological heights. At first it was only athletic apparel companies like Reebok, Lady Footlocker, and Champs, but after the 1996 Olympics the athletic female body was paired with everything from Evian ("Within me lives a superhero") to Diet Mountain Dew and Movado watches. As a result, the athletic female body has finally made it on the cultural scene. For those of us who have been athletes for a long time, it's a bit like what feminist rocker-actress Courtney Love says of her recent spate of cover appearances: After years of invisibility or vilification, "[I]t's like being popular all of a sudden. You know?" (Dunn 1997, 166). We know. After years of being told that we are too muscular or too big, too aggressive and domineering, our bodies and the attitudes that go with them have been accepted and even glorified, offered in the mass media as models of strength, possibility, and personal integrity for young women, as an example of our growing power in the world. How could the situation be any better? Powerful body equals cultural power, so the equation goes. We're hooked.

Looking Too Good, Maybe

So, yeah sports! Yeah to the cultural acceptance of strong women! Say yeah to improved self-esteem for girls, the opportunity to learn competitive skills transferable to the business world, sports showing us that there's no limit to what we can do. Things are looking pretty good for girls it seems. Now we can have it both ways. According to Gabrielle Reece, the poster girl for the new version of athletic femininity, a.k.a. Nike femininity, "I get out of bed, throw on the Lycra, pull my hair back, lace up my shoes and oh-so-deliberately apply my lashes. Then I go out and spike the ball into my opponent's face. This open display of schizophrenia is fun. Men aren't so lucky. They generally aren't allowed to wear lipstick with their work suits" (1997, 78). We have it all! Things are looking very good, too good.

Throughout the mass media, and particularly in the Nike ads, which function as lightning rods for the latest ideological trends, sports, and the body image that goes with them have taken a turn beyond validating women's athletic participation. Recently sports and working out are offered as a cure-all for systematic inequalities of all kinds. There is a logical leap that is made from the premise that participation in sports provides a host of positive experiences that will build character and give everyone the opportunity to compete to the conclusion that having a strong body will automatically get a girl (or a boy, for that matter) a significant place in the culture. Mass media focused on sports presents a world in which systematic inequalities don't exist—it's a level playing field and we're all out there doing our best. Sports are the great equalizer, the inclusive haven that now gives us all a leg up, the thinking goes, an equal chance to strut our stuff. Whatever race, whatever gender, we all can play and reap the benefits.

"I can do anything I want to do," a young Hispanic girl tells the viewer forcefully in a recent Nike television spot, which, with striking, inclusive images of mixed races, genders, and ages, presents athletics as an arena in which all personal pains, fears, and inadequacies are overcome. But what about the lack of opportunity that a young Hispanic woman, born to less than privileged economic circumstances and deprived of affirmative-action legislation, may very well face no matter how great her legs and lats are from playing sports? What about the very real forms of discrimination faced by older women? All social problems cannot be solved by simply lacing up the latest Nike shoe named after a woman—such as the Air Skeek named for skier Picabo Street—and getting your body out to the slopes or the soccer field or the track.

All this yeah-saying, which presents itself as a solution for political problems like structural inequality, has an unmarked, profoundly political dimension. It makes us feel good. It makes us feel great. That's how it works. Whoo-hoo! You, go, girl! But it's a double-edged sword, a pill that might kill, and a recent turn in athletic advertising makes these darker political implications explicit. Lately, female athletic participation has been joined to the political discourse of women's rights, suggesting that to further our position and power as women in this culture, all

FIGURE 7.4

Sports as the solution to all girls' woes: Nike ad.

Women's Sport and Fitness, October 1998. Author's collection.

we need to do is work out. Forget political activism of the type that got us Title IX in the first place—girls just wanna get pecs. I have made the argument elsewhere that physical activity such as women's bodybuilding can function as a form of political activism, a way of developing self and consciousness that can lead to larger, structural changes and heal past abuses; but I was careful to emphasize that these individual forms of development could not take the place of organized, concrete activisms of the kind that led to the implementation of Title IX, which was a major factor behind the fact that so many women today do have the possibility to work out and play sports (Heywood 1998a). Contemporary advertisements—as well as magazine articles, books, sports videos, and other forms of mass media—make the argument that working out is the only form of activism we need.

A Reebok insert which appeared in the February 1998 issue of *Condé Nast Sports for Women* is a striking example in this trend. The insert is a booklet of fourteen pages and comes with a women's training CD for your personal computer. The first image on the insert is a female hand, white against a black background, fingers raised as if to take an oath. The text, in red, is spread across her knuckles: "please repeat after me." Inside, we have a woman in an orange Reebok bra top lifting weights, and on the facing page the words "I take me, to have and to hold, from this day forward, for better or worse, for richer, for poorer, in sickness and in health, to love and to cherish, till death do us part, so help me, god. I do."

This woman-affirming parody of the conventional wedding vows is followed by political discourse that borrows both from the Declaration of Independence and that milestone treatise of first-wave feminism, the Declaration of Sentiments: "We hold these truths to be self-evident: that all women are created equal and independent, that from that equal creation they derive rights inherent and inalienable, among which are the preservation of life, liberty, and the pursuit of happiness." Clearly, according to the ad, those rights and the pursuit of happiness are bound up with working out, for the following page, interspersed with more images of women running and walking, says "[O]n my honor I will try to make my health a priority, make it to the gym, vote women into office, balance work, kids, relationships, and all my other roles without losing my mind and live by the make-myself-happy-law."

What looks like a kind of politics, voting women into office, is undercut by the insistence that making oneself happy means going to the gym in addition to balancing traditional roles. Happiness, self-fulfillment, and progressive politics come from working out—get it? More shiny images, more cleverly appropriated political texts, and then we have the caveat, a woman kickboxing to this text: "I have the right not to remain silent, to put myself first, be sexy, intelligent, and tough all at the same time. To be rich and happy. Anything I desire may not be held against me. Do you understand these rights?"

Well, yes, actually I think I do: the concept of rights has become a matter of isolated self-fulfillment, which keeps women working on themselves rather than working together to really change anything. (Everything's great. What do we need to change? Never mind attacks on welfare mothers, affirmative action, abortion legislation—we get to have muscles now. We get to be tough chicks—tough and sexy at the same time. We've got it all.) I understand that the desires the ad seems to applaud—the expansion and development of the individual woman—are undercut by the all-too-familiar, not very individual script haunting the ad's surface: a happiness which is dependent upon wealth and which follows the gender script of the nineties, i.e., femininity Nike/Reebok/Gabby style—"women we love who kick ass." So are all women really getting the chance to kick ass? I wish I could be as reassured as most of the other female athletes and their fans around me seem to be, and rest easy that our cultural moment has come.

Nonetheless, athleticism as fashion has had profound social consequences. Today, women nationwide are participating in classes like kickboxing, spinning, rock climbing, and boxing, relegating to the cultural dustbin mythologies of the "weaker" sex and assumptions of female incompetence. Any day you can walk into your local gym and see the women sweating alongside the men and walking in the same proud way, owning their bodies like never before. Since the 1996 Olympics and the national interest in the women, the WNBA is enjoying unprecedented success, and national attention has turned toward women's college basketball. A women's sports magazine, *Condé Nast Sports for Women,* was launched to immediate acclaim and a subscription list of over three million. These changes in cultural iconography had a profound impact on the attention given to women in the 1996 Olympics, from the relative amount of airtime to the politics of representation, to the cultural changes that have happened since. The stage is set for a true marriage between feminism and female athletes for the first time, but it remains to be seen whether we will really "seal the deal."

Women's Athletics as "Stealth Feminism"

Clearly sports are an arena where feminist questions emerge, but it has not always been defined or considered as such. Athletes do not necessarily consider themselves feminists, and many feminists would not consider themselves athletes.[3] Though the female physical educators who largely oversaw women's athletics until the 1980s were reluctant to embrace feminism through the mid-seventies, the cause of women's sports most dear to them was given its biggest boost by the passage of Title IX, and the feminist movement was largely responsible for its passage. Clearly, female athletes needed feminism then. According to sports historian Mary Jo Festle, "[P]assage of Title IX reflected the feminist tenor of the early 1970's. . . . The women's liberation movement had begun encouraging women to demand more opportunities, break free of stereotypes, reclaim their bodies, and exercise their strength" (1996, 113). But now, in the context of the mid-nineties, the situation is reversed. Now feminism needs female athletes.

Feminism in the nineties suffers from as much (perhaps even more) bad public relations and media representation as ever, with pundits claiming that younger women disassociate themselves from the term in record numbers. Feminism is the new "f" word, that thing you just don't want to be. From the faux feminist posturings of Katie Roiphe and Camile Paglia to the anti-sex/pro-sex, victim feminist/power feminist debates, for many young women "the word *feminist* conjures up a very different image from the powerful, exhilarating one it once did" (Baroni 1994, 196). Accusations of feminists as man haters became louder than ever in the mass media of the mid-nineties, often mouthed by women who claimed to be part of a "new feminism" (what Anna Quindlen called "babe feminism" and Susan Faludi called "pod feminism") (Quindlen 1996, 3–5). Within the academy, evermore acrimoniously divided by the arguments between feminists who fall under the label of poststructuralism and those who follow identity politics, and by splits along the lines of race, sexuality, class, and even generational lines, there is little sense of unifying cause, direction, or collective movement. Since the 1996 Olympics, female athletes are giving feminism a platform that cuts across the acrimonious divisions of race, class, and sexual orientation that continue to fracture the movement. As the editors of *Teen People* wrote in October 1998, "[F]ew people would argue against school sport"; and there are increasingly productive alliances of feminist organizations around issues related to women's sports, as well

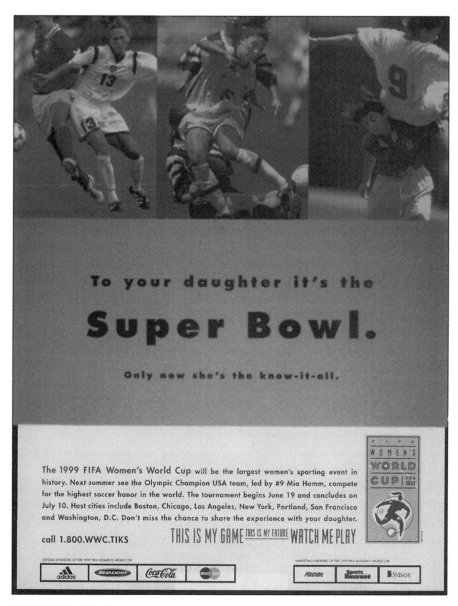

FIGURE 7.5

Authorizing girls: women's sports as the new feminist frontier,
an ad for the Women's World Cup Soccer.

Sports Illustrated for Women, spring 1999. Author's collection.

as significant feminist ideology in organizations like the Women's Sports Foundation. Through their work on women's sports issues, feminists are advancing their ideologies and causes in a kind of stealth feminism that draws attention to key feminist issues and goals without provoking the knee-jerk social stigmas attached to the word "feminist," which has been so maligned and so discredited in the popular imagination. At this historical moment, feminists need athletics, among other things, to advance such agendas as equal opportunity and self-esteem for women and girls.

It's a reciprocal relationship. Athletes need feminism because some disquieting realities persist between the pro-women's sports rhetoric and hype. While many parents and the community at large seem to assume that sports is a golden world unto itself, exempt from the problems people face elsewhere in their daily lives, the same issues of racism, sexism, and class bias inform what happens in sports. For women, that means negotiating a set of gender-specific issues first brought to national attention by feminists: issues like sexual harassment and sexual abuse; and women's health issues, like the female athlete triad, a syndrome, associated with overtraining, that is characterized by disordered eating, amenorrhea (cessation of menstruation), and osteoporosis (bone loss).

A recent lawsuit began to focus national attention on a problem that those of us who participated in organized sports were long aware of, though it rarely made its way into the media: the problem of sexual harassment and abuse of women athletes. Two former soccer players at the University of North Carolina, Chapel Hill, one of whom is a member of the U.S. women's national team, filed a $12 million lawsuit against their coach, Anson Dorrance, alleging "inappropriate conduct and unwelcome harassment" such as uninvited sexual advances, sexually explicit comments about team members, and interrogations of team members about their sexual activities (Haworth 1998, 1).

This case will have a significant impact on the future of women's sports because Dorrance is one of the most prominent coaches, known for coming up with a coaching style specifically geared to women. Citing Deborah Tannen and Carol Gilligan, Dorrance writes in *Training Soccer Champions* that "the great leaders of men ... are strong personalities who lead with a powerful presence and will. Their effectiveness comes through their resolve. With women, your effectiveness is through your ability to relate. They have to feel that you care about them personally or have some kind of connection with them beyond the game. Women want to experience a coach's humanity" (Dorrance with Nash 1996, 65). Gender-based assumptions such as these may well lead to the kinds of behaviors alleged in the suit. Just what does it mean to "experience a coach's humanity"? What kinds of "connections" might coaches assume that women want? Under the guise of difference-based feminist theory, this particular application of "difference" raises unsettling questions about coaching practices, but those questions are rarely part of public discourse about women in sports. While the problem of sexual harassment and abuse has been widespread enough for the Women's Sports Foundation to have a special task force devoted to it and specific guidelines for coaches, it is rarely mentioned in media discussions, or in books and articles about women's athletics.

In my own interviews with female athletes, stories of sexual harassment and abuse were part of almost every woman's experience. One athlete, Michelle Hite, a former University of Kentucky track standout, claimed that "sexual harassment was as much part of the daily routine as practice" (personal interview, June 1998). She and many other women speak of coaches who came on to them sexually, who made comments about their bodies and interrogated them about their sexual lives, and who put them on restrictive diets or assigned extra training to make them lose weight. Such coaching practices undoubtedly contribute to health risks like female athlete triad, and the media is so ignorant about these risks that one article on Dorrance cites his practice of "display[ing] charts of player's body fat percentages" in the soccer office in an approving tone (Stancill 1998, 4). Such practices are themselves a form of harassment. But even if we adhere to a stricter definition restricted to sexual suggestiveness, most women I have spoken to have either experienced harassment or abuse or know someone who has. A paradise exempt from problems associated with sexism sports isn't. If the actual experience of female athletes is one of harassment and abuse, without systematic attention to these issues the self-esteem so touted in the media for women and girls in sports is not realizable.

The Atlanta games were the focal point of a growing trend in support of athletic women, a trend that has since grown into a successful women's professional league, a mainstream women's sports magazine, images of athletic women throughout the media, a new athletic body ideal, and a growing industry in literature about women's sports. National attention has turned to women's sports, and sports for women is being offered as the contemporary cure-all for social problems affecting women. Yet the same social problems that affect women in the world at large affect women in sports. We are poised at a time when the phenomenon of women's sports could go either way: it could prove to be a fickle advertising trend, a Band-Aid that directs attention away from the real kinds of political activism necessary for social change, or it could build on the activism of women's organizations that have embraced the cause of sports, inaugurating the kinds of real change that are claimed for sports. Whichever way it goes, the 1996 Olympic games will be remembered as the games that brought women athletes to the fore, as a moment when sports became as accepted for women as blow-drying their hair.

NOTES

1. On this alternative tradition see Mary Jo Festle (1996), *Playing Nice: Politics and Apologies in Women's Sports,* especially chap. 1 and 5; Susan K. Cahn (1994), *Coming on Strong: Gender and Sexuality in Twentieth Century Women's Sport,* chap. 3; and Mariah Burton Nelson (1998), *Embracing Victory: Life Lessons in Competition and Compassion.*

2. The "mannish lesbian" stereotype still circulates in the "lesbian baiting" characteristic of sports today (the subtle and not-so-subtle accusations that female athletes are necessarily lesbian). Old assumptions that women who excel at sports are really more like men (and must therefore be lesbians because they're not conventionally feminine) show a profound disrespect for female athletes of whatever social or sexual orientation because they assume that, on the one hand, good athletes are not "real women" and, on the other, that lesbianism is something to fear; this undermines the fundamental dignity and worth of all female athletes and fosters a homophobia that may discourage sports participation.

3. I've found, in my interviews with former or current athletes, that roughly the same percentage protest "I'm not a feminist!" compared to the number of the general student population that does so (one-half to two-thirds). Like many other researchers have found, however, once you explain that feminism means only a commitment to equality between men and women, most would then agree to call themselves feminists.

CHAPTER 8

Y₁ˢ

Women's Sports:

Coming of Age in the

Third Millennium

↑ participation

DONNA A. LOPIANO

The growth of women's sports in the Olympic Games during the last fifty years has been stunning.[1] Women were excluded from Olympic participation from ancient times through the advent of the modern Olympics in 1896. In 1896, Melpomene petitioned to compete in the marathon and was denied entry. Against the wishes of both the Olympic Committee and Olympic organizers, she unofficially ran the forty-kilometer race from Marathon to Athens in four hours and thirty minutes. In the 1900 Paris games, eleven women, less than 1 percent of all participating athletes, were allowed to compete in golf, tennis, and yachting, but most didn't even realize that their events were considered an official part of the Olympic schedule. It took a half century for the female athlete participation rate to rise to over 10 percent (11.1 percent in 1952, Helsinki), only twenty-five years to rise to over 20 percent (20.1 percent in 1976, Montreal), and twenty more years to rise another 15 percentage points to almost 35 percent of all participants in the 1996 Atlanta games. The growth of participation is clearly accelerating.

This limited participation of women in the Olympics over the first century of the modern Olympic Games is a reflection of sex discrimination in the larger society. The progress made in sports parallels and oftentimes plays a leading role in the advance of women's rights and women's participation in other cultural institutions. There is one prediction we can confidently make. When women are given the opportunity to perform in sports, their achievements will produce a

steady elimination of barriers preventing their full participation and an
increased public awareness of the lack of gender equality. Stereotypes and myths
that diminish the abilities of females will disappear. We cannot look at the role
of women in sports without an understanding of the larger society in which
sports reside. The advances made by women, particularly in developed nations,
over the last decades of the second millennium clearly predict a developing global
enlightenment—an era of sports opportunity.

There are at least eleven major factors aiding the emergence of the female
athlete as shown by her increased participation in the Olympic Games:

1. The movement toward capitalism and the global marketplace, demanding
   recognition of any market as large as the female sports market.
2. The advantage of socioeconomic class in permitting some women in some
   sports in all countries to pursue elite-level participation.
3. The equality of gender in socialist societies and the role of sports in the political ideology of those countries.
4. The recognition, by most nations, that success on the playing fields of international sports translates into national pride which has no gender boundary.
5. Advances in promotion of female sports participation worldwide through
   the power of television, the Internet, and other global communications.
6. The gradual evolution of the female role from sex object, decorative object,
   and caretaker subject to male dominance and control to a more independent, broadly involved, and powerful role with cooperative gender relations.
7. The realization that sports participation produces beneficial social, psychological, and physiological benefits to individual participants.
8. A more activist and organized global feminist sports movement.
9. The coming of age of social justice as a global value.
10. Male self-aggrandizement and pride in paternity and/or teaching that
    allows transcendence of social mores prohibiting female participation.
11. The idiosyncratic role of powerful and visionary individuals in the hierar-
    chy of amateur and professional sports in setting gender policy or remov-
    ing barriers to the commercial exploitation of women in sports.

Capitalism and the Global Marketplace

The global marketplace will greatly affect gender equity in sports in the coming
millennium as society is propelled toward capitalism and global markets. From the
stunning demise of a socialist economy in the USSR, and its lurching giant steps
into capitalism, to the positioning of global corporations to enter socialist enclaves
such as China, to the creation of the Eurodollar and the European Common Market, capitalism will be the story of the third millennium.

Nothing could be a better template predictor of the probable impact of a global
marketplace on the expanded role of women in sports than the occurrences of
the last quarter century in the United States. Unlocked in 1972 by Title IX, a federal law outlawing sexual discrimination in educational institutions, the doors of

educational sports were flung open for girls and women, when they had previously been closing due to diminished federal funding. In each succeeding generation of girls, the number of women in America who are actively involved in sports and fitness has increased. As a result, over a twenty-five-year period, the number of girls playing varsity high school sports went from one in twenty-seven to one in three (for boys, participation is one in two). Participation of girls in high school sports grew from 7 percent to 40 percent of all female students. At the college level, participation of women grew from 16 percent to 38 percent of all athletes. As important is the fact that girls' and women's sports budgets expanded dramatically. Well-trained coaches were provided to this previously disadvantaged population, and athletic financial assistance to female athletes went from being almost nonexistent to over $180 million per year.

Fifty-five million women now regularly participate in sports or fitness activities in the United States. Thirty-one million girls play team sports. Women represent 55 percent of all volleyball players, 43 percent of all runners, and 41 percent of all soccer players. These mandated educational institution sports opportunities were directly responsible for U.S. domination in the new team sports of the 1996 Summer Olympics (soccer and softball) and the 1998 Winter Olympics (ice hockey). The result of these opportunities has been the development of three very different new, large, and potentially lucrative sports marketplaces: (1) the active female market, (2) the female as a spectator of men's sports, and (3) male and female spectators of women's sports.

ACTIVE FEMALE MARKET

Even though the physically active female consumer is less than forty years old, she has entered the critical consumer demographic of "18–34 female," the most desired and prolific consumer in America. As a result, U.S. corporations are rapidly repositioning to exploit and develop this market, which has the potential of doubling the existing sporting goods industry. The U.S. female was once a relatively narrow consumer, buying mainly goods that enhanced her image as sex object, decorative object, or caretaker and purchaser for other members of her family. She is now buying athletic shoes and apparel, and sports equipment, and moving into product categories where she was never before considered to be a major force—from cars and automotive accessories to hardware and building materials.

This active female consumer is also more eclectic in her sports participation than her male counterpart, making her an even more lucrative customer. American males are pressured from a very early age to participate in one of three or four of the most popular men's professional sports. Females are under no such constraints. Therefore, American girls and women explore the worlds of dance, sports, and exercise and are more eclectic and more likely to participate in more activities than males. Each of these activities requires different shoes, apparel, and equipment.

The new female consumer also appears to have retained the decorative relics of the feminine stereotype. She buys athletic shoes, apparel, and related items disproportionate to her participation in sports. For example, while only 20 percent of all golfers in America are female, they purchase 50 percent of all golf products with the exception of clubs. The active female still cares about how she looks when she plays sports, which makes her an even more lucrative consumer.

Since 1994, the active female has demonstrated her sports consumer potential by outspending the American male in athletic shoes and apparel. Still, only 20 percent of all schools and colleges are complying with Title IX. Boys are still receiving twice the participation opportunities, scholarship dollars, and athletic programs benefits. In fact, we are only halfway down the road to equal opportunity for women in sports in the United States. The purchasing power demonstrated by women to date is only the tip of the iceberg when you consider that the active female consumer is forty years old and under.

This growth trend will continue for at least another forty years as women catch up to men in education-based sport opportunities. The buying power of the active female will continue to grow as equity in the workplace better balances earning power. Female worker income in the United States currently exceeds $1 trillion annually, 80 percent of all retail purchase decisions are being made by women, and in 33 percent of dual income families, the woman is earning more than the man. Her expendable income in later years will exceed that of her male counterpart, simply because of her longer lifespan and inherited wealth, and the advent of a more active population of seniors.

FEMALE FANS OF MEN'S SPORTS

An unanticipated consequence of Title IX and the American gender-equity sports movement has been an increase in the number of female sports fans consuming men's professional sports products and licensed merchandise. When women were given the opportunity to play sports, they became as knowledgeable and as passionate about sports as their male counterparts. The female spectator currently comprises 35 to 45 percent of the in-arena and television-viewing audience of men's professional sports today. Every major men's professional league (NHL, NBA, MLB, NFL) has sports-marketing staff specifically dedicated to the women's market.

MALES AND FEMALES AS SPECTATORS OF WOMEN'S SPORTS

The current women's professional team sports explosion in the United States, the performance of women's teams in the 1996 Olympics, and the growing popularity of collegiate women's sports are other results of Title IX. Few realize that it takes fifteen to twenty years to develop an Olympic-level or professional athlete. The American public is just beginning to see the results of female athletes receiving quality coaching, access to weight rooms, college athletic scholarships, national- and international-level competitive experiences, and the encouragement of their parents and society at large. These benefits were never present prior to the 1970s. Not only is there a large enough pool of elite athletes to support professional sports leagues, there is an eager, loyal, and interested spectator pool of males and females to support them.

This spectator pool for women's sports is a separate market from the spectator pool for men's sports. The spectators who watch women's sports and the spectators who watch men's sports are not the same people. This results in an expanding sports spectator market that attracts investors and sponsors to women's professional sports leagues.

Thus, the most significant factor in igniting an international gender-equity movement and the strongest impetus to creating expanded opportunities for women to play sports may well be the economic forces evolving from a global marketplace.

Key point

Socioeconomic Class and Opportunity

Both men and women of leisure, necessarily from privileged social classes, formed the core of participants in the Olympic Games in the early twentieth century. The concept of "amateur athlete" revolved around the participation of classes whose need for financial support in order to train, travel, and compete was not an issue. Until the 1970s, when the feminist movement began to question mainstream social values based on class and gender, women of means were more likely to appear at the games than their lower socioeconomic counterparts. [See chapter 1—eds.]

The ability of women of means to avoid gender discrimination in sports and to become Olympic champions supports the possibility that even nations that disapprove of female participation in sports will rally around the idiosyncratic Olympic champion. At these historic moments, national pride supersedes the conflict of gender and, sometimes, even religion, making it possible for an athletic daughter of a ruling family to establish the Muslim Women's Games.

Women from the higher socioeconomic classes who have access to power and resources have used their influence in both national and global arenas to affect social change. Coupled with other forces advocating gender equality, these women of means will continue to play a pivotal role in the next millennium's global efforts toward greater gender equity.

The Impact of Socialist Societies

Key 2 extremes

Once women were admitted into the Olympic Games, their participation was an interesting combination of two extremes. Initially, only women of higher socioeconomic class from developed countries were permitted by their nations to participate in "feminine" sports (sports which emphasized grace and skill and did not require extreme demonstrations of strength, endurance, physical contact, or group bonding). Only they could afford the time and expense of training. Socialism ushered in a new era of female athletes who were, in reality, genderless pawns set up to express the superiority of a political ideology. Socialist governments undertook the expenses of training and coaches. They engaged in extraordinary procedures to select the most talented athletes to enter training at early ages. This focus and emphasis produced startling results.

The international success of female athletes from socialist countries forced non-socialist nations to examine their opportunities and training programs for women and to ease their more sophisticated forms of gender (and race) discrimination in favor of winning on the political playing fields of the Olympic Games. While mass participation rights for females and gender discrimination laws did not necessarily follow in those countries, the obsessive pursuit of victory enabled many talented female athletes momentarily to leave the obscurity of their national sports experience to pursue Olympic glory on international playing fields.

In the 1960s and 1970s (in Eastern Bloc countries), and again in the 1990s (in China), the success of female athletes from socialist countries in international competition was overshadowed by allegations of the use of performance-enhancing drugs and other questionable practices (i.e., delaying the onset of puberty, inducing abortions in order to derive performance-enhancing benefits, etc.). The dominance of socialist women, especially in strength-based sports, unwittingly played into Western nations' preoccupation with more feminine sports, induced gender testing, and reinforced the stereotype of a "feminine" body shape. This backlash delayed the Olympic offering of team sports such as ice hockey, softball, and soccer until the 1990s. That barrier is now broken, however, and it would not be surprising to see the more traditionally male sports such as boxing, weight lifting, and wrestling become recognized Olympic sports for women in the next millennium.

Few would refute the contention that the gender equality of socialist nations and subsequent success of their female athletes resulted in non-socialist countries expanding sports opportunities for women in both numbers of participants and types of sports. There is reason to believe that these pressures will continue, especially as China becomes a dominant force in sports.

National Pride

Sports are a global cultural institution. In all sports, regular periodic competition between national teams, promoted by the print and electronic media, ignites passionate nationalism like no other human endeavor, save war. Indeed, the playing fields of sports have been likened to the battlefields of war. As societies become more fragmented by pace, the complexity of knowledge, the merging of races and ethnicities, and the extension of business, art, and other human pursuits into global markets, sports become one of the few activities that can focus a population on a common interest and transcend the bias, stereotypes, and other barriers that divide human beings rather than unite them.

National pride has simple dividing lines—they, us, theirs, and ours. It matters not what color, ethnicity, gender, or other criteria "we" are. There is no reason to believe that the millennium will see any diminishment of national pride. To the contrary, the more the nations of the world become globally interdependent, the greater the need for pride and more "politically correct" sources of differentiation. National pride in flag, dance, heritage, and sports assists people in defining their place in the world and creating a comfort zone in a world which they seem to find much too complex. As women's achievements in sports and contributions to national pride increase, pressure is placed on anachronistic beliefs that the female athlete is less worthy of support, less productive or less important than the male athlete, and the myths promulgating gender inequality in sports begin to dissipate.

Olympic purists agree that an ideal Olympic Games would be a gathering of the best athletes in the world. The selection of these athletes would be unencumbered by limitations of nationalism or other non-sports-related criteria. Yet the games are inexorably bound by a structure that is nationalistic at its core (National Olympic Committees, a definition of the Olympic family as a collection of countries, etc.). As long as this Olympic structure is country-based and our global society increases in complexity, these factors will be positive forces promulgating gender equity, increasing participation opportunities for female athletes, and expanding the public's appreciation of the achievements of women in sports.

Influence of Global Communications

As developing countries generate sufficient wealth to give their citizens the means to access television and the Internet, and as global literacy and access to the print media extends the dissemination of the images and achievements of female athletes on a global scale, considerable pressure to change will be placed on societies that are currently discouraging females' interest and participation in sports. Televised sports events and print and Internet news coverage of sports competitions are the most easily translatable programming that can cross barriers of custom and language. The Olympics, world championship competition, and continental and international league play are all highly desirable events of worldwide interest, events that will continue to be embraced by the media.

From a practical perspective, televised women's sports events and news coverage of women's sports are, at their core, advertisements promoting the women's sports product. While this communication is essential to the success of feminist agents of change, such distribution of images of competent, successful, and highly skilled women creates its own momentum.

In the United States, we are starting to see the beginning of female sports-specific magazines and cable television networks delivering programming to women with sports as a core element. Even the very top non-sports women's magazines (*Glamour, Vogue,* etc.) have full-time health and fitness editors who cover sports and exercise as regular features.

As female audiences for male and female sports events increase, economic pressure in support of women's sports also increases. Advertisers of products utilized by female consumers begin sponsoring sports events for women and targeting women who watch sports on television and in arenas. This investment fuels continued growth of women's sports and women's sports participation. In the United States, 1996 NBC Olympic female spectators made up 65 percent of the TV-viewing audience, and women in the most desirable female demographic categories for advertisers increased by 40 percent from the Barcelona games (1992) to the Atlanta games (1996).

Inevitable Change in Female Role and Stereotype

It is reasonable to assume that the barriers currently limiting the full and equal development of girls and women in sports and other human pursuits will continue to disintegrate. As nations move from agrarian to industrial and technology/service economies, male dominance derived from physiological advantage declines and the need to maximize the intellectual capacity and productivity of the workforce increases. Economies choosing to ignore half the talent of their population fall behind. As women become more educated and their value and status in the workforce becomes more equal, stereotypical views and myths of female deficiencies, physical and intellectual, decline. In this environment, the female athlete will come of age in the new millennium.

Knowledge of Sport Benefits

Until the twentieth century, the popular justification for the value of sports participation was the training of males for war and business competition. Only during the last several decades have the positive physiological, psychological, and sociological benefits of exercise and sports participation for both genders been touted to the public. If the U.S. experience is an indicator of the impact of health knowledge, the millennium will see an all-time high in print and electronic media coverage of the benefits of exercise, health research results, and the promotion of physically active lifestyles. There is also good reason to believe that the millennium will champion a cultural and economic shift to preventive medicine, with exercise and sports participation as essential elements of that approach.

Global Feminist Sports Movement

Feminist movements throughout history have been both cyclical and national in scope. However, it appears that the global economy and global communications will create a fertile ground for a global gender-equity movement in the new millennium. Sports are a mainstay cultural institution in most societies, and gender equity in sports participation does not require the sharing of real power. (Men can still govern sports and hold the highest positions of authority.) Allowing women to achieve success in sports is more palatable than allowing their full participation in other cultural institutions such as religion, the military, or government. However, once a female athlete achieves the status of champion or celebrity, her power is conferred by the public and the media and derived from earned status (which is irrevocable) as opposed to an assignment of title or position by someone else. Thus, this celebrity foothold can often be parleyed to propel a gender-equity movement at an extraordinary pace. For example, the Billie Jean King versus Bobby Riggs 1973 "battle of the sexes" generated a television audience of 50 million viewers and the largest crowd ever to view a tennis match. There is no reason to doubt that sports will be a central battleground in the next wave of feminism early in the new millennium.

Social Justice as a Global Value

2000

As nations move away from war and violence as means of conflict resolution, social justice ascends the value hierarchy. At its heart, social justice demands the cessation of inequality and discrimination on the basis of race, gender, ethnicity, economic class, and other differences among human beings. Social justice as a priority value in the third millennium is both a hope and a prediction. The weapons of war and violence have become too potent to permit their continued dominance. A social justice environment must fuel more equitable participation by women in all aspects of society—play, work and family.

It is even reasonable to predict that the new millennium will see a renewed emphasis on civility and skill as the primary determinants of sports victory instead of equating competition with violent behavior and antagonism against opponents. During the 1998 Winter Olympics, the media suggested that preoccupation of North American ice hockey teams with committing violence against opponents had diminished their skating speed, agility, and skills. On that same global stage, the world was embarrassed by the U.S. ice hockey players' trashing of their living quarters. Does the millennium portend a swing back toward the more noble notions of sports? If so, values traditionally deemed feminine will play a major role in determining the speed of this swing back to civility in sports performance and spectatorship.

Male Pride

One of the most surprising occurrences in the recent American experience of the impact of Title IX on gender equity in sports was that "Dad" became the leader of the gender equity in sports movement. The recent generation of mothers and fathers—products of the feminist movement of the 1970s—raised their daughters to believe that there were no barriers to women achieving their aspirations. A daughter could be a doctor, lawyer, astronaut, or athlete. But it was Dad who encouraged, taught, and championed the participation of his daughter in sports because, unfortunately, this first generation of moms who supported sports participation for girls did not have the chance to play and therefore lacked the skill and knowledge to coach their children. That will change as the first generation of female athletes begins to bear children.

The sports feminism of dads with athletic daughters has inexorably changed the nature of the battle for sports resources. This power struggle ceased being gender-based and became age-based. The athletic directors, school principals, and college presidents of the 1970s, 1980s and 1990s were people who grew up in a culture which taught them that "women aren't—or should not be—interested in sports," "girls can't throw," and "no one will pay to see women play sports." As the members of this "dinosaur" generation retire and dads and moms with athletic daughters assume the reins of power in sports, the dynamics of the gender-equity struggle will change dramatically. This new generation of men will demonstrate that pride in the abilities of their athlete daughters is more important than support of male dominance in sports.

Idiosyncratic Role of Powerful Individuals

Ultimately, minorities deprived of equal treatment or benefits are liberated or held hostage by the action or lack of action of the majority in power. This majority does not act without "key influencer" catalysts—individuals who hold power because of their position, expertise, or respect. Would Martin Luther King's efforts or the Civil Rights movement have been successful if George Wallace rather than Lyndon Johnson had been the president? Would the modern era of professional women's basketball and the success of the WNBA have occurred if David Stern was not the NBA commissioner? Would the International Olympic Committee have adopted numerous gender-equity policies, such as 10 percent representation of women on National Olympic Committees or no new sports without both male and female events, without Samaranch as the IOC president or Anita DeFrantz as a powerful member of the IOC executive committee? Would the economic viability of the female sports television-viewing audience have been demonstrated without NBC Sports president Dick Ebersol creating an Olympic programming schedule and features specifically designed to attract the interest of women? Would Lifetime Television for Women have succeeded without the blessing and vision of CEO Doug McCormick?

Predictions for the Third Millennium

The powerful forces detailed above will ensure the continued growth of opportunities for women to participate in sports in the new millennium, including the achievement of equality of participation and medal opportunities in the Olympic Games. And, if the explosive growth and popularity of women's sports participation in the United States is any reflection of what will happen to this participation when social justice is reinforced by national law, and when women take on increasingly important roles in society, then the future of women's sports in the new millennium will be a bright one indeed.

It is also reasonable to expect that the new millennium will usher in new roles for men and women in sports. Women will break significant barriers by participating in nontraditional sports from boxing to weight lifting and wrestling. There will be no sport that is closed to a woman because of her gender. Both male and female values will change, bringing both genders to more common and different ground. Sports will have more rules that prohibit violence and random physical assault. Women's sports will become more commercialized. There will be an increase of participation in coed and lifetime sports. More families will participate in sports together. The number of men participating in fitness activities will increase and the number of women in team sports will likewise grow.

The difficulties involved in sharing political power and mobilizing institutional commitment to gender equality will be the highest barriers to the full participation of females in sports and society. Progress will be slow and flawed with the expression of anger and sexism by generations of men and women who grew up in a different time and place and who were taught different beliefs about the role and capabilities of men and women. This cauldron of conflict, fueled by power, pride, and insecurity, is an inevitable outcome of major social change. The good news is that major social change in gender roles will occur globally in the coming millennium; the bad news is that it will not come easily.

However, if there are four stages to social change—anger, backlash, acceptance, and celebration—the end of the new millennium will display the acceptance and celebration of women's sports and gender differences. We will realize that sports are not where men prove that they are better than women. We will learn that "different" is not "less than." We will learn that "different" means "not the same as." We will learn to celebrate our diversity.

In the new millennium, there is no doubt that opportunities for the female athlete to participate and achieve success in the Olympic Games will match those of her male counterpart and that the participation of women in sports worldwide and at all levels of skill will blossom. The real question is not "whether" but "when."

NOTE

1. This article draws on information included in the following: National Association of State High School Athletic Associations, participation data; National Collegiate Athletic Association, participation data; and United States Olympic Committee, Olympic participation data.

CHAPTER 9

Yes!

Sex Testing

One Chromosome

Too Many?

CHERYL L. COLE

_____

1966. Budapest. The European Track-and-Field Championships. A new event
has been added to the program. Before the more familiar competition begins,
three female gynecologists take their places . . . in the gender control facility.
These three doctors were charged with making critical decisions about the sex
of the female athletes. Two hundred and forty-three women athletes. All would
participate in this initial qualifying event. Two hundred and forty-three unclothed
athletes paraded into the room and stood still for inspection. Just what was it
that the gynecologists had been trained to see? And what were they looking for
at this first meeting?

Although the literature offers no easy way to understand precisely "what" the
gynecologists were assessing, their method implied that "true sex" was there to
be seen. The judges could "see" what they were looking for. Perhaps they were
looking for familiar and easily *recognized* bodily differences that mark off female
bodies from male bodies. Perhaps they were searching for bodily anomalies—signs
that betrayed the female body, erasing basic and fundamental distinctions between
the sexes.

Diagnosis? All 243 athletes were pronounced "female." Still, numerous journalists and scientific critics asked their readers to think about those who did not
compete in the games. Unexpected absences betrayed suspect athletes and suspect bodies. According to these reviewers, absence confirmed guilt. In the United

States, for example, those accusations were explicitly directed at Soviet female athletes. That the Soviet athletes had not failed the test "in fact" only enhanced their position in America's fantasy.

Almost immediately after the European Track and Field Championships, the International Amateur Athletic Federation (IAAF) extended its sex-testing mission. This time, they called for pelvic examinations at the Commonwealth Games in Jamaica. Now, instead of merely looking at bodies from a presumably tolerable proximity, these examiners would probe bodies. This new approach to testing implied that the criteria for qualifying as female had changed. Yet again, the literature on testing offers no description of what exactly was examined, nor what it was meant to reveal, nor what acceptable results would be. Now athletes bared their genitalia for inspection (Ljungqvist and Simpson 1992, 850). At their second meeting, once again, all the women competitors passed. All were diagnosed "female."

The procedural shift from the body's surface to its interior took a more radical turn the following year at the 1967 European Cup Track and Field events in Kiev. By now, officials had added a different, even more "scientific" strategy for visualizing and documenting sexual status—chromosomal screening. It was the combination of exterior inspection and chromosomal screening that changed the outcome of the examination.

Ewa Klobukowska, Olympic champion and co-world record holder for the one hundred meters, failed the analysis. She became the first "woman" to be disqualified from competition on the basis of her "sex." She had, in the IAAF's words, "one chromosome too many to be declared a woman for the purposes of athletic competition" (cited in Turnbull 1988, 64).

While the criteria for determining sex in Kiev were seemingly more clearly linked to chromosomes than genitals, reports of what decided Klobukowska's disqualification differ. The American gynecologist and obstetrician Alan Ryan (1976) concluded that "one sex chromosome too many" meant that Klobukowska had been diagnosed with a triple X chromosome pattern. Ryan and a British gynecologist and medical advisor to the British Amateur Athletic Board, John S. Fox (1993), argued that the gynecologists' observation of her masculine genital characteristics, rather than chromosomes, led to her ineligibility. Other critics claimed that Klobukowska was suspended because of some sort of chromosomal mosaicism. That is, these critics speculated that Klobukowska was neither absolutely XX nor XY. Offering the most detailed explanation, Elizabeth A. Ferris (1992) contended that Klobukowska had an XX/XXY mosaicism. According to Ferris, Klobukowska "was aware and had taken steps, surgically and medically, to correct" this condition. Perhaps the exam had documented traces of "abdominal testes" that "had been removed." Perhaps it had revealed that Klobukowska was taking "female" hormones (686).

Regardless of the specific condition behind the disqualification, the IAAF barred Klobukowska from all future competitions. The IOC revoked the gold and

FIGURE 9.1

"Klobukowska in Action: One too many."

Courtesy of Archive Photos.

bronze medals that she had won in the 1960 Olympics. And, in 1970, the IAAF voided her records and erased her name from their record books. Not surprisingly, the popular media represented the results of Klobukowska's sex test as "news." In the United States for example, reports of Klobukowska's sex ambiguity and her ineligibility for competition appeared in *Time* (September 29, 1967) and *Newsweek* (September 25, 1967). Recalling the fantasy of suspicious and guilty Soviet athletes whose duplicity had been enlisted for a national project, *Time* observed that because Klobukowska had passed previous exams she "saw no reason to duck the test" (70). But according to *Time*, "science" defeated such duplicity: "On the basis of microscope's evidence, three Russian and three Hungarian doctors gave the fatal verdict" (70). An in-action, full-body photograph of Klobukowska accompanied the article. The photo captures her just prior to crossing the finish line and accentuates what appears to be her stunning muscular development. Quite clearly, the image is meant to render her suspect. *Newsweek* simply asked, "Who goes there? Ex-miss or missing-x?" (97). *She wasn't missing an X*

Moreover, the popular media represented chromosomal assessment through the familiar terms of "scientific progress" by portraying sex chromatin as capable of establishing a level of truth previously unobtainable in sex testing. "Doubtful femaleness" could now be uncovered. That it could now be uncovered, however, implied that it had not been uncovered through earlier tests (*Time*, September 25, 1967, 70).

In the words of *Time*, some "dames" apparently resemble, but are not, real dames because "nature has scrambled their chromosomes" (70). Klobukowska, as *Time*'s representative case of "scrambled chromosomes," clarified the doubters' doubts. In effect, she was used to confirm the victory of the technology of sex testing. With the aid of scientific technology the boundary separating the sexes could be fixed in ways that were useful for sports competition.

Twenty years after Klobukowska's sexual exile, Alison Turnbull (1988) named Ewa Klobukowska "an early and very public victim of the sex chromatin test," in an article entitled "Woman Enough for the Games?" published in Britain's *New Scientist* (63). In an effort to underscore Klobukowska's victim status and, by extension, earn readers' immediate sympathies, Turnbull stresses Klobukowska's strikingly ordinary appearance. A "victory shot" of Klobukowska (the quintessential victorious extension of the arms, accentuating her slenderness) centered on the article's opening page, apparently documents, at the level of the body, Turnbull's claim. Its caption reads: "Innocent victim: Eva [*sic*] Klobukowska was a champion sprinter until a sex test deemed that she had 'one chromosome too many'" (61).

As the innocent victim, "Klobukowska" takes on a dual narrative function. Most explicitly, her body is established as the normal female body. Less explicitly, but no less effective, it becomes the background against which other female bodies are judged as normal or deviant. Thus, Turnbull's argument is effectively made concrete as it is translated through visual terms.

FIGURE 9.2

Ewa Klobukowska, innocent victim.

Courtesy of *New Scientist,* September 15, 1988.

The photographs which follow include a full-body image of U.S. track athlete Florence Griffith-Joyner, who appears, but only appears to be, in action. Joyner, an African American, is, quite significantly, encoded as immodest, the willing object of the voyeur's gaze. The image of Joyner in a bodysuit, which "seems to leave observers in little doubt of the wearer's gender" (Turnbull 1988, 61), is situated next to a full-body, in-action photograph of Czech runner and eight hundred meter world record holder Jarmila Kratochvilova. Kratochvilova's physicality offers readers a look at a concentrated and highly visible collection of "masculine" features: broad shoulders, exceptional muscular development and definition, overall comportment. The side-by-side images of Kratochvilova and Joyner are framed through the authoritative voice of Finnish geneticist Albert de la Chappelle, a prominent critic of the current testing procedures. By his view, the test unfairly discriminates against women like Klobukowska while failing to detect those who are truly advantaged. His testimony about the virilizing effects of congenital adrenal hyperplasia, which he claims is a relatively common heredity disorder, gives meaning to Kratochvilova's hypermuscularity.[1] At the same time, Kratochvilova's masculine physique lends credibility to de la Chappelle's claim about what and who the test does and does not detect.

Klobukowska as a sign of the victimized ordinary feminine; expert commentary about the virilizing effects and pervasiveness of congenital adrenal hyperplasia; photographs which appear to simply document bodies "as they really are"—this combination is convincing and extremely compelling. Together they leave no doubt that an injustice has occurred. And they leave no doubt about which of the bodies in the photographs needs policing. Turnbull had intended to clarify the natural variance of female physiques and hoped to offer new views about testing. Ironically, her narrative relies on and reinforces the fundamental

FIGURE 9.3

Czech runner Jarmila Kratochvilova and American runner Florence Griffith Joyner: contrasting styles of body.

Courtesy of *New Scientist*, September 15, 1988.

Fair ? Clothing make up

categories justifying sex testing in the first place. In so doing, she demonstrates the difficulty of thinking outside of the familiar terms which govern sports and sexual difference.

Thirty years have elapsed since sex testing was first introduced into international sports competition. In those thirty years, the overlapping constructs which link biology, sports, and equality, made explicit by Turnbull's narrative of the Klobukowska case, have continued to animate ongoing debates for and against the IOC's gender verification policy. Common sense suggests that proving one's sex would be quite simple and straightforward. Sex testing in the Olympic Games challenges that belief. Common sense suggests that science simply documents sex. I investigate, in what follows, how the scientific methods used by the IOC never simply "reveal" but also shape how sex as well as its "threats" are imagined. I draw attention to explicit claims about the needs of sports for normative bodies and the deep trauma that results from athletes who receive unsatisfactory results. More specifically, I draw attention to the rhetorical uses of the categories of equality, femaleness, and trauma through the "case" of Maria Patino, the second and only other woman athlete to receive public attention after being disqualified on the basis of her sex test. My goal is not to confirm nor dispute claims about trauma, but to draw attention to the ways in which those categories establish and extend the IOC's heroic image and its authority as well as the policy's apparent reasonableness. I conclude by examining the different responses of the IAAF and IOC to the very real uncertainties and contradictions that sex testing has produced, the problems of trying to ground sex in the body, and the continuing difficulty of thinking outside of the familiar terms which govern sports and sexual difference.

The Fundamentalism of Sports

The 1960 Rome Olympics were notable for rumors and speculations about the role of drugs and sex in counterfeit performances. Drug panic was heightened by media coverage surrounding the amphetamine-related death of a cyclist; sex panic, by rumors of men competing as women. The IOC reacted by becoming the first sports organization to establish a medical commission charged with the medical control of doping and sex. Not surprisingly, the need for a mandatory sex-testing policy has been routinely justified as a means for preventing men from competing as women. The International Athletic Foundation's (IAF) Work Group on Gender Verification Testing, to take one example, argues that "rumors that men were masquerading as women poisoned the atmosphere of high-level competitive sports." As they explained it, "[t]esting was thus introduced as a preventative measure . . . to eliminate . . . any inappropriate competitor" (Ljungqvist and Simpson 1992, 850).

Despite legendary rumors, there are only two cases, for which there is only anecdotal evidence, about men masquerading as women. Most frequently iden-

tified is Hermann Ratjen. According to popular accounts (which were often reproduced in science-based publications), the Nazis coerced Ratjen into passing and
competing as a woman. He competed, as Dora Ratjen, in the high jump for three
years, including the 1936 Olympics.[2] Accounts of Ratjen's coercion typically
include a photograph of Dora Ratjen, full-body, in mid-air, crossing over the high
jump bar. Dora/Hermann Ratjen is, in fact, most often represented as the first
and only man to pass successfully as a woman in the Olympic Games. Given this,
it seems that the actual number of men impersonating women was not the issue.
Instead, what mattered was the perception, rumors, and possibilities of passing.
Temptations to cheat, defined exclusively through "doping" and passing, were attributed to the growing importance of sports in wider international politics.

Prior to the adoption of mandatory sex testing at the international level, one
national governing body, the British Women's Amateur Athletic Association, had
sought to eliminate the possibility of female impostures. They required that each
woman athlete submit a letter signed by a doctor verifying her sex. Recognizing the possibility of falsified letters, the IAAF initiated the "on-site inspection"
discussed in the introduction. Following the IAAF's example and their own random sampling at the Tenth Winter Olympics, the IOC adopted what it calls its
gender verification policy. The policy requires that all women competitors
undergo gender verification from an IOC-approved organization prior to their
participation in the games.

From its first required exam at the 1968 Mexico City Olympics until 1992,
the IOC used sex chromatin exams, and, more specifically, a procedure called the
buccal smear, to determine the sex of the female athletes.[3] From the IOC's perspective, the buccal smear offered several advantages. Among its most important,
according to the IOC, was that it was less invasive than previous tests. It involves
only scraping buccal epithelial cells (from inside the cheek). Whereas the earlier
1966 and 1967 exams brought women athletes under the immediate gaze of physicians and had been depicted as invasive, degrading, and humiliating, the buccal smear
sustained a reassuring distance from the medical gaze. Moreover, the laboratory-
based test placed physical distance between the athlete and the actual test. And
it deflected attention away from the whole body while not reducing the body
to genitals.

The buccal smear is a well-known technique that visualizes chromosomal
constitution, presumed to be the fundamental expression of sexual difference. By
making visible the inactive X chromosome (called the Barr body), it indicates
the number of X chromosomes. Since the inactive X chromosome only exists
in the XX pair, chromosomally XX women test chromatin positive. Those who
are XY, test chromatin negative. Since males are understood to be constitution-
ally XY, XY women are disqualified from competing as women. Thus, the exam
relies on a logic which links chromosomal characteristics to the authenticity of
athletic performance. Those competitors who successfully meet the IOC Medical Commission's model of femininity (femininity is the term repeatedly used

by the IOC) based on chromosomal pattern are issued what the IOC named its "certificate of femininity." Once issued, the certificate, which is actually a wallet-size card signed by the president of the IOC Medical Commission, becomes the object inspected at those competitions requiring gender verification. Indeed, Fox (1993) claims that some competitors carry several certificates issued by various governance bodies because of the variability of screening procedures and qualifying criteria across competitions.

Interestingly, from its earliest accounts, the IOC used sex testing to announce its (imagined) alliance with women. That is, through its narration of sex testing, the IOC presented itself as aware of and opposed to the historical injustices that excluded women from the Olympics or that limited the events in which women could compete. Mandatory sex testing, according to the IOC, was a means of protecting new opportunities that had opened up for women. From the IOC's perspective, both the IOC and mandatory testing were depicted as responding to a larger historical struggle associated with women's rights (Hay 1974). In the IOC's words, "the purpose of the femininity tests . . . [is] to make sure all female athletes compete under identical anatomical conditions." Thus, what/who needs policing is that which "threatens" fairness—defined in terms of identical anatomical conditions. Paradoxically, biology, the IOC's basis for its previous discrimination against women would now ground its assessment of equality—as well as the sincerity and heroism of its efforts.

Eduardo Hay, gynecologist and obstetrician at the Faculty of Medicine, Mexico, and a spokesperson for the IOC Medical Commission, suggests that what and who were threatening to women's sports would—in the final instance—be evaluated through sports, not science. To a great extent, his statement makes explicit that the IOC would depend upon science, but that the IOC's decisions and needs would override scientific discussions about sexual difference. It also implies that the body's compatibility with the fundamental demands of sports would be decisive in determining sex and fairness. Rather than explaining what he imagines to be the relevant relations and differences between the sports and science, Hay moves his argument forward by offering a "clarifying" example: the intersexual and hermaphroditic athlete. Such athletes, Hay contends, "must be barred from competition in order to ensure fair play" (1972, 998). "Such anomalies" would "give the woman athlete endowed with these masculine anatomical conditions, an unfair and unlawful advantage over the anatomically normal woman athlete" (Hay 1974, 119). From this perspective, those unnatural bodies would compromise and contaminate the foundational principles of sports. Moreover, they would make normal women athletes the victims of unnatural bodies holding "unlawful" advantages.

Hay extends his rationale for necessarily excluding hermaphrodites by linking hermaphroditism, anatomical physical advantages, and illicit doping practices. Doping and genetic advantage are, from his perspective, moral equivalents. Both doping and hermaphrodism, according to Hay, violate the principle of fairness,

Propaganda [handwritten marginal note]

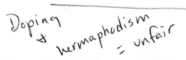

the apparent site of consensus around sport. Both are illicit and unsportsmanlike. Hay argues that doping and its imagined genetic counterpart are more frequent and enticing in a context in which athletic performance is an agent of nationalism, an expression of the superiority of the state.

Although sex testing seems to depend upon the scientific documentation of femaleness, the narrations of sex testing routinely invoke curious slippages. For example, Turnbull's narrative is marked by the easy slippage from deviant femaleness to muscularity. The IAAF's statement moves easily from men masquerading as women to "any inappropriate competitor." Hay quickly moves from hermaphrodism to drugs. Overall, the sex-testing narrative relies on and facilitates slippages between male masquerade and hermaphrodism, intersexuality, muscularity, female masculinity, drugs, nationalism, and victimization. Thus, the issue organizing sex testing is not restricted to men impersonating women. Instead, the multiple categories that displace and replace one another imply a persistent and chronic passing that demands preventative measures—particularly measures that will render deviance visible.

Reasonable Procedures and Rational Actions

Evaluations of the IOC's gender verification policy are routinely facilitated, as I suggested above, through interdependent categories related to normal/deviant and fairness/victimization. Psychic repercussions of abnormal results, articulated in terms of shame, humiliation, trauma, and violations of privacy, are typically asserted under the guise of explanation in sex-testing narratives. For example, in their response to a *Nature* editorial on sex testing, Ferguson-Smith et al. simply claim that "[i]t is not hard to imagine the distress and humiliation felt by an athlete confronted with failure to pass a sex test" (1992, 10). Declarations of the obviousness of distress and humiliation, and their correlate psychic content, exemplify routine assertions in the sex-testing literature. In this section, I want to consider the rhetorical role that these categories play in imagining what is considered responsible behavior and who is considered rational.

In the 1992 issue of the *British Medical Bulletin,* Ferris sets out to challenge the IOC's testing policy. Her opposition to the policy is based on its "unfair disqualification of women athletes" and the "untold psychological harm" it has produced (683). Despite her intention to denounce the policy, she (like Turnbull) actually does otherwise. Ferris undermines her criticisms of the policy as she challenges, through the category of trauma, the prominent understanding of the IOC sex-testing protocol. Sex chromatin, she explains, was intended to be the IOC's initial, not definitive, step in a multiprocedure process. Deficiencies lie not with the protocol, but with athletes who, "traumatized" by inconclusive screenings, terminate the process. Ferris's translation of the "repercussions of irrationality" produces an otherwise rational and reasonable procedure: "Affected women athletes, in a state of severe shock at failing the chromatin screening test taken on the eve of an Olympic or other major competition, and lacking the medical expertise necessary to evaluate its implications, have declined to undergo the complete procedure of chromosomal, hormonal and gynaecological examinations" (688). Hence, the impediment in the procedure, construed as the athlete's unwillingness to proceed, is attributed to a combination of psychic numbness and insufficient information, a disorientation and alienation induced through the sudden instability of one's sex identity.[4]

The IOC and IAAF justify their *posttest* advice and procedures through categories connected to psychic trauma. According to the IOC and IAAF, they advise an athlete who receives an unsatisfactory result to feign a warm-up injury that requires withdrawal from competition. From their view, this advice is given to help athletes avoid speculative publicity and curiosity. Indeed, their efforts to guarantee confidentiality and to help athletes avoid embarrassment and irreparable psychic damage that would ensue from publicity appears responsible and rational. In the IOC's "heroic" accounts, both precautionary mechanisms—designed to assure equality and to alleviate public humiliation—are evidence of their reasonableness and of the reasonableness of the procedures. Since only two athletes' results have been publicized, I imagine that other disqualified athletes have participated in the IOC's recommended performance.

Although not initially identified by name, a Spanish hurdler, Maria José Martinez Patino, was among those ruled ineligible based on the results of the sex chromatin test at the 1985 University Games in Kobe, Japan. Consistent with tactics allegedly designed to protect the athlete's privacy and to manage the psychic trauma certain to result from publicity, Patino was advised by event officials to feign a warm-up injury and withdraw from competition. She took their advice. Like her predecessors and successors she enacted a performance that left her status and the exam which determined it, at least temporarily, unchallenged.

In a 1991 story in *Women Sports and Fitness* entitled "When Is a Woman Not a Woman?" Alison Carlson narrates Patino's later efforts to challenge the diagnosis. By emphasizing Patino's determination, despite seemingly insurmountable obstacles, and her perseverance, in the face of humiliation, Carlson builds on and advances the terms organizing the female victim of the sex test narrative. Carlson traces Patino's quest to regain her sex status, beginning with Patino's expensive but successful search for an expert who could explain the conditions under which she could fail the sex test. The expert, an endocrinologist, identified the problem as androgen insensitivity. Because Patino is unable to respond to testosterone, she is, we are told, unquestionably female and chromosomally XY. Carlson emphasizes Patino's victimization by drawing attention to the directive issued to her, despite the new knowledge of the condition shaping the test's outcome, at her next competition. Patino was told to repeat what would this time be a career-ending, injury performance. Carlson depicts Patino's refusal to comply in heroic terms: Patino's willingness to face public humiliation as the Spanish Athletic Federation publicly disqualified her, erased her records from the record books, and banned her for life from future competition. Carlson's narration is one that portrays Patino as a brave and independent actor whose ability to overcome obstacles culminates in the IAAF declaring her eligible to compete as a women and reinstating her records.

Given this narrative, it seems as if Patino's efforts made the IAAF and IOC accountable in ways that had been delayed by earlier management techniques. Indeed, although criticisms of the specific technique and general procedure were advanced prior to Patino's challenge, those criticisms had been given limited attention. Yet, while Patino's efforts seem to be individualized and localized (a familiar effect of the highly seductive narrative of the athlete overcoming insurmountable odds), I think that it is a mistake to imagine this story to be that of Patino's alone. The results of Patino's efforts are symptomatic of, located within, and shaped by the broader forces behind the growing intersexual and transsexual movements. For example, and relatedly, by the time Patino challenged the IAAF's decision, the New York courts had decided that Renee Richards, a male-to-female transsexual, was legally female and did not have to undergo the Barr body exam in order to qualify to play on the women's professional tennis tour. Thus, although the challenge that Patino presented to the IAAF was narrower in scope, far less significant in its consequences, and perhaps even antithetical to the demands being made by the growing intersexual and transsexual movements, the outcome of Patino's challenge cannot be understood apart from the broader conditions which brought the larger social movements into being.

At the same time that I argue that it is a mistake to imagine this story to be that of Patino's alone, I think that the narrative effectively demonstrates the individualizing effects of sex testing and its related strategies. That is, the contest over Patino's true sex suggests the normalizing and individualizing effects of the strategies mobilized under the guise of compassion and concern, heroism, reasonability, responsibility, and rationality. It allows us to see how "secrecy," maintained in the name of easing individual suffering and shame, performed the work of diverting attention from the contradictions and criticisms of gender verification. It also allows us to imagine how secrecy worked to isolate from one another those declared anatomically advantaged. I should be clear here: by pointing to secrecy, I do not mean to suggest personal failing or passivity on the part of those athletes who did not challenge the test. Nor do I mean to imply that medical commissions were ethically responsible for publicizing their results. Instead, I am suggesting that secrecy played a crucial role in enabling and extending the authority of the various medical commissions and their governance organizations.

Additionally, Carlson's narration of Patino's struggle clearly remains, like those previously discussed, enabled and limited by the larger categories which shape ways of thinking about sexual difference and sports. Similar to Turnbull's narrative of Klobukowska as victim, "When Is a Woman Not a Woman?" relies on the mutually reinforcing and interdependent categories of the normal/deviant and fairness/victimization. Thus, what appears to be a sympathetic description is, again, an expression that is symptomatic of the logic of sex testing: "She has no uterus and is sterile, but she has female genitalia, feminine body proportions and normal sexual response. Significantly, even if she took steroids, she couldn't benefit from them" (Carlson 1991, 27).

Hence, for Carlson, Patino's disqualification was unjust because Patino, symbolically (in terms of her external appearance) and functionally (defined in terms of normal sex response), is a real woman. Even more significant for Carlson, any confusion about Patino's sex could be sorted out by her complete inability to benefit from steroids. To be sure, Patino's inability to profit from steroid use becomes the crucial link for situating her athletic performance as one of unquestionable integrity. And, by extension, it ensures her the full moral weight of victim status. Such narrations, exemplified in previously discussed statements by Turnbull and Ferris, rely on and reinstate the categories of the normal and abnormal, categories which lie behind moralizing assessments of athletic performance and the body. From Carlson's perspective, the purity of Patino's body and her athletic performance (both of which she defines in terms of the complete absence of the masculine), entitles her to full membership in women's competition. For Carlson, the implication is clear: if Patino does not qualify as a woman, no one would. The IAAF agreed.

In their moment of accountability, the IAAF and IOC reevaluated, albeit in different ways, their mandatory sex-testing policies and their favored techniques. Given that Patino's immediate challenge was restricted to her right to inclusion based on the claim that she was a true female, the IAAF revisions were, at least at first glance, remarkable. Of course, the IAAF revisions are less remarkable if we recognize Patino's story as a momentary magnification of the contradictions and criticisms that had been produced by and were accumulating around sex testing. And they are even less remarkable if we consider the broader social movements and larger debates that shaped the outcome of Patino's petition. For the IAAF, the mounting contradictions, including the diminished capacity to easily distinguish between two distinct sexes, required revising their approach. As we will see, the IOC would hold onto its chromosomal icon.

Gender Verification: Revisited and Revised

The IAF convened what it called a Work Group on Gender Verification in Monte Carlo, Monaco, on November 10 through 11, 1990. Closing the supposed distance between sports and science, the work group included representatives from medical genetics, gynecology, pediatrics, endocrinology, pathology, biochemistry, psychiatry, psychology, and sports medicine, and athletes. Its purpose was to provide a public space to consider alternatives to current practices used by the IOC, IAAF, and other international federations. Their deliberations and recommendations were released in a statement published in *JAMA* (February 12, 1992,

850–852). Among those present were Eduardo Hay, from the IOC Medical Commission, and Bernard Dingeon, charged with overseeing gender verification at the 1992 Albertville Winter Olympics. Both IOC representatives refused to add their signatures to the report (Dingeon 1993, 357).

The report was divided into sections which emphasized historical considerations, objectives, and alternative approaches. Three interrelated themes shaped their overall recommendations. One of the first tasks that the work group assigned itself was determining the original intent of sex testing. Their proposals would follow from its purpose, which, in their view, was exclusively to prevent men from masquerading as women. Invoking science's authoritative voice, they disputed the validity of "sex chromatin analysis as used for gender verification ... long ... abandoned by the genetic community" (Ljungqvist and Simpson 1992, 851). Relatedly, they opposed privileging chromosomal (genetic) sex over, or excluding, anatomical, psychological, or sociological sex status. Here, they stressed the often repeated worry about possible psychological damage: "the profound consequences on the person's mental health ... and tragic effects on her life" likely to result from queries about an individual's sex (Ljungqvist and Simpson 1992, 851). Moreover, they asserted that the occasional individuals with disorders of sexual development such as XY gonadal dysgenesis "possess no unfair advantage ... no physical attribute relevant to sports performance that is not attainable by or present in other 46, XX women" (Ljungqvist and Simpson 1992, 851).[5]

On a different level, their published statement implied that they recognized the medical and scientific establishments' repeated, but finally failed, attempts to develop a rigorous and closed definition of sex. Science, they stated quite precisely, would not be capable of "assess[ing] the sex of all individuals" (Ljungqvist and Simpson 1992, 851). Thus, they too were giving up—or at least modifying their efforts—on reigning in the criteria determining sex.

Based on their "doctrine of original intent" and the above arguments, including what they understood to be a historical line of unfair disqualifications, the work group advocated abolishing the gender verification examination. Under newly enacted drug-testing guidelines, the IAAF could "incidentally" gain the knowledge they believed they still needed to disclose male masquerade. Doping control now required that all competitors urinate under close observation to ensure that urine was being delivered from the urethra. Thus, this simple but powerful form of observation would be used to detect men trying to pass as females.

Remarkably, or at least seemingly so, the work group did not simply try to find a new way to purify the category of female. Instead they worked with the category's elasticity to "accommodate" intersexuals and transsexuals.[6] They recommended that individuals (46, XY) with gonadal or genital variations (they actually use the term "defects") raised as girls and individuals having prepubescent sex reassignment should be eligible for competition. Decisions about individuals who had postpubescent sex reassignment would be delegated to the appropriate sports' governance medical body. Finally, the work group advised that a medical exam be required for all athletes. Such exams, the report clearly states, "would, of course, include simple inspection of external genitals" (Ljungqvist and Simpson 1992, 852). Consequently, as the IAAF went on record as disbanding gender verification, it reinvested in a clear and verifiable difference. Their "less ambitious" project relied on the emphatic reemergence of genitals as the proper marker of sex.

Moreover, several comments in the report appear to be responses to the IOC's position on sex testing. For example, the report disputes the utility of accrediting laboratories and standardizing protocols (apparently a recommendation forwarded by the IOC) since neither addressed the problem of sex testing itself. Comparably, they opposed activating more recent or advanced forms of chromosomal analysis. Moreover, the IAF work group sent a candid message in which they endorsed the plan as "a model for all international competitions in which gender verification is needed" (Ljungqvist and Simpson 1992, 850). In January 1991, the IAAF Council adopted the recommendations. Finally, the report verified that "[t]he plan ha[d] been well accepted by almost all athletes, physicians, and sport authorities" (852).

Unlike the IAAF, which imagined that international sports and competitors had been ill-served by the sex chromatin examinations, the IOC reconfirmed its early understanding and dedication to mandatory sex testing. According to a letter published in *Nature,* the IOC's "sole aim is to find an efficient solution to the practical problems of fraud screening before competitions" (Dingeon et al. 1992, 447). In a previous publication, Eduardo Hay, who had worked with the IOC from the beginning of its gender verification project, expressed not so subtly what and who the IOC's sex test was meant to address: "If the Medical Commission of the International Olympic Committee had wanted to satisfy everybody, we would undoubtedly, at the present moment, have Olympic Games divided into chromosomic groups. For it is easily forgotten, at this stage, 'that the sole purpose of the Medical Commission in this investigation of femininity, is to ensure the physical equality of the women athletes competing against one another'" (1974, 122).

For the IOC, the matter governing the exam was clear. Establishing a tone that intimately connected femaleness and physical equality, the project sought to maintain the rights of "true" female athletes. By banning those who violated the so-called basic laws of sexual difference, the IOC preserved the basic laws of sports. With sex testing advanced as a basic need and its continued optimism about science's ability to reveal sex, the IOC would continue to deploy science as part of its self-governing and regulation. Femaleness and equality remained joined in the icon of the chromosome.

The IOC sought to improve and standardize laboratory-based testing and the "reliability of the verification method" (Dingeon 1993, 357). In 1992 it adopted a new technology called polymerase chain reaction (PCR). PCR works by amplifying the DNA sequence on the Y chromosome to test for the presence of SRY (the gene thought to determine maleness). Recent work on chromosomal analysis had shown that absence of the SRY gene was the key element in determining sex. Bernard Dingeon had attended the IAAF workshop in order to discuss "preliminary findings" that demonstrated the "advantages of polymerase chain reaction (PCR) gender verification" (Dingeon 1993, 357). PCR, according to Dingeon, "assesses the sex of individuals very adequately in over 99% of those enjoying perfect health" (1993, 357). The IAAF report argued that "PCR-based testing to identify those athletes with a Y chromosome would seem especially hazardous in the setting of sports competition" (Ljungqvist and Simpson 1992, 851). Why it was "especially hazardous in the setting of sports" remained unexplained.

Dingeon's position clearly differs from that of the IAAF. He explained that "the 601 female athletes at the Albertville games confirm that jugal sampling . . . now both quick and painless, is extremely well received by women because it respects these concerns, sporting ethics are upheld, and competitors are shielded from rumors of their sex" (1993, 357). He defended PCR's value over and against the IAAF's medical exam. The exam would be too costly; the emphasis on genitals would not screen out transsexuals; and, once again naming the athletes as empowered agents, gynecological exams were humiliating (Dingeon 1993, 357). Curiously, despite his defense of PCR, Dingeon indicated that the classification of male pseudohermaphrodites needed updating and the physiological basis of the testing remained insufficient. The IAAF predictably, seized on the inconsistencies in Dingeon's argument (Simpson et al. 1993).

Conclusion: The Heroic IOC and Genetic Doping

Motives for sex testing in high-profile, international sports, as I have tried to show in this chapter, resist being reduced to a single event or purpose. Threats to the foundations of sexual difference and sports are expressed in regulatory narratives through various categories that displace and replace one another: male impostors, hermaphrodites, transsexuals, female masculinity, muscularity, nationalism, and doping. From a perspective that acknowledges gender verification's roaming and frequently contradictory rationale, the project's coherence would be seemingly undermined. Yet for the last thirty years those confusing categorical overlaps have been and remain negotiated through a narrative which speaks compulsively to fairness. In this case, sports' egalitarian code produces the illusion of a unified object of concern, located in the female body. Moreover, chromosomes have been produced as the iconic representation of sexual difference and equality.

For more than thirty years, a substantial number of professionals and organizations have publicly denounced or refused to participate in sex-testing procedures. During the 1950s, Lawson Wilkins writing in *Pediatrics* and Murray L. Barr writing in the *Lancet* "explicitly warned against the use of sex chromatin testing in sports" (de la Chappelle and Genel 1987). Prior to the testing policy, Bunge (1960) predicted the problems that would be encountered if sex testing were introduced into the Olympic Games. As I discussed in a footnote, immediately following the IOC's implementation of the Barr body test, Keith L. Moore (1968), one of the first to describe the Barr body procedure, published an editorial in *JAMA* denouncing its use. Geneticists in Finland refused to perform sex chromatin testing at the 1983 World Championships in Helsinki. De la Chappelle and Genel also cite as having "condemned its use" the Lawson Wilkins Pediatric Endocrine Society, the Endocrine Society, the Australian Society of Human Genetics, the American Academy of Pediatrics, and the American Society of Human Genetics (1987, 1266). In 1992, a group of twenty-two French biologists and geneticists asked the French government to ban the IOC's tests because it violated the rules set out by the National Ethics Committee and the French Constitution. The French Medical Association voiced the familiar argument that "Knowledge of a genetic characteristic may infringe on the intimacy and dignity of individuals and disturb them irremediably" (Anderson 1992, 784). Xavier Estrivill, a Spanish geneticist, refused the IOC's request to conduct gene amplification on a trial basis. Most recently, the following groups announced their support of the IAAF's 1992 decision to recommend but not require "health" tests: the American College of Obstetricians and Gynecologists, the American Fertility Society, the American Society of Human Genetics, and the Endocrine Society.

Interestingly, more recent commentary suggests that above all else, the IOC saw gender verification as a powerful means for "controlling rumors" about female masculinity. Ferguson-Smith and Ferris (1991) attribute the IOC's resistance to suspending sex testing to its successful role "in removing scandal and innuendo from international sport" (20). Fox contends that sex testing was implemented "to allay public anxiety that had been engendered by women athletes whose physiques were considered to be more masculine than feminine" (1993, 148). Thus, by Fox's view, the IOC used gender verification to mediate the relationship between the Olympic athletes and the public. More specifically, he frames gender verification in terms of its long-term success in tempering "anxieties" related to viewing performances by women with masculine physiques. How are we to understand this sort of spectatorial anxiety? Is this spectatorial anxiety a universal problem that transcends geopolitical borders? What are we to make of an examination that addresses a deep unease with female masculinity, that is apparently successful in removing innuendo and scandal, but that remains an ongoing need? Do we need to think more about the ways in which universal categories like sex gain their meaning within national contexts? In this chapter, my comments have focused on the discussion as it has appeared in medical publications. The few popular articles referred to in this paper do indeed suggest that sex as a "universal category" accrues meaning in historically specific contexts related to nation.[7]

In his response to the IAF work group, Jean D. Wilson, of the department of internal medicine at the University of Texas Southwestern Medical Center, called the plan "a genuine reform in amateur sports" (1992, 853). Still, he sees the recommendations as "only a first step" in the sort of changes needed (853). By his view, for example, intersexuals and transsexuals should be permitted to determine their own identities. Moreover, in his effort to further clarify the inadequacy of the logic behind the sex-testing policies still enforced by some organizations, he points to the parallels between variations made visible in sex testing and the ever present inequalities defined by "height, weight, coordination, or any other parameters" (853).

Perhaps Wilson is onto something when he calls attention to the discrepancy in the forms of diversity that are and are not respected. Like Wilson, de la Chappelle and Genel argue that "equality among competitors is impossible to achieve." To underscore what they call the "natural biological variability of individuals," they point to height and proportion of fast- and slow-twitch muscle fibers (1987, 1265–66). They even argue that conditions such as congenital hyperplasia create only modest increases in androgens and, therefore, are no more advantageous than other "medical conditions that might naturally alter physical stature" (1266). Yet, they displace and contain their doubts (about the possibility of sports' foundational concepts) through the figure of the muscular female. In the final instance, they charge that "overtly masculinized women should probably be excluded from competing on medical grounds alone" (1266). Similarly, Fox contends, "One has only to look at the enormous variation in physique in both sexes to appreciate that 'unfairness' is more often attributable to autosomal genetic variation, irrespective of the sex chromosome complement" (1993, 149). But, like de la Chappelle and Genel, Fox eases the doubt he has introduced by arguing that it is still appropriate to screen females for conditions that "offer a degree of performance enhancement" (149). It is quite remarkable that all too many critics reenter the terms on which sex testing is founded, despite their attempts to do otherwise.

One way to take seriously the inconsistent treatment of physical variations noted by Wilson and the inconsistent recognition of those variations by critics such as de la Chappelle and Genel and Fox is to consider how those inconsistencies are regularly helped along by aligning female anomalies with drug use in sports. In narratives on gender verification, "drug use" is a prominent sign that is regularly invoked, to a great extent, because of its ease of reference.[8] The commonplace acceptance of the terms that ground the prohibition of drug use in sports quickly divides and recodes those "medical conditions that naturally alter physical stature." In this way, what are initially recognized as gender anomalies are reimagined as forms of genetic doping. Thus, the particularly and apparently principled opposition to drugs as a technology of performance enhancement works to ease the burden of the contradictions that continually crowd into the discourse on gender verification. Relatedly, the optimism about the ability of science to reveal drug use lends confidence to scientific attempts to locate sex in the body.

Indeed, the discursive conflation of illicit drugs and illicit sexed bodies is convincing and compelling. Together, illicit drugs and biological sex stimulate "our" imaginations and anxieties about the authenticity of athletic and sexual performances. By providing scientific evidence and visual testimony of counterfeit performances, drug- and sex-testing technologies reinscribe the line between the natural and unnatural, the human and the hybrid. Not only do particular visualizations leave no doubt that injustices have occurred, but they leave no doubt that the vulnerable and innocent Olympic body, the universal body, in both its individual and collective form, has been protected. In short, the rhetoric of doping—in its explicitly and insidiously sexed forms—is perhaps the single most important element in shoring up the boundaries of "the natural" on which the IOC's promises and heroic tales of "saving sports from corruption" depend.

NOTES

1. Congenital adrenal hyperplasia refers to a condition in which an XX fetus's development is shaped (masculinized) by the high volume of androgen produced by fetus's adrenal gland. It is considered to be the most common form of female pseudohermaphrodism.

2. The story which appears less frequently is that of Sin Kim Dan, who, when competing for North Korea in 1964, set records in the 400- and 800-meter running events. Sin Kim Dan was apparently revealed to be male when his father identified him as a son that he thought he had lost in the war (Ferris 1992; Ryan 1976). Interestingly, no photographs of Sin Kim Dan appear in the text.

3. For Moore (1968), the sex chromatin exams led to "grossly unfair" disqualifications because the IOC's definition of sex underestimated its complexity. Based on the evaluation of numerous cases of abnormal sexual development, Moore argues that "no single index or criterion" displays an individual's sex. Thus, buccal smears, which indicate chromosomal sex "can not be used as indicators of 'true sex'" (164). Moreover, Moore points to those anomalous cases in which women could be justifiably declared eligible or ineligible. Not surprisingly (as we will see), his conclusions are linked to the anomalies' virilizing effects.

4. Similarly, the IAAF cites "distressed athletes" as the reason that the "intentions of the IOC have not been realized in practice" (Ljungqvist and Simpson 1992, 851). Later in the same article, the IAAF asserts that "[e]xact diagnoses are rarely available, as most competitors are told to feign injury and withdraw. Thereafter, information on these athletes is, unfortunately, not readily obtainable" (Ljungqvist and Simpson 1992, 851).

5. Gonadal dysgenesis is considered to be an intersexual condition defined by undifferentiated gonads. In some cases, it results in external genitals that deviate from what is considered normal.

6. Although no mention of the Renee Richards case appears in the report, I imagine that the New York court's decision heightened their incentive to deal with the issue.

7. I consider the relation between "America" and sex testing in high-profile international sports in my forthcoming book on embodied deviance and national identity in postwar America.

8. I offer a critique of the logic behind drug testing and the impossibility of the "natural" body on which that logic relies in Cole (1998).

CHAPTER 10

Cool stuff

The Gay Games:

Creating Our Own

Sports Culture

VIKKI KRANE

JENNIFER WALDRON

Stephane and Tony had been training and looking forward to participating in this ice skating competition for the past year and a half. They had raised enough money to offset the expenses of traveling to New York City and staying there for ten days. Now Tony could barely lift his head without getting dizzy from the flu. Regretfully, Stephane went to the ice arena and told a referee that they were withdrawing from the competition because Tony was ill. However, the official had a different idea. Rather than simply allowing them to withdraw, the official sought to allow Stephane to continue in the competition. The official went into the stands and made the following announcement: "I have a skater here whose partner is ill. Is there any one here who can complete level 4 waltz patterns and is willing to skate with him in this competition?" Amazingly, Charles emerged from the stands and said that he knew the moves well. However, he was here as a coach and did not have any skates with him. So the official made another announcement: "We found a skater, but now we need a pair of skates in size 9." Again, the audience pulled through and a skater came forward: "I already competed, so use my skates." Charles and Stephane had only about fifteen minutes to practice, yet they were both incredibly excited simply to be able to complete. As it turned out, the two very talented skaters were quite compatible and skated to a gold medal (adapted from Feder, 1994a).

The experience of these two men, one gay, one heterosexual, epitomizes the essence and spirit of the Gay Games. Besides being the only place where we find two men participating in pairs figure skating, the Gay Games also turn upside down the whole traditional culture of sports competition. At the Gay Games, the spirit of participation far eclipses the need for winning. As seen in this example, skaters are willing to share equipment. An ill competitor can be replaced at the last minute without penalty. And judges are willing to turn a coach into a skater so that another skater can participate.

The Gay Games were the vision of Tom Waddell, who dreamed of a sports environment characterized by inclusion, a space free from prejudice of any kind. Waddell wanted to overcome what he saw as the sexism, racism, heterosexism, and nationalism that permeates the traditional Olympic Games: "Let's look at the Olympics. The Olympics are racist, the Olympics are exclusive, they're national-istic, they pit one group against another, and only for the very best athletes. That doesn't describe our Games" (quoted in Coe 1986, 13).[1] For Waddell, "[doing] one's personal best is the ultimate goal of all human achievement" (quoted in Clark 1994b, 12). So he wanted to differentiate the Gay Games from the culture of the traditional Olympic Games: "Anyone from anywhere is welcome to participate in this event" (quoted in Clark 1994b, 12).

Specifically, the Gay Games provide the opportunity for gay, lesbian, bisexual, and transgendered (GLBT) athletes to participate in an affirming and empower-ing environment. We are a community who has been marginalized and even dis-missed by mainstream sports, thus it is especially important to be privileged and to champion all athletes who wish to participate in these games. In doing so, we eschew many of the values of traditional sports, such as the need to dominate and conquer our opponent, the view of opponents as the enemy, and applause only for the winner. The emphasis of the Gay Games is on participation and the pursuit of personal bests, not on winning and establishing superiority. This is not to say that high-level competition does not occur. Athletes set many official records during the Gay Games. In 1998, for instance, participants set over one hundred meet, gay, and Master's records (of many countries) in just the swimming and track-and-field events (Uncle Donald's Castro Street 1998). But while the inclu-sive nature of the Gay Games recognizes and supports those individuals whose goals include competitive success and setting national and international records, the spirit of the games ensures that any interested person can participate. There are no exclusions based on age, competitive level, nationality, race, sexual orien-tation, gender, religion, political belief, HIV status, or bodily condition. Medals are given and records are maintained, consistent with traditional sports values, while the inclusiveness and expressiveness of the Gay Games more fully embrace our queer sports culture.

By using sports as the vehicle for social change, the Gay Games challenge the dominant sports culture as well as the dominant culture in society at large. Therefore, we frame our discussion within the broad perspective of construct-ing culture, specifically, queer culture (Desert 1997). Sometimes the word "queer" means a sweeping category of all gay male, lesbian, bisexual, and transgendered people. This is its most encompassing definition. However, queer has additional meanings. We use the term "queer" to denote our political identity as well as to indicate a non-heterosexual orientation. Although not all participants at the Gay Games have political motives, simply participating in such an event has political, social, and cultural implications. We also use queer to disrupt the normal assumptions of heterosexuality (or heterosexism) prevalent in our society. Heterosexism is the conviction that heterosexuality is the only acceptable mode of social interaction and sexuality. It leads to marginalizing and stigmatizing nonheterosexual relationships, identities, and communities (Herek 1992). Clearly, we do not agree that heterosexuality is the only socially acceptable sexual orientation. So with the term queer, we contest the heterosexism that is common in our society. Further, we do not want to exclude, nor perpetuate prejudice against, non-heterosexuals. Thus for us, queer refers to non-heterosexual identities and community that are inherently disruptive to heterosexism in our society. Defined as such, the Gay Games are a queer event, taking place in a queer space (Ingram et al. 1997) while challenging heterosexism and developing an alternate sports culture.

A Brief History of the Gay Games

In his opening address at Gay Games I in San Francisco, Tom Waddell offered the following welcome: "Welcome to a dream that is now reality. Welcome to a celebration of freedom. These Gay Games, the first of their kind, are offered to gay and enlightened people from all over the world. They are a departure from other events of this scope and magnitude in that the underlying philosophy is one of self-fulfillment and a spirit of friendship. This is a first; it is our beginning, and as such, we expect these games to set a solid precedent for future games that are exemplary for wholesome and healthy athletics, devoid of the notion that beating someone is the sole criterion for winning. Participation makes us all winners" (cited in Uncle Donald's Castro Street 1998).

The first Gay Games, titled Challenge '82, were held in San Francisco in August of 1982. To organize them, the San Francisco Arts and Athletics (SFAA) was created in 1980. The SFAA oversaw all administration and organization of Gay Games I and II. Gay Games I was a huge success: 1,350 athletes from twelve nations competed in fourteen sports. As in the Olympics, the arrival of a lighted torch, brought from New York City to San Francisco by runners, announced the opening of the Gay Games (Uncle Donald's Castro Street 1998). At the opening ceremony, Tom Waddell spoke about the inclusive, participatory philosophy of the Gay Games.

Gay Games II, Triumph in '86, was held in August of 1986, again in San Francisco. These games drew 3,482 athletes from seventeen countries to the seventeen events. The SFAA added to the 1986 games a "Procession of the Arts," a series of cultural events that included conferences, concerts, plays, exhibits, films, dances, and cabarets (Uncle Donald's Castro Street 1998). At the closing ceremonies, Tom Waddell announced that Gay Games III would move from San Francisco to Vancouver, British Columbia, Canada.

Yet two major events occurred before Gay Games III took place. In July 1987, Tom Waddell died of AIDS-related pneumonia. At the 1986 games, Waddell was a source of inspiration when he won a gold medal in the javelin event even though he was critically ill from AIDS (Labrecque 1994). Now his death would have a profound impact on the queer community that would dedicate itself to keeping his dream of an inclusive athletic event alive. Barry McDell, chairman of the Vancouver Athletics and Arts Association, testified to Waddell's impact on that community: "Tom was an international hero to thousands and thousands of gay men and women. Gay Games I gave us the most significant gay or lesbian experience of our lives. Tom taught us not to fear being gay" (quoted in Waddell and Schaap 1996, 228).

The second significant event that occurred before Gay Games III was that the SFAA disbanded and became the Federation of the Gay Games (FGG). Consistent with Tom Waddell's ideals, the change in the organizing body resulted in a more inclusive and international umbrella organization. An elected fifty-five member board is charged with remaining true to the fundamental principles of inclusion and participation, choosing the site for each Gay Games, and reaching out to the international queer community to promote the games (Federation of Gay Games 1997; Labrecque 1994). The FGG seeks "to foster and augment the self-respect of lesbians and gay men throughout the world and to engender respect and understanding from the nongay world, primarily through an organized international participatory athletic and cultural event held every four years, and commonly known as the Gay Games" (Federation of Gay Games 1997, 1). (Currently, nine different committees compose the FGG: cultural, membership, outreach, policy and procedures, site selection, sports, strategic planning, task force on AIDS and breast cancer education, and computer and technology task force.)

Gay Games III, Celebration '90, was the first to receive federal funding when the Canadian federal government contributed toward the $2.1 million budget. In addition, the city of Vancouver allowed participants free public transportation. At the 1990 games, the pattern of doubling in size from the previous games continued: seventy-five hundred athletes from thirty-nine countries participated in twenty-three athletic events in Vancouver; two thousand people participated in the cultural festival. Opening and closing ceremonies, as well as related social events, were held in public venues. Thousands of local volunteers helped the games to proceed smoothly. And for the first time, new national and international athletic records set during the games were recognized by international sports governing bodies. In Vancouver, the Gay Games achieved the status of a world-class event (Uncle Donald's Castro Street 1998).

Gay Games IV, held in June of 1994, brought together more athletes to compete in an athletic event than in any other previous athletic event, including the

1994 Olympic Games in Atlanta: 10,864 athletes from forty countries, participated in thirty-one events; 250,000 spectators came to New York for the Gay Games and Cultural Festival; seven thousand volunteers ensured that the games ran smoothly (Uncle Donald's Castro Street 1998). By 1994, the games' budget had grown to $7 million, and the event brought upwards of $316 million into New York City. Though previous Gay Games had been held during August, the FGG decided to hold Unity '94 in conjunction with the commemoration of the twenty-fifth anniversary of the Stonewall Riots. At the Stonewall Bar in 1969, a group of drag queens and other gay men and lesbians fought back against police brutality and intolerance toward GLBTs. For many people, the Stonewall Riots mark the beginning of the Gay Liberation movement in the United States. So the eight days of Gay Games IV ended with the sold-out closing ceremonies in Yankee Stadium, followed by the Stonewall "March on the United Nations" the next day.

Gay Games V were the first to take place outside of North America and were held in Amsterdam, Netherlands, a city known for its tolerance. Friendship '98 successfully lived up to the motto of "friendship through culture and sports" as 14,715 participants from five continents and sixty-eight countries competed in twenty-nine events, plus six exhibition events (Uncle Donald's Castro Street 1998). Participants included 250 "special needs" persons (e.g., individuals in wheelchairs, athletes who are deaf). Two hundred and fifty thousand spectators attended the games. Additionally, thirty-two choirs and two international marching bands performed at fifty-two venues. Fourteen artist workshops were offered. Amsterdam's concert hall, the Musiektheater, became Friendship Village, a central meeting place during the games. Here people registered for all athletic and cultural events. They congregated, bought souvenirs, and obtained Gay Games and local information, volunteered, and enjoyed free live entertainment. Each day participants and spectators could get the free newspaper, the *Daily Friendship,* to keep up to date on all the athletic and cultural events. A task force on AIDS and breast cancer education sponsored events focused on education, awareness, and prevention. One of the high-profile events at Gay Games V was the International Memorial Run commemorating individuals lost to AIDS and breast cancer. Participants walked, ran, cycled, skated, or raced their wheelchairs along the course. The enormous Rainbow Flag, brought to Amsterdam from San Francisco, was displayed. The International AIDS Memorial Quilt hung as a memorial.

The Gay Games V Outreach Program focused on increasing participation of individuals from developing countries and increasing participation by women (Uncle Donald's Castro Street 1998). Committee members sought sponsorship to defray the costs for these individuals, and to assist them to participate in the games. These efforts brought 238 non-Western participants to the games. The Women's Issues subcommittee of the Outreach Program also sponsored road shows to reach women throughout Europe, created special literature aimed at women, and provided discounts, low-cost housing, and day care for women participants. Because of the efforts of the Women's Outreach Committee, women's participation increased to 42 percent at Gay Games V, up from 35 percent at previous games (Uncle Donald's Castro Street 1998).

Gay Games VI will be held in Sydney, Australia, in September 2002. The theme of the games will be "Under New Skies." The FFG and Sydney Gay Games organizers are looking forward to having the games in the Southern Hemisphere where they will attract more individuals from Australia, the Pacific Rim, and other Asian countries. The athletic and cultural events of the sixth games will take place in the facilities being built for the 2000 Olympics.

The Unique Sports Culture of the Gay Games

[At the open workout day] already the spirit was more comradely than combative. Athletes offered applause—and pointers—to the opponents we'd face the next day. On Wednesday, organizer Teresa Galetti set the tone with her welcome: Dangling some Gay Games medals in the air, she said that if any participants wanted one so badly that they had to cheat . . . they should just come see her and she'd happily *give* them one. In other words, the Gay Games—at least in this event—built a sports culture based not on winning at all costs, not on revving up hatred toward opponents, not on glorifying the victor and reviling the loser. . . . In this celebratory atmosphere, we lived a vision of competition that couldn't possibly inspire anyone to respond to losing, as Penn State coach Joe Paterno once did, by saying he'd go home and beat his wife. The sports culture that teaches men to dominate and coerce—and that teaches winners they can just take whatever they want—was roundly defeated in this [martial arts], the most seemingly violent of sports. That was the victory all of us walked away with.

(lesbian participant, quoted in Solomon 1994, 140)

To create a uniquely queer sports culture is to establish a culture as different from the dominant sports culture. Queer sports culture exists as the "other" to traditional sports culture. Another way to think of the effect of the Gay Games is to think of them as composing what has been called "queer space." Queer space designates spaces that contest traditional heterosexist assumptions and practices (Desert 1997; Ingram et al. 1997). Queer space also provides opportunities for homoerotic expression and builds alliances and community among GLBTs. It is a site of cultural expression and community action. Such sites emerge from individual experiences (which then translate into an increased sense of community) or through group actions leading to increased camaraderie. For one week every four years, the Gay Games provide a truly queer sports environment that contests the heterosexism of traditional sports culture. The games allow GLBTs to express ourselves in sports in ways we typically cannot in traditional sports settings. As well, they create an increased sense of community.

Perhaps figure skating offers the quintessential example of the way the Gay Games help create a truly unique, queer sports culture. Arthur Luiz, cochair of figure-skating competition, explains: "The sport of figure skating, as the world knows it, has been transfigured. Gay skaters and promoters and coaches and choreographers and costumers have forged a new direction in figure skating, one that encompasses the meaningful theme of Gay Games IV—that of Unity. Figure skaters of the same gender have united, and in doing so have forged a heightened level of artistic and athletic expression" (quoted in Labrecque, 1994, 30). Many aspects of Gay Games skating are incompatible with traditional skating culture. As journalist Abigail Feder suggests: "The Gay Games, by freeing skaters from the usual strict rules about music, costuming, and gendered moves, opened up the very idea of what skating could be. For these competitors, skating became a forum for personal, political, and artistic explorations before a crowd looking for more than whether or not they could land their triple jumps" (1994a, 140).

Expressiveness, and even playfulness, in attire was prevalent on the ice in New York (Feder 1994a, 1994b). Some male participants skated in drag and some female skaters wore pants. All participants skated to music with lyrics. Additionally, female pair skaters toyed with traditional gender roles by switching who had the "lead role" during their routine. In the '94 games, one male skater emerged on the ice dressed as half man/half woman and then proceeded to do a solo "dirty dance" to the song "I've Had the Time of My Life" (Labrecque 1994). Male pairs, in romantically charged moves, engaged in lifts, throws, and spin moves that traditionally demarcate masculine and feminine roles in figure skating. In mixed-gender pair skaters, female partners lifted their male partners. Skaters wore personally meaningful attire. Matthew Hall, an internationally ranked Canadian skater, wore the red AIDS ribbon prominently displayed on his outfit. An American skater wore a rainbow-sequined vest and hat. A former U.S. national competitor, Wynn Miller, sported a Mohawk and nose ring and wore leather, reflecting his involvement in the sadomasochistic community. (Not suprisingly, after a magazine displayed a photograph of him in this attire, his home skating rink posted a dress code forbidding this type of costume.) Skaters also selected politically expressive music, such as "A Whole New World." Further working the crowd, a skater from Seattle began his individual routine to "Singing in the Rain." He then segued into a favorite in the gay community, "It's Raining Men." All of these actions stand in direct contrast to the strict regulations of traditionally sanctioned figure skating.

Trevor Kruse and Darren Singbeil of Toronto expressed their views on the "gays in the military" controversy (Labrecque 1994). 1994 marked the height of the controversy in America, so in New York they took to the ice dressed in camouflage T-shirts and black tights. They also donned black tape, X'ed over their mouths: "Don't ask, don't tell." Through their poignant skating performance, they overtly challenged the enforced silence of GLBT military personnel. The audience overwhelmingly appreciated their stance, showering them with applause.

Although the Gay Games initiated same-sex pair figure-skating competition in 1994, the Gay Games organizers did not seek official sanctioning (i.e., recognition by the international skating governing body) at that time. Officially sanctioned rules would not have accommodated these personally, socially, and politically meaningful sports behaviors. But in 1998, the Gay Games did seek official recognition of the event by the International Skating Union (ISU). This request led to one of the biggest controversies at Gay Games V. Official sanctioning has its advantages—a single set of official rules for all competitors, a pool of officials who are familiar with this set of rules and know how to conduct the events, and, some would say, instant credibility. Further, in ISU-sanctioned events, participants' performances can count toward their official standing in international skating. However, ISU regulations do not allow same-sex couples in competition. Ultimately, the ISU did not officially recognize the Gay Games. This decision was especially harmful for the elite skaters who participated in the 1998 Gay Games competitions because they risked being expelled from subsequent ISU-sanctioned competitions. Of the one hundred skaters registered at the games, about twenty-five of them could have been seriously affected by this ruling. Eventually, Gay Games organizers canceled the competitive skating event and instead arranged a "public practice." This allowed the skaters to perform their routines, but in a noncompetitive event without standings or medals, so as not to violate the ISU ruling. Not surprisingly, the actions of the ISU only heightened support for the Gay Games skaters. The public practice events were presented in sold-out venues. The mayor of Amsterdam came to show his support of the skaters and of the games in general. And during the closing ceremonies, the skaters received a standing ovation after an exhibition performance.

This appreciation of our queer sports culture reverberated throughout all the Gay Games sports venues. The energy and excitement of such an inclusive and compassionate environment was extraordinary. It was not unusual for the crowd to cheer for all participants, no matter whether they were in first place or last place or anywhere in between. During the long-distance road races (i.e., ten kilometer, half and full marathon), the crowd cheered for all runners. They were especially encouraging and high spirited when partners crossed the finish line hand in hand, something inconceivable in traditional races.

Competitors also felt this energy. For example, Kara and Dana arrived from South Africa after training for six months for the ten-kilometer race. Although neither runner considered herself "a competitive athlete," both were excited to be part of the Gay Games. Proudly, they were part of the small contingent from South Africa. All week, Kara and Dana wore the South African Gay Games team warm-up jackets and the matching traditional African caps (which they sold during the games in their continued fund-raising efforts).

Prior to the race they were nervous, yet excited. All week long the anticipation of the event built, as the distance-running events were held on the last day of the games. The crowd was building along the course, especially near the start and finish lines. Soon people were lined up five and six deep trying to get a glimpse of the runners. The media and people with friends in the races jockeyed for position with their cameras poised. First the runners in the marathon began, followed twenty minutes later by the half marathoners, and then the ten-kilometer race was to begin. In all, over twenty-five hundred runners were there.

Kara and Dana lined up at the start for the ten-kilometer race with hundreds of other runners. The starting gun blasted, and off they ran. Since Dana had not been feeling well the past two weeks, they knew they would not be running together, so Kara ran ahead. The crowd energized each of them as they were loudly applauded throughout the course. Kara was the first to come to the final stretch leading to the finish line. Friends strained to get her photograph. The crowd was roaring for all runners. Kara's pace increased. Any fatigue was replaced with excitement and energy and she sprinted for the finish line. Dana soon followed. Although initially feeling rundown from being sick, she, too, was energized by the crowd. Kara was waiting for Dana, who ran into her arms as she crossed the finish line. Both runners were elated by their races. Even before they knew their times, they knew that they had had great races. The actual time didn't even matter. They were successful competitors in the Gay Games.

Part of the distinctiveness of the Gay Games sports culture is that it wholly embraces all facets of the queer community, including gay male camp and lesbian butch. A prime example of embracing a characteristically queer sensibility is the Pink Flamingo Relay Event. This is a relay swimming race where participants dress up, often in drag. Predicated on "camp," this sports event contrasts with the exceedingly masculine nature of traditional sports. A common social commentary about gay males, leveled by those in the traditional, heterosexist sports culture, is that gay males are effeminate, that they are not "masculine enough." In the queer space of the Gay Games, participants celebrate this, highlighting how we differ from the norms of the dominant culture. As journalist Joe Clark notes, "Complaints that the Games exist to show straight people that fags aren't all sissies are entirely irrelevant; many Gay Games boys are sissies even when decked out in the butchest jock gear" (1994a, 142).

This is part of the beauty of the games. Participants do not have to fit the stereotyped image of a traditionally masculine athletic male or a traditionally feminine female. In fact, it is expected that we do not fit heterosexist stereotypes. In women's power lifting at Gay Games IV, ironically, the largest, most muscular man in the venue sat throughout the competition and judged the event, while a small woman loaded and unloaded heavy weight plates onto the bar (Clark 1994a). Further, the audience seemed to bask in the notion that power lifting is not a traditionally acceptable sport for women. They applauded every lift attempt and went wild with applause when the lift was successful.

The Gay Games provide a queer space where participants and spectators can celebrate our difference from the dominant culture. As Clark concluded, "Gay Games IV showed once and for all that gay people should take part in sports because we are so very good at them," especially within our own unique sports culture (1994a, 140).

The Gay Games and Queer Culture

Bruce Hayes has competed in both the traditional Olympics (winning a gold medal in swimming) and the Gay Games. In 1985, he retired from competitive swimming after participating in the Los Angeles Olympics. Of that decision, he has said: "I was sure I would never compete again. I told myself it was because I was tired and burned out—which I was—but I was also convinced that I could not continue to compete and be an active homosexual at the same time. And I wanted to 'activate' a lot more than I wanted to swim. So I gave it up" (quoted in Labrecque 1994, 28). Yet Hayes missed swimming—that is until he found Team New York Aquatics (TNYA). Here he felt he could combine his gay and athletic lives. As part of Team New York, Hayes competed in Gay Games III and IV:

> In the nearly four years we spent planning [the 1994] Gay Games in New York City, the question we were asked most often—by gays and straights alike—was "Why a Gay Games?" At a time when the gay community's political plate is so full, should we really be pouring so much money and effort into a sports event that is not overtly political? My response is an unqualified yes. I speak only from my own experience. The Gay Games changed my life, as I'm sure they changed the lives of all who have participated in them. They gave me the courage to come out and the awareness and willingness to get involved in our community's political struggles, things I sorely lacked during my years in the closet. But in a larger sense, the Gay Games give us an opportunity to show ourselves to the world in a way the world is not accustomed to seeing us—as athletes.
>
> (quoted in Labrecque 1994, 28)

Learning about and participating in our culture provides queer people a stronger sense of belonging. It also lays the foundation for development of our social identity. For individuals in marginalized social groups, social identification or a sense of community is especially important for several reasons. First, social identity ultimately becomes a strong source of self-esteem. Second, being part of the larger culture is empowering. Third, gaining a sense of the history of the queer community is critical to understanding our community. Finally, social change occurs only with increased self-esteem and empowerment, and an understanding of our culture and history. The Gay Games promote these outcomes. Athletes who participate in the Games generally describe their experiences in very positive terms. Often, as Bruce Hayes described, it is transformational. Additionally, the cultural festivals associated with the Gay Games celebrate queer culture and reconstruct our history. Tom Waddell captured the Gay Games celebratory relationship to queer culture: "We have culture. We have a bona fide culture. It exists because the dominant elements in our society have told us that we're different, so we have been *exploiting* our differences. We *are* different. We're wonderful! And we're worth knowing" (quoted in Coe 1986, 13). Similarly, at the opening ceremonies in 1998, Harvey Fierstein said, "We have arrived here on the backs of generations before us. When you step into the spotlight, stand proud for the generations to come that will be riding on your backs! . . . Stand proud! We are not different. We are extraordinary!" (quoted in Uncle Donald's Castro Street 1998).

For many individuals, the Gay Games enable participants and spectators to become fully enmeshed in a queer environment for one week, without concern for heterosexist prejudice and discrimination. This experience enhances self-esteem and promotes empowerment. This alone is reason for many individuals to participate in the Gay Games. Ann Northrup, member of the Board of Directors of Gay Games IV and Cultural Festival, affirmed: "The Gay Games define us as a coherent, diverse population of our own, asserting our right to celebrate ourselves—not ask for someone else's approval. It is the ultimate manifestation of self-esteem" (Northrup 1994).

Interviews with lesbian athletes who competed in the '94 games reveal the degree to which their participation led to a heightened sense of belonging to a larger community (Krane and Romont 1997). These women described the importance of participation in an inclusive, nonbiased, and comfortable sports environment. They expressed feelings of empowerment and self-enhancement because of participation in the games. And they described feelings of unity with and pride in the GLBT community. All but one of the 132 respondents in this study noted that they would participate in the Gay Games again if money and other constraints were not prohibiting. As one of the athletes responded, "I feel it is an experience everyone should have. It is a week to feel proud and out and free and complete" (Krane and Romont 1997, 135).

When asked to describe the most significant event that occurred during her participation in the 1994 Gay Games, one woman described the difficult path she traveled to get here. "The last time I was in New York I was 16. I had run away from an abusive home and was on the streets. I return to the Gay Games as a strong, healthy, business owner, Ph.D. and not the same person—that's been the best part, by a long shot" (unpublished data from Krane and Romont 1997). This is the epitome of the spirit of the games: celebration of the strength of our community in spite of forbidding circumstances.

As individuals feel personally empowered and their self-esteem as queer individuals increases, they are more likely to reach out to, and participate in, the larger queer community. This interaction with the community will reduce feelings of isolation and alienation, further enhancing individual self-esteem: "By creating a safe and accepting environment, the Gay Games offers participants the opportunity to express themselves openly and to experience the camaraderie and validation of art, culture, and sports. The experience can be a highlight in one's lifetime. While individually, participants celebrate personal achievement, collectively, we experience the solidarity of community and celebrate the diversity and scope of the gay, lesbian, bisexual, and transgender community" (Federation of Gay Games 1997, 1).

The Gay Games are an important component of queer culture. This is emphasized in the cultural festivals that document and celebrate queer history and culture. This cultural component of the games is important for two reasons. First, it allows us to uncover and publicly express our own queer values, practices, beliefs, and interests that often are silenced by dominant, heterosexist cultural practices. Second, much of our queer history has been invisible. Queer individuals often attempt to avoid prejudice and discrimination by concealing their sexual orientation from the general population. This "closeting" led to the development of a hidden past, overtly known only to those queer people already enmeshed in queer culture. The cultural festival contributes to ending this silence and invisibility as singers, dancers, actors, and other artists entertain and educate participants and spectators.

In 1998, the Amsterdam games included the largest cultural festival yet. There were art projects, a choir festival, marching bands, a storytelling festival, an international women's festival, an open-air film festival, and a myriad of music and theater productions. The choir festival and lesbian marching bands were at many sports and cultural venues. Exhibits were not aimed at Gay Games participants and visitors only, however. They were integrated throughout the daily life of Amsterdam and thus reached a much larger audience. In cooperation with the city of Amsterdam, thirteen museums and over thirty galleries mounted exhibits relating to the Gay Games. For example, the National Trade Museum displayed the photo exhibition "Gays and Lesbians at Work." The Jewish Historical Museum exhibited photographs of Jewish gay and lesbian groups.

By being visible and proud, the queer community begins to affect change within the larger community. Becoming more involved in our community, we become empowered to speak out and reach out to the broader society. The Gay Games and Cultural Festival displays our culture in positive ways and allows the society at large to visualize us in more complex ways than stereotypic depictions. As stereotypes break down, prejudice, too, diminishes.

HIV and the Gay Games

"I always liked sports and competition, AIDS/HIV is also a kind of competition and I've learned a lot from that. I don't have to win as long as I'm strong enough to stand up and being in the Gay Games is already winning for me" (cited in Swatling 1998, 15). In 1996, Han Reymann was uncertain whether or not he would still be alive to see the 1998 Gay Games in Amsterdam. He was quite ill with HIV. Though he had tried many different treatments, he had lost a lot of weight and was so weak that he could not walk. So he was preparing for the worst. However, a new drug treatment gave him a new lease on life. With this therapy, Reymann's health greatly improved. During a celebratory trip to Italy, Reymann visited with friends who were training for the Gay Games swimming competition. Just for fun, he joined in one of their training races and realized that he was faster than these men who had been in training. So, Reymann set his sights on Amsterdam. This gave him a new goal as he continued to improve. He took pride in his status as an HIV-positive athlete. And at the Gay Games he swam in the butterfly and backstroke competitions and was a member of the Dutch water polo team (adapted from Swatling 1998).

For HIV-positive athletes, the Gay Games can be a very empowering experience. For some athletes, like Reymann, simply being healthy enough to participate is an incredible boost to self-esteem and dignity. Michael Frantz, a bowler, described his satisfaction in being at the 1998 games: "I have been HIV positive since 1986, and I was diagnosed with AIDS in July 1994. I'm grateful for my time on this earth, and my achievement at the Games is accomplishment enough" (quoted in Athletes of the Gay Games 1998, 80). Another athlete testified to the transformative experience of the games. Where before he had focused on dying, now, with the medical advances and new drug cocktails, he has changed his focus to living: "This triathlon is a way to prove that I am alive" (van Dam 1998, 1). Ultimately, Gay Games participation for HIV-positive individuals is a display of strength and well-being in the face of adversity and illness. It also provides tremendous hope and strength for the entire queer community (Coe 1986).

In the 1980s, the AIDS crisis drew together lesbians, bisexuals, and gay males in a united effort. AIDS was a catalyst for the political coming-of-age of the gay community. The epidemic created a sense of urgency and militancy and brought together the community in a way never before imagined. As local and national agencies were slow to react to the crisis that initially centered on the gay community, GLBTs responded to the challenge by taking care of our own and working to affect social and political responses (Paul et al. 1995). In the face of prejudice and discrimination, they came together to fight for their collective lives. The queer community was catapulted into national awareness in an unprecedented manner. Enormous numbers of gay men and lesbians volunteered for various AIDS-related causes. New social and political networks were formed. The discrimination routinely experienced was exposed. The queer community united to become highly visible in a positive and productive manner (Paul et al. 1995). Ultimately, HIV and AIDS accentuated the importance of social networks and social support for both the individual and community. This consciousness was embraced by the Gay Games.

In 1986, Gay Games organizers were committed to encouraging HIV-positive people to participate in the games, in any capacity. Nonetheless, garnering support for Gay Games II was challenging because of the overwhelming concerns about HIV and AIDS in the GLBT community. For obvious reasons, individuals who were donating substantial resources to HIV-related causes expressed skepticism about the need to donate money for a sports event: "It was hard to tap emotional support for the Gay Games when friends and loved ones were dying" (Coe 1986, 14). Organizers, however, felt the games could provide important social support for the queer community, as well as induce a sense of community pride. The games also could be a source of motivation for HIV-positive participants and an inspiration for spectators. Thus, HIV-positive people were encouraged to participate in the games. Accordingly, organizers worked closely with AIDS groups in San Francisco (Coe 1986). Inevitably, Gay Games II was psychologically helpful for the community as it demonstrated our strength, spirit, and unity in the midst of the AIDS epidemic (Uncle Donald's Castro Street 1998). Dianne Feinstein, mayor of San Francisco, welcomed the crowd at the 1986 opening ceremonies with the following remarks: "I am so pleased to be here! Welcome to San Francisco and these Gay Games. They are very important, and don't let anybody tell you they are not. One of the things it has been a privilege for me to see is the spirit and talent that resides in this community—special spirit, special talent, a coming together in times of trial with the idea that 'We Shall Overcome.' What's important is that you are here; What's important is that you are good; What's important is that you are coming together from all over the world in peace and love to demonstrate to all who are willing to see that you are energetic, enthusiastic, and that you have much to give to this needy world" (Uncle Donald's Castro Street 1998).

We now know that HIV-positive individuals can lead long, healthy, and prosperous lives. In the 1980s, early in the epidemic, not only were there many misconceptions about HIV, but the span between an HIV-positive diagnosis and catastrophic illness was much shorter than it is today. Today, participation in the Games provides the opportunity to highlight healthy and active HIV-positive athletes. This is just as important for other queer and HIV-positive individuals as it is for society at large. As Clifford Ueltschey, a participant in the 1998 physique competition, testified, "I also want to demonstrate that it is possible to create a muscular physique in spite of this disease" (quoted in Athletes of the Gay Games 1998, 83).

Conceivably, one of the most important social outcomes of Gay Games IV in New York was that HIV-positive athletes from other countries were allowed into the United States for the games. The law in 1993 did not allow HIV-positive individuals to enter the United States without a special visa or a special application indicating their HIV status. At this time there was much discrimination against HIV-positive people, who, accordingly, were not likely to disclose their HIV status. Additionally, many people expressed concern that HIV/AIDS would be spread during the games. Some hotels were wary of serving gay visitors. In the spirit of inclusion, social justice, and political action, the Federation of Gay Games (FGG) requested that the government classify the Gay Games as a "designated event." This status would allow HIV-positive individuals to enter the United States for the period of the games. To coordinate this effort, FGG worked diligently with the U.S. State Department, the Department of Health and Human Services, and Immigration and Naturalization Services. The final outcome of these deliberations was that in March 1994, Janet Reno, U.S. attorney general, signed a ten-day blanket waiver that allowed HIV-positive individuals to enter the United States to attend the Gay Games. No special visas or applications were needed. This blanket waiver was a social and political statement by the FGG and the U.S.

government and furthered the ideal that no person shall be excluded from the Gay Games.

Although the efficacy of organizing the Gay Games in the face of the HIV/AIDS crisis was questioned by some, the games have had a long-term positive impact on HIV-positive individuals. Healthy and vibrant HIV-positive role models met the press and received extensive coverage in the media. The notion that someone could not be HIV positive and participate in athletics was dispelled.

Gay Games and Social Change

Throughout his competitive career, rumors that he was gay surrounded Greg Louganis, Olympic diving champion. He only acknowledged that this was true to a small circle of very close friends. Louganis was convinced that to reveal publicly his gay identity would be devastating to his status as an internationally acclaimed diver. So he remained closeted throughout his competitive diving career. However, Louganis did attend the 1994 Gay Games in New York. Although he was unable to attend the opening ceremonies in person, he greeted the crowd with a videotaped message. Louganis ended his welcome with "Welcome to the Games! It's great to be out and proud" (Louganis and Marcus 1996, 276). The crowd, who enthusiastically began applauding upon Greg's appearance on the large screen, then went wild.

Later in 1994, Greg Louganis was awarded the Robert J. Kane Award, one of the highest honors given by the U.S. Olympic Committee (USOC). Inspired by his participation in Gay Games IV, in his acceptance speech to the USOC and approximately a thousand people in the audience, Louganis dedicated his award to Tom Waddell (Louganis and Marcus 1996). Then he requested that the USOC strongly consider moving the volleyball venue from Cobb County, Georgia, where it was slated for the 1996 Olympics. Cobb County had recently passed a resolution condemning "lifestyles advocated by the gay community." Louganis explained that because of this it would not be an appropriate location for Olympic athletes, some of whom may be GLBT. After this speech, and with the urging of other queer individuals and organizations, the USOC and the Atlanta Organizing Committee did move the volleyball venue out of Cobb County.

This is just one example of social change prompted by the Gay Games. In this situation, it is important to know that the relationship between the Gay Games and the USOC was not always so affable. In fact, the history of the two organizations has quite a rocky past. Initially, the USOC fought the use of the word "Olympic" in the title "Gay Olympics" (the original name of the event). Just three weeks before the first games were to take place, the USOC received an injunction forbidding the use of the word "Olympic" by the SFAA. This action was based on the Amateur Sports Act of 1978 that gave the USOC exclusive rights to the word "Olympic." The result of this confrontation was that the SFAA had to eliminate the word "Olympic" from all signage, medals, souvenir items, advertising, and written materials (Uncle Donald's Castro Street 1998). This action nearly bank-rupted the SFAA and Gay Games. Along with the logistical problems this court action posed, it was a strong political statement from the USOC. Obviously, the term "Olympic" has been used in other capacities—Special Olympics, Senior Olympics, Dog Olympics, Police Olympics, and even Nude Olympics and Rat Olympics. As Waddell eloquently stated, "It seems that the USOC is using its con-trol over the term 'Olympic' to promote the very image of homosexuals that the SFAA seeks to combat" (quoted in Coe 1986, 11). After a five-year lawsuit that went to the U.S. Supreme Court, it was determined that the USOC did have rights to the term "Olympic." Thus, the name of the event became the Gay Games. Fur-ther, the unrelenting USOC put a lien on Waddell's home for $92,000 in legal fees. Eventually, in 1993 they waived these legal fees.

More recently the USOC became more amicable toward the Gay Games. First, in 1992 the USOC invited the FGG Executive Committee to meet with USOC representatives in Colorado Springs. The goal of this meeting was to facil-itate a more positive relationship (Federation of Gay Games 1998). In 1994, Gay Games IV was listed in their annual handbook under the heading of noteworthy events. And in 1994, the USOC awarded now openly gay Greg Louganis one of its highest honors.

Overall, the Gay Games help debunk stereotypes and increase the status, recog-nition, and legitimacy of the GLBT community. They present the queer com-munity as energetic and strong, cultured and talented, an image that makes it more difficult for the wider society to ignore. Journalist Anna Quindlen recognized this capacity of the games to challenge prejudiced perceptions: "The Games, which have been going on at pools, skating rinks and gymnasiums throughout the area, are a terrible threat to those who believe that America's house needs more clos-ets. Because as men and women in warm-up clothes have stepped onto subway trains, gay cops have helped out with security and gay athletes have challenged world records, the Games have come to illustrate the myriad ways in which gay men and lesbians are now part of the mainstream" (quoted in Waddell and Schaap 1996, 234–235).

The need for social change was seen during the opening ceremony. For one athlete, participation was paradoxical. He was excited to be a Gay Games par-ticipant, yet he also was frightened of the consequences should he be recog-nized. This explains the mask over his head as he carried the sign recognizing his country, Iraq, into the stadium. He was the sole representative from his country, and the spectators recognized his courage and gave him an especially energetic welcome. Even here, in highly tolerant Amsterdam, the Gay Games participants were reminded of the lack of tolerance toward GLBTs in other countries—places where severe punishments are handed out as a matter of course for simply being queer.

The Gay Games promote social change through activities aimed at learning about social justice activities and strategies. In 1998, the social issues programs within the cultural festival included a series of workshops that addressed important social issues of the queer community and provided information about working for social change. The cultural program included a conference on "Trade Unions, Homosexuality, and Work," a capacity-building program for improved GLBT organizing, and a workshop entitled "Organizing Is a Sport." There was also a special joint human-rights program cosponsored with Amnesty International and Hivos (the Humanist Institute for Co-operation with Developing Countries). The goals of this program were to "draw international attention to the lack of safeguards to protect human rights of lesbians and gays, create a forum for the exchange of personal experiences for the benefit of Gay Games participants and especially those from developing countries, facilitate the exchange of information between grassroots and mainstream human rights organizations, [and] build the necessary networks in (especially) developing countries" (Voss and van Yperen 1998). Topics covered by the fourteen workshops included in this program were lesbian and gays and the law; refugees; HIV/AIDS; human rights activism; lesbian and gay activism and new technologies; activism and fundraising; lesbian and gay antiviolence; and gender, sexual orientation, and human rights.

Although the Gay Games seek to affect social change outside of the queer community, there are challenges within our community also. No event of this magnitude occurs without some internal conflict. While inclusiveness is the primary theme of the Gay Games, it is difficult to ensure that no one is marginalized. In particular, bisexual and transgendered individuals often feel excluded from the queer community. Ironically, because some queer people do not understand bisexuality and transgendered identities, we sometimes fall into the same patterns that are pushed upon us: stigmatizing those who are different. While the Gay Games have made the effort to be inclusive of bisexuals and transgendered people in all written literature, controversies still erupt. For example, in Amsterdam, controversy arose around the ballroom dance competition (Newsplanet Staff and McMullen 1998). The international rules for ballroom dance require that all participants dress in gender-appropriate costumes. Following those rules, Gay Games rules initially stated that individuals who violated this policy would not be scored in the competition. This led to complaints from transgendered dancers, drag queens, and other outraged people. Eventually, the protests paid off—this international rule was repealed for Gay Games competition and all entrants were guaranteed fair judging regardless of their attire.

Another area of controversy related to the Gay Games is financial. Inherently, there are many costs associated with attending the Gay Games—travel, accommodation, registration, and so on—thus many people are excluded due to their economic circumstances. Since in most countries males tend to have more wealth than females, males are more likely to be able to afford to come to the games. This is one reason that the games have a larger percentage of male participants than female participants. Similarly, all individuals from lower socioeconomic classes or economically depressed countries may be unable to attend the Gay Games.

However, through the Outreach Program, Gay Games organizers provide financial assistance for some women and individuals from developing countries, but this doesn't cover all those who can't afford to attend.

Altogether, the Gay Games compel social change and address social justice issues across a wide range of areas and through a broad range of activities. These changes may be seen in the queer community, the sports culture, and society at large. Just as critical as broad social change is the change in individual people's lives. As journalist Joe Clark concluded, "Would it really be a disappointment if the only effect of the Games were to leave over 10,000 athletes with memories they will cherish for a lifetime?" (1994a, 142). Likewise, participants in the cultural festival, spectators, and media representatives are similarly affected.

Upon returning home from the games, participants feel energized and inspired. This leads some of them to come out to more people around them. This, in turn, increases the visibility of the queer community. While not everyone can become overtly involved in the politics of the queer community, simply being honest with the people around us is an important step. Social change begins as we tell our family and friends that we are queer. Our pride empowers us; their knowledge stimulates them. Both result in continued efforts to reduce prejudice. Social change continues as people like Greg Louganis, Martina Navratilova, Billie Jean King, Bruce Hayes, and Matthew Hall speak out publicly. Their openness then encourages others, and the trend continues. Social change begins with small but important steps right in our own backyards. Through the Gay Games, we all learn more about each other and grow in our acceptance of those different from ourselves. As the motto of Gay Games IV proclaimed, "Games can change the world."

NOTE

1. This article also draws on information contained in the following web sites: www.backdoor.com/CASTRO/gaygames.html; www.gaygames.nl/info/us/social.html.; and www.backdoor.com/CASTRO/gaygamesI.html2.

PART THREE

THE OLYMPICS:

DRAMA,

SPECTACLE,

MEDIA

CHAPTER 11

Carrying the Torch

for Whom?

Symbolic Power and

Olympic Ceremony

ALAN TOMLINSON

___

The World's Old Flame

When Muhammad Ali staggered up the steps toward the cauldron in which the Olympic flame would be ignited at the beginning of the Atlanta Summer Olympic Games in 1996, commentators drooled over the emotive impact of the great boxer's gesture. Here, after solemn pronouncements of the voice-over on British television—telling the viewer that Atlanta was truly proud, "genuinely delighted, that the Games were taking place for the first time in a city where most of the people are black"—one of the greatest legends of twentieth-century sports pulled at the heartstrings of the global television audience. Barely able to coordinate the ascent of his once majestically lithe, athletic, and powerful body up the steps whilst brandishing the flame ("Just at least hold it," the worldwide audience was muttering under its collective breath), Ali, with his wracked and shaking body, seemed out of joint with the context of physical supremacy so characteristic of Olympic achievement and ideals. Carried across more than forty states by a relay of ten thousand people during the few weeks preceding the start of the games, the torch, now, in its last short but inestimably high-profile lap, looked roaringly threatening to the ambling and uncertain figure. Every jogger in the world who happened to be looking on at this moment felt for the boxing great—an Olympic gold champion in 1960—as he faced this normally trivial but in this case daunting test. Yet as he mounted the steps, to an authentic, far from manufactured

167

FIGURE 11.1

Muhammad Ali lighting the Olympic torch at the Atlanta games.

Photograph by Michael Cooper, courtesy of Allsport, UK Limited.

roar of appreciation which dwarfed the reception received by Samaranch, the IOC president, or the United States' own president, Bill Clinton, a remarkable metamorphosis materialized.

Ali seemed to transcend this moment of everyday life and this physical condition of the day. He didn't suddenly come alive in some Lourdes-like miracle of transformation. He didn't suddenly look like the irrepressible, hyperactive sports colossus of his young manhood. But his act achieved a sort of triumph over the mundanity of the merely mortal. Far more than the gold medal of his youth in his physical prime when all was possible, his stumbling and uncertain lighting of Atlanta's Olympic flame achieved an Olympian heroism. Ali's wife, Lonnie, recalls the response of her husband to his Atlantan torch bearing: "He was floating on air. He just sat in a chair back at the hotel holding the torch in his hands. It was like he'd won the heavyweight title back a fourth time" (qtd. in Remnick 1998, 67).

No one witnessing this Ali-an act of reaffirmation could forget it. And it was great television. Like no sportsman before or since, Ali has had a political, historical, worldwide resonance. It was like watching family and history together reach unknown heights of collective catharsis. It brought a lump to the throat. It made you want to reach out and touch. It made you *want* to believe in the authenticity of the Olympic spirit.

No doubt those staging the spectacle were holding their breath, too. Would Ali make it? What would the audience response be? Would the lighting be hailed as a sick public relations gesture? Or as a magnificent reassertion of a universalist Olympian aesthetics of the physical? The dignity of the man and the sheer global charisma of the Ali personality and legend ensured that the ceremony would be greeted positively, would be hailed as a symbol of Olympic ideals, would be judged on the good-taste side of the showbiz tendency in big-time sports in the United States.

But another reading is possible, a reading beyond the official rhetoric of the event, apart, too, from the sentimental memories of spectators in the stadium and television viewers in their homes.[1] In this other reading Muhammad Ali is reduced from a figure of complex oppositional cultural politics—"I ain't goin' to Vietnam. I ain't got no argument with no Vietcong"—to little more than a simple apologist for the cultural and political powers that be. Go see Ali in the remarkable film documentary *When We Were Kings;* read or reread Mailer or Plimpton on the regal Ali in his prime. Think about *Sports Illustrated*'s Gary Smith's reminder that the source of Ali's greatness and moral strength was that he "was fighting for more than himself." Listen to Ali's own words of 1978: "I'm a representative of black people . . . it's more than a sport when I get involved." Then sit in front of your VCR and play back his part of the Olympic opening ceremony.

One of the few truly memorable and dignified moments in an elongated event of tattiness and tawdriness from the beginning of the Atlanta Olympics to the end, Ali's torch bearing and flame lighting were more true to the hypocrisies of the day than to the ideals of his phenomenal life. This has been the true power of the Olympics—not to bring the youth of the world together in the pursuit of international harmony, but to use the youth of the world, and in Ali's case the remnants of that youth, to transmit cultural, political, and economic meanings and values. For a Parkinson-afflicted, slow-smiling, and terminal-looking Ali to lend himself to the trite and predictable rhetoric of the Olympics was an ironic volte-face from that time when he used his Olympic gold medal to launch his meteoric, culturally challenging, and politically significant career. The Olympics become what successive political or economic ideologues and entrepreneurs have wanted them to become. As Ali hauled his weary and uncoordinated limbs up those Olympic steps, the whole thing came over as ultimately no less overtly ideological than the last Olympics held in the United States, in Los Angeles in 1984; no less even than the first truly visualized Olympics, Hitler's Nazi games in Berlin in 1936, captured in gripping close-up detail by filmmaker Leni Riefenstahl. Everyday spectacle works to produce ideological effects most effectively precisely when it seems to have an other-worldly innocence.

Olympic Screenings

Outside of unscheduled accidents such as the death—which really meant the funeral—of Sir Elton John's "England's rose" Diana, Princess of Wales, Olympic screenings have produced the highest television viewing figures in the history of the world. The sports and media industries see the Olympic Games and the football World Cup as the most widely watched—and therefore in a sense the biggest—television media events in the history of humankind. Statistics are presented which indicate the grip of these sports events upon the popular consciousness of peoples throughout the contemporary world. The IOC (International Olympic Committee) produces its own publications on the place of the Olympic Games in the viewings/ratings hierarchy of the global television industry. In the preface to its broadcast analysis report, the IOC president, Juan Antonio Samaranch, claimed that, following on from the 1992 Winter Olympics (in Albertville, Savoie, France) and Summer Olympics (in Barcelona, Catalonia, Spain), they "achieved the highest level of interest in Olympic history ... best evidenced by the television coverage, as it is through television that the world experiences the Olympics."

The winter games were seen by a gross cumulative television audience of 8 billion viewers in 86 countries; the summer games, by a cumulative audience of 16.6 billion in "a record 193 countries ... Barcelona, as host city, provided 2,800 hours of live sports coverage. In several countries, ratings records were set." These records represented 2.3 billion people, 85 percent of all people with televisions. The gross cumulative figure of 24.6 billion for 1992 was an increase of 44.7 percent on the cumulative figure of 17 billion for the 1988 games (10.4 billion for Seoul, 6.6 billion for Calgary). In its bullet-pointed summary entitled "The Whole World Watches the Olympics," the report positioned the Olympic Games right at the top of the global ratings, the Barcelona games being "televised in more countries than any other event, including the World Cup Soccer Tournament, the Super Bowl, and the Formula 1 Grand Prix Series." Surveys in the United States, Spain, and the United Kingdom are cited, indicating that in those countries nine out of ten people "tuned in to watch" the Barcelona games. Such impact prompts television companies to invest huge amounts of money in television rights to the games. North American giant NBC Sports won the rights, in 1994, to the 1996 Atlanta Summer Olympics, with a record bid of $456 million. NBC was confident that such outlay would be repaid by advertisers unable to resist the profiling guaranteed by the anticipated viewing figures for the North American–based games, which would be broadcast so comprehensively worldwide. Three and a half billion viewers were anticipated for the event.

Most importantly, for media professionals, the Olympics—unlike the death of Diana, say—can be planned and scheduled. In fact, the winter games and summer games were separated after 1992 in order to avoid saturation coverage in any one year, and to spread out the value of what Olympic sponsors were buying. Why waste such a god-sent opportunity by using it all up once every four years? A context in which histories can be developed, soap-operatic narratives fostered, and the intensifying symbiosis of top-level performance sports and television reaffirmed is not one to be taken lightly.

Television has enabled global sports events to be projected on an increasingly grand and spectacular scale. The flickering black and white television images of the 1960 Rome Olympics were revelatory in their time. More sophisticated broadcasting techniques and the advent of color television have meant that those innovative images of 1960 now appear as quaint and inadequate records of sports events for the worldwide sports audience. Fueled by cold war rivalry throughout the 1970s and the 1980s, made-for-television Olympic ceremonies became a major source of audience figures, justifying the investments of the television industry and the main sponsors of the games.

The Los Angeles Olympic Games of 1984 can now be seen as a watershed in this regard, providing spectacular opening and closing ceremonies to assert the superiority of the Western, capitalist, free American way over the oppressive Eastern, communist, totalitarian Soviet way. The Soviet Union and many of its allies boycotted the 1984 games in a direct response to the United States' boycott of the Moscow Olympics in 1980 (in response to the Soviet invasion of Afghanistan). In this context, the Los Angeles games in 1984 were a statement of the strength of U.S. ideals, ever stronger in the face of Soviet disruption. Allying Hollywood showbiz flair with U.S. political rhetoric and ideology, the ceremonies set a standard and an expectation for spectacle that succeeding host nations have felt compelled to emulate or to surpass. In Seoul in 1988 and in Barcelona in 1992, the summer games opened to magnificent ceremonies celebratory of the different levels of the regional, the national, and the supranational—and simultaneously resonant of some central tensions within an increasingly globalized world of sports consumption. Aware that

Barcelona was a hard act to follow—"We're not Barcelona," pronounced one awestruck Atlantan after the Barcelona ceremony, "but we'll give it our best shot"— Atlanta served up its own blend of mythmaking and local cultural celebration.

The winter games—in Calgary, Canada, in 1988; in Albertville, France, in 1992, in Lillehammer, Norway, in 1994 (the latter the first to be separated from the calendar year of the Summer Olympics, in order to spread the investment of television moguls and sports sponsors), and in Nagano, Japan, in 1998—also became increasingly concerned with the symbolic impact of the pageantry, ceremony, and message making of the games' televised opening and closing moments. Seoul's games were a statement of the political and economic accomplishments and aspirations of an aggressive and thrusting, emergent political power, as well as a statement, by contrast with North Korea, of the superiority of a capitalist model of development over a communist model. Barcelona's games were symbolic of the rehabilitation of Spain in the post-Franco period, and of the Catalan region's and the city of Barcelona's status, vis-à-vis the central state and the metropolitan center, Madrid. For Calgary, the staging of successful winter games in 1988 was not only an internal political statement of its own capacity to rival western (Vancouver) and eastern (Toronto) neighbors, and of its attractions as a long-haul tourist destination, but a statement of the country's capacity to do just as well what cities and regions in the United States were able to do. In Albertville, Savoie, and the surrounding Alpes-Rhône region, the winter games were a pretext for improving the transport infrastructure and tourist potential of the area, opening up still more effectively routes between the area and the powerful industrial and commercial centers of northern Italy. The winter games of 1994 in Lillehammer showcased a different kind of politics and aspiration, with the politically democratic Norwegians offering a more modestly scaled event rooted in environmental consciousness and an independence of thought and expression which proved far from conducive to the dictatorial style of the IOC president, Juan Antonio Samaranch. The opening ceremony of Atlanta's summer games of 1996—the centennial Olympics, Atlanta having come strongly from behind in the bidding process to narrowly beat an overconfident and sloppy Athens bid based on history and sentiment—featured a form of spiritualism, five Olympic spirits symbolizing the universalism of the movement and its ideals. The made-for-media ritual and ceremonial surrounding the opening of the events attracted the largest share of the global audience, and it has to be said that not just a few in that audience must have looked on in puzzlement at some of the most magnificently trite spectacles in history.

Los Angeles '84: The Box of Spielbergian Tricks

The 1984 opening ceremony marked the beginning of the Summer Olympic Games in Los Angeles, California: a deep, resonant, and melodramatic voice from the heavens (referred to hereafter as god-tone) bid the world welcome to a "wedding of image and sound." In the view of award-winning film and TV producer David Wolper (the designer of the designer Olympics), "The world expects more from Hollywood." In the words of British BBC commentator David Coleman, the coliseum mixed history, myth, and politics: "In the sunshine of this Californian afternoon, ancient Greek rites, Hollywood fantasy and the reality of life in 1984 will find common ground."

This "common ground" comprised a huge cast of regimented extras, including one thousand vocalists, eight hundred marching musicians and fifteen hundred dancers. The ugly urban landscape receded as the god-tone was joined by Rocket Man (a black man in a silver suit) flying into the stadium. A launch of huge balloons made way for marching bands piping a repertoire of well-known U.S. tunes. The scene was then set for a preschool, illustrated history of American culture; the god-tone prefaced this with the claim that we were about to be told of the making of one nation out of many.

The stadium was overrun by covered wagons "thundering across a map of America from west to east," as one British television reviewer pointed out, with designer cowboys performing dexterous tricks of acrobatics and musicianship and dancing away the conquest of the frontier with wholesome-looking young women. Even Coleman was a little lost for words here, but he soon found some: "[T]hey pushed onward across the continent—relying on music for relaxation and fun." His task—unless it were to be critical and myth-exploding or intertextual (with references, say, to the 1954 Hollywood musical *Seven Brides for Seven Brothers*) in a truly contextualising way—was simply impossible. What is there to say about a caricature of caricatures, prepared as mass spectacle for 2.5 billion viewers worldwide, particularly if one of those caricatures is a B-movie cowboy figure (an antiseptic version of the Marlboro man) and the country's then president, Ronald Reagan? The designer cowboys were followed by a concession to black culture: the steamboat of the South was traced out in formation by the marching bands, and that most indigenous of cultural legacies—jazz—was brought onto the stage. But it did not take long to refocus on the mainstream (in god-tone's words, "[J]azz soon moved from the streets of New Orleans to the concert halls of New York"). And from under two headless bronze statues queues of blue-clad female dancers emerged to the music of George Gershwin, to be followed by eighty-four grand pianos. The voice from the heavens then reminded us of the cultural sources of the main motifs of the ceremony: the world of movies and the musical—"[T]he stage is the world of entertainment. Let's play the music and dance." Close-ups of celebrated individuals in the stadium audience, after the Reagans, showcased Hollywood heroes Gene Kelly and Cary Grant, not exactly stars of the sports world.

Finally, the stage filled out with males and females clad in white, flowing evening attire, with the stadium audience joining in the singing of "God Bless America" and the performers producing, in Coleman's words, "a glittering climax to the theme of the XXIII Olympiad—within a human outline of the map of America." This task was accomplished with the help of twelve hundred extras/performers and prefaced, again in Coleman's words, "the biggest piece of audience participation in Olympic history, if it works." All the spectators in the stadium stood up at the command of god-tone, held up colored cards, and produced a salute to the world, a human display of the flags of all the countries competing in the games. Two countdowns later (with god-tone commanding, like in a space-center operation) it was over to the athletes. Two female swimmers of the U.S. women's diving team at the 1920 games in Antwerp were led in to feature in the flag-exchanging part of the official opening ceremony—human relics, reminders of the U.S. link with the first occasion on which the "flag" ceremony had taken place.

Though the Soviets and many of their allies did not make it to Los Angeles, the movement had come through. Again, "America" (the United States) had saved the free world and in so doing had reinflated the currency of Olympism. But wasn't there more to it than this? The spectacle was unashamedly patriotic, to the point of crude ethnocentrism. The version of history offered in the opening ceremony was both highly selective and phantasmagoric: the presentation of history as a series of shifting illusions, marginalizing minorities and celebrating the dominant. And the opening ceremony was culturally solipsistic and self-indulgent, the United States celebrating itself and its we-can-do-it spirit much more than the Olympic spirit or ideals, in playful images and with a childlike pleasure at performing the trick in public—the gleeful dressing up as cowboy or rocket man; the physical exuberance; and, all embracing, the naiveté (or simple-mindedness) of the messages offered to the world. The blend of the patriotic and the ethnocentric was manifest in controversy over Los Angeles' commercialization of the torch relay, enthusiasm for which was interpreted by President Reagan as an "outpouring" which "reflects the new patriotism which has swept our land." Thus is a universalizing symbol—the ritual transportation of the "sacred" Olympic flame from the site of the original Olympiad to the modern site of contest (an invention for the 1936 Berlin Olympics, introduced to dignify Aryan elitism)—transformed into a nationalist icon.

The spectacle was what Gilbert Adair has called "Spielbergian" or "para-Spielbergian," mixing visions of a simple, untainted, and yet retrievable past with the impact of new and sometimes alien forces, in an optimistic blend for the future, exemplified in the closing ceremony by Wolper's spaceman (the grandaddy of ET), hailing the games as an example of "the family of men involved in the limitless possibilities of human achievement. For almost 100 years you have celebrated the best that humanity has to offer. You call it the Olympic Games, and for that and the cities that have kept the Olympic ideal alive, I salute you." For Adair, the Spielberg film, which "was predicated on a universe of infinite spiritual consciousness" and "grop[ed] towards a literal *theology* of space," is a form of Christian Science–fiction. The 1984 Los Angeles Olympics' opening ceremony, and persisting themes in its closing ceremony, addressed the world in an accessible

language of popular entertainment, offering their own version of the miracu-
lous route to future salvation.

Go South Young Man: Atlanta's Olympic Symbols and Ceremonies

Atlanta's problem was that it did not want to appear as simply another part of the
United States. Los Angeles had set the pace in 1984 and ten years later had even
hosted (well, close enough, it was in the Rose Bowl, Pasadena) the final of soccer's World Cup. Things were beginning to look like a U.S. monopoly. And, of
course, the Olympics' and soccer's longest-running sponsor, Coca-Cola, had its
headquarters in downtown Atlanta. Coke was the longest-running Olympic
sponsor, ever since 1928 when the flame first featured in Olympic ritual. As
1981–1993 Coke president Donald R. Keough proudly boasted in 1994, adding
that now that the number of Olympic countries has risen to 190, "Coca-Cola
thank god is available in each and every one of those countries . . . and we're so
proud that the Games are coming home at last, for sports are embedded into
the paradigm of this company." But the organizers knew better than this. There
wasn't to be a dominant Coke motif in welcoming the world to the games. At
the same time, Atlanta didn't want to be subsumed under an homogenizing U.S.
identity. Barcelona's ritzy blend of contemporary cultural politics and mythical
narrative, though, was scary for the Atlanta ceremony makers. How could Atlanta
be both American and global and follow on at all credibly from 1992, when
Barcelona's historical and mythical sense of its own history and identity provided
a tough act to follow?

Atlanta needed a vision. The success of the Atlanta bid was the personal coup
of Billy Payne, real-estate developer and lawyer, who claimed that he had a dream
one (Sunday) morning of how he could win the Olympics for Atlanta. Payne re-
counted his revelation, which came to him that Sunday morning in February 1987,
while driving home with his wife, feeling good after some successful fund-raising for the local church. The "deeetaiiil" is best left to the man himself, heard in
a deep Southern drawl with a preacher's pitch and a salesman's sincerity: Payne said,

> I had a sense of how wonderful it is to see the end result, to see the sacrifices of
> so many people . . . a great feelin', not religious. In my office the next day I wrote
> down projects on sheets from a legal pad, threw them all away and then pulled
> all of the pieces of paper out of the trash can. All of them had something to do
> with sport and my love of the community. . . . I said to Martha in the kitchen,
> "I've got it . . . we're gonna bring the Olympics to Atlanta." "You've gotta call
> Peter," she said. Peter's the grandson of the founder of Coke, and he's my best
> friend, we fish together. And he's the most conservative figure ever, who'll walk
> six stores to find the 59c deal. I put the idea to Peter. He said "That is a won-
> derful idea. How much money can I give you?" Peter is also my richest friend.
> He hung up when I named the figure, and then brought by a cheque for the
> ridiculous amount.   (Author's field notes)

Well done, Billy, Martha, and Peter. No doubt the check was signed on the kitchen table and they all ate muffins and Martha's momma's apple pie and toasted the plan with root beer. Payne's engaging sentimentalism had its honest side, too. In September 1990 Atlanta beat Athens for the right to host the games. Payne recalled ruefully, "We came back euphoric, but knowing nothing whatsoever about what we would do next." No wonder Atlanta became notorious for sloppy organization, unreliable transport and communications infrastructure, as well as the bomb in the Olympic Park.

At the Olympic Experience exhibition, a buildup to the games, a letter from Payne articulated the pitch to the few browsers (a crowd hugely outnumbered by the queues clamoring for entry into Coca-Cola's own theme museum a little way down the road) curious enough to see what lay behind the images of the mascot Izzy and the torch/flame logo. We were rewarded for our efforts with a call to dream with Izzy, "our fun-filled Olympic character, of what might be in 1996, when the Olympic Games come to the American South for the first time ever." The letter from Payne, and associated literature, were at pains to mark out something—anything—special about Atlanta's success and forthcoming challenge. Payne the dreamer drew upon the platitudes of official Olympic history: "Our mission is to conduct the Centennial Olympic Games with sensitivity, integrity, fiscal responsibility and commitment to the needs of athletes . . . to share with the world the spirit of America, the experience of the American South and the vision of Atlanta . . . and to leave a positive physical and spiritual legacy and an indelible mark upon Olympic history by staging the most memorable Games ever. . . . I hope you will sense the anticipation we feel and return in 1996 for the "Celebration of the Century"—the 100th anniversary of the modern Olympic Games." Thanks, but I think I'll have to stay at home and catch what I can on the TV. I know you beat Athens, Belgrade, Manchester, Melbourne, and Toronto, so that, as one of your copy-chaps put it for me, displaying a very special grasp of geography, "for the first time in Olympic history, the games are awarded to a US city east of the Mississippi River and the Olympic Movement will touch the American South for the first time ever." Well, that one sent us scrambling for our atlases. Clutching at historical and geographical straws such as this, how could the games be kicked off with a ceremony meeting the expectations of its predecessors and portraying a distinctive and attractive image of Atlanta?

Atlanta's bid logo was a play of sorts on the five Olympic rings. Described as a "star on the rise," it comprised five loosely sketched swish-like As in the form of a star in the five Olympic colors; the As stood for Access, Accommodation, Athletic facilities, Attitude, and Ability. The event logo featured the five rings of the Olympics in the swirling shape of a flame atop a torch. It was designed by Launder Associates and proudly presented as the second games logo ever to have the five rings in the design. The figure 100 (the centenary motif), drawn as a column, represented the handle of the Olympic torch; the column is said to be a feature of both southern United States and Greek architecture. The rings pro-

vided the top of the column, a base for the five-pronged flame. The flame—embodying "the enduring nature of the Olympic Movement and the purity of athletic
competition"—gradually takes the shape of a perfect star, supposed to symbol-
ize the athlete striving for excellence. The logo colors were inspired by Deep South
connotations (as Launder Associates so helpfully elaborated): a green background
for the lush foliage of the trees of the Atlanta area; red for the southern region;
orange for the people of Atlanta; magenta, blue green, and lavender to represent
the energy of the Atlanta community. It made you ache for the simplicity of the
Olympic rings themselves.

The two prominent Olympic symbols, the flame and the torch, dominated
the opening ceremony that was to culminate in Ali's ascent to light the flame. Hometown boy Billy Payne had never traveled abroad, beyond the shores of the Americas. This was perfect for him in an era of globalization; he could show Atlanta
to the world by bringing to Atlanta one of the world's biggest cultural events. Payne's
dream came true. The opening of the Atlanta games had something of the continuation of a dream about it in its mixture of fantasy and light entertainment,
absurd storytelling, and clichéd mythmaking.

The most representative images of the city of Atlanta must be the Coca-Cola
bottle, the archetypally ugly urban landscape and skylines, and the inspiring image
of the black Civil Rights martyr Martin Luther King Jr., whose dream was more
sincere, more necessary, and more noble than anything that went on in Billy Payne's
head. At least the organizers showed some good taste in leaving Coca-Cola out
of the ceremonial reckoning—the IOC still prides itself on keeping advertising
boards out of the Olympic arena, so seeking to purvey a pure, pristine message
of an untainted, uncommercialized sports contest. The proceedings began with
five Olympic spirits—each one a color of the five Olympic rings, red, black, green,
yellow, blue—bursting out of the perimeter walls of the Olympic stadium. The
colors represented the five continents, and the stadium surface was draped in these
colors as golden singer-dancers looking like robotic sunflowers writhed their way
through their itinerary. The television commentator noted, "[Y]oung tribes of
the various continents flood the arena"; this was as good a description as any of
the amorphous blob of colorful and chaotic dancers, drummers, and gymnasts
who gradually assumed a recognizable shape as fliers descended from the stadium
rim, in respective Olympic colors, and five ragged rings and a wobbly 100 (the
latter made up of children in white garb) materialized uncertainly in the heart
of the stadium.

At this point John Williams—longtime collaborator and score-scribe of
Spielberg the moviemaker—brought some cadence if not credence to the proceedings and conducted the centennial Olympic theme, "Some of the Heroes,"
whilst the figure 100 reshaped into a dove of peace. The participants left the stadium for all the world like a drug-crazed exodus of refugees. The stage was now
set—with flags of the Atlantic paramilitary and U.S. army bands—for Payne's biggest
buzz. Bill Clinton walked into the arena and up to IOC president Samaranch and

Payne himself. Twilight was falling as Clinton was trumpeted in to the U.S. national anthem, and six fighter pilots executed a flyby. An Atlanta welcome wave gave all present a slice of the action. Atlantan culture was now center stage. Mixed-race gospel singing, frenetic aerobic dance (Jane Fonda's a local celebrity, remember), and cheerleaders were illuminated by the headlights of pickup trucks which had rumbled into the stadium.

The pace slowed as locally born Gladys Knight sang the anthem of the state, "Georgia on My Mind," and a sequence revolving around "Summertime" was offered as a "tribute to the beauty of the South, its volatility of climate, its history, spirit and culture." Things were certainly heating up: a year or two before, Billy Payne had joked about how he had lied to the IOC about the climate, saying that it would be "75 degrees (not 92 degrees) for the Opening Ceremony." An elaborate dance drama then symbolized the birth of the South, issuing from the new day generated by the meeting of the moon and the sun. For this serious generative moment the musical accompaniment was a haunting aria. The set changed dramatically with the arrival of a huge scaffolding trimmed at its bottom edge by what seemed to be rolls of barbed wire. This was real hometown stuff, though, and turned out to be a representation of a giant catfish pulling "Old Man River" and one of his riverboats (no slave ships here). Stilted southern gents patrolled the river edges as "When the Saints" played, to be interrupted by a violent storm of thunder and lightning. To the recitation of the words of William Faulkner on the American South's qualities as "something that did not exist before," the Southern Spirit appeared to reclaim the landscape from the storm. The "landscape bursts with new life," spluttered the television commentator, and a hallelujah refrain celebrated the restoration. A little more audience participation with flashlights after a countdown, and then the gospel singers really let go, and dancers with headgear sprouting several flagpoles offered a spectacular accompaniment.

The theme moved back toward the broad Olympic theme as the building of a Greek temple was reenacted, the Greek poet Pindar was quoted on the greatness of the Olympic Games, and the set was transformed into a cast of silhouettes of archers, discus throwers, jumpers, wrestlers, and dancers, resonant of the Greek statues of the athlete, and of Leni Riefenstahl's cinematic representation of those representations. This was a truly striking set and heralded tributes to the achievement of de Coubertin, the founder. It was he who rekindled the flame of the Olympic idea, we are reminded if not informed. The fabric flames came to life at this point as the first and succeeding games were represented by runners with flags of the host cities. As the Atlanta runner sprinted to the front of the procession and approached the representation of the stadium at Olympus, the pillars collapsed backwards, a triumphalist anthem blared out, young black women carried the Atlanta flag up the steps, and the interminable march of the nations began. After that fashion parade of participants, Muhammad Ali emerged to play his paradoxical part.

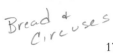

Seeing through Olympic Spectacles

Analysis of opening ceremonies confirms that the Olympic idea is no simple, pure, and untainted set of values. Indeed, from its very inception in the modern historical period, the Olympic ideal has been wracked by tensions and contradictions, surviving a succession of reformations, ursurpations and, in a very real sense, a necessary series of what I like to call arrogations. What I mean by this is simple enough: the allegedly pure Olympic ideal has always been molded in the image of the time and place of the particular Olympiad or games, rendering all claims to the representation or protection of some set of pure Olympic ideals unjustifiable. The ceremonies capture this. In the song to round off the opening ceremonies (both pre-opening and once the games were officially open) at Los Angeles, the stadium swayed to the tune of "Reach Out and Touch" with adapted lyrics stressing international friendship:

> Reach out and touch somebody's hand,
> Make the world a better place if you can;
> Come join the celebration as we salute the unity of every nation . . .
> That we all care and it's love and people everywhere . . .
> We can change things if we start giving;
> Why don't you . . . Reach out and touch?

Inherent in the birth of the Olympic movement were some fascinating contradictions: the founder de Coubertin's para-populist educational reformism was rooted in his own aristocratic privilege; his pacifism derived from France's military humiliation in the Franco-Prussian War of 1870; and his declared egalitarianism concerning the politics of the body was bounded by principles of privilege, patronage, and misogyny. Discussion of the meaning of the Olympics will be sterile if it lacks a sense of such a complex history. Despite the early Olympic message calling for peace and cooperation amongst the youth of the world, the local celebration of the games as expressed in ceremonies leads inevitably to forms of nationalism and nationalist self-aggrandizement.

The harnessing of the mass media in the cause of particular nationalist ideologies is hardly a new phenomenon in sports. Leni Riefenstahl's film of the 1936 Berlin Olympics (*Olympia*) presented to the world a technologically innovative and brilliant encomium to the aesthetics of the body. She also produced political propaganda. In an earlier film of the 1930s (a mountain film, clearly consonant with the primitivist Wandervogel element in early Nazi ideology) Riefenstahl, in Susan Sontag's words, "devised for herself" the role of "a primitive creature who has a unique relation to a destructive power." In retrospective accounts of the making of her 3.5-hour Olympic film, Riefenstahl has often been presented as the individualist genius, the romantic artist, uninvolved in any political process. She herself has further vivified this interpretation, as related by Sontag: "Riefenstahl has maintained in interviews since the 1950s that *Olympia* was commissioned by the International Olympic Committee, produced by her own company and made over Goebbels' protests. The truth is that *Olympia* was commissioned and entirely financed by the Nazi government (a dummy company was set up in Riefenstahl's name because it was thought unwise for the government to appear as the producer) and facilitated by Goebbels' ministry at every stage of the shooting" (1983, 79–80).

Riefenstahl's film reworked Olympic icons—statues, ruins, physical grace—to fit an elitist politics of racist superiority. The image of Germany, in both her film of the Nuremberg rally (*Triumph of the Will*) and the Olympic work, was unashamedly ideological. The medieval spires and the outdoor camaraderie of the body in political camp or sports village shroud the reality of a modern Germany, in which industrial production was geared to ambitions of world conquest. The innocence of the bucolic fronted the most ruthless and tyrannical political regime of modern times.

It would be meaningless to seek to understand the relationship between this example of representation of the Olympics and the process of arrogation of Olympic ideals with no reference to either the filmmaker's other works or the political context in which the work was done. Similarly, the Los Angeles games must be seen as a social production, staged by professional experts groomed in Hollywood and the entertainment industry, in one of the most powerful capitalist societies on earth. The Atlanta games were another U.S. production, a politics of popular song and dance merged effortlessly with a regional identity politics, fronting a bonanza for the speculators and developers of the city of Atlanta and the state of Georgia.

Billy Payne was one of a network of white males to take from as well as give to the Olympic dream. He placed his old friend Bob Holder in the position of cochairman of the games' organizing committee, along with former United Nations ambassador and former Atlanta mayor Andrew Young. Holder made sure that deals came Payne's professional way from the state's input into the games. And the organizers redesigned downtown Atlanta, seeking to connect the campus of Georgia Tech with the city center, eliminating housing projects which prior to the games sat between the campus, Coca-Cola headquarters, and downtown Atlanta. The development projects of the organizers of the games were lucrative, indeed, for them and other members of what was known in the city as the "Georgia Tech Mafia." Some commentators have seen the relatively peaceful transition to full black citizenship, during the Civil Rights movement of the 1960s, as the key to Atlanta's emergence as such a dominant city of the American South. The prospect that Atlanta would soon be led politically by a black mayor was not contested by the white economic elite, so long as it could retain control of the local economy. True to this long-standing truce, Payne and his associates benefited from state construction projects. Others benefited much more sensationally from the deals that underlay the Centennial Olympic Park, in a classic diversion of public resources to private gain, a "well-designed rape of the public" as one anonymous commentator has so graphically put it. Forty thousand volunteers, "reflecting the true Olympic spirit," as ACOG (Atlanta Committee for the Olympic Games) put it, will have helped show a smiling face of the South to the world, fronting the bigger smiles of those at the heart of the property heist.

That a figure of such potent cultural politics as Muhammad Ali could carry a torch for a city of greed, ruthlessness, and rapacious ambition says much about the malleability of so-called Olympic ideals, the persisting power of Olympic ideology, and the recurring and uncanny capacity of Olympic ceremonies to veil the real interests that lie behind their enduring appeal. It shows, too, that we should not idolize or idealize our contemporary heroes, vulnerable as their profiles are to appropriation by the commercial, cultural, and political logic of the Olympics.

Sydney 2000 will be no different. Whatever national or regional themes are mobilized—secession from the British Commonwealth, celebration of the new Republic of Australia, complex relations with Southeast Asian neighbors, and internal controversies over race discrimination—a selective cultural politics will be at work, glossing the seamier realities of the history of a racially prejudiced former slave colony. Sydney is some spectacular setting. The ceremony will be magnificent (and no doubt millennial). It will also be absurd. It will be typical of the ceremony that frames the sports spectacle of the modern era, whose recurrent trait is a jingoistic hypocrisy. There could be no more telling testimony to this than the unwitting figure of Muhammad Ali, mounting haltingly those Atlantan steps, and in the very act masking the deals and the realities by which the Atlantan dream of 1996 was really motivated, and on which its tawdry implementation was based. The final Olympics of the twentieth century reduced the majestic figure of Ali to a butterfly barely able to fly, let alone float—an apposite epigraph to a centenary Olympics on the eve of the fin de siècle confirmation of the rottenness and corruption at the heart of the Olympic movement.

NOTES

I am very grateful to my colleague Ben Carrington for very useful suggestions in response to the first draft, almost all of which have been absorbed into the text.

1. I have drawn upon previously unpublished material, including observational data and documentation collected in Atlanta itself (author's field notes, Atlanta Marriott Hotel, October 1994); documentary sources acquired on the basis of investigative research; and, of course, the television broadcasts on the basis of which most people across the world watch the Olympic Games, in my own case the transmission of the ceremonies on BBC network television in the United Kingdom. Other readings are, of course, possible by commentators with backgrounds different from mine and with access to different and distinctive forms of transmission of the spectacle. I would be very interested in hearing from such commentators.

CHAPTER 12

Whose Ceremony

Is It Anyway?

Indigenous and Olympic

Interests in the

Festival of the Dreaming

Sydney Aborigines

LISA MEEKISON

On a cool September evening in 1997, ten thousand people packed the forecourt of the Sydney Opera House at Bennelong Point on Sydney Harbour for the opening ceremony of the Festival of the Dreaming, the first of Sydney's four annual Olympic Arts Festivals. The Festival of the Dreaming was billed as a celebration of indigenous arts and cultures in Australia and abroad. This first event was the Awakening Ceremony, ostensibly held to reanimate the Aboriginal spirits of the city and to kindle public interest in the festival.[1]

While the Awakening Ceremony was a spectacular artistic event, I suggest that it can also be understood as an event where different and sometimes competing sets of interests collided. Within the Festival of the Dreaming as a whole, and strikingly within the Awakening Ceremony, an intersection of agendas broadly cast as indigenous and nonindigenous came to the fore. The indigenous interests, represented by the artistic direc-

[F]rom the time that it was announced, it was like, this is an opportunity for people, Aboriginal people, to really hold their head up high.

—*Indigenous arts worker*

They're going to use it. They're going to use the Aboriginal culture because it's a seller for them and it fills their pockets up.

—*Indigenous arts worker*

To all of you . . . supporters of the Olympics, supporters of the arts, supporters of the Aboriginal people, welcome to this Ceremony.

—*Michael Knight*

182

tors of the Awakening Ceremony and the Festival of the Dreaming and the performers therein, used the ceremony to make reference to indigenous identity, history, locality, and social justice. The nonindigenous interests, specifically represented by the minister for the Olympics but also by the very frame of the ceremony as an Olympic event, used the Ceremony to create excitement about the coming 2000 games and to reaffirm the supposedly universal values of Olympism. In this case, this competition of interests between the global, as represented by Olympism, and the local, as represented by indigenous performers, is not indicative of antagonism or opposition between the two. I suggest rather that this conscious pursuit of differing agendas points to the power of local agency even within large and powerful institutions.[2]

The Awakening Ceremony

Festival of the Dreaming posters started appearing in Sydney at train stations and bus shelters in the weeks before the festival. The poster, done in black and blue and fire-scorched orange, featured a single, confronting eye staring out from a crack in corrugated iron, challenging the viewer to attend festival events. The Sydney Organising Committee for the Olympic Games (SOCOG) hung Festival of the Dreaming banners from the streetlights on major thoroughfares, at the state library

FIGURE 12.1

The Awakening Ceremony, the Festival of the Dreaming, 1997 Olympic Arts Festival.

Courtesy of James Pozarik.

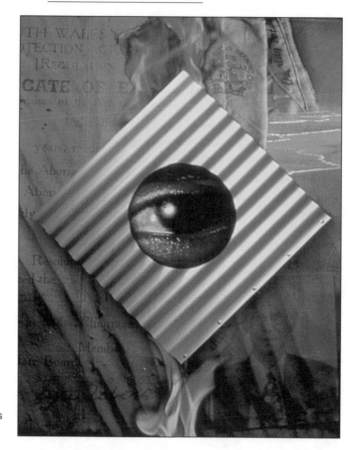

FIGURE 12.2

Olympic arts festival poster.

Courtesy of the Sydney Organising Committee for the Olympic Games (SOCOG).

and at festival venues. The *Sydney Morning Herald,* Sydney's major newspaper and a Sydney 2000 sponsor, ran frequent articles on many of the upcoming shows and exhibits in a run of pre-festival publicity.

Downtown at the SOCOG offices on Kent Street, Festival of the Dreaming staff worked long hours on scheduling, ticketing, marketing, and logistics. In numerous studios and rehearsal spaces around the city, actors, dancers, street performers, artists, and curators polished artworks, exhibition spaces, and performances in preparation for the series of opening dates which would follow the Awakening Ceremony on September 14.

By late afternoon on September 14, thousands of people had crammed onto the steps of the Sydney Opera House, indigenous and nonindigenous, locals and tourists. People called out greetings to friends, herded children through the throng, maneuvered baby strollers up the steep steps, and accidentally stepped on the hands and feet of those already seated. Some people attempted to clear enough space to consume their picnic sandwiches and wine. Audience members chattered excitedly and peered down at the extraordinary stage—a giant circle of sand flanked by oil drums.

Dusk fell and the sense of festivity heightened. A group of dancers filed onto the stage and stepped up onto a platform which ran along the back of the stage and abutted the cliff wall that leads up to Sydney's Botanical Gardens. Then they stepped into hessian bags and lay down, becoming a new and strange part of the scenery. Other dancers discretely took up places behind the oil drums that ringed the stage.

Suddenly lights illuminated the stage and the crowd stilled as the first notes of a loud, low didgeridoo sounded. Djakapurra Munyarryun, a principal dancer with Sydney's Bangarra Dance Theatre, appeared downstage left, beating a pair of clap sticks and singing. His brother, John Munyarryun, followed him, playing the didgeridoo. The two, in body paint of white ochre, walked slowly across the stage until they came to a stop in the center.

When the two musicians reached the center, the male dancers behind the oil drums bent down and set fire to the drums' contents. Great clouds of smoke spilled forth. The breeze caught the smoke and swept it northwest, over the performers, the audiences, and the opera house, where it finally dispersed over Sydney Harbour. Some in the audience blinked back tears from the smoke. Others shivered at the sound of the didgeridoo and Munyarryun's singing. One man sitting in front of me, slightly awed, whispered to his friend, "It's eerie, isn't it?"

The music stopped abruptly and someone on stage—it was impossible to see who because of the smoke—howled. Everyone craned to see what was going to happen next. Colored lights, run from the two giant stacks that flanked the stage, shone through the smoke and lit the dancers' body paint, making them gleam.

Women clad in red dresses appeared on stage and began to dance counterclockwise around the two musicians. They moved in the characteristic steps of some traditional Aboriginal women's dances: eyes downcast, left arms behind their backs, they clasped gum leaves in their right hands, bringing them up over their shoulders in little flicking movements. Finally, the didgeridoo and clap sticks fell silent and the dancers ceased their movements. The audience, sensing the end of the solemn music, burst into applause and screamed their appreciation.

Music started again, but now from a synthesizer. This composition was by David Page, the musical director for the ceremony. While the first performers remained on stage, dancers from Bangarra appeared downstage left, the women in silver dresses, the men in silver pants and body paint. They danced in the Bangarra style of "fusion" between contemporary western and classic Aboriginal dance steps. They drifted stage right, toward the center, where they met up with the dancers already there. All the dancers started moving en masse, combining traditional and fusion movements in a stunning array of styles.

When the music changed slightly, the dancers on the back platforms finally stepped from their hessian coverings and danced in place, each movement elegant, restrained, slow, and strong. The wind blew their dresses against their bodies as they reached up, down, and out, and echoed the gestures of traditional dance by flicking their arms up over their shoulders.

The ceremony built to a crescendo and the music shifted back to the didgeri-doo. Through the smoke one could see mischievous Mimi spirits, evoked by fan-tastically costumed stilt walkers from the Stalker Theatre Company, looming above the dancers. It felt as if the ceremony had indeed woken the spiritual world as well as audience enthusiasm.

And then—abruptly—it all stopped. The audience was silent for a moment and then burst into sustained applause. As people clapped and smoke contin-ued to fan out over the stage, someone whisked a podium, emblazoned with the Millennium Athlete logo of SOCOG, onto the stage. A man stepped up to the podium and began to speak. He was Ossie Cruse, a member of the New South Wales Aboriginal Land Council and one of SOCOG's indigenous or "Gamarada" dignitaries.[3] At first it was difficult to hear him, but suddenly the sound came true. "It's my job then to welcome you . . . to Koori country," he said, suggesting in a double entendre that not only was the land upon which we were all seated "Koori country" but that through the performance we had just witnessed we had effectively entered a place and time where things were done the indigenous way.[4]

Cruse continued:

> The folk that are with me . . . there are a number of people that have been cho-sen as the Gamarada program, and in recognition of the protocols, we together would like to welcome you. Because we come from all different parts of the state of New South Wales. But indeed, I'm not only welcoming you on behalf of the people of New South Wales, but indeed of the people of Australia. Because we as Aboriginal people, regardless to our language, regardless to our skin grouping, indeed we are one people. Therefore, I'd like to welcome you as the people of this country, the indigenous Australians, and the Festival of the Dreaming, to the land of the Eora, the Gadigal/Cadigal people, the Darug people, the Gandangara people, and the Dharawal people.   (1997)

The audience responded enthusiastically to Cruse, interrupting his welcome several times to applaud a particular point, such as his comment that all indige-nous people in Australia are "one people."

Michael Knight, the New South Wales minister for the Olympics and presi-dent of SOCOG, took the podium after Cruse. Smoke still drifted over the dancers as Knight began to speak. First, he thanked Cruse for his welcome, then he intro-duced himself. He acknowledged representatives from SOCOG and the artists and performers of the festival, then welcomed the audience, "[T]o all of you: supporters of the Olympics, supporters of the Arts, supporters of the Aboriginal people, wel-come to this ceremony" (1997).

Knight then spoke of the significance of the Awakening Ceremony and indeed the whole Festival of the Dreaming: "[T]oday we've been privileged to be part and to witness this very special contemporary version of a traditional smoking ceremony. And the purpose of such a ceremony is to awaken and cleanse the country as it begins a new journey. And the new journey that we begin as a result of this ceremony is the Festival of the Dreaming, this three week Festival that takes us through the first of our Cultural activities for the Olympics [and] a journey that takes us right through to the Olympics." Knight also explicitly stated the reason for having the Festival of the Dreaming as the first of the four Olympic Arts Festivals: "[T]he team entrusted with this responsibility of organizing the Sydney Olympics made a very deliberate decision to begin our Cultural Program with the Festival of the Dreaming. . . . We did that for two reasons. Firstly to recognize the primacy of Aboriginal culture and Aboriginal civilization in this country. Secondly, to reach out, to give the message of reconciliation: to say that the Sydney Olympics are inclusive not exclusive, and to give the message that these are the Games for all Australians. . . . There is important significance to the Festival of the Dreaming . . . and that alone is reason to attend." Knight concluded his speech by exhorting the audience, "Be a part of it. Enjoy it," and then strode off the stage, beaming.

Next, Rhoda Roberts, artistic director of the festival, leapt up to the podium. She smiled, grabbed the mike, adjusted it, and made her own welcome to the audience, first in the Bundjalung language, then in English, "Gee egala witha. Welcome to Eora country, Darug land" (1997). She made her acknowledgments and then, like Knight, described the Festival of the Dreaming as a journey: "As Michael said . . . the next three weeks are the journey. What it is, to me, is the journey of walking through tall grass. Please explain. The tall grass . . . we look at our Australian bush . . . when you walk through the grass, it takes many, many generations for the tracks and the trails to be laid. This [festival] has been 209 years in the making. The tracks are now flattened, and we want you to come on a journey with us for the next three weeks and flatten those tracks even further." Roberts then talked about the site of the Sydney Opera House, and about Bennelong, the Aboriginal man for whom the point was named: "This is known as Bennelong Point; originally it was known as Tyubow-gule. Bennelong was one of our very first interpreters on this land. He was very misunderstood. For many months he was shackled . . . so that he would interpret for Governor Phillip. I hope we have cleansed and awakened his spirit to begin this journey on this very special point of Sydney Harbour." Roberts concluded her talk with thanks to all those who contributed to the ceremony and an invitation to Stephen Page, the artistic director of the ceremony itself, to take the stage.

Page took a few minutes to get to the podium, but the audience clapped while they waited. Finally Page, his young son clasped in his arms, reached the stage and said: "I've got nothing to say . . . I just think it's a bit overwhelming and I'd just like to thank Rhoda for the opportunity and obviously all these wonderful artists who I love very much. . . . And it is about passing on now to our next generation. This is my son Hunter, and he'll take all this goodness and share it with everyone. Thank you" (1997). And with that, the Awakening Ceremony was over. Indigenous and nonindigenous audience members clapped and whistled and the last clouds of smoke drifted over all of us.

Smoke and Fire: The Awakening
Ceremony in Context

Even as the spectacle of the Awakening Ceremony dazzled the audience, participants acted out specific sociopolitical and/or corporate agendas. To understand these agendas, we need to explore the context of the Festival of the Dreaming as both a major Australian event and as the first of the Olympic Arts Festivals.

The first fact behind the Festival of the Dreaming is that Aborigines and Torres Strait Islanders are in a position of genuine social disenfranchisement in Australia. Due to the efforts of several generations of indigenous activists, and to gradual social policy reform in the last several decades, some of the worst manifestations of the repression of indigenous peoples have been ameliorated. For example, since 1967 indigenous people have been counted in the national census. Nevertheless, racism and social and economic disadvantage endure in many forms. For example, recent inquiries such as the 1991 *Royal Commission Report into Aboriginal Deaths in Custody* and the 1997 *Bringing Them Home: National Inquiry into the Separation of Aboriginal and Torres Strait Islander Children from Their Families* have found that indigenous people still suffer poorer health, higher infant mortality, higher rates of incarceration, lower life expectancy, and lower incomes than their non-indigenous counterparts.

Further, many significant gains made by indigenous people in the last decade have recently been erased or cut back. For example, since getting elected in 1996, John Howard's Coalition government has created legislation to reduce indigenous peoples' scope to make native title claims. It has also drastically cut funding to the Aboriginal and Torres Strait Islander Commission (ATSIC).[5] In addition, in early 1997 an independent member of Parliament, Pauline Hanson, founded her own ultraright wing One Nation party, which has made consistent vocal attacks against Aboriginal and Torres Strait Islander people.

Such cultural and political currents are contributing to a breakdown of what has been dubbed "reconciliation," that is, the process through which indigenous and nonindigenous people have been coming to terms with the reality of the history of white Australian settlement and through which they have been developing terms of rapprochement. Indeed, the perilous state of this process was amply demonstrated at the Reconciliation Conference in Melbourne four months before the Festival of the Dreaming when conference delegates turned their backs to Prime Minister Howard in a gesture of despair and contempt.

In addition to this immediate sociopolitical context, however, the frame for the Festival of the Dreaming was set also by its role as the first of Sydney's four Olympic Arts Festivals and, by extension, its relation to Olympism. Although usually overshadowed by the games themselves, Olympic Arts Festivals are an integral part of any Olympic program. The founder of the modern Olympics, Pierre de Coubertin, referred to the ancient games for his model of an integrated festival of arts and athletics. In Olympia, intellectuals, philosophers, and artists attended the games. Sculptures showed off the "beauty in athletics" and poets "sang the praises of Olympic visitors" (Segrave and Chu 1988, 3). Coubertin wrote, "[I]f the modern Games are to exercise the influence I desire for them they must in their turn show beauty and inspire reverence" (de Coubertin 1988, 104). He added, "Thus on all sides individual efforts are ready to converge toward an ideal of general harmony. The arts are drawing together; sound, line, color, and form seem to be preparing to associate once more in movement, which is living beauty, and thus to constitute the spectacular element of the modern Olympiad. With their aid may be framed a worthy setting for the Games" (de Coubertin 1988, 105).

In accordance with Coubertin's vision, from 1912 to 1948 the "Pentathlon of the Muses," an arts competition encompassing such fields as drama, choreography, and sculpture, took place alongside the sports events (Bandy 1988, 166). After 1948 the International Olympic Committee (IOC) decided to change the emphasis from artistic competitions to exhibitions, and after 1968 the IOC recommended that these exhibitions be conducted by only the nation hosting any given Olympic Games (Bandy 1988, 167). Thus the emphasis now is to use the arts to disseminate some of the more refined goals of Olympism, such as the "brotherhood of man" and the pursuit of world friendship and peace. Further, Olympic cultural programs provide host nations with a chance to show off their arts and culture and to add to the spectacle of the games.

According to SOCOG staff, the Sydney Olympic Arts program is the biggest since Berlin '36, and it is the first time in Olympic history that a cultural Olympiad will run over four years as four distinct festivals. This unique festival design was a key element of Sydney's Olympic bid in Monte Carlo in 1993. The four festivals, the Festival of the Dreaming, A Sea Change, Reaching the World, and Harbour of Life, were designed to feature different aspects of Australia's history, cultural life, and artistic strength and to appeal to both Australian and world audiences. In 1997 the Festival of the Dreaming celebrated indigenous art and culture. In 1998 A Sea Change looked at exploration, immigration, and the development of Australian settler society. Reaching the World in 1999 was a touring program that "expresses the spirit of Australia . . . to the continents of the world" (SOCOG 1993). The final festival, Harbour of Life, which will be staged during the games, will include *la crème de la crème* of Australian art and culture and will "celebrate a world of lasting peace, security, and friendship" (SOCOG 1993). Judging from their themes, it appears that SOCOG is using the festivals to discuss, explore, present, and celebrate "Australian-ness" as well as Olympic values.

Thus we see that the Awakening Ceremony was framed not only by the Sydney games, but by contemporary Australian sociopolitics and by the *relationship* of those sociopolitics to Olympism and European ideas about the role of the arts in bettering humanity and furthering world understanding. I now want to consider how each of these frames represents certain sets of interests, and to look at how these interests were made manifest within the ceremony itself.

A Pas de Deux of Interests

SOCOG has been unambiguous in its aim to use the Olympic Arts Festivals to further Olympic values. In fact sheets, SOCOG has stated explicitly that "The Olympic Arts Festivals will celebrate excellence in the arts and demonstrate the unifying force of the Olympic Movement in blending sport, culture and education" (1993). Further, SOCOG has always made it clear that the Festival of the Dreaming was a key part of its vision for the Olympic cultural program. As far back as July 1996 a SOCOG web site stated: "The success of the first year of the Cultural Olympiad will set the tone for a uniquely Australian Olympic Games in 2000. Australia's indigenous peoples will receive their highest exposure, significantly, in this first year; *The Festival of the Dreaming* will celebrate the world's indigenous cultures, highlighting Aboriginal and Torres Strait Islander peoples and the indigenous peoples of Oceania" (1993).

Notwithstanding SOCOG's espousal of Olympic ideals, and its desire to "celebrate" Australia's indigenous people, there were also certain practical gains to be made by staging an indigenous arts festival. For example, as the person quoted at the beginning of the paper mused, it is within the realm of possibility that SOCOG wanted to cash in on the visibility and popularity of indigenous art, which has a high value in Australia even though its creators are not always treated with the same respect. It is also possible that SOCOG made a strategic choice to produce a well-resourced indigenous arts festival in order to circumvent indigenous opposition to the games or even the possibility of a call for boycotts.

However, indigenous participants in the festival continually resisted being absorbed into any agenda not of their own making and tried to redefine what the festival was about and to whom it was directed. For example, in newspaper interviews, speeches, and meetings, Rhoda Roberts made it very clear that she intended to use the festival to raise issues that she felt to be important to indigenous people: "So look out: we're hitting the place in a big, black way, and things are going to get a good shaking-up. . . . This is the first time ever the Aboriginal people have owned something like this—it's about us, not about how other people see us—so it's going to be a very passionate experience. . . . We had to own it, to prevent it being presented in a tokenistic way: 'Hey, come and do a corroboree for us, will you?'" (Roberts in Burchall 1997, C5). SOCOG permitted Roberts the latitude to speak out and the larger body of SOCOG did not appear to want to contradict Roberts' vision (although they appeared to want to temper it at times); rather, it seemed like the officialdom of SOCOG had its idea of what the festival was for, the indigenous producers/participants had theirs, and the two communities decided to pursue their agendas more or less independently.

Of course the Olympics and the Olympic Arts Festivals are complex events. There is every probability that SOCOG was motivated by a whole range of desires—as were the participants in the Festival of the Dreaming. In the Awakening Ceremony, however, performers and speech givers did articulate certain themes and by so doing supported the idea that within the ceremony there were two sets of interests, one defined and voiced by Michael Knight, the other defined and voiced by the indigenous organizers and performers. These were not necessarily oppositional interests; rather, they suggest different concerns and ideas of what the ceremony was about.

As I described above, the ceremony had two key parts: the dance performance and the speeches. The former was evocative, seeming to suggest a number of things but also open to multiple interpretations. For example, in my reading, the traditional and "fusion" dance styles signaled the diversity of contemporary indigenous cultures: there is no one indigenous culture just as there is no one indigenous dance, and contemporary indigenous peoples live a variety of experiences, not one of which is more "authentic" than another. Second, the ceremony also proved the breadth of talent and expertise present in the indigenous arts world as the musical composition and direction, the choreography and the dancing were all by indigenous artists. Third, the ceremony indicated the strength and vitality of indigenous traditions in that, according to the participants, it really was a ceremony. It brought together the elements of fire, water, and earth, paid tribute to Bennelong and began a spiritual cleansing of the site.

In the speeches, however, participants were much more explicit about what they believed the ceremony was for and what they hoped to achieve. They thus highlighted the contrast between "Olympic" and indigenous intentions for the festival. For example, although Koori spokesperson Ossie Cruse mentioned the Sydney 2000 games in passing, only SOCOG representative Michael Knight foregrounded the games as the raison d'être for the Awakening Ceremony: "Welcome to this Ceremony.... Tomorrow marks the three years out from the Opening Ceremony of the Sydney 2000 Olympics, the most important and largest event in the world in the year 2000" (1997). Knight's double use of the word "ceremony" here accomplished a very neat trick, for it conflated the opening ceremony of the 2000 games with the indigenous ceremony just performed. The word "ceremony" has a certain weight and authority; I would venture to say that this quality is heightened—at least for nonindigenous people—when it is associated with Aboriginality and/or indigenous people. Thus the coming Olympic Games appropriated, or in Knight's estimation were bequeathed, an almost religious degree of solemnity and importance by the Awakening Ceremony. Further, the juxtaposition of the two ceremonies in Knight's speech created the impression that indigenous people not only supported the Olympic cause, they were willing to contribute their artistic and spiritual resources to prepare the way for successful Sydney games.

Rhoda Roberts also used the word "ceremony" in her speech. She referred to the ceremony as a "gift" from choreographer Stephen Page and thanked the Munyarryun family "for joining the north and south as Aboriginal people" through the Ceremony. These thanks have nothing to do with the Olympics and everything to do with indigenous politics, which tends to see a division between the generally urban indigenous peoples of the southeast and the more "traditional" peoples of the center and north of Australia.[6] The Munyarryuns, from Yirrkala in the far north of Australia, provided a corporeal link between north and south. Roberts's words also added weight to Cruse's sentiment that "regardless to our language, regardless to our skin grouping, indeed we are one people." Thus Knight and Roberts made reference to ceremony and the power thereof in substantially different ways: Knight used it to connect times and events, and Roberts used it to connect places and people.

Another word that both Roberts and Knight used was "journey." Knight said the purpose of the ceremony was to cleanse the country as it began a journey, an odyssey beginning with the Festival of the Dreaming and culminating in the Olympic Games. Once again Knight was purposefully connecting the Awakening Ceremony and the Festival of the Dreaming to the 2000 Olympic Games. In Knight's vision, SOCOG and ceremony performers and audiences were participants in a journey that linked that festival moment to the Olympic Arts Festivals of the years ahead, to the games themselves, and, by extension, to the whole spirit of Olympism.

Roberts struck a very interesting counternote. She, too, referred to the Festival of the Dreaming as a journey, but for her it was a journey through "tall grass" in which the way was not at all clear. The journey to which Roberts refers also looks back as well as forward: "[T]his [ceremony] has been 209 years in the making," she said, making an explicit reference to 1788, the year that the British invaded Australia and the dispossession of indigenous people began. She also brought the past into the present by acknowledging the efforts of a previous indigenous generation, the "elders who fought very hard for us . . . to be able to stand here in 1997 and welcome you to this Festival." Indeed, this statement is very powerful, for she tacitly credited the festival's existence to the political and social effort put in by indigenous elders over time rather than to SOCOG's spirit of inclusiveness. Roberts looked forward, too, but her vision was more modest. She invited the audience to join her for "three weeks [to] flatten those tracks even further." She voiced interest in a social journey, one of truth telling about the lives of indigenous Australians, not an epic journey to the grand spectacle of the games. While not using the word "journey," Steven Page echoed this sentiment in his brief speech, saying that for him, the festival was about generating goodwill to pass on to "our next generation."

Roberts and Cruse also grounded their speeches with literal and metaphorical references to place and locality. The Olympic movement is inherently ambivalent about place. On the one hand, the very philosophy of Olympism is internationalism; it is about collapsing the difference between peoples and between places to find commonality in sports and achievement. On the other hand, however, there is an intense focus on host cities, both practically, in terms of how cities present the games, and ideologically, in terms of what cities present about themselves. Knight acknowledged place mostly in terms of this latter point; that is, he referenced it in terms of the Sydney games and what sort of games they were going to be. Cruse, however, gently drew the audience's attention to what surrounded them and hinted at its Aboriginal past when he commented, "You can imagine what it was like before the big buildings went up, couldn't ya . . . here on the shores of this beautiful inlet." While an acknowledgment of pretty surroundings is hardly an atypical public speaking event, in this instance it had the effect of reminding people that the location has an indigenous history independent of the iconic Sydney Opera House.

Roberts, too, referenced place and with it, history. First, she identified herself as a "Bundjalung woman from northern New South Wales," specifying not only her language group affiliation but also the region from which she comes. Second, as described above, she talked about the tall grass of "*our* Australian bush," connecting indigenous and nonindigenous people together in a vision of the history of country—of laying tracks and trails—and relationship to place. Third and most significantly, like Cruse she talked about the specific site of the ceremony, although she was far more overtly political about it: "This is known as Bennelong Point; originally it was known as Tyubow-Gule." By giving these two names, Roberts was taking people back to two distinct eras of the Aboriginal history of the site, as Tyubow-Gule is the Eora name for the site. By using it in that context, Roberts asserted a right to identify one of Australia's most famous sites as indigenous land—a not inconsequential action in a time of fervent debate over native title. Second, Roberts talked about Bennelong, the Aboriginal man for whom the spot was renamed by the British. Bennelong is often cast as Australia's Uncle Tom, an Aboriginal man who betrayed his countrymen by becoming infatuated with the British after their arrival. However, while he eventually did take up residency with them, it was only after a long period of brutality in which he was kept shackled in leg irons and forced to learn English so that he could interpret for them. In these few references, Roberts deftly uncovered the layers of history of the site, making it clear that the ceremony was specifically about recalling and cleansing that history.

In this vein, it was also significant that both Cruse and Roberts identified some of the Aboriginal language groups of the Sydney region, groups such as the Darug, Eora, Dharawal, and Gandangara peoples. Roberts even used the Eora language to welcome people to the ceremony, again referencing precontact history and asserting rights to place by doing so. Further, as most nonindigenous residents of Sydney could not name one, let alone several, of the indigenous language groups who occupied the region before British settlement, Roberts and Cruse seized a platform to begin a little elementary education about the land's history, as well as indigenous protocol, which specifies that owners of land must be acknowledged and must welcome visitors to their country.[7] Thus Roberts and Cruse drew on the ceremony to illuminate indigenous history as well as contemporary ways of doing things, as opposed to merely pointing to the journey toward 2000.

Conclusion

The quotations at the beginning of this paper capture some of the ambivalences and contradictions that surrounded the festival and shaped the way it was perceived by participants and audiences: one member of the indigenous arts community described the Festival of the Dreaming as a cynical move on SOCOG's part to appropriate and sell indigenous arts because they have value and "will fill [SOCOG's] pockets up"; and she also credited the festival as an opportunity for indigenous people to show off their cultures and to "hold their heads up high."

The Awakening Ceremony was both of these things. Certainly SOCOG was trying to capitalize on certain aspects of the ceremony. SOCOG wanted to use the ceremony, and the Festival of the Dreaming as a whole, as a vehicle for the expression of Olympic values such as inclusiveness, tolerance, fairness, and artistic excellence. Irrespective of any larger agenda to whip up enthusiasm for Olympism and the games by so doing, credit is due to SOCOG for attempting this within a political climate that is essentially intolerant of difference in general, and of indigenous people in particular. However, SOCOG did try to appropriate a degree of symbolic capital from the ceremony. For example, Knight spoke as if the ceremony had given a blessing and a sense of spiritual import to the Sydney Olympics and also had created the momentum to carry the Olympic program through to 2000. Knight also tried to appropriate interest in and support for indigenous people so that, in Knight's telling sentence, "supporters" of the arts and of Aboriginal people became supporters of the Olympics.

Despite the Sydney Olympics frame, however, there was no sense that nonindigenous interests controlled either the event itself or subsequent interpretations. The ceremony's participants "held their heads high," performed what they wanted, and resisted being interpreted only according to SOCOG's agenda. As anthropologist Corrine Kratz (1994) has suggested, performances allow for multiple interpretations, notwithstanding the fact that everyone knows what the "official" interpretation is supposed to be. The Awakening Ceremony was very good proof of that. Whatever SOCOG might have wanted from it, Cruse, Roberts, Page, and the performers made it their own and used it to talk about indigenous history and relationship to place, and to present both the diversity and unity of indigenous cultures.

Of course, it is difficult to predict the effectiveness of this sort of social agency. What is the significance of proudly stating the names of the Aboriginal language groups of Sydney if nonindigenous audiences are so unfamiliar with them that they literally do not even hear them? I was disheartened to see that this was the case with one nonindigenous critic who quoted Roberts as saying, "Welcome to Eora country, dark land." That sounds spooky and exotic to nonindigenous ears and fits the mood of the ceremony very well, but it wasn't what Roberts said. She said, "Welcome to Eora country, Darug land." Granted it was just one critic, but it is still disappointing to think that nonindigenous Australians have trouble hearing indigenous people even when they are speaking loud and clear.

Further, not all indigenous people in the audience felt that the ceremony spoke for them. While many enjoyed it and found it powerful and moving, others questioned the appropriateness of Roberts, the Pages, and the Munyarryuns, people not originally *from* Sydney, having such prominent positions in the event. Others disputed the notion of a pan-Australian indigeneity, arguing that indigenous cultures are too diverse to be dealt with as one category of people. A handful of people even expressed concern that the amalgam of spirituality and spectacle in fact made the ceremony at best unseemly and, at worst, dangerous.

Thus the Awakening Ceremony, and, by extension, the Festival of the Dreaming, could not presume to represent the entirety of diverse indigenous peoples, experiences, and interests. Nor could they negate or overwhelm the frame that the Olympics provided and the power and interests that such a frame represents. Nevertheless, judging from the Awakening Ceremony, they might have tempered that frame, expanded it even, and made the festival something more politically and socially charged than just a bland cultural show. To some degree then, perhaps both "sides" got something they wanted. With the Festival of the Dreaming in general, and the Awakening Ceremony in particular, SOCOG not only had a critical and commercial success, but also got to advertise Olympic values via support for indigenous arts and attach itself to a spiritual awakening. Yet Roberts, Cruse, the Pages, the Munyarryuns, and other performers were able to take charge of a site and opportunity offered to them by SOCOG: the Awakening Ceremony was a place for indigenous response. In it, participants referred to history, politics, and a vision of the future that had little to do with the Olympic Games themselves and everything to do with social justice and the visibility of indigenous people. If one takes the ceremony as a synecdoche for relationships between indigenous and nonindigenous Australians or, on an even bigger scale, for relations between global movements like the Olympics and specific local interests, one sees a certain flexibility in the structure. These relations might have giddy power imbalances, but they are not necessarily immutable. Indigenous or local agency can inform and perhaps even transform internationalist agendas.

NOTES

I would like to thank the Commonwealth Scholarship Commission and the Social Sciences and Humanities Research Council of Canada for helping to fund this research.

1. The indigenous people of Australia are Aborigines and Torres Strait Islanders and the Festival of the Dreaming showcased the arts of both peoples as well as the arts of indigenous people from the United States, Canada, New Zealand, and so on.

2. At the time of the Awakening Ceremony, I was engaged in participant observation research with several of the protagonists of the festival, including the Sydney Organising Committee for the Olympic Games (SOCOG), which produced the festival, and the Bangarra Dance Theatre, whose artistic director, Stephen Page, choreographed the Awakening Ceremony. This paper is based upon this research as well as information obtained through extensive interviews within the indigenous arts community in

Sydney. When speeches or statements have been made in public and on the record, I have quoted people directly. Otherwise, people who contributed to this research remain anonymous to protect their privacy.

3. The Gamarada dignitaries were indigenous statesmen and women whom SOCOG selected to represent the indigenous community at various Olympic functions.

4. "Koori" or "Koorie" is the chosen collective title for indigenous people in New South Wales and Victoria, especially those who live in urban areas.

5. The Aboriginal and Torres Strait Islander Commission is the "peak representative indigenous agency in Australia. It is also a Commonwealth statutory authority responsible for administering many programs for Aboriginal and Torres Strait Islander people." For more information, see the ATSIC web site at http://www.atsic.gov.au.

6. By using the word "traditional" in this context I do not mean to impose a Western category on the indigenous people of the north, center, and so on; rather, this is the term that many urban indigenous people with whom I worked use to describe indigenous people who continue to live in their familial country, speak their own languages, and so on. Of course, many of the other dancers in the ceremony would also have been from areas outside of Sydney; Roberts likely singled out the Munyarryuns because of their prominent role within the event.

7. Knight's acquiescence to this protocol when he thanked Cruse for the welcome to "his" lands was striking, given the Commonwealth's contemporaneous efforts to reduce or erase the scope of the Native Title Act.

CHAPTER 13

Yes

Who's Sorry Now?

Drugs, Sports, and the

Media toward 2000

ANDREA MITCHELL

HELEN YEATES

It is 1998 at the World Swimming Championships in Perth, Australia. On January 5, Germany's head swimming coach, Winfried Leopold, is disqualified from the world championships after confessing to involvement "in the doping of former East German swimmers" (*Courier Mail,* Jan. 5, 1998). On January 8, the front pages cry foul as they accuse China of having a "secret drug lab," in an apparent attempt to "circumvent official doping tests" (*Courier Mail,* Jan. 8, 1998). On January 9, a drug bust takes place at Sydney airport. Police take one Chinese swimmer, Yuan Yuan, into custody. The headlines trumpet: "World Swim Crisis over Growth Hormone Haul" and "Busted: A Bagful of Hormones" (*Australian,* Jan. 9, 1998). On January 12, reports circulate that the International Swimming Federation (FINA, Fédération Internationale de Natation Amateur) will widen the "Chinese doping inquiry" (*Australian,* Jan. 12, 1998). On January 15, four Chinese swimmers are banned from the World Swimming Championships: "Swimming drug net lands four more Chinese" (*Courier Mail,* Jan. 15, 1998). Meanwhile, images of the splendid Caucasian bodies of the Australian swimmers receive extraordinary coverage in print and on television. The *Sydney Morning Herald* features Michael Klim, Australia's sensational star, as "a man with a mission"—to win (Jan. 12, 1998).

Explosive articles fuel the controversy sparked by the headlines. Cameras study the unnaturally well-developed shoulders of Le Jingyi, the woman with "China's

racism?. (margin note)

hopes on her shoulders." The headlines, her photograph, and the story on secret drugs implicate her in drug cover-ups (*Sydney Morning Herald,* Jan. 8, 1998). The media seizes on this international sports crisis. As "anger grows" and "officials step up testing," the media reports that the "plucky" Aussie team is determined to "defy the Chinese cheats." A front-page picture in the *Australian* shows Aussie swimmer Michael Klim with fist raised, captioned by "I'm the best in the world" (Jan. 14, 1998). The following day the Australian relay team wins gold and is called "fearless, all-conquering, awesome." Feature articles reflect on the "sports doping storm that has enveloped the Chinese team" (*Sydney Morning Herald,* Jan. 14, 1998). The "race" war is on, in every sense of the word, and the media is in the thick of it.

Drugs in sports is a pressing issue confronting the world today. The media's construction of drug misuse in sports revolves around such issues as the chemically enhanced transformation of athletes' bodies and notions of winning, losing, cheating, national pride, and shame. In the long history of human drug taking, performance boosting in sports via chemical means goes back to the earliest Olympics of ancient Greece. Athletes quite openly used alcoholic pick-me-ups laced with strychnine during the marathons in the early modern Olympics. When a cyclist collapsed and died during the 1960 Rome Olympics after taking nicotinic acid and amphetamines and when heroin was identified as the cause of hurdler Dick Howard's death, public and official concern finally resulted in the introduction of drug testing in 1968 (Donohew et al. 1989, 226).

Despite being illegal, anabolic steroid use was and still is part of a training program for some sports people, helping them to build the musculature required for high-level success. Drug taking has been long documented in bodybuilding, football, cycling, weight lifting, and field events such as shot put and discus. A program of steroid use during training can also help athletes with the explosive starts required for success in the sprint events. To avoid detection, and a drop in performance caused by what is referred to as "hormone crash," athletes taper off their drug program anywhere from fourteen to twenty-eight days prior to competition. This allows any banned substances to metabolize and pass from their system, thus remaining undetected. Excessive and prolonged steroid use can lead to health problems, such as gynaeco-mastia ("bitch tits"), liver cancer, and mood and personality changes. It is now recognized that coaches and swimmers from the East German swimming teams of the late 1970s and early 1980s used steroids. The performance-boosting drugs of choice of the late 1990s, such as Human Growth Hormone (HGH) and Erythropoietin (EPO) are currently almost impossible to detect, and "for many athletes, impossible to resist" (Blair 1998, 43). For some athletes and their coaches, sports "norms" about what constitutes cheating are ignored in the desire to win. Despite also knowing the harmful effects of drugs, many prefer to take the risk of impaired health in favor of the chance to win, thus overriding common sense about self-preservation and harmful behavior.

The viewing public is supposed to support the moral high ground of "zero tolerance," eschewing all forms of cheating in organized sports. However, many insiders attest to endemic drug taking within sports circles. A former champion bodybuilder, David Shaw, claims controversial, firsthand knowledge of doping in elite sports in Australia: "Because of our liberal use of drugs, it's unfair and inaccurate to say that we are one of the best sporting nations on this planet." He looks at the history of the Olympic medal tally, pointing to Australia's phenomenal improvement for a small nation: "[N]ow we're fifth and we're clearly competing against countries that have all but institutionalized doping." Athletes who claim not to have taken performance-enhancing drugs feel cheated, and as the money stakes get higher, the financial losses are considerable. As Shaw states, "Sport equals money. The governing bodies want the drugs. They merely require athletes to be clever and discreet" (quoted in Drane 1997, 37).

The political twists and turns surrounding drug testing of athletes over the last thirty years have made uniform procedures across the sports federations almost impossible, while the list of banned substances grows daily. The International Olympic Committee's (IOC) Medical Commission is also confronted with the increasing possibility that athletes banned under their rulings may take civil action against what can be seen as an invasion of their human rights and dignity. Loss of income and reputation, especially given the difficulties of proving actual intentional substance abuse, are also crucial issues. Drug testing itself acts as a gatekeeping device, a kind of floodgate valve, keeping back wholesale substance abuse by athletes. At the same time, it allows through those athletes supposedly worthy of heroic adulation (McKay 1991).

Heroes are differentiated from antiheroes who use problematic and questionable practices. Critics, such as Mark Spitz, point out that inequities arise when only five substances are tested for, when it is well known that twenty-five are in use (*Sydney Morning Herald,* January 8, 1998). What trust can or should the public place in the "heroic" achievements of sports stars if their success is gained illegally or because of a double standard in the rules regarding drug taking and testing? In a letter written to Daniel Kowalski (Australian fifteen-hundred-meter swimmer) a six year old asked if the swimmer had taken pills to make him go faster (*Sports Factor,* Radio National, July 17, 1998). A growing public cynicism about the Olympic ideal threatens to undermine the overall popularity of the games. The Olympic movement, as Segrave notes, is the only international sports institution which explicitly pursues particular social values based on human betterment through moral sports behavior and participation (Segrave and Chu 1988, 151). As a self-professed sports educator and moral guardian, the IOC itself has a duty to uphold community values regarding drug use in Olympic sports. The challenge for the media in the drug debate is to represent the views of all stakeholders in the face of conflicting interests, beliefs, and attitudes.

Media Countdown and Economic Meltdown

In mid-December 1997, the *Sydney Morning Herald* newspaper produced a special feature on the 2000 Olympics, entitled "1000 Days to 2000." This feature highlighted Sydney's pre-Olympic preparations, as the city heads toward what the media
pundits say may be an Olympic triumph greater than Barcelona, probably the "greatest" ever. Such "hype" mirrors the euphoria that swamped the Australian media
and the citizens of Sydney at the time of the announcement that they had
beaten their toughest rival, Beijing, for the staging of the 2000 Olympics. By mid-
January 1998, the mass media added a new perspective to the Olympic bid outcome by framing the drugs scandal as yet another Chinese/Australian battle, with
potent ramifications for Olympics 2000.

When five Chinese swimmers tested positive at the Perth World Swimming
Championships to a drug used to disguise the effects of steroids, the media
indulged in what could be termed a form of xenophobia. Reactions varied from
"They should be put on a plane and sent home. When you're caught with that
amount of drugs on your person and you are part of a team, the whole team
is implicated," to the "Chinese [are] caught with their hand in the cookie jar"
(*Courier Mail*, Jan. 9, 1998). However, a few contradictions started to surface on
the media margins. Chinese swimmer Shan Ying spoke of the Australian media
which "had gone too far in its reporting of the Chinese scandal" (*Australian*,
Jan. 1998). Her protest fell on seemingly deaf ears. One letter to the editor in
the *Sydney Morning Herald* complained that there was a double standard emerging from the "hypocritical" media reportage on the drugs issue: "When (Australian swimming star) Samantha Riley tested positive for a banned substance
we were quick to cover her tracks, and the fact that it was 'accidental' led to
a short ban, allowing her to race in Atlanta. Here we have . . . positive tests for
a drug that masks steroids, so one can argue that they are effectively, but not
technically, positive steroid tests. And so Don Talbot (Australian swimming
coach) calls for the expulsion of the Chinese team" (D. Colebatch, Jan. 16, 1998).
Another article, reprinted from the British Guardian, argued for drugs at the
Olympics. The writer, Jonathan Freedland, claimed, "The automatic response
is to condemn the Chinese, as with the East Germans before them, as schem-
ing commie cheats. But there is another way of looking at the whole business"
(*Sydney Morning Herald*, Jan. 16, 1998). Freedland cited the British science
writer Oliver Morton, "who argues that drugs should take up their rightful place
in physical competition. Why, he asks, should athletes be denied the pharma-
ceutical help the rest of us turn to routinely? Why can't sprinters use pills to
boost their speed?" (*Sydney Morning Herald*, Jan. 16, 1998).

Mostly, however, the media reportage does not present such radical, minor-
ity views, tending to move immediately into a "zero-tolerance" mode, thereby
becoming automatically anti-Chinese, with few shades of gray in the whole issue
admitted. When FINA banned the Chinese swimmers and their coaches for two
years, it unleashed a furor, with most pundits claiming that they should have been

FIGURE 13.1

"Asian Economies."

Reprinted from the original, courtesy of Sean Leahy, *Courier-Mail* (Brisbane), December 1, 1998.

banned for four years and calling on them to leave the championships. Demanding an "apology" and "giving medals back" were recurring themes in the media during this drugs scandal.

While the headlines blazed over charges of the Chinese swimmers' drug abuse, the mainstream media ran parallel stories about the overheating and bankruptcy of the Asian economies. This juxtaposition paired the alleged corruption and excesses of the economic managers in Asian countries with the corruption and excesses of the swimmers and their coaches in China. The ideological and racial divisions of East/West, Oriental/Caucasian were writ large in the public consciousness as the drugs scandal story broke. Direct connections between the overblown bodies of the Chinese swimmers and the overblown economies of the Asian region were not made explicitly in the media (except Leahy's cartoon, see fig. 13.1). However, as the narrative of the World Championship drugs scandal unfolded, an atmosphere of fear and distrust of all things Asian was created daily. Cartoonists produced images of the pumped up, drugged Chinese swimmers' disgrace and deceit one day, and the Asian tiger economy "blow-out" the next.

The so-called "miracle" economies of Asia plunged into currency meltdown mode during 1997 and 1998. By January 1998, the Asian economic crisis showed no signs of abating, and, indeed, in some commentators' minds it had reached "apocalyptic proportions" (*Australian,* January 14, 1998). Reports were rife that the economic consequences were impacting strongly on Western economies such as those of the United Kingdom, United States, Australia, and New Zealand. Common headlines were "Peril of the Orient," "Fresh Scandal Rocks Besieged Japanese Brokerages," "Asian Nerves Have Wall Street Trading Like Rabbits." A barrage of emotive and panic-ridden phrases backed these headlines: "Asian financial turmoil," "Asia bailout," "Asia fallout," "inferno," "scenes of eye-popping panic," "economic turbulence," "Indonesia's civil unrest," "negative inflation," "dollar at eleven-year low," and "US fear of Asian contagion." Reports circulated that China itself wrote off bad debts to prevent the country's banking system from becoming the "biggest casualty" of Asia's financial crisis. The popular media reports generally swept aside individual countries' differences, thereby, in a sense, conflating all things "Asian" as being in critical disarray, even though, according to some expert commentators, China was actually maintaining economic stability.

In this inflamed context, the Chinese drugs narrative in the media reached a certain xenophobic "apocalypse" of its own. Like the bodies of the Chinese swimmers, the economies of Asia were represented as unnaturally inflated. The photographs of the women swimmers and the media narratives around them emphasized their physical attributes, implying the sexist notion that they were particularly transgressive for having breached traditional sexual/gender boundaries.

The economic pages of the media played out the West's moral ascendancy over the East. Articles discussed how Western countries such as the United States (along with the International Monetary Fund) were attempting to bail out the transgressive Asian countries from their "follies" and "excesses."

Certain dichotomies developed in the media along ideological, racist axes: West/East, Caucasian/Oriental, moderate/immoderate, natural/unnatural. The barely restrained theme was that Western officials have to keep the Asian athletes' inflated bodies in line, just as the economic moderators in the West have to reign in the transgressive and unnaturally "melting down" Asian economies. This is in a sense a debate concerning definitions of "truth" about athletes' bodies. The traditional boundaries between male and female, masculinity/"musculinity"/femininity are blurring and breaking down as more women enter sports seriously (Hargreaves 1994). This "fearful" trend challenges conventional notions of "safe" bodies. The Western media frames the Chinese as having "unsafe" bodies brought on directly by "unsafe" drug use. The threat posed is that these duplicitous, subversive bodies may swamp the authentic, "safe" bodies of normal athletes.

Subsequent to the media hysteria outlined here, the doping panel of FINA decreed in late April 1998 that the Chinese swimmers banned in Perth should be allowed back in the water, making them temporarily eligible for international competition. The two-year ban on the swimmers was nullified, pending further investigations into Chinese claims that the swimmers had used a legal Chinese herbal medicine rather than a banned drug. The Australian media highlighted the

FIGURE 13.2

Zhang Yi's pumped-up body on display after testing positive to banned substances.

Reprinted from the original, courtesy of the *Courier-Mail* (Brisbane).

lifting of the ban as "a joke." Australian swimming star and Olympic gold medal-ist Kieren Perkins, quoted extensively in the media, asserted that athletes only have to make sure they have "good political friends who can put the right pressure on the right people so that they can get away with [testing positive]." Thus the media generally framed the ban-lifting decision as a political favor to the unrepentant Chinese.

No Shame, No Apology:
The Search for Lost Glory

In 1997 the media exposed another (former) communist country for its supposedly systematic illegal use of performance-enhancing drugs. One dramatic story went to air in an Australian *Sixty Minutes* television segment. The program, provoca-tively entitled "No Shame," promised confrontation and crisis. It featured reporter Richard Carleton accompanying former Australian sports stars, swimmer Lisa Curry-Kenny and runner Raelene Boyle, to the new Germany with the purpose of con-fronting former East German athletes, Christiane Knacke-Sommer and Renate Stecher, who "stole" Olympic medals from Australia's disappointed heroes through allegedly taking illegal drugs.

Mimicking the style of the U.S. *Sixty Minutes* show, reporter Carleton declared emotively, "For both athletes [Curry-Kenny and Boyle] it's a search for truth and vindication, a chance to prove how the drug cheats robbed them of Olympic glory" (*Sixty Minutes* [Australian], Nov. 23, 1997). Assuming the moral high ground, Carleton took a "trial by media" approach, determined to right the supposed wrongs of earlier Olympic games, when drug tests were either less rig-orously applied or less scientifically accurate than today's tests. The program did not clarify this issue; it simply cut to the chase.

In a Western-style, "shoot-out" situation, Carleton set up the East European medal winners in a confrontation with the two Australians, whose "career dreams were shattered" by losing to the ostensibly "pumped up" women from the for-mer East Germany. In a sense, of course, the two Australians were also set up, and the whole program became a shameful accusatory/denial scenario in which there were no real winners.

At the 1972 Munich Olympic Games Australian sprinter Raelene Boyle gained two silver medals in the one-hindred- and two-hundred-meter track-and-field events. The powerful Renate Stecher from East Germany narrowly beat her in both events. In her 1997 meeting with Renate Stecher, Raelene Boyle did not gain the satisfaction she and the *Sixty Minutes* team sought—an admission and an apology. Neither was forthcoming from Stecher, who maintained that she never took any substances and that both events were fought and won honestly. The doc-uments available from the once-secret East German files are ambiguous: one says that Stecher was doped; another, that she refused drugs (*Sixty Minutes* [Australian], Nov. 23, 1997).

At the Moscow Olympics in 1980, Lisa Curry-Kenny came in a disappointing fifth in her main butterfly event. Drawing the long bow, the *Sixty Minutes* team pushed this theory: had the three East German medalists in her race been disqualified for taking drugs, then Curry-Kenny would have been the silver medalist. Early in the program, Curry-Kenny raised suspicions about the testosterone levels of her fierce rivals, stating that the East German girls were "awesome-looking, big, muscly . . . with deep voices." A German microbiologist, Dr. Franker, also declared that the female athletes had been put through a "sexual transformation," with their testosterone level being lifted "to a male level" (*Sixty Minutes* [Australian], Nov. 23, 1997).

When interviewed, the bronze medalist Christiane Knacke-Sommer claimed that she had been doped systematically since she was twelve and that they all swam "by remote control." However, she then asserted that she was redeemed because she was actually "clean for Moscow." As a small gesture of reconciliation, Knacke-Sommer handed over her swimming suit to Curry-Kenny—but not the medal. The weeping Curry-Kenny blamed Knacke-Sommer herself, saying that a sixteen-year-old should stand up and refuse the drugs administered by her coach. Such a simplistic response overlooks the whole context of the nationalistic training culture of the former East German Olympic team, where winning was all and the individual had little or no power.

One purpose of the trip was to elicit apologies. However, the German Dr. Franker stated that there was no word for "sorry" in the German language; that not saying sorry is a "national characteristic." This sweeping comment remained unquestioned for both its generalization and, as stated by a German person, its ironic xenophobia. In effect, the people from the former communist state of East Germany are portrayed as unnaturally cold and driven, incapable of shame or remorse. It is possible, of course, that Franker qualified his statement about himself and his compatriots regarding the German language not having a word for "sorry," and the *Sixty Minutes* producers may well have edited out such qualifications. There are in fact a number of phrases that express such a sentiment in German: two translate as "we beg to be excused" and "it does me great pain."

The narrative presented in this *Sixty Minutes* report was vindicated in a way by the subsequent contrite action of Knacke-Sommer, who, in June 1998, "planned to return all her medals." While Curry-Kenny will probably not get her Olympic medal, this action shows that the media is playing both a responsible and an irresponsible role in writing and rewriting Olympic drugs history. It is ironic, also, that someone like Lisa Curry-Kenny is presented in the Australian media as "normal," despite her attempts to push the boundaries of her own body when it suited her (McKay 1994). In the 1980s she transformed herself into a sleek, muscular "winning" machine. Then, after becoming a mother, she submitted her body to plastic surgery, remolding her breasts into acceptable, pert, rounded ones, more authentically feminine in the media's eyes. In some ways, Curry-Kenny embodies a personal crusade for the willful transformation of the female body, perhaps unwittingly tracing the problematic margins where surgery, drugs, and sports training may be deemed legitimate or where slip fall into an illegitimate, unsafe space.

The Taunts and the Taints: Ben Johnson and Michelle Smith/de Bruin

Another controversial athlete, Ben Johnson, a Jamaican Canadian, was stripped of his gold medal for the one-hundred-meter men's sprint at the 1988 Seoul Olympics after testing positive to a banned substance, Stanozolol. His name has become shorthand in the media for "drug cheat," with his misdemeanors inevitably arising in much media coverage of drug taking in sports.

Despite persistent rumors about Johnson's incredible performance, the athlete managed to clear numerous drug tests in the lead up to Seoul. According to his coach, Charlie Francis, Johnson was not a cheat; he was simply unlucky enough to get caught. He argues that, although the rules may be clear about substance abuse, the practices that enforce these rules are inconsistent, unfairly applied, and open to subversion. In a book published in 1990, Francis opined that most of the elite sprinters who lined up with Johnson at the starting line in Seoul would have been on some drug program for enhanced performance.

Ben Johnson's positive drug test and subsequent loss of his Olympic medal supposedly cost him over $25 million worth of sponsorship deals, while gaining him worldwide opprobrium. Terms such as "national embarrassment" were added to "cheat," "doping sinner" and "disgusting vile coward." As Francis notes, "the biggest story in Olympic history required the worst knave (Ben), the most Faganesque coach (me) and the most malevolent witch doctor (Astaphan, Johnson's medical supervisor)" (1990, 11). The incident sparked the Dubin Inquiry into drug taking in Canadian athletics. Yet, according to Johnson's coach, it is simply the greater technical expertise enabled by higher funding for sports which allows many U.S. athletes to avoid being caught. According to Tim Blair, writing in *Time,* the Atlanta Olympics "were known among the athletes as the 'HGH games'" (i.e., the human growth hormone games). Cleaners allegedly got tired of finding syringes in athletes' rooms. In 1997, Carl Lewis accused U.S. athletic authorities of hiding the extent of drug use, with doping being "ignored and sometimes supported" (Blair 1998, 44–46). Johnson's attempts to return to elite-level sports ended in 1993, with a lifetime ban being imposed when he again tested positive to steroid use. According to Johnson, this second ban was the result of faulty testing. He is currently appealing in an attempt to clear his name and reenter the sport.

Other writers support Francis's claims that Johnson was unfairly victimized and suffered a "trial by media." *The New Lords of the Rings,* first published on the eve of the 1992 Barcelona Olympic Games, created a furor with its allegations of drug taking, medal buying, and general corruption amongst the officials at the top of the Olympic movement (Jennings 1996). Recently, *New Scientist* magazine revealed that samples which tested positive from five unidentified athletes during the 1996 Atlanta games were not taken to the next, or B, sample-testing stage. The IOC justified this lapse in standard practice by citing concerns about the reliability of the sample-handling procedures. According to the medical director of the IOC's Medical Commission, "[W]e had worries about how samples had been extracted and prepared, [and] we didn't want to proceed with the cases" (*New Scientist,* December 7, 1996, 15). The five athletes remain protected from any suspicion, as their names were not revealed. By contrast, Johnson's name was leaked to the media prior to his B sample being tested.

Like Johnson, Michelle Smith/de Bruin, the Irish triple gold medalist, has faced many a taunt and taint. Initially, the Irish euphoria, as reported in the international media, centered on her being the first Irish woman to win gold in the pool. However, this achievement was immediately sullied by an unprecedented media barrage of accusations regarding drug-enhanced performance. These accusations have pursued Smith/de Bruin since the 1996 Atlanta games. The diminutive star of just 157 centimeters (five feet, two inches), small in a sport where many of the female swimmers are nearing the six-foot mark, came out of nowhere, if prerace pundits were to be believed. Nobody predicted her extraordinary three gold medals in the four-hundred-meter women's medley, four-hundred-meter freestyle, two-hundred-meter medley, and a bronze in the two-hundred-meter butterfly.

Naturally enough, Smith/de Bruin's fans at the 1996 Atlanta games, including her husband and coach, Erik de Bruin, reacted angrily to accusations of her cheating. Some media reports commented on her "surprisingly" calm ability to field the journalists' endless questions about how she had improved so much. Her seemingly "rehearsed" aplomb at handling the media was used to reinforce the drug rumors surrounding her career.

The level of innuendo reached such a crescendo during the swimming competition at Atlanta that the BBC felt compelled to put together an in-depth report, looking at some of the accusations in detail. Interrupting coverage of the swimming, the BBC's three-minute apologia took a pro-Smith/de Bruin approach, stressing that there were absolutely no problems with Smith/de Bruin's drug tests. Other media commentary, such as articles in the British *Guardian,* talked about the "whining yanks" displaying their hometown bias by supporting American Janet Evans, Smith/de Bruin's defeated rival.

Despite some supportive early coverage, the international media seized on the story of Smith's marriage to her coach, Erik de Bruin, a Dutch discus and shot-put champion serving a four-year ban for drug offenses. In a European/American divide, the press lined up to either laud or denounce Smith/de Bruin's achievements. The Australian media, with its strong Irish-Australian readership, was more moderate in its assessment of Smith/de Bruin, despite the Irish swimmer being in a position to topple Australia's own golden girl, Susie O'Neill, in the two-hundred-meter butterfly. Another example of the Australian media's evenhandedness was that, although Erik de Bruin's four-year ban was discussed, they also noted that the Dutch federation later reversed his suspension, due to irregularities in the drug-testing procedures and other legal problems. Counting on Australia's reputation for drug-free swimming, some journalists went so far as to connect Smith/de Bruin's achievements to those of Aussie wonderboy Kieren Perkins, commenting that "if dramatic time drops are indicative of steroid use, then Kieren Perkins is the guiltiest swimmer around. No one attacks the world record books with a sharper cleaver" (Smith 1996, 52).

At the end of April 1998, Smith/de Bruin was again in the drugs-testing limelight for allegedly manipulating a sample collected in January 1998. Australian media coverage of this new stage in the Smith/de Bruin saga discussed the problems of testing her in her home in Ireland and then returning the samples to an IOC-accredited laboratory in Switzerland. Doubts over the security of samples en route echo the concerns over sample-handling procedures that enabled some unnamed athletes to go free at Atlanta. The 1998 Smith/de Bruin drug controversy provided an opportunity for the media to raise some of the structural difficulties underlying the whole drugs-in-sports debate. Radio sports commentators expressed concerns about the ongoing "harassment" and invasion of privacy which year-round testing places on athletes. According to one journalist on the ABC (Australian Broadcasting Corporation), no other group of professional entertainers would allow the indignities which power sports people are subjected to, because of the need to continually assuage public concern about alleged drug taking.

Sports have always provided entertainment for the viewer, but this explicit recognition of the connections between athletes and other paid entertainers marks a change in the media presentation of the drugs-in-sports debate. All too often, the media coverage remains at the level of the guilty individual "cheat," with the inevitably blinkered win/lose mentality going unquestioned. If, as many inquiries have discovered, 75 percent of top-class athletes take performance-improving drugs, it is reasonable to ask why only the exposed medal winners are vilified. However, ignoring the reality of high-level sports, journalists tend to support a drug-free "level playing field," claiming to protect the athletes who don't cheat from those who do.

This cheat-free zone, supposedly inhabited by a "superbreed" of squeaky clean, healthy athletes, is an essential part of the mythology of the sports economy. Individual athletes wanting to attract corporate sponsorship must live up to an ideal, "all-natural" advertising image. Smith/de Bruin's sponsorship potential, initially thought to be substantial (as the *Times* noted in the July 26, 1996, headline "Smith Plunges into Deep Pool of Money"), has not in fact been realized. One of Smith/de Bruin's major sponsors, TNT, chose not to renew her sponsorship in August 1997, declining at the time to comment on the reasons.

FIGURE 13.3

The rise and fall of an Irish heroine, Michelle Smith/de Bruin.
Courtesy of the *Weekend Australian*.

The issues surrounding the cases of Smith/de Bruin and her husband/coach appear to be too multilayered for the mainstream sports media to cover adequately. Perhaps fear of litigation has stopped further investigative reporting, but the legal and medical technicalities of the cases do not fare well in the black/white, goodies/baddies atmosphere of everyday journalism.

In August 1998, Michelle Smith/de Bruin was found guilty of manipulating her sample and banned from competition for four years. The *Australian* noted, with some satisfaction, that finally what we had all suspected was out in the open, headlining the story with "De Bruin Pays the Price of Deception" and "The Rise and Fall of an Irish Heroine" (*Australian,* April 30, 1998).

The *Sunday Mail* refused the narrative closure of the *Australian*'s interpretation and ran their coverage under the banner headline "I'm Innocent," signaling

Smith/de Bruin's intention to appeal the decision (April 30, 1998). Obviously the media is still divided regarding this complex case.

Whatever the outcome of the appeal, the concept of the level playing field and the high ideals of Olympic competition regarding dignity and morality are further devalued and damaged in the public's eyes. The stories of Michelle Smith/de Bruin, as well as those of the individual East German and Chinese swimmers, are symptomatic of sports in the late 1990s, just as Ben Johnson's story epitomized the 1980s. Such personalization is a media phenomenon, where all too often, for the sake of both simplicity and sensationalism, the individual bears the brunt of a much wider cultural problem.

1990s Drugs Scandals: What Is Going On?

As we are reminded biennially, during the staging of the Summer and Winter Olympics, the motto for the modern games is "*citius, altius, fortius:* faster, higher, stronger." Such a motto seems to reflect what many claim is a competitive human instinct, and it is this "natural" urge which motivates athletes to perform to their utmost. There is a wide gulf between the rhetoric and the reality of the Olympic movement. The populist rhetoric surrounding the games talks about personal bests, being a contender, and the universal peace brought about through sports participation in this global event. This idealism is at odds with the increasing commercialization and professional athleticism of many elite performers. To use the old cliché, what really matters, and what everyone knows matters, is winning. Athletes who manage to grab gold on the day bring to themselves not only individual glory and public recognition, but also, in the media–saturated environment of the late twentieth century, extremely lucrative sponsorship deals. In the scramble to claim responsibility for producing such prodigies, many first world countries, somewhat like proud parents, have created sports institutions, the sole purpose of which is to identify, cultivate, and groom future sports "super stars," gladiators for their countries in the sports arena.

Due to the repeated scandals and furors about athletes who supposedly "cheat" by taking drugs, there is growing recognition that the level playing field metaphor is in many ways a convenient myth. Countries such as Australia and France have specifically allocated funding to research the various ways in which medal-winning performances can be achieved and have fostered young athletes at educational establishments such as the Australian Institute of Sport. As a result of this increased research activity, many assumptions about "natural" physical aptitude have been revised. Certain individuals succeed not only because of such basic physical attributes as body size and shape and general good health, but also because of material benefits such as access to training facilities, income support, and quality coaching/mentoring programs.

Since the Ben Johnson furor in 1988, doping in sports has become even more technical, with the drug testing always seemingly one step behind the athletes, who know exactly what the Olympic laboratories can and can't test for. Complex medical, ethical, and legal arguments are involved, arguments which the mainstream media tends to gloss over. However, difficult as it is to investigate the political machinations behind the official Olympic façade, some intrepid journalists claim that the IOC cannot afford to have it widely known just how prevalent drug taking is at "the top." A conference in February 1999 was held to look into this vexed issue. Since urine samples are becoming inadequate to detect pharmacological interventions, blood testing is being suggested, raising the thorny problem of the infringement of basic human rights when invasive bodily testing is undertaken.

Of particular concern are the ways the Western media tends to create oppositions that can be tied to political agendas. Elite sports people, such as Michelle Smith/de Bruin, are from countries which, despite being considered Western, First World nations, are still on the periphery when compared to competitors from major nations such as the United States, Britain, France, Russia, Italy, and even Australia. Drug cheats who are outed by the Western media tend to belong mainly to this marginal category or to former Eastern bloc or communist countries. At the time of his drug bust, Johnson was doubly marginal as he is Jamaican-born and represents Canada, a country without a powerful, national athletic federation at that time (Coplon and Francis 1991, 12). Michelle Smith/de Bruin is also, of course, a woman, which tends to place her in a troublesome category in relation to Olympic competition, where femininity control, in the form of the notorious sex test, is imposed on women only. The media tends to ignore gender, race, and nationalistic discrimination in the drugs-in-sports debate.

A further example of an asymmetrical approach to drug taking by the media is the lack of attention given to the two U.S. athletes who tested positive at the 1992 Olympic Games, from a total of only five athletes who were eventually "caught." A cursory glance at the history of the positive tests since 1968 presents a much broader picture, with athletes from a wide cross-section of nations represented. Seemingly racist, ethnocentric, and sexist assumptions and biases may be traced in some of the media coverage, especially when looked at in conjunction with the political climate surrounding particular Olympic Games.

Truth and Reconciliation: The Significance of the "Sorry" Drugs Spectacle

The media hypocrisy in Australia regarding drug taking by the unrepentant Chinese athletes during the 1998 World Swimming Championships in Perth was exposed when the media played down Australian swimmer Richard Upton's severe reprimand and fine after banned substances were detected in his urine sample in April 1998. Despite this, he was still allowed to compete in the Commonwealth Games. Such seeming discrepancies are rife in the world of swimming. American Olympic gold medalist Gary Hall Jr. was banned from competition after he tested positive to marijuana in 1998. The ban was later lifted and he was allowed to reenter competition pending further investigations by FINA.

The Australian swimming establishment has long made clear its antipathy toward drug taking by other national swimming teams, maintaining that Australia's prominence in the pool is attributable solely to talent and hard work. While chinks are appearing in the armor, the media tends to have a conveniently selective memory in relation to the drugs-in-sports debate of which the East/West controversy is a part. The rather "sorry" attempt by a hyped-up *Sixty Minutes* team to extract an artificial apology from two former East German medalists feeds beyond the simplistic them/us, East/West divide into a broader, more serious debate in Australia and other nations around truth and reconciliation. For instance, unlike the Canadian government, the Australian federal government has refused to say "sorry" to the indigenous population for having removed children forcibly from their parents, as generations known as "the stolen children." In 2000, the world will witness more closely the host country, Australia, deeply divided over human rights issues and unreconciled past excesses, the playing out of which will inevitably color the world's view of Australian athletes.

Against such a complex background of racism, nationalism, and sexism (especially concerning certain women athletes' bodies), the media's often contradictory coverage of the drugs-in-sports issue is provocative.

In the new millennium, the media as well as the other stakeholders, such as the coaches and the athletes themselves, have a shared responsibility to ensure that the drugs-in-sports debate is handled in a balanced way. Simplistic sloganizing still seems to be readily and thoughtlessly taken up by the world media eager for "quick fix" stories about drugs. Beamed out to billions by television companies as a hugely engaging, massively lucrative spectacle, the sports/political oppositions are writ large in the Olympic media arena. The media rarely probes behind the scenes to uncover the political and sports issues that really count in the debate over drugs. At the same time, the Olympic Games audiences seem to oblige the media by wanting to "get high" on the excitement of drugs scandals, without ever fully understanding the bigger picture.

CHAPTER 14

The Olympics

of the Everyday

[handwritten margin notes: "Amateurism & Modern Mythology", "City Bids"]

KAY SCHAFFER

SIDONIE SMITH

The Olympics and Everyday Life: Defining Values

At the millennium, the Olympic Games remain, as they have always been, a fascinating spectacle of both the ideal realm of athletic competition and prowess and realpolitik of gritty national and international intrigue. But they remain as well a spectacle of so much more. The games are always more than carefully choreographed contests of skill and drive. They are about boycotts and bids, about buildings and regulations, about the spectacular hoopla of opening and closing ceremonies and the crass commercialism of souvenirs, about celebrity and national sports policy, about urban construction and artistic performances, and, sadly, about bribery and corruption. They're about everyday life.

Even if we're not obviously aware of the impact of the Olympics in our everyday lives, the impact is there nonetheless. It's not just the games we watch every two years. It's also the effects of the Olympic Games that surround us.

Take, for instance, the notion of "fair play." Olympians and their audiences universally applaud the virtue of fair play. It signifies a cultural code of appropriate behavior, behavior not only assumed on the playing fields but translated into other arenas of life, into the worlds of business, public life, and international trade. But the notion of fair play has a history, and a history that is tied to a nineteenth-century form of nationalism. Although it appears to be an egalitarian principle today (until corruption of drugs and money-tainted athletes' performances and bidding strategies), leveling the differences among the contestants through a universal code of conduct, its history in relation to the modern games is tied to notions of gentlemanly conduct promulgated by the social institution of the British public school.

In the British public school, sports became a training ground for the nineteenth-century English gentleman. With its invocation of neo-Grecian and neoclassical attributes of the beautiful, controlled, clean body, sports helped to discipline the body of young boys and men and to teach them the proper ways to use that body. Around the 1880s the concept of fair play became a part of the curriculum in the British public schools. It came to distinguish the British school chap and his future as a British gentleman from the identity and scripts of masculinity of other men. The virtue of fair play came to mark the difference of the British gentlemen from the men of the lower and middling classes. As the property of the well-educated British gentleman, the virtue of fair play was a guarantee of his superiority within his own country and the superiority of his class around the world.

It was also believed to be a guarantee of his imperial success in the conquest of nations through colonization and settlement. Education in the virtues of fair play was a necessary prerequisite for the British gentleman's successful conquest and colonization of the "backward races." In this British context, then, fair play was a virtue of gentlemanly masculinity, a differentiating rather than leveling virtue. As J. A. Mangan argues so persuasively, training in sports at the British public school was training for leadership of an empire. The spectators who watched these sporting boys and the enactment of this fair play witnessed to the community the rituals of gentlemanly masculinity. In this way they played their part as "supporters" of empire.

But it was not only in Britain that these aristocratic, gentlemanly values were extolled. They were acknowledged more broadly within the elite circles of European politics and civil life. There they formed the pretext for Coubertin's vision of the nobility of the Olympian, the diplomat of an ideal world community of respect.

Other motivations have shaped the cultural embrace of sports culture and sports events. In Coubertin's France the goal of encouraging communal sports activities was not tied to a public school system. Rather, emphasis on sports, on honing the athletic body, had to do with readiness for war. In the last half of the nineteenth century social disruption threatened the body politic in France. Riots and insurrections broke out throughout the country in the wake of French defeat in the Franco-Prussian War; the most significant riot was that of the Paris Commune of 1870. For French conservatives, the Paris Commune riot symbolized the threat of social revolution within the country. In the wake of defeat after the Franco-Prussian War, the riots also served as a reminder of the failure of French militarism abroad. Collective participation in sports thus became a means to instill the values of discipline and restraint in French citizens as well as a means to promote the codes of engagement that are preparatory to combat.

Moreover, athletic competition was understood to unify crowds of strangers around communal rituals of confrontation. In this way athletic competitions became means to unify the unruly mob and to contain that unruliness through organized spectacle. The otherwise suspect mob could cohere as a unified force of national will. The Olympic Games could thereby function as a key event in the promotion of social cohesion, specifically, national cohesion, and the mobilization of the masses (Faure 1996, 81–85).

From the outset, a welter of chauvinistic motivations shaped the modern Olympic movement: moral superiority/authority, social cohesion, national progress, rehearsals of competition, readiness for war. In the everyday life of the nation, sports and that pinnacle of sports competition, the Olympic Games, have done and continue to do much cultural work in terms of defining, promoting, and reproducing broadly accepted and extolled cultural values.

Good

Everyday Life before, during, and after the Games

But let's draw back from these defining values to the nitty-gritty impact of the games on an Olympic city before, during, and after the games.

Bidding

EVERYDAY LIFE BEFORE THE GAMES

In order to prepare a potentially winning bid, key organizers in hopeful cities mobilize expanding coalitions of people and organizations in many sectors of local and national life—business and industry, government, sports, the nonprofit sector, arts and entertainment. And who is chosen to represent the host city on the bidding committee? One economic commentator writing for the *Australian* (Sept. 21, 1993) colorfully described the Sydney bid team as representing the "boomtime tourist industry, the jackals and cheerleaders of business and the media, small time politicians operating on a big stage, property speculators, marketing and PR spivs, junketeers of all creeds," a list which Macquarie University's politics professor Colin Tatz agrees is "fairly accurate." (qtd. in Booth and Tatz 1994, 7). The money, glory, and publicity to be had from steering a successful bid brings strange bedfellows together to do the "business" of attracting the games.

Selling the idea of hosting the Olympics to the IOC organizers and coalition partners sets a massive game plan in motion. The big business of image making pushes into high gear. Promotional materials must be developed, slogans tested, logos designed, mascots imagined, and activities carefully choreographed. The image of the host city must jive with ideals befitting the host country. In the case of Sydney and Australia, key organizers could play upon the radical transformation wrought in the image of Australia at mid century when Melbourne hosted the '56 games.

With those games Melbourne shifted in its own imagination from a provincial town to a cosmopolitan city. The '56 games were dubbed "the friendly games" after Australian Olympians broke the disciplined ranks of the march of nations in the closing ceremonies. This action enhanced Australia's reputation for irreverent, antiauthoritarian behavior, as well as the nation's reputation for casual and open hospitality. These national attributes were invoked by international promoters for the 2000 games as well.

For the 2000 games the Sydney Olympic Bid Committee structured its entire game plan around the promotion of a city committed to Olympic ideals. It chose the twin themes of environmental responsibility and friendly athleticism to enhance its bid. That meant promoting Australia's climate, clean air, and concern for ecology as well as its laid-back urban life and its exotic "outback." It meant concealing the fact that the main stadium at Homebush, fourteen kilometers from the city center, would be built on a toxic postindustrial site next to a polluted river. It also meant promoting Australian multiculturalism and Australia's indigenous people and their participation in the games.

To enhance the multicultural theme, key organizers enlisted 160,000 schoolchildren to sign petitions supporting the games, petitions that were then sent to IOC members. One hundred and twenty schools, specially selected for their multicultural mix as well as excellence in their academic and sports programs, were chosen to be "twinned," one to each IOC official, who, when visiting Sydney, would be taken to "his" or "her" school and presented with scrapbooks full of student messages of support for the games.

The games would also be a "showcase" for Aboriginal culture. To this end the Sydney Olympic Bid Committee employed prominent Aboriginal spokespersons to campaign for the games and pressed an obliging media to douse the flames of racial protest and dissent. In a last ditch, cynical bid for votes, it played the racial card, sending Aboriginal dancers to Monaco—like so many "tourist curios," as one Aboriginal leader noted—to perform for the IOC members.

Like every other aspirant host city, Sydney engaged in strategies to laud, pamper, coddle, and indulge IOC members in every imaginable way. Committees in every hopeful city researched the personal lives of IOC members and their families—even their sexual preferences. China topped the gift-giving extravaganza by sending a priceless 2,200-year-old terra-cotta soldier from the Ch'in tomb. Other cities offered all-expense-paid trips, jewelry, clothing, cars. Rumors that bidding countries offered funding for athletic programs, as well as jobs and scholarships for IOC members' relatives, are widely alleged and under investigation. The rumors, initially in relation to Salt Lake City's bid for the 2002 Winter Olympics, quickly spread to questions about the Sydney and Nagano bids as well. The IOC does not condone such activities, which verge on bribery, but neither does it routinely monitor them. (Only with the Salt Lake City scandals grabbing so much headline space did the IOC press hard on the abuses. Heads have rolled in the organizing committee. A mayor has decided not to run for reelection. And behind the scenes, would-be pretenders for Samaranch's crown dodge the heat as they jockey for position. Every day there's a new installment in the saga of the Olympics scandal.) Nor is there a structure for reporting and adjudicating abuses to the IOC code. Far from models of peace, tolerance, unity, goodwill, and understanding between nations, the games and the bidding strategies which bring them to life foster rivalry, greed, corruption, and international competition.

key

Once the frenzied strategies employed to win the bid have been successful, the chosen city fills with the euphoria of civic and national pride—and a sense of communal anticipation. But that's the emotional affect that comes with the announcement. That emotional affect must be translated into the hard work of the long haul. For as a result of winning the bid, the city must be transformed. Transformation involves the development of urban renewal plans for the city spaces where sports facilities will be built. It involves designing and building futuristic sports facilities large enough and technologically advanced enough to serve as venues for world-class competition for upwards of fifteen thousand athletes and officials—and as signs of the host country's preeminence in the architecture of public spaces. It involves development of massive communications and transportation infrastructures. A host city such as Sydney, already cosmopolitan on an international scale, fast becomes the nexus of a massive media information network and flow of capital.

changing city

Architects, city planners, construction workers, and tradespeople of all kinds go to work on the Olympics. New jobs are created, jobs which lead to new economic and political relationships as laborers and unions do the work of transforming the city. Neighborhood residents go to work as well, although with different motives, for during the process of transformation whole neighborhoods are sometimes relocated, drastically affecting the everyday lives of neighborhood peoples—usually lower-income people with limited political clout. In preparation of the '96 games an inner-city neighborhood of Atlanta disappeared into the concrete, steel beams, and grass of the Olympic Ring, a geographical area in the heart of Atlanta with a radius of one and a half miles. When this happens, local community groups and civic associations, neighborhood activists, and the clergy mobilize, organize, and lobby to protest against or claim the benefit of the kinds of dislocation that Olympic construction brings with it.

Whatever's happening on the ground, over the airwaves, and on billboards and television sets, the work of the image makers continues. Competitions are held for the design of mascots. For Atlanta organizers John Ryan came up with what would become a ubiquitous presence at the 1996 games—Izzy, the multicolored, unisex creature wearing the Olympics rings and sporting a big grin and oversized sneakers. But as early as 1972 when the Munich games offered Waldi the Dachshund, mascots have given the games a kind of readymade personality. Then, too, advertisers and promoters, sportscasters and politicians saturate commercial television, billboards, radio, magazines, newspapers with sports hype, sports figures,

Hype

Media Blitz

and sports images. Vignettes of athletes, moments from games past, and projections of records to come become the staple fare of everyday life.

The roster of popular icons expands to include an increasing number of athletes preparing for the games. These icons bring new styles onto the playing fields. Recall "Flo Jo" (Florence Griffith-Joyner) bringing ultrafeminine fashion onto the running field with her long nails, impeccable makeup, and figure-hugging Lycra bodysuits. And they bring new styles of the flesh and fashions onto the streets. Young people and weekend athletes sport new styles of athletic wear and gear. In turn the increasingly close links between sports and fashion influence what events and what athletes become fashionable in the long run up to the games and the long denouement after. And image making and trend setting are just two of the big businesses that take home the loot of the games.

Always the sound of money in the tills can be heard as the background noise of Olympic preparation. Winning the 2000 bid cost Sydney organizers A$28 million (U.S. $17 million). Estimates put the cost of staging the Sydney games at well over A$1,600 billion (U.S. $990 billion) and the cost of running the games at A$3,000 billion dollars (U.S. $1860 billion) (including infrastructure costs). The taxpayers of New South Wales will incur an enormous tax debt for some years to come. But the bid committees know that one of Samaranch's achievements over the past twenty years has been to make the games a winning bet for the host city. The 1986 Los Angeles games netted a profit of some U.S. $240 million. And the profits have been rolling since then—what with television and satellite contracts and contracts for the sale of tourist items of all kinds.

This money has to be raised by any means available. New organizations assume responsibility for securing sponsorships and brokering deals. Due to the unveiling of corrupt bidding practices which came on the heels of drug scandals, finding sponsorship for the 2000 games proved difficult indeed. Barely five hundred days from the opening of the games, reports indicate that Sydney was likely to fall well short of its target sponsorship revenue of A$854 million (U.S. $547 million)—possibly short up to A$200 million. This corporate and donor money contributed to the Olympics could otherwise support such publicly sponsored activities as art exhibitions, book fairs, conferences, and publicly funded companies like orchestras, opera companies, and theaters. Diversion of money from arts organizations, nonprofit agencies, and medical research goes on for the four to six years prior to the games. From this perspective an incredible amount of money is siphoned off into sports training and the Olympic Games, especially when we remember that Australia has a population of only 18 million.

What are the rewards? Well, let's take the per medal cost of the games. According to a recent research report (*Advertiser,* December 15, 1998), Australian taxpayers will be dishing out $51.8 million Australian dollars for each medal that will be awarded at the 2000 games. Even more distressing, around the city and the nation, graft, greed, and corruption follow from the seductions and the spoils of hosting the games.

Even as money is diverted from arts institutions in the run up to the games, artists, draftspersons, and sculptors are enlisted to promote the games and the athletic ideal. Art, as Coubertin understood from the very beginning of the modern games, can be used to elevate sports and bodily discipline. Harking back to the early festival of the games in Greece, a festival that involved not only athletic contests but also artistic contests, Coubertin hailed art as the setting for the modern games. Every Olympic event since 1896 has involved new displays of public art and sculpture and a cultural Olympiad—a multitude of arts festivals and activities designed to promote the finest in artistic endeavor in the years leading up to the games.

Early in the century at the 1920 games in Paris a festival of the arts presented the sports ballet *Le train bleu,* a production of the Ballet Russe de Monte Carlo. Named for the famous blue train that took French vacationers south from Paris, *Le train bleu* brought together Jean Cocteau as set designer and Coco Chanel as the costumer. In 1998 dance choreographer Meryl Tankard presented a new performance, in anticipation of the Sydney games, entitled *Possessed.* Inspired by photographs from the 1936 games in Berlin, Tankard created a series of gymnastic movements that recall for the audience photographs of similar movements in the 1936 games. As the earlier work of Riefenstahl in photographing the 1936 Olympics was the epitome of a modernist aesthetic in service to a fascist state, this Tankard work is the epitome of a postmodern aesthetic, a pastiche of bodies, gestures, and cultural quotations in service to an emergent multicultural society. In addition to the Tankard piece, Olympic organizers in Australia orchestrated a series of four arts festivals in the four years leading up to the games. These festivals showcased Australia's indigenous artists and accentuated the nation's multicultural diversity. They were meant to project an Australia welcoming of all the different people who might attend the games.

That's because hundreds of thousands of tourists will pour into the Olympic city. To handle the crowds, thousands of volunteers are enlisted from around the country to augment the activities without even a promise of a free ticket or preferential seating at the games. Travel agencies package tours and print glossy brochures that advertise the lures of the host city around the world. At one and the same time they trumpet the tradition of the games and the modernity of the host city, promising tourists the most updated accommodations as they attend the events of this oldest of competitions. As the packagers of the nation beckon potential visitors, they use the seductive images of national icons, the language of Olympic ideals, the lure of national traditions.

As the eyes of the world turn more purposefully toward the Olympic city, issues of national identity take on new urgency and increasing visibility. This has certainly been the case in Australia in the last several years. One of the salient political controversies surrounding the games in Australia has to do with who will preside over the opening ceremony. Since Australia will not yet have become a republic by the time the 2000 games begin, protocol demands that

Queen Elizabeth, as Queen of Australia, open the event. Monarchists among the Australian citizens would see this as only fitting. But other Australians, probably the majority of them, would see the official role of the queen as a sign of Australia's continuing colonial status and its continuing dependence upon "the mother country." For many Australians this continuing relationship with England seems fundamentally anachronistic in light of the multicultural society that Australia has become, particularly since the Second World War. As it turns out, John Howard, the prime minister of Australia, seized the republican controversy of 1999 to secure his bid to open the games. Given the fact that Howard is an avowed monarchist, this was a supreme irony. He revoked his decision, however, in favor of the governor general (the queen's representative in Australia) after the republican referendum failed and his political opponents rebuked him for his duplicity.

Another political issue concerns racial politics in Australia. Aboriginal leaders have called for their people to boycott the games in protest against the stalled processes of reconciliation between indigenous and nonindigenous peoples, particularly in relation to land rights. The runner Cathy Freeman has distanced herself from a possible boycott, publicly stating her intentions to compete in the Sydney games. But Aboriginal spokespersons may try to use the games to put their case to the world. This would contravene the Olympic Security Plan, demanded by the IOC, which ensures "no disruptions" and no political meetings or protests in the vicinity of the games. In the past, countries have taken draconian measures to quell possible protests. In 1980 Moscow cleared the city of Jews; in 1982 the premier of Queensland gave the police state-of-emergency powers to delimit and control activities of Aborigines in the vicinity of the Commonwealth Games (Booth and Tatz 1994, 11). How these politics are played out at the games remains to be seen. But the times are uneasy.

How will the nation represent itself to the world? The people charged with producing the opening ceremony at the Sydney games have to find a spectacular way to capture the national spirit in the context of international pageantry. When the dancers and jugglers, the singers and twirlers run onto the Olympic field, when they gyrate in a spectacle of glitz, glimmer, and throbbing music, and when the athletes play their appointed part in the spectacle of international unity by marching solemnly into the stadium, what message about ethnic and racial identity will be beamed around the world, bouncing from satellite to satellite in an ideological dance of athletic politics?

EVERYDAY LIFE DURING THE GAMES

As the games approach, everyday life must adjust to the arrival of tourists, athletes, and the media. The festivals that mark the beginning and end of the Olympics capture the spirit of international celebration with all the energy, excitement, glitz (and problems) associated with such spectacles as the Mardi Gras, the Superbowl, the Grand Final, and political conventions. Crowds cheer. Bands play. Entertainers perform. Athletes march.

Well before the opening ceremony and after the closing ceremony, everyday life is disrupted. Work patterns have to be shifted, weddings and special events postponed, crops left untended. Traffic patterns must be reorganized so that people can get to work. Public transportation suddenly gains in popularity. Restaurants pack in provisions for full houses. Caterers cook the extra millions of meals. Launderers clean the linen and make up the rooms of the thousands of athletes housed in the Olympic Village. Train stations announce additional trains and new routes. Banners and emblems appear. Buskers congregate. Hawkers of souvenirs set up their displays. Scalpers bark out inflated ticket prices. Every kind of public space fills with crowds of people—eating and drinking, gossiping and storytelling, exchanging badges and emblems. They spill onto sidewalks and roadways, relax in parks, dance late into the nights, sleep in public spaces. The people of the games disrupt the normal patterns of communal life. Hotels, cabs, parking lots, and convenience stores now become so many necessities that move and service hordes of people. It's like the strange disruptions of an El Niño that comes every two years.

And in the Olympic Village? Coaches give their last minute instructions. Athletes rehearse their rituals for calming nerves. Rehearsing their routines, they close their eyes and "see" the event unfold before them. Runners-up swallow disappointment, smiling their good-natured smiles. Parents cross their fingers and yell their encouragement. Bodies give out. Legs swell. Hamstrings pull taut. Athletes take inelegant spills. Breaths are held.

All this activity promotes the "joyfulness" at the heart of Coubertin's vision. Since the unforgettable terror of Munich in 1972, however, an element of fear has invaded the atmosphere as well. Tourists and athletes move from venue to venue, watch an event or an arts performance, take a cab or eat a meal, always carrying with them a heightened awareness of the potential for violence.

The rush is on. And then it's gone.

AFTER THE GAMES

Life in the Olympic city returns to "normal." Parking spots suddenly materialize. Traffic flows more smoothly. Dancers in the opening and closing ceremonies place their photos into albums. Athletes pack up their gear and return home to a hero's welcome or to the humdrum of everyday life. Merchants tally their earnings. Tourists get on with the tour or return home exhausted but exhilarated.

The Afterlife of the Olympic Athlete

A few of the Olympic athletes become celebrities—sometimes just at home, sometimes abroad as well. Honors bring celebrity, sometimes instantly. And once an athlete turns into a "celebrity" the dance between star athlete and the media begins,

Celebrity

for there can be no celebrity without publicity, and publicity can become unsparing. Then, too, the media like particular types of athletes and like these stars to act and appear in particular ways. Celebrity also brings lucrative sponsorships; but sponsorship, in turn, creates its own expectations. Sponsors have to be satisfied. They have to be appeased. They have the power to withdraw sponsorship. And so the star athlete dances in the spotlight with wanna-be partners in the shadows. If honors pressage lucrative sponsorship deals, the promises are precarious. They can be bestowed, and withheld, almost on a whim. In all these ways, marketing takes over the athletic body, the personality, the name.

The fate of Australian swimmer Dawn Fraser is a case in point. Having won the one-hundred-meter freestyle in a record three Olympics and taken home four gold medals from the Tokyo games in 1964, just seven months after she broke her neck in a car crash that killed her mother, she is the most successful swimmer of all time. In the early years of the 1960s she was everyone's darling girl, as close as one could come in those days to an international celebrity. But her independent, antiauthoritarian spirit tested Olympic officials to the limit. On the evening before her triumphant return to Australia she and a dorm mate got up to some high jinks that would end her athletic career. In exuberant prank mode, the two broke curfew, escaping their watchers to snatch a Japanese flag from a display in front of the Imperial Palace as a souvenir. Upon her return home she was virtually ostracized for her actions. The Australian Olympic Committee suspended her from competition for ten years. Dawn Fraser's Olympic career came to an end because she failed to conform to expectations of proper Olympic behavior in star athletes.

The public giveth. And it taketh away.

In modern times the public's insatiable lust for "celebrities" has thrust the athletes into strange arenas. Their status as sports champions blurs into that of glamour magazine cover girls or inspirational spokespersons for any number of products: Nike, Wheaties, Uncle Toby's Health Foods, milk, meat, Nautilus sports equipment, Toyota high-performance vehicles—the list goes on. These days their muscular, rippled bodies are as likely to appear in aestheticized nude shots in trendy magazines like *Black and White.* Or their bodies are erotically displayed as "cheesecake" calendar guys and girls on boxes of breakfast food. These disciplined, athletic bodies have become the new benchmarks for youthful beauty. They mark out the cultural equation of physical power with sexual power (Hargreaves 1997).

We conclude this meditation on the everyday effects of the Olympic Games by recalling how the celebrity body shows up in the most prosaic of places—the calendar that marks off everyday time. In 1994 the first of the "Golden Girls of Sport" calendars appeared in Australia and the United Kingdom. Redolent of pinup calendars, the first Golden Girls was greeted with outrage from feminist groups and sports organizations alike. But today, at the turn of the millennium, the arguments about the exploitation of women's bodies seem curiously schoolmarmish and outdated. The Golden Girls have become an accepted feature of athletic celebrity. A new generation of postfeminist women actively promote their bodies as signifiers of freedom, happiness, and healthy sexuality. Sports organizations themselves design figure-enhancing uniforms intended to eroticize the sports body and swell the audience of television viewers. Sex sells; and sportswomen as well as men celebrate sexual display, with a privileged few making more money from their promotions than their performances.

Anna Kournikova, the goddess of center court, recently commented, "Ten years from now it won't be enough that we, as ladies, only play tennis. The public wants to see more. We are the possession of the public. They make us stars and let us earn money. In about ten years every woman tennis player will play topless" ("This Is What They Said" 1998, 18). This is the kind of quote that sports magazines adore. And this is the kind of quote that reveals the dynamic ways in which celebrity athleticism, cultural politics, commodity capitalism, and international nationalisms conjoin to make the Olympic Games a Rorschach test of athleticism and modernity in everyday life.

CHAPTER 15

No

Terrorism, "Killing Events," and Their Audience: Fear of Crime at the 2000 Olympics

Pre 9/11

JOHN TULLOCH

We all have our resilient images of terrorism at the Olympics. Some of us are old enough to have seen the television coverage of the Munich Olympics live. I remember the sombre, haunting images of stark concrete balconies in the Olympic village, of hooded Palestinian gunmen and white-shirted Israeli hostages, and over the images the voice of the well-known BBC commentator David Coleman adopting a new gravity (and acquiring an international currency) as he helped construct a new television genre of public terrorism. Prior to this event our images of "politics" intruding directly into international sports tended to be at the level of a few people invading the center court at Wimbledon. But this was the first major modern instance of "terrorism at the Olympics," and Coleman capitalized on it.

Then more recently, there were the Atlanta images: American swimming champion Janet Evans reeling away from a live interview on German television as a terrorist bomb exploded in a telephone box somewhere beyond the window behind her; and also the images accompanying the assumed terrorism behind the destruction of an airliner just out from New York. In this latter case we saw, again and again, computer simulations of a supposed ground-to-air rocket attack on the plane. In this case it was later shown that there was no terrorist attack at all; but in both these instances the media's initial construction of terrorism at the Atlanta Olympics was as a series of repeated images of what could not be seen—a rocket attack which never happened, a bomb explosion whose perpetrator was never discovered.

later

Perhaps this absence of representation is inevitable? Analyzing media images of the kidnapping and subsequent murder of Jamie Bolger in an English shopping mall—an event perhaps even more emotionally resonant than Olympics terrorism—Alison Young argues that "no explanation can ever soothe the intense anxiety that the event inspired. Thus all we are left with is a realization of the limits of representation, the words of pain and loss, and the narratives of blame" (Young 1996, 97). That issue in the media of a public killing event and the limits of representation in the Bolger case are emphasized by the fact that the technology (and point of view) of the image—in this case the shopping-mall video camera—is not designed to see killers and abductors, but rather to catch shoplifters. In place of a seen crime (the kidnapping), the television public was given repeated narratives of absent images (the video camera) and faulty memory (the eyewitnesses who initially "saw" a young boy with his family or friends).

Terrorist acts at the Olympic Games, as reported in the media, are part of a genre of "big killing" television events, and each has its legacy of images that can haunt us. These are narratives of blame where crazed or fanatical people—adults armed with the latest technology of weaponry (or perhaps worse, young children armed with whatever comes to hand on the railway line or riverbank)—are "seen" to shoot, blow up, beat and maim an "innocent public." Seldom, of course, are these killings actually seen by the camera, even when they really happen (unlike the airliner simulations). In other instances of mass public killing, we are left to visualize for ourselves (via vivid oral testimony) the young crazed man who gunned down so many people in so few seconds in the tourist café at Port Arthur, or the disturbed man who massacred young children in a Dunblane elementary school while they were exercising their fragile, growing bodies.

These actions are represented as all the more fearful and reprehensible because they burst unexpectedly and without warning into the routine lives of people going about their daily business: the Israeli weight lifters competing at the Munich Olympics; people in streets, shopping malls, and offices (Melbourne's Hoddle Street massacre on a train line, the Bolger case in Britain, Sydney's Strathfield shopping mall massacre, and the Oklahoma City bombing); children doing physical education in the school hall at Dunblane, Scotland, while their professional, middle-class parents were starting their workday as travel agents, lawyers, or university lecturers; tourists buying souvenirs of the heritage penal colony site at Port Arthur, Tasmania. All of these were events that resulted in symptomatic media constructions of big killings as "unrepresentable, unthinkable, unimaginable."

Often—as in the Atlanta Olympic Games example—the technologies of the image (the live interview; the computer simulations) simply draw attention, as Young says, to the limits, the breaching, of representation (1996). Rather than "see" the Atlanta event or the perpetrator, we are treated to a repeated and ritualized proliferation of media images of terrorist breaching of cultural limits. It is this repetition that initially replaces any image (or secure explanation) of the moment and meaning of the crime. We see the images again and again, but seldom the criminal act itself. Perhaps the lasting mythological status of the Munich terror-ist images does not mainly depend on the fact that the criminals were caught and killed. Rather, the lasting resonance may depend more on the fact that the images were caught and then instantly converted into an appropriate (manage-able) television genre by the suitably modulated voice of a well-known sports com-mentator. Thus the proliferation was closed off, the certainty of representation contained rather than breached.

All of these are terrifying moments, some of them graphically conveyed and hauntingly remembered. But if we stay at the level of media images only, we will not go very far in understanding how graphically they mean things in our var-ious individual lives. If the media images convey the unrepresentable and unthink-able, how are they "thought" by the public? If part of the shock of the image is conveyed by the sudden, unimaginable eruption of aggression into daily routines, we need to get back into people's daily lives to find out what they mean there.

To illustrate what these things mean in people's daily lives, let us turn from graphic media images to an equally graphic account by a group of older people: first about their fear of crime generally and then particularly about big killing events like the Munich shooting, the Atlanta terrorist bombing, and the Dunblane or Port Arthur massacres. We will see here how deeply people may respond to media images of these events and how they weave these events into a whole world of other anxieties.

A team of researchers from the Centre for Cultural Risk at Charles Sturt Uni-versity conducted interviews about these events as a part of a study of fear of crime (including big killing events) with two hundred people (Tulloch et al. 1998). I was interested in examining the way in which these shocking media events impacted on people's own temporal biographies—on their changing sense of them-selves and of the world around them. The first interview I will quote was recorded in Bathurst, New South Wales, with people over the age of sixty. Bathurst (two hundred kilometers west of Sydney) is Australia's earliest settled inland town, but it is also (with a population of thirty thousand) still perceived very much as a rural place by its inhabitants—with many of the traditional Australian "city versus country" implications that this involves. But the mythical implication of city/country difference is changing.

I begin by quoting a lengthy extract from this interview to illustrate the deeply felt emotion and its context, as these older people respond to questions about fear of crime and the various crime epidemics which they feel surround them, including terrorism. We will see that Olympic terrorism means to these people just one of a whole world picture of growing fears.

> *Joan:* I will say that one thing that crime has done for me is the fear of AIDS. Now you always had a fear of rape, though it wasn't a thing you went to bed and slept and ate and breathed and died with, but when I'm on my own now I make sure that I've got hair spray or something beside me because I am *petrified* of AIDS, because I think that that is a death sentence.

      Bob: It's the same when you're traveling on suburban trains, isn't it?

    Joan: Oh, suburban trains now are just a nightmare. I'm down in Sydney regularly every month, and you find you're [looking round] like this—who's sitting this side of me, who's sitting that side of me. My sister was not only attacked in the train, but this girl went berserk and bruised her everywhere. There was also a man—he had just been clawed, with blood pouring, and not one person came to his assistance. No one is game to move to help anybody because you don't know if you'll be jabbed with a needle. This is *now*, and if this same fear that I and my family have in Sydney reaches out into Bathurst, heaven help us.

     Ron: Yeah, and if there's a noise of a night, I have a club handy, and I'll get up at the ready and go around and check the doors upstairs. I've got a plan, you know.

Interviewer: Do you think television has contributed to your fear?

     Ron: No, it was just the break-in. Just that the people broke in, and up until then we were sort of quite blasé, weren't we?

   Anne: Yes, very.

     Ron: We'd got nothing, we thought that nobody . . .

   Anne: You think that nothing will happen to you. The thing I do most now is always take the phone with me to bed, so that if I'm there by myself and I hear a noise I can either ring the police or ring my son Peter. It's right beside us.

    John: You know, in a full lifetime span, and that's a fair time for me, the thing that shifted it without doubt is drugs. Because I think that even criminals behaved in some sort of a human manner twenty or thirty years ago if they broke in. But I've got the feeling now that if a person's under the influence of drugs, he's just an impossible animal to deal with. He could be that savage he could kill you in a second because he's under the influence of drugs. Now, I've had no experience with drugs directly or anyone under drugs, but television has taught me that people under the influence of drugs that break into your house are just maniacs . . . and that's my big fear. . . . I've learnt that in later life, since the drug situation came in, and with television.

Interviewer: Do others share that sort of view?

 General: Yes, it's a problem, yes.

     Jan: And television does make you aware of it. You can read a newspaper, but it's just you reading that section. But when it's images . . .

    Joan: Where it's TV images . . .

    John: Yes.

     Jan: . . . that's what reinforces it.

 General: Yes. Absolutely.

Interviewer: Do you think rural communities are relatively drug free?

 General: No!

    Pam: Not where a parent of a child is a drug addict. [A woman I know] said it takes her about five minutes in any street she likes to name in Bathurst to get drugs—and she's a very respectable person in Bathurst. Their daughter was at school with my daughter. Five minutes, she said.

Interviewer: Well, let's move the subject slightly and think about some of the bigger news events—you know, Port Arthur, Dunblane, the Atlanta bombing, those sorts of things. If you watch those sorts of reports on television, how does that make you feel?

Pam: It just makes you feel that you're not insulated, that that could happen here.

Interviewer: Do you think that it changes anything over the longer term for you, or is it just an isolated incident?

General: No, it changes things for me, changes your thinking for the rest of your life.

John: I think it makes you fearful.

Joan: I found that Dunblane and Port Arthur—but every bit as much the Strathfield Plaza [massacre]—I found I couldn't go in a shopping center, and I really do go to Sydney a lot, and like in Westfield shopping center I was just petrified. I'm looking up and down escalators thinking what's this person . . . ? And yet you have to go and do that shopping. It had a tremendous impact.

Interviewer: Do you talk about these big killing events a lot?

General: Oh yes.

Interviewer: And what kinds of things are they saying to you? Is it just a one off, or . . . ?

Ron: No, no, I think everyone is really frightened of those sort of events. Even the children, I think, take it in as being absolutely terrifying. I'm sure they do . . .

Interviewer: Well, staying with the big events, we've got the Olympics coming up, which is a joyous occasion, a wonderful thing for Sydney and Australia. Do you think that's going to make you . . . ?

Anne: I believe China or somewhere else should have it.

General: Yeah (laughter).

Jan: I'm not happy about it. . . . I get to think of Munich!

General: Yes.

Joan: Atlanta.

Jan: And I know this idea "this can't happen here." And for a long time I guess I was the ostrich—that rural upbringing, rural living—you know, "these things just don't happen here, don't happen in Australia." *No one* can tell me that there won't be another Port Arthur, that there won't be a scare in the Olympic games. No, I wish they weren't coming.

Pam: To be quite honest, while they're on I wouldn't even contemplate going to Sydney.

Anne: I wouldn't either.

Jan: No, I feel like that, too.

Interviewer: Is that right?

Joan: And so are Sydney people fearful. My family live in Sydney, and they're fearful.

Interviewer: And that's because of Atlanta and Munich, etc.?

General: Yes.

There is plenty of graphic imagery in this conversation, just as in the media itself. But here the imagery is built into a changing biographical and social narrative. Through this emphasis on the audience rather than on the media images of big killing events on television, we become aware of the way in which our perception of potential crime or terrorism at the Sydney 2000 Olympics is inevitably embedded in our own much more routine daily knowledge, experiences, and anxieties. We found from talking to people (particularly older people, but to some extent parents of teenagers, too) in the Olympic city of Sydney and its environs that "other" Sydneys are increasingly added in people's minds to the opera house logos on "Sydney-2000" T-shirts. And these other Sydneys are linked in as "landscapes of fear" in both media and everyday life representations.

Older people derive—both from their own experience (e.g., in this interview, from break-ins), from family and friends' narratives (about attacks on Sydney trains, about the availability of street drugs "in five minutes," about their fears of Olympics terrorism), and from television (the drug economy, home invasions, etc.)—a set of understandings about how they believe the world of Sydney works. For example, older people quite generally have a perception of the threat to them from the "new immigrant" economies of drugs, prostitution, and Asian gang crime, and also from what they see as the "young people's" economy, as structural unemployment leads to drugs and home invasions. Asians and young people become an other which can make them very fearful indeed, and their fear of Olympics terrorism is linked to this as another big fear. In contrast, young people themselves, as we will see, tend to see the Olympics leading to an increase in the kind of petty crime which they or their friends routinely experience, like theft, mugging, and harassment in particular places and times.

It is these very particular landscapes of fear in Sydney which have begun to weaken among older people the earlier "lucky country" perception and the "violent crime doesn't happen to us in Australia" narratives. In this context of local landscapes of fear, big killing media events have prepared many (particularly older) people for the possibility of terrorism at the Sydney Olympics.

Of course, even within one age group, different situational circumstances will help inflect this fear in particular ways. Take Tom for instance. Tom had been a chemical engineer and an executive in a large company until retrenched. His wife is a social worker who worries about the government's new policy of leaving psychiatric patients out in the community. Tom (still living in an affluent beach suburb of Sydney) combines all of these experiences and perceptions in his own fear about Olympics and other terrorism.

He began our long interview discussion by focusing on media reports of deliberate chemical poisoning of foodstuffs in Japan and Australia: "You get more people in society who become disenfranchised in the sense of not having access to money or any of the pleasures of life. Some of these people may well be sufficiently highly trained to cook up the equivalent of a botulism." As a retrenched worker himself, Tom felt that much of this economic formula of disenfranchisement comes from America, along with the downsizing business practices from there. But he was aware that other things—like terrorism—could spread from the United

States, too. As a chemical engineer, he has long been amazed at the "killing inefficiency" of terrorism. He knows how easy it would be to poison millions by introducing botulism into Sydney's water supply. And through his wife he is aware of more "unhinged" people now wandering around the streets of Sydney. So, he said, the Olympics "will make Sydney more dangerous because of what has happened in Atlanta. . . . It's a draw card for the extremists. . . . It is so easy to make a bomb."

Similarly, a group of parents (of teenagers) that we interviewed in Sydney also emphasized the recent food/chemical poisonings. One female in this group said she would not go to the Olympics because of the increased risk; and one of the males agreed that he would not go to a large, exposed place like the Olympic stadium and its surrounds because of his fear of acts of terrorism and violence: "I think possibly the media is going to enhance that. Why do people do those sorts of things in the first place—it's to get coverage. And of course when the whole world is focused on Sydney in 2000, well, what a golden opportunity! I mean, every city that hosts the Olympics must go through exactly that and no matter what they do as far as security is concerned, people will succeed. There'll be crazy people who will slip through the loop and pull the trigger—whatever that trigger may be. . . . It's a dangerous situation, and it's dangerous because the media will cover it." We found that this view that the media encourage terrorism at the Olympics was part of a wider fear—especially prevalent among the retired, older people (often grandparents) whom we interviewed. This broader fear was that the conjunction of new immigrant crime (drugs, etc.), of increasing structural unemployment among the young, and of increasing TV violence was leading to a much meaner world, stretching from home invasion to big killing and terrorist events.

Many older people have, in other words, constructed a crime-wave landscape. They picture parts of Sydney being "infected" by Asian (and/or American) style crime. This urban environment increasingly threatens the once relatively innocent suburban and country areas. The memory that "once I never ever locked my door when I went out" has become a recurrent trope in this narrative of a golden past. It is within this construction of new and very specific landscapes of fear in people's daily biographies that any understanding of the "meaning" of crime and terrorism at the Sydney 2000 Olympic Games needs to be embedded.

As we will see, this crime-wave understanding of the Sydney Olympics is less common in younger people—and, of course, it is not shared by all older people either. To get a sense of these differences, we need to attend to "situated stories."

Situated Stories: The Sydney Olympics

Ang writes, "the contemporary cultural condition—postcolonial, postindustrial, postmodern, postcommunist—forms the historical backdrop for the urgency of rethinking the significance of ethnography, away from its status as realist knowledge in the direction of its quality as a form of storytelling, as narrative. This does not mean that descriptions cease to be more or less true; criteria such as accurate data gathering and careful inference making remain applicable" (1996, 75). To explore further the meanings of Olympics terrorism and other big killing events in people's daily lives, let us look more closely at the narratives people tell. Following Ang, this will focus on "storytelling, as narrative"; and having begun with older people, I will now look at the stories of one mother and then teenagers from very different backgrounds.

My choice of these particular stories prompts three theoretical observations before proceeding. First, like Ang, who asks the question, "[W]hat kind of representational order . . . should [we] establish in our stories about media consumption?" (1996, 77), I recognize that it is important for researchers to be reflexive about their own (theoretical and methodological) stories. My overt methodological ordering device is a cultural studies one—foregrounding in my choice of storytellers' issues of gender, age, sexual preference, and ethnicity. Secondly, this is, nevertheless, also a choice based on the actual narratives of fearful "lay" storytellers, rather than one focused simply on my "expert" analysis of texts. Thirdly, I further agree with Ang that their stories—and our stories, too—can never be simply in conditions of their own making. I take seriously Ang's point that our stories must "enter the uneven, power-laden field of social discourse" (1996, 76). A particularly powerful social discourse when we (researchers, the media, our respondents) talk about terrorism, the media, and the Olympics is the issue of TV violence. The TV-violence debate has been both one of the longer lasting and one of the more socially pervasive of the moral frames within which the media and contemporary cultures have been conceived (Alasuutari forthcoming).

So, rather than attempt either a textualist account (for example, of recent Sydney newspapers predicting a link between Asian drug gangs and Olympics terrorism) or an objectivist account (of how many of this or that public thought this or that about terrorism at the Olympics), this chapter tells situated stories (in relation to gender, age, sexual preference, and ethnicity), particularly in the context of the social discourse of TV violence. But in doing so, it studies how "terrorism, television, and violence" get framed in stories of "lay knowledgeability" (Wynne 1996) rather than the narratives of its traditional, expert (often quantitative) researchers.

VIOLENCE AND PLEASURE: ROB AT THE COMPUTER AND AT THE CROSS

Rob is a sixteen year old who lives with his mother, a lawyer, and his young sister in an inner-west suburb of Sydney (not far in fact from the future Olympic Games site at Homebush). Previously, they lived on the South Coast where Rob's mother worked for a neighborhood community center.

At first glance, Rob seems a likely candidate for all those experts' negative accounts about young males, television, computer games, and violence, accounts with which we are familiar. Asked, for example, about his media role models, Rob said that he liked Arnold Schwarzenegger's films for "the violence I guess. I have seen basically every one of his movies. . . . I like the story line of the violence. . . . It's the way people get hurt. Seeing people in pain. That's fun." Rob also enjoys playing violent computer games: "*Diablo, Doom, Quake,* different war games like *Command and Conquer.* Just different games, different degrees of violence." Moving on from his discussion of Schwarzenegger movies to his favorite television series, *Good Guys, Bad Guys,* Rob said that he prefers this series because good guys don't always win. Instead of happy endings in cop shows he "would rather see a dramatic ending—like the good guys getting hurt at the end. Adds more spirit to it."

For Rob, violent shows are pleasurable, especially when the good guys are vanquished: "Yeah, it's the level of violence. I like watching violent shows . . . It's the action scenes, and whether somebody gets hurt . . . You see somebody get shot— it's good when a cop gets killed because you know it's one for the bad guys, finally . . . It's the same with computer games, like *Command and Conquer.* It's a war game where you can either be the good guys or the bad guys. I always like to be the bad guys so that I can beat the good guys." Olympics terrorists are bad guys, so where will Rob stand on this issue? To understand that, we need to dig a bit deeper into Rob's use of violent crime.

Rob's pleasure in violence is, of course, gendered and not unexpected. He is, in fact, exactly the kind of male teenager, playing with violent computer games, about whom many parents and older people that we interviewed most worried. However, if we look at the various circuits of meaning (not just television and computer games) that Rob draws on in relation to his different emotions and fears, at his conceptual strategies for managing them, and at the various images, rhetorics, and narratives that he tests out against his experience, Rob appears in a much less macho guise.

This is evident, first of all, in not only what he said about his enjoyment of computer games ("I would not say that it reflects on the personality. I'm not a violent person. It doesn't really influence me"), but also *how* he talked about his "fun" in the violence of Schwarzenegger movies. Rob finds his fun in the *unreality* of the violence: "That's why maybe it could be fun. It doesn't seem real. . . . Like if somebody was in pain on the ground I wouldn't know what to do. But people on TV, because they are actors, they mightn't have the experience about what pain's like. It might seem funny. I just like seeing the good guy lose for once."

When we hear Rob say, with real feeling, that he would not be able to handle real-life pain on the ground in front of him, we believe him. And part of his fun in violence is clearly a narrative one: he is sick and tired of the clichéd too-pure hero always winning.

Rob's fear of real-life violence is also evident in his use of the media for strategies he might use when he goes to risky places. He said that media coverage of certain problem areas that he occasionally visits does make him fearful: "Kings Cross—sometimes they talk about that and occasionally I go there to see friends or something. I worry about people there. Like you get bad news on a certain area, when you go there you worry about what's going to happen to you. . . . Occasionally I hear something about a stabbing or a mugging. I walk down the street with nice clothes on, good target. I get worried about that." Like older people, then, Rob has his Sydney landscapes of fear. Because of media influence, he said that he would never go to Cabramatta, an outer-city suburb of Sydney known for its Vietnamese population and its crime: "Different gangs or drugs. See images of lots of syringes. Just the images and interviews about it." Rob does have a few fears about his own inner-west Sydney suburb (the bank across the road has been held up, and there was a killing at the local ice rink), but overall, he said, this area "doesn't really worry me a lot. Sometimes the police are there. I know that if anything goes wrong, there is always somebody there to help me." In contrast, he has only once seen a policeman at Kings Cross and would not go there alone, even in the daytime.

On the other hand, sometimes the media can offer useful strategies, Rob believes: "When they interview a guy . . . on TV about how he mugs people, at least [you hear] different strategies, so if somebody actually came up to me and tried to mug me . . . [I know] things like walk, side swipe and duck easily, like different strategies, how you approach them." Having some strategies, and looking around himself all the time, gives Rob the confidence to walk home from parties in Canterbury (inner-west Sydney) at one o'clock in the morning: "If the media report they are putting more police on the beat, you feel a bit more secure. . . . So I'm still walking alone at night, whereas that sometimes used to get me a bit worried."

This mix of lay and media knowledge gives him a geography of places to avoid. Some of this map comes from the media, and it is often a map of the (sexual and racial) "other": Kings Cross (Sydney's red-light area), Cabramatta, Redfern (an inner-city suburb with a predominantly Aboriginal community). But some of the map also comes from local talk and gossip: "Certain areas in Sydney—Hyde Park. I have heard people say you don't go there at night." If to our interviewer, Nicky, Hyde Park "is beautiful at night . . . beautiful fairy lights—it looks magical," Rob has more realistic local knowledge. Staying at the Whitlam Square YMCA in Sydney recently, Rob was warned by "students who lived in the area" not to walk in Hyde Park at night.

He argued that the media do not seriously represent issues of safety in public city places: "You hear bits and pieces, but there is no real focus that I know of. You don't hear them talking about certain open areas like Hyde Park—I've never heard that one on the news. The only way I hear about it is that people told me not to go there at night." Rob feels that in this place (Hyde Park) and places like it there will be an increase in crime in Sydney during the Olympics, because "we will have more people in the city and therefore more opportunities for criminals or whoever to strike—muggings. More people who do not know the area, do not know where not to go at certain times. . . . Some might go to Hyde Park at night and say, 'Nice park.' "

Clearly, Rob draws on both media and local talk to construct his map of which parts of the city to avoid, the strategies to adopt, and so on. Consequently, his response to crime at the Sydney Olympics is entirely situated. Unlike many of our older respondents, he doesn't worry about terrorism at the Olympics at all, because "that wouldn't happen in Australia." In this respect Rob is fairly typical of the other male teenagers whom we interviewed, who have a far more localized and "anthropological" knowledge of specific subgroups that might harm them (for example, "Home Boys" on trains at night and at specific North Shore and Outer West stations) than their parents and elders do. Teenagers generally feel less worried by the "global wave" theory which many older people extended to Olympic terrorism.

As we can see from his earlier comment about feeling safer personally where police are on the beat, and from his localized knowledge of landscapes of fear, like Hyde Park in Sydney, Rob's response to crime at the Olympics is best understood *not* in terms of his preference for violent computer games, his liking for Schwarzenegger movies, or his preference for "bad guy" winning, but in terms of his own, very particular experiential landscape. Even his response to the question, "What do you think could actually be done to make public spaces more safe and carefree where people could actually enjoy themselves day and night during the Olympics?" is strongly embedded in the situated understandings of this inner-city sixteen-year-old Sydney boy: "You could get more beat police, police who walk the streets. But there is nothing you can really do about it. You can only warn people, but that's hard to do with tourists."

A LESBIAN MUM AND ONE BLACK MAN: "THERE'S NO SAFETY ANYWHERE, ANYTIME"

Julie has encountered violence all her life. Her communist father philosophized anarchy when she was a child, but when he was drunk he beat her "to the wall and back." Later, as a community group protester on the steps of Parliament House, Canberra, Julie met other "rogue-males," on one occasion physically swinging away at an out-of-control policeman who had seriously injured one of her smaller female companions. Nowadays, she is prepared to move through the trains at night to sit and talk with nervous women passengers. Her female partner has boxed, her teenage daughter has more than once attacked males who were physically assaulting her, and together this group of women has recently stood up to a group of men planning to rob a drunken woman on the train. Overall, people who encounter her know, Julie says, "Don't mess with me."

One of Julie's most formative experiences as a woman in this world of violence was in her early twenties when she joined a feminist discussion group. Here she learned "there is no safety anywhere, anytime, so you may as well live your life and not let the fear control you." Since then, she feels, she has been able to reassess the violence that she knows so well: "I know about violence, it can't scare me.... For me it has taken ... a lot of ingrained fear that I had to learn about in order to get past it so I could say 'I will never fear again.' ... Mine was a long term project to get there. But that feeling at the end ... is very real for me."

Yet, despite this long-term biographical project, Julie is very aware of the power of the media to reduce her feeling of self control. She will not, for instance, watch films with stalking themes because she feels that they disempower her psychologically. And she feels that her experience of American "big killing" event media has been negative in distancing her from black people, despite her best intentions and awareness of their oppression.

This revealed itself very clearly on an occasion when she was a tourist in the United States, walking through the unfamiliar landscape of Seattle at night. She said that as she did so, she could not get out of her head the portrayals of American race violence and death that she had seen on television: "I was very conscious that it had gone into my head. So when I was walking through an area that had a lot of black people in it I was much more conscious of the fear then." Her ensuing encounter with a black pedestrian on those streets indicates that, despite her public confidence on Australian trains, the issue of the media, big killing events, and one's sense of fear have to be renegotiated in each new, fine-grained, localized experience:

> A black man was walking towards me. He had a piece of paper wrapping up something in his hand. As he got fairly close to me he crumpled it up and threw it at my feet. He was directing it at my feet, at the ground right in front of me. I didn't look at him but I stepped around it, sort of slightly bowed my head in his direction, and kept him in sight as I walked past him. I didn't turn my back on him until I knew he was past me, and continuing on his way; and then I turned around and kept walking. At this point I brought my eyes up again to assess the crowd around me, and the next black man, who was maybe twenty feet behind the first one, looked at me and met my eyes and smiled. . . . I have no idea how my reaction was perceived by either man. It was a completely instant reaction. . . . I was in a way acknowledging the first man's presence by half-nodding my head, stepping around the paper. . . . It was an unusual situation. I didn't know the ground rules. I was very conscious of the media's portrayal of race violence, and I didn't *know* how much of it was true, how much wasn't. . . . My conditioning was a very, very big factor there. . . . And the second man's smile—I was trying to read so much into two seconds. But I would say I saw a slight humor in it; I would say I saw a slight appreciation of my tactics; I would say I saw a slight reassurance, "I'm not going to do the same thing." Who knows how much of that was real, but I looked up, and I met his eye, and he smiled, and I gave a half-smile, and I nodded again, and kept going—and thought, "Whew, calm down now."

This particular narrative is a very clear example of the situated nature of media effects—how, in this case, media discourses (about racial violence in the United States), reflexive thinking (Julie's own use of memory and experience to assess the actual situation), and nonverbal circuits of communication like body language and facial expression are all woven together in dealing both behaviorally and emotionally with fear.

Equally, big killing events like the Atlanta terrorism and the Port Arthur massacre are negotiated, contained, and controlled in terms of Julie's deeply held feminist values and experience:

> The terrorism at the Atlanta Olympics and those other things didn't really make me more fearful. Particularly the Port Arthur one made me stop and think a lot, but once again it was like "I can't let the fear control me because that would be ridiculous." We talked a lot amongst the female staff here at work; you know that we could be sitting here at our desks right at this minute having a normal conversation and someone could walk in with a gun—what are we going to do? Flip out about it? No, you get on with it. Some people in the office were freaked out after the Strathfield shooting [in an inner-city Sydney shopping mall] because it was much closer to home. You can think of Port Arthur as being down there [in Tasmania], it's a tourist resort, you don't go there every day. But the Strathfield shopping center you go to every day. . . . So people were more worried about that. . . . With me it was more like a looking around and thinking, "Who could do it? It could happen right now." It was more like a testing out of my feelings about the situation. But it wasn't that all of a sudden I became too scared to go to Strathfield shopping center. . . . It created a lot of discussion, some of the other women were expressing fear, usually I provided a reality check. . . . It's partly my cynicism—I know there's violence out there all the time.

Providing a "reality check" is also what Julie offers to scared women traveling alone on the trains at night. This is the context—and also her cynicism about "rogue-male" policemen who are not even in control of themselves, let alone other people's security—of her response to the question about terrorism at the Sydney Olympics: "I think there is a potential for people wanting to make statements about things—as in the Atlanta Olympics terrorism. I think those big international events attract that sort of attention. Whether it will happen or not is another matter. Whether security can do anything about it or not is another matter. . . . I suppose if you had really top-notch security people who really knew what they were doing they might be able to see an event happening and nip it in the bud. . . . But I'm not sure you could say there would be safety anyway. My attitude is there is no safety anywhere, anytime."

In this, Julie's response is quite similar to the general anxieties, among parents and older people, that I quoted earlier about the media encouraging extremists at the Sydney Olympics. Looking at Julie individually, however, we can also see how her particular encoding philosophy ("there is no safety anywhere, anytime") makes this interpretation specific to her. She has a particular set of subjectivities as a woman. This is not, as we have seen, a recipe for (female) fear, passivity, and inaction, whether on the train at night or at the Olympics; just as Rob's (male) love of violent movies is not a clue to his attitude to crime at the Olympics.

BLACK BOYCOTTERS: THE OLYMPICS
AND VIOLENCE AT REDFERN

Our earlier teenage narrative was that of an inner-city, middle-class white boy who included Redfern among his landscapes of fear. How would a group of inner-city Aboriginal and Pacific Islander students who came from "near Redfern" respond to our same questions about violence, crime, and the Sydney Olympics? Violence—routine threat, harassment, or actual assault—is almost a daily ritual for many young Aboriginal Australians. At the same time, TV violence—consisting of good cops chasing bad guys—is also a daily media event for them.

Terrorism is one familiar social discourse among Aboriginal Australians about the Olympics; but another is boycotts, especially by the black nations. Extremes of opinion in Australia around the current conservative Australian government's policy on native Aboriginal title to land, or around the racist politics of Pauline Hanson's new One Nation party, have already led to Aboriginal threats to boycott the Sydney Olympics. We found these two social discourses—about violence and about boycotts—come together in the stories of one group of mainly Aboriginal students with whom we talked.

It is not just Rob who worries about Redfern. This inner-city Sydney suburb (together with Cabramatta, and certain western suburbs, localities like Mt. Druitt as well as the Sydney red-light district of Kings Cross) composes the media's landscape of fear in relation to this Olympic city. Indeed, our quantitative survey of respondents in two Australian states (New South Wales and Tasmania) indicated that these same Sydney localities are the most feared places in Australia.

Our teenagers near Redfern, however, challenged a particular part of that map of fear, blaming media stereotyping of "one particular race. . . . There's a lot of drugs here but there's a lot of other suburbs. Like Cabramatta—it's not in the media as Redfern is." Other comments were as follows: "And all those other areas are worse than Redfern." "There is drugs there." "Not all the people in Redfern are dogs, like alcoholics." "It's not like people say it is in the media." "They say all the bad points, they don't say the good points." "Redfern's a real strong black community, like they're all helping each other out and that. . . . Besides the drugs and stuff, everybody sticks together. . . . You don't get very many black communities ever like that. There might be drug addicts and that, but there's Aboriginals in Redfern that work hard just as much as other people do." These students are not naively idealistic about Redfern, and they are made fearful by TV violence.

"On television they just talk about murders and that's it." The teenagers commented on this: "I get scared when I watch *Australia's Most Wanted* when I'm walking about by myself. That's scary, eh. . . . There's heaps of deviates about." "Yes there's a lot of devos, men . . . who are in late night cars and when they see girls sitting there by themselves they stop." But these teenagers don't think that the many other urban environments where these things happen attract the same image that Redfern does, and one student said that Redfern even got shown in a bad light on the news in America. These students said, "We know what Redfern's like because we come out of there." But the bad media images stop other people from coming there. One Aboriginal girl noted that if you are black and live near this suburban area (she is from Waterloo), even well-meaning people ask if you are from Redfern. These teenagers have plenty of fears of crime—"A junkie coming up like to get money trying to stab me with a needle"—but in their view the local economic reality underpinning drugs is not covered in the media.

Whereas the middle-class Rob welcomed police on the beat in his area, the Aboriginal/Islander group of teenagers felt that much of the risk to them came *from* the police. They had direct experience of police. One boy said, "When the police pick you up they're all racist." A girl interjected, "With media they try to make out that police are really caring." A boy added, "Real heroes!" A girl said that she heard a policeman say to a neighbor, "Get inside you black slut, you're nothing, you're scum." Two of the students said that they had been assaulted by the police. A girl recalled how her older uncle was choked in jail by a police officer. She said that her uncle was vomiting blood and had red marks around his neck. They argued that none of this is reported in the media: "They don't show the things that we go through." "They show like this court case about murder but they don't show a case about three Aboriginal boys getting threatened by police. But in the media they show like this happened *to* police." Like Rob and Julie, but even more negatively, they are deeply suspicious of "heroic white male" police images on television. The media bias against them affects their behavior, they believe. Teenagers on the streets will retaliate against the police by throwing bricks at cars. "It happens, now, today." Like the older people, but in a very different way, these teenagers emphasize the *now* of their local knowledge.

It is in this relationship between situated local knowledge and mass media context that these students will respond to questions about big killing events on television, such as the Atlanta Olympics terrorism or the Port Arthur massacre. Symptomatically, it was not Atlanta or Dunblane which this group chose to comment on, but Port Arthur in Tasmania, a state known deeply (regarded angrily?) in this community for its genocide of the Aboriginal people. Via this choice of Port Arthur, these teenagers would remember a very different historical tale.

An Aboriginal girl in the group immediately responded to the big killing TV question: "You know the Port Arthur massacre? See how that was all big, and all in the media and that. Well, see there's things like the Myall Creek massacre, the Oyster Bay massacre [both sites of past mass killings of Aboriginal people in Tasmania]; they're all big massacres but they happened to Aboriginal people and so they don't do those in the media." Overall, the big killing reports neither affect them nor change anything for them. They said there is little talk about them after a couple of days, though the Aboriginal students said that their parents do tend to contextualize them in terms of their own history—and one of the boys humorously said that they are planning their own terrorism: blowing up Redfern police station. But this joke became more serious as the students were asked about the Sydney Olympics.

When asked specifically about potential crime and terrorism at the Sydney Olympics, all of the groups of teenagers with whom we talked (whether in city or rural areas) tended to deny that there will be any terrorism but suggested that there will be a lot more petty crime and mugging because of "all those loaded people from overseas." While agreeing with this, however, the teenagers from near Redfern gave it their own symptomatic spin: "All the rich people coming here from Asia, from Japan, they'll be robbed." But there is a different sense here of these Asians not as others (or tourists who "can't be told" about Hyde Park, in Rob's account) but as brothers. The group went on to talk about bomb threats and potential Olympic boycotts (from South Africans, from Canadian Native Americans, and from Australian Aboriginal people) "because of the way they've been treating the black fellas and the Asians . . . because of all Pauline Hanson's stuff."

The city of Sydney is a different place for Rob, for Julie, and for these teenagers near Redfern. So, too, are their perceptions and stories of terrorism, crime, and the Sydney Olympics different.

Conclusion

This chapter opened with comments about the media's limits of representation in relation to big killing events. Theorists of the postmodern would take this further, arguing that the postmodern condition itself is one of social and representational fragmentation. Apparently random violence and crime within national and social communities, perpetual fear and fragmentation, and the media's limits of representation, are all part of a perceived maelstrom of social melancholy and cynicism.

Osborne goes as far as to suggest that criminality itself has become the focus of the media's emphasis, in the absence of any sense of the "truth" of representation: "What makes criminality the perfect metaphor for post-modernism is precisely the way that media narratives encode crime and disorder as the representations of fragmentation rendered coherent" (1995, 27–28). In a situation where both the moral and representational orders are breached, the "obsessive . . . and hysterical replaying of the possibility of being a victim and staving it off" becomes the central way through which the media institutionalize (and reorder) the postmodern condition (Osborne 1995, 29). In this context, it can be argued that media terrorism and other big killing events are one of a number of crime genres through which the conditions of postmodern fragmentation are rehearsed, played, and repeated, over and over again.

But it is clear, from the case studies of this chapter, that people do find ways to represent and understand acts of terror—we all, as Julie put it, have our "long term project to get there." But people do this in very different ways according to their gender, sexual preference, age, ethnicity, and socioeconomic background. Moreover, they do so in multiple ways, drawing on different aspects of their social, environmental, and biographical identities. Thus we might further argue that these multiple representations are themselves part of the wider postmodern condition, composed of a vast range of local, fragmented, and partial "micro-narratives."

It is for this reason that (in the "post-" situation, as Ang describes it in our earlier quotation) there is an urgent need for an ethnography of storytelling. An important feature of this storytelling is to expose the relationship between people's individual (but situated) long-term projects and the media's "hysterical replaying of the possibility of becoming a victim." The stories I have told—of Julie, Rob, the near Redfern teenagers, and the Bathurst seniors—are situated stories of this kind. It is their localized micro-narratives which tell us what Olympics terrorism means in different Australian landscapes of fear.

PART FOUR

POLITICS AT

THE GAMES

The Olympic Branding of Aborigines: The 2000 Olympic Games and Australia's Indigenous Peoples

DARREN J. GODWELL

Within the politics of Australian indigenous affairs Murrandoo Yanner and Lowitja O'Donoghue are poles apart. Yanner is characterized as a young, assertive leader of a new generation of indigenous politics, whilst O'Donoghue is at the end of an illustrious public career committed to securing citizenship rights for Australia's Aboriginal and Torres Strait Islander peoples. In spite of their politics, when commenting about the Sydney 2000 Olympic Games both personalities forecast mass protests and public demonstrations if Australian race relations don't improve.

At a national level, the 2000 Olympic Games have provided a symbolic deadline to benchmark improvements for indigenous peoples and in broader race relations within Australia. It is within this climate that I will consider questions surrounding indigenous peoples' involvement with the Sydney 2000 Olympic Games. What influence will Aboriginal and Torres Strait Islander peoples'

But should the Government continue its mistreatment of Aboriginal people, you'll find a million people lining up at the gates of the Olympic stadium.
—*Murrandoo Yanner*

If governments can't change their attitudes, it will lead to boycotts and the indigenous people would be calling out black athletes.
—*Lowitja O'Donoghue*

involvement in the Olympic Games have? Are broader political goals furthered through individual agency within the structures of the Olympic Games? What will be the lasting consequences for Australia's indigenous peoples after the Olympics leave town?

Firstly, I'd like to outline some occasions where indigenous peoples have been involved with Sydney's Olympic Games organizations. Secondly, I'll speculate on what implications this intense national and international exposure may have on Australia's Aboriginal and Torres Strait Islander peoples and broader race relations in Australia beyond 2000.

Avoiding Protests

In the last week of September 1998, two years before the 2000 Olympic Games, the chairwoman of the National Indigenous Advisory Committee (an advisory group that reports to the Sydney Organising Committee for the Olympic Games [SOCOG]), Lowitja O'Donoghue, forecast a black boycott of the games. This speculation came from the committee responsible for improving relations between the indigenous community and the Sydney Olympic Games. The spectre of indigenous dissatisfaction was again outlined in late November 1998 in comments by Murrandoo Yanner, who also called for a black boycott. In the face of these public comments, SOCOG remained tight-lipped as the threat of political demonstration began materializing before their very eyes. Neither the Sydney 2000 Bid Committee nor SOCOG have ever had an indigenous director on their boards. In both organizations though, committees have been established to provide advice to the boards on numerous issues and topics. In this vein, SOCOG has created the National Indigenous Advisory Committee and created a list of indigenous "elders" to assist with indigenous community relations.

From the earliest days, the Sydney 2000 Bid Committee—the organization responsible for winning the 2000 Olympic Games for Sydney—sought to include Australia's indigenous peoples in advisory/community relations roles. Rod McGeoch, chair of the Sydney 2000 Bid Committee, in his book about the Sydney 2000 lobbying campaign, wrote, "There was a very conscious view from the start that the bid should involve all Australians. We were particularly keen to have the involvement and support of the Aboriginal community" (McGeoch and Korporaal 1994, 144).

Consistent with this objective, Aboriginal rights campaigner and former senior government bureaucrat Charles Perkins was appointed to the bid committee and indigenous actor Justine Saunders was appointed to the Sydney 2000 Bid Committee's Cultural Committee. Other prominent indigenous personalities, such as high-profile professional football player Ricky Walford and David Clark, were also enlisted as spokespersons and promoters of the 2000 bid campaign. Perkins and Aboriginal international tennis champion Evonne Goolagong-Cawley were also part of the final presentation team to the IOC in September 1993. On numerous occasions, indigenous peoples were engaged to perform at official bid campaign functions. The Sydney 2000 Bid Committee also sent Aboriginal performers, including a didgeridoo player, to Monte Carlo as part of the final presentation team. Even at this early stage of development of the Sydney Olympics, indigenous peoples were raising concerns about how and where indigenous association and involvement was being orchestrated. The then deputy chair of ATSIC (Aboriginal and Torres Strait Islander Commission), Commissioner Sol Bellear commented in a radio interview at the time that these performers in Monte Carlo were "tourist curios—like koalas and kangaroos" (AM Program, ABC Radio, September 25, 1993). The presence of this criticism about the extent and nature of indigenous participation is an important marker of how, or if, the Sydney Olympics' organizations have registered and responded to concerns voiced by the indigenous community. In contrast to this criticism has been the implicit approval of the Sydney 2000 Bid Committee, and SOCOG, with the participation of Aborigines and Torres Strait Islanders who have accepted commissions, positions, or roles within these SOCOG-affiliated agencies. Yet it is difficult to find evidence that suggests indigenous participation with the Sydney 2000 Olympic organizations has been raised beyond the bounds of tokenism to which Sol Bellear objected.

There have been few occasions for Australia's indigenous peoples to raise our domestic struggle for justice on our own land onto an international stage. In 1982, the Brisbane Commonwealth Games provided just such an international platform. Many protests and demonstrations were conducted during the games and many people were arrested. The most disturbing feature of the 1982 Commonwealth Games, though, was the readiness of the then state government to assign the powers of martial law to the police. Avoiding a repeat of the street scenes of protest in Brisbane in 1982 has always been a priority for the Sydney 2000 Olympic organizations. Accordingly, strict provisions have been outlined in the "security" plans developed for the Sydney Olympic Games.

At a fundamental level, the association of Australia's Aboriginal and Torres Strait Islander peoples with the Olympic Games is about politics: identity politics (both Australian and indigenous), Australian race politics, and general politics. Any issue about race relations in Australia is going to involve politics. It is within this climate that the participation and activities of indigenous peoples with the Sydney 2000 Olympic Games must considered.

"Something with Aboriginality"

Big international events like the Olympics, World Expos, and World Cup Soccer championships all seek to deliver the blockbuster public spectacle to better earlier shows. Stagings must be bigger, better, showier, cleaner—even greener—in order to upstage previous offerings. Organizers believe that better shows will entice visitors and generate larger television contracts. In particular, events are designed to seize the imagination of the television viewing public.

With the spread of the ideology of globalization and improvements in television broadcasting and information technology, the Olympic Games of the later twentieth century are like never before. The Olympics are packaged for various audiences to elicit various responses, e.g., athletic prestige, corporate sponsorship, nationalism, civic reinvention, and/or national unity. The 2000 Olympic Games are being customized deliberately to relate to select audiences. The games have been portrayed as the "Green Games," the "Athletes' Games," "Oceania's Games," "Australia's Games," or simply as the "Sydney Olympics." This manipulation is being facilitated by the ready application of marketing, labeling, and televisual strategies.

The biggest challenge for the modern Olympics, as opposed to the ancient Olympics of Greece, has been to distinguish the same "product"—an athletics meet—every four years as being a unique offering from each respective host city. Every conceivable distinguishing feature is seized upon, repackaged, and subsequently launched as a unique quality peculiar to these particular games. Geography is co-opted, architecture symbolized, national values reframed to reinforce Olympic ideals, national politics suspended to fabricate nonpartisan support, and cultures essentialized to serve every occasion. In this effort to brand successive Olympic Games, strategic outlets are engaged to release evidence of uniqueness, including the uniqueness of the host nation's indigenous peoples.

After researching the 1976 Olympics in Montreal, the Commonwealth Games of Edmonton in 1978, the Calgary Winter Olympics of 1988, and the 1994 Commonwealth Games in British Columbia, Paraschak observes that "analysis revealed that while token Native participation has been present in all of the festivals, more prominent Native images have been included within the two Olympics Games, as well as the most recent Commonwealth Games. However, these images have been selectively constructed to fit within the naturalized, dominant images already existent in [the nation states], which portray Native cultures in a static, 'pre-history' state" (1995, 1). For Australia's indigenous peoples this strategic promotion of the indigenous population is evident on each occasion when indigenous performers—dancers, singers, musicians, or artistic images—were/are engaged to support the Sydney 2000 bid. Obvious examples include the bid committee's and SOCOG's selection of logos. Rod McGeoch recalls the logo selection process: "There seemed to be about 20 winning entries. . . . There was a lot of deep consideration and milling around. All of a sudden Leo Schofield said, 'It isn't here. It simply isn't here. Tell them to do it again.' There were discussions about how there was no Aboriginality in the designs and that nothing just jumped off the page. So the firms were asked to resubmit designs by the end of the week. We gave a few hints such as the importance of including something with Aboriginality but we left it open" (McGeoch and Korporaal 1994, 68). The winning design selected was a rainbow ribbon, arranged as the silhouette of the Sydney Opera House, with the colors merging into each other using alternating dots. The dots were reminiscent of stylized paintings from Aboriginal artists of central Australia. Aboriginal artist Ron Hurley was credited with suggesting the use of dots in the winning concept design for the Sydney 2000 Bid Committee's logo.

Through the introduction of visual elements linked to Australia's indigenous peoples and cultures, the Sydney 2000 Olympic organization laid some claim to being unique or "peculiar to Australia." This branding sought to help International Olympic Committee (IOC) members distinguish the Sydney 2000 bid campaign from other bids. Accordingly, the primary carriage of the Sydney 2000 Bid Committee's image observed "the importance of including something with Aboriginality" (McGeoch and Korporaal 1994, 68). This sense of the unique was reinforced when indigenous performers were engaged for official Sydney Olympics organizations' functions, presentations, or displays. The making of the images and designs for SOCOG involved the appropriation of indigenous motifs, designs, and styles. Inevitably, this leads to an implication that indigenous peoples have authorized appropriation of their cultures in support of the Olympic bid. On occasion this appropriation has occurred with the full participation of at least some prominent Aboriginals and Torres Strait Islanders. This process of branding is being used in order to set the Australian or Sydney Olympics apart from previous Olympics. As Paraschak's (1995) research demonstrates, this process of appropriation is by no means confined to Australia.

"And the Winner Is Syd·en·ney!"

Juan Antonio Samaranch proclaimed Sydney, Australia, host city for the 2000 Olympic Games on September 23, 1993. After this announcement, the bid committee was dissolved and the Sydney Organising Committee for the Olympic Games (SOCOG) was duly constituted. SOCOG's board appointments reflected a confluence of interests, for example, the lord mayor of the host city as well as the state premier's and prime ministerial representatives. Although the considerations were complex, Aboriginal and Torres Strait Islander peoples were not included in the Australian Olympic Committee (AOC) formula for SOCOG's board appointments. In the time since SOCOG's creation, five developments have been particularly relevant: (1) the appointment of an Aboriginal Affairs manager; (2) Sydney's contribution to the 1996 Atlanta Olympic Games closing ceremony; (3) the new logo launched by SOCOG in September 1996; (4) the Festival of the Dreaming, and (5) a failed bid to have an indigenous person appointed to the SOCOG board. After the appointment of the chief executive officer for SOCOG, the filling of the Aboriginal Affairs manager came next. SOCOG appointed Steve Comeagain to this critical position. As with anything new, you get only one start. The manager for Aboriginal Affairs was responsible for setting the tone of the relationship between the broader indigenous community and SOCOG.

Comeagain had little or no previous experience in sports management, major event management, arts administration, or community relations—all essential areas for SOCOG. Comeagain was also unfamiliar with the national networks in sports, the Olympic movement, or Aboriginal affairs. Ultimately, this inadequacy would limit the extent to which indigenous views were incorporated into policies, contracts, and early developments within SOCOG. SOCOG made early assurances to the local Aboriginal and Torres Strait Islander Commission (ATSIC) and the New South Wales Aboriginal Land Council to involve them in the recruitment and appointments to key positions concerning indigenous people within the organization. SOCOG did not honor this assurance in the recruitment of the Aboriginal Affairs manager. One must surely question the selection process used to make this appointment. Placing an ill-equipped individual in such a key position also draws attention to SOCOG's motives. Comeagain has since resigned from SOCOG.

Another major occasion occurred in 1996 at the closing ceremony for the Atlanta Olympic Games. Within each closing ceremony the next host city for the Summer Olympics is given a small window to preview what people can expect from the next host city. The director of Opening and Closing Ceremonies for Sydney 2000, Australian Ric Burch, delivered a teaser for the worldwide television audience numbering 1 billion.

The performance began with an Aboriginal didgeridoo player seated on a platform that was turned into a figurative fire with wind blown shreds of red cloth. The event was dominated by the Bangarra Dance Theatre completing a short performance, enlivened by inflatable kangeroos carried by people riding bicycles, and concluded with a billowing sail replica symbolizing the Sydney Opera House. In Philip Batty's analysis, "the organizers chose to represent 'Australia,' through a pageant of the 'indigenous,' heavily laced with the associated signs of the 'primordial' and the 'natural'" (1998). Keep in the mind that these images are intended to introduce the tone of the next Olympic Games for the billion-strong, worldwide television audience. So the world was introduced to Sydney's Olympics by alien images of sparsely clothed Aborigines dancing around a fire to the tunes of a didgeridoo.

After the Atlanta closing performance, the next milestone for SOCOG was the launching of a new logo (see fig. 16.1). This symbol identifies the Sydney 2000 Olympics as opposed to the bid effort. SOCOG's explanation of the Millennium Athlete logo stated: "The boomerangs and suggestions of sun and rocks, together with colors of the Harbour, beaches and red interior invoke the unique Australian landscape and its original inhabitants." A designer who contributed to the logo added, "[T]he boomerang was a real inspiration for us. It deals with speed and comes from ancient land."

The language employed to describe and explain the Millennium Athlete portrays Australia's indigenous peoples in a peculiar, fixed existence with the symbols and colors that "invoke the unique Australian landscape and its original inhabitants." The boomerang is affixed to the "ancient land," and by association so, too, are the creators of this implement—the "original inhabitants." From the

FIGURE 16.1

Millennium Athlete, the Sydney 2000 logo.

Courtesy of the Sidney Organising Committee for the Olympic Games (SOCOG).

designers' evocations of landscape, artifacts, and "suggestions of sun and rocks," Australia's indigenous peoples are set into the past of ancient history. This dating process inadvertently (or maybe intentionally) challenges the existence of Aboriginal and Torres Strait Islander peoples in contemporary Australian society. This false impression undermines progressive race relations, yet it is consistent with racist assumptions about Aboriginal and Torres Strait Islander peoples. What's more, such racial stereotypes are often reinforced by indigenous peoples who accept rewards to behave in ways which do not confront these racial stereotypes. Paraschak makes a similar point about the images presented of First Nations peoples from Canada: "The images of native culture provided through the opening and closing ceremonies of multi-sport international games clearly are limited as well to a 'prehistorical' time, as evidenced by the stereotypical demeanor and dress of the native participants. This contributes to a colourful display, and fits within naturalized eurocanadian sensibilities" (1995, 8).

As opposed to the earlier design process, and without any specific acknowledgment, we must assume that no indigenous artists or designers were involved in the design of the Millennium Athlete logo. If this is true, then it rounds out the conclusion, ultimately, that indigenous peoples' involvement has been marginal, reduced, and eventually omitted and can be distilled to the point of stereotype. Yet the symbols or artifacts of indigenous peoples' existence are readily incorporated or appropriated to give the logo that "original Australian feel."

The Olympic Games are a celebration of the physical, but the modern Olympic movement also seeks to celebrate the artistic. This celebration is called the Cultural Olympiad. Sydney submitted a plan to have four cultural festivals in each year of the Olympiad. The first of these festivals was held in 1997—The Festival of the Dreaming. SOCOG's promotion of the festival proclaimed: "The Festival of the Dreaming promoted a greater awareness and appreciation of Australian indigenous heritage. This is one of the oldest known to man, but a culture which is constantly developing and evolving. The festival had thirty exhibitions, fourteen dance and theater productions, eight performance troupes, fifty films, a literature program, three concerts and a number of special commissions."

As Lisa Meekison's chapter in this book also discusses the Festival of the Dreaming, I'll limit my discussion to some of the promotional images used for the festival. Specifically, I'd like to consider the festival's official poster (see fig. 16.2) and an image used for the promotion of one of the feature events of the Festival of the Dreaming—Bangarra Dance Theatre's commissioned production entitled "Fish" (see fig. 16.3). The return of the gaze, presented in the black eye at the center of the poster, proved provocative, although not altogether challenging. This reversal of the objectifying gaze confronted the more familiar politics of representation in Australian race relations and supported a sense of agency for Australia's indigenous peoples. The appointment of indigenous peoples as managers of the Festival of the Dreaming also supported the notion of indigenous agency. Rhoda Roberts, an Aboriginal Australian, accepted the position of director of the festival,

FIGURE 16.2

Festival of the Dreaming poster.

Courtesy of the Sidney Organising Committee for the Olympic Games (SOCOG).

reportedly with some reluctance. Roberts commented, "It took quite a few meetings before I felt safe this wasn't just a token gesture—that authorship and control would be in the hands of indigenous people." But whilst the "black eye" marked off new territory for indigenous agency, the promotional poster for one of the feature events of the festival—Bangarra's "Fish"—returned to familiar contradictions.

FIGURE 16.3

"Fish" poster. Frances Rings, dancer.

Courtesy of the Bangarra Dance Company. Greg Barrett, photographer.

Here (see fig. 16.3) we had a black female in center frame. With a rear view, it presents the voyeur with a glimpse of what is to come, or to be imagined, from the near naked performer. The absence of a face spares the viewer any confronting human expression or nonverbal messages delivered by facial expressions. This returns viewers to the more familiar objectification of black people. Yet, at the same time, the physical form of the muscular back challenges traditional constructions of femininity.

In late 1998, the SOCOG board accepted the resignation of Director Rod McGeoch. For many years, many indigenous leaders argued that an indigenous person should be on the SOCOG board in a sincere acknowledgment of Australia's indigenous peoples. Such a demand was consistently rebuffed by governments, both state and Commonwealth, the SOCOG organization, and responsible government ministers on the basis that there were no available vacancies. With McGeoch's departure the SOCOG-commissioned National Indigenous Advisory Committee renewed its call for an indigenous director. The chairperson of the committee, Lowitja O'Donoghue, again made the case to the minister for Olympics, "[T]he Games are being held in Australia and we are the original owners of Australia and we should have some say" (*Sydney Morning Herald,* September 25, 1998). In the face of a threatened mass resignation of the National Indigenous Advisory Committee, the minister for the Olympics, the Honorable Micheal Knight, joined by the premier of New South Wales, the Honorable Bob Carr, announced on November 26, 1998, that Marjorie Jackson-Nelson, an Australian double Olympic gold medalist, would be appointed to the SOCOG board. Although Jackson-Nelson was not an indigenous person, not one member of the National Indigenous Advisory Committee resigned.

These primary events—the appointment of the Aboriginal Affairs manager, the preview at the Atlanta closing ceremony, SOCOG's new logo, the Festival of the Dreaming promotional material, and the failure to appoint an indigenous person to the SOCOG board—all provide insights into the contests over indigenous /nonindigenous control and power, indigenous representation, and the Sydney Olympic movements' co-option of indigenous images, motifs, and artistic representations and of indigenous peoples themselves.

Beyond 2000: Implications for Australia's Race Relations

Over the last thirty years Australia has witnessed a boom in the generation of aesthetic and artistic images, expressions, representations, symbols, and motifs inspired by, or directly created by, indigenous peoples. This proliferation has grown exponentially from the days of department store promotions in the 1950s. Australia's colonialization has been, and continues to be, well served by artists and those industries drawing from aesthetic images. Dinah Dysart notes in her essay "Émigré Artists": "The Europeans knew little about Australia; many of them arrived purely by chance. They had no preconceived ideas to color their perceptions, and their reactions were many and varied. Gert Sellheim, for instance, responded to Aboriginal art, using it as a source of inspiration. In his designs for posters to encourage tourism, he drew on Aboriginal motifs to signify a sense of place" (192–193).

Dysart's views reflect the colonization of Australia through the construction of a sense of place. Ironically though, while this colonization comes at the expense of indigenous peoples, it is "Aboriginal motifs" that Sellheim uses "to signify a sense of place." At this point, I would also like register that I take exception to Dysart's claim that these immigrant artists had no preconceived ideas. The antipodes have a long-established philosophical and ideological foundation in European thought reaching back centuries to the ancient Greeks. It was this influence that migrants carried with them to Australian shores.

As part of the settling of Australia, immigrant artists sought to create the geographic and symbolic spaces that were made into "Australia." Anne-Marie van de Ven draws our attention to this colonization in her essay "Images of the Fifties: Design and Advertising": "Artists and mural workers in Australia were actively encouraged to exploit the many aspects of the local design source of Aboriginal art in order to avoid the necessity of paying heavily to other countries for the right to use their designs in commercial work" (1993, 38).

As the physical landscape was being invaded by settlers and would-be pastoralists, and thus alienated from indigenous interests, so, too, were the aesthetic expressions of Australia's indigenous peoples being appropriated. This appropriation was, and remains, an essential experience in the shaping of Australia and an Australian identity. Again, van de Ven writes: "Throughout the fifties, designs derived from Australian Aboriginal art were popularly used to market a distinctive Australian identity. . . . Aboriginal imagery gave a distinctively Australian 'look' to local advertising imagery . . . this look was also defined by the repeated use of images thought to typify 'the Australia way of life' and by depiction of the physical 'oddities' of the Australian environment" (1993, 39). While these representations were being stolen from Aboriginal people, they were denied any money for their work. This should not surprise us, considering that in the 1950s Australia's indigenous peoples were subject to popular philosophy and government policy that barely recognized Aborigines and Torres Strait Islanders as human. Richard White, in his essay "The Shock of Affluence: The Fifties in Australia" recalls that "Aboriginal people were isolated from the mainstream, despite the popularity of Aboriginal motifs in mainstream Australian culture" (1993, 19).

Aboriginal people were excluded from the affluent society, continued to live in appalling conditions on the fringes of white society, and were denied full citizenship. But official segregationist policies were slowly giving way to a new policy of assimilation: Aboriginal people were being encouraged to abandon their culture in favor of the "Australian way of life." Yet, white culture ransacked Aboriginal cultures for motifs—elite culture in works such as John Antill's ballet *Corroboree* and popular culture in tea towels and garden ornaments.

None of this would be news to those who have read the work of Australia's foremost art historian and theorist, Bernard Smith (1989). Smith has examined the "imaging" process emergent in European contact with the peoples and lands of the South Pacific. Building on this foundation, Ian McLean has recently focused the argument onto the inextricable bond between indigenous peoples' presence and Australian identity. In *White Aborigines,* McLean discusses Russell Ward's formative 1958 essay *The Australian Legend:* "[Ward's] new Australia was a white Aborigine sprung from the land itself—namely, 'the outback ethos' and the 'nomad tribe' of bushmen being formed by 'the struggle to assimilate' to 'the brute facts of Australian geography'" (1998, 88).

Drawing us back to Australian art, McLean offers some insight into the contribution of white artist Margaret Preston. He writes:"Preston contributed four articles to *Art and Australia* between 1925 and 1941, urging that Aboriginal art become the foundation and inspiration of a modern, national Australian art" (1998, 90).The construction of identity and reality occurs primarily in the mind of the image maker and the focus of this imagination is objectified to fit within this imagination. A feature of this process is the dissociation of the object of the imagination from the actual life of the object.

Marcia Langton expanded this idea in an indigenous context in her speech to the Global Diversity Conference in 1995. Langton commented that "Aboriginality ... is a field of intersubjectivity in that it is remade over and over again in a process of dialogue, of imagination, of representation and interpretation," but this stereotype of Aboriginal peoples fulfills a special role:"a deliberate, shameless and calculated use of a long tradition of images and ideas that had been carefully constructed over nearly 200 years of occupation of this country. It is a tradition that has been created to justify a history of dispossession: in a land of terra nullius, it has been necessary to invent and elaborate a received and unquestioned stereotype of Aboriginal people" (1995).

Yet in spite of people reading and, I assume, understanding the critiques of Bernard Smith, Ian McLean, and Marcia Langton, we see Australia's visual colonialization proceeding into the twenty-first century, albeit in new forms.With the Sydney Olympic Games it appears that Australia's indigenous cultures continue to be coopted and represented as the one original Australian expression on an international stage.With a media spin machine perpetually looking for an angle, the unique Australian angle has been increasingly framed by so-called "unique" indigenous artistic images, representations, or sound bites. What's more, this process is being supported and promoted by indigenous and nonindigenous peoples alike.The presence of indigenous peoples in such a process could be interpreted as a sign of legitimation and validation of the behavior associated with and corresponding to images generated over the last fifty years.

The logical conclusion: the "image" is perceived as having more legitimacy than the "reality."The image and the nonindigenous imagination which created its boundaries assume the measure of authenticity against which contemporary activity, behavior, and images are considered. The danger in this process is that Aboriginals and Torres Strait Islanders could be characterized, or typecast, by these broader "paintin' and dancin'" stereotypes. Subsequently, indigenous cultures are distilled into a narrow definition of "real Aboriginal culture" as portrayed in overt artistic displays. This predicament has already befallen other indigenous peoples around the world.

These Aboriginal stereotypes are permitted because they do not challenge fundamental nonindigenous assumptions about race. These assumptions are the pillars of eighteenth-century racism and nineteenth-century imperialism—and now seem to undergird twentieth-century globalization. Such stereotypes fail to challenge the fundamental power relations between peoples of privilege and peoples of disadvantage.

In Australia, the stereotypes of the primitive abound. The absence of indigenous voices affirms the colonial claim to the legitimacy of dispossession. These assumptions are left unchallenged by simplistic characterizations of artistic expression and marginalization of political demands. The challenge that confronts our indigenous leaders then becomes a question of how do we cope, manage, or prevent any further descent on this path of cultural prostitution? What overt elements of our image and representation will we permit for external use? How will these images be developed by and with us so that they don't confine us?

Conclusion

The Olympic Games of 2000 place Australia in a difficult situation. The unresolved nature of race relations in Australia is a major factor in this difficulty. The public attention generated and the promises made while preparing for the Olympics exacerbate the dissonance. While mainstream Australia may not see any link between Australia's race relations and the Olympics, Australia's indigenous peoples are regularly reminded of the link every time they see a Sydney 2000 Olympic Games logo and are confronted with another form of appropriation.

I would contend that the representation of indigenous peoples in the Australian public domain is consistent with an underlying avoidance of these complex questions. To date, the selection and display of images of Australia's indigenous peoples are consistent with fundamental assumptions and stereotypes of race relations in Australia. Underpinning these relations are ideological beliefs about physicality and intelligence being determined by "race," thereby predetermining the extent and nature of relations between these races. In the past such ideas in the name of concepts that rationalized inhumane treatment under the guise of civilization, concepts which justified injustice, concepts which affirmed the unequal treatment of equal peoples.

This process continues the reduction of Australia's indigenous cultures to palatable expressions which are consistent with, and reinforce, nonindigenous constructions of what it means to be Aboriginal or Torres Strait Islander. This reduction thereby sustains the status quo of race relations in Australia by failing to challenge the fundamental assumptions of power relations between indigenous and nonindigenous peoples. To date, the Sydney 2000 Olympic Games have reinforced this deficiency. This, in a sense, frustrates sincere efforts to improve relations between Australians—indigenous and nonindigenous. The cost of the Olympics may extend beyond the acknowledged bill of $3 billion.

Bidding for the

Olympics:

Site Selection

and Sydney 2000

IAN JOBLING

Sydney's bid to host the Olympic Games in the year 2000 was the third attempt in successive Olympiads by Australian cities. Brisbane and Melbourne bid for the 1992 and 1996 Olympics, respectively. However, the history of Australian cities proposing and bidding to host the Olympic Games goes back to soon after the modern Olympic Games were held in 1896. (A proposal is an informal expression of interest in hosting the games; it is not fully developed, whereas a bid is presented to the International Olympic Committee [IOC].) Indeed, after Edwin Flack, the sole Australian at those inaugural games in Athens, won both the eight-hundred- and fifteen-hundred-meter track events, the Melbourne *Argus* (April 11, 1896) speculated that these "new" Olympic Games "may even in due course offer themselves to the delighted gaze of Melbourne."

In the 1920s the first advocates for Sydney as host got it wrong from the outset. They proposed to celebrate the planned opening of the Sydney Harbour Bridge in 1930 with the Olympic Games. Unfortunately, 1930 was not designated an Olympic year. Had they put forward a bid for 1932 (ironically also the year of the bridge's actual opening), there might have been some chance of success. There would be no games in Sydney for another seventy years.

In February 1946, Melbourne gave the bid a go. Frank Beaurepaire, the great swimmer of the 1908, 1920, and 1924 Olympic Games, reportedly called for a sports stadium in Melbourne with "all facilities for holding the Olympic Games in Australia." When the Victorian State Olympic Council (VOC) met in 1946, its first meeting in seven years because of World War II, they agreed to seek further information from the Australian Olympic Federation (AOF) on how to go about bidding for an Olympic Games. Incredibly, the federation held only just over six pounds (i.e., less than thirteen dollars) in reserves for its project! By January 1948 the federation sent a bid to the IOC proposing to celebrate the sixteenth Olympiad in Melbourne in 1956.

According to newspaper articles in Victorian newspapers, the VOC mounted several arguments for its bid. If the Olympics were to be a truly "world" games, then it was time for them to be held in the Southern Hemisphere. Australian athletes had participated in every Summer Olympics since the 1896 games. Australia was one of only four nations with this record. Thus it could claim a more senior position in the Olympic movement than the other competitor in the Southern Hemisphere—i.e., Buenos Aires. With the development of pressurized aircraft, it would take at most a mere thirty hours for athletes and spectators to reach Melbourne. Criticism that Northern Hemisphere athletes would be competing "out of season" was met with the reaction that this was something Southern Hemisphere athletes had always had to endure.

By October 1948, Frank Beaurepaire quoted the "betting odds" in *Argus* (October 28, 1948) as "Melbourne—even money; Buenos Aires—6/4 against; Detroit—2/1; All others—Buckley's chance."

On April 30, 1949, the front-page banners of the Victorian press read "Melbourne Gets the Games." It took four ballots for Melbourne to receive twenty-one votes to Buenos Aires' twenty; other bidding cities were Detroit, Los Angeles, Mexico City, and London. The bid was successful and that should be the end of this aspect of the story. But aspects of the Melbourne games may have had a bearing on the failure of future bids by Australian cities (of which there were several before Sydney 2000). The strategy of the Melbourne Invitation Committee before "decision day" had been to proceed with any promises likely to convince the IOC to award the games to Melbourne. The extravagant plans for a new Olympic stadium and swimming pool complex were two examples. When site construction stalled and the Olympic Organising Committee vacillated over the site for the main stadium (Would it be Olympic Park, Princes Park, the show grounds, or perhaps the Melbourne Cricket Ground?), IOC president Avery Brundage visited Australia to express his deep concern over the lack of progress. Another issue, which had significant implications for future bids, was the revelation that Australia's strict quarantine laws would prevent equestrian events being staged in Melbourne (they were held in Stockholm). Despite these difficulties, the Melbourne games were a most successful sixteenth Olympics. In fact, they have been heralded as "the friendly games" ever since.

In the run up to the 1972 games, Sydney made its bid for a return of the Olympics to Australia. The proposal for Sydney to host the 1972 Olympic Games was an interesting one because, even by May 1965, it seems that no other nation had indicated a wish to stage them (the Olympics did not make profits in those days). International politics at the time played a key role in the decision. The international sports federations, meeting in Lausanne, Switzerland, decided that the country staging the 1972 Olympic Games must issue visas to all athletes entitled to compete. This automatically eliminated NATO countries as possible organizers because they would not issue visas to East German athletes. Avery Brundage was reported to be receptive to an Australian bid and his "Sydney can do it" comment was headlined in the *Sydney Mirror* on May 20, 1965. Not all comments were favorable, however. The sports editor of Sydney's *Sun Herald* (May 2, 1965) wrote that it was "crazy to suggest Sydney could stage the Games on a scale as grand as Tokyo . . . to get the Games ahead of other nations whose visa restrictions would rule them ineligible, would be a pyrrhic victory." It should be noted that the Australian government, like the NATO countries, had a policy that prevented it from issuing visas to an East German team. Nonetheless, the AOF decided unanimously in May 1965 to support an application by Sydney even though it was considered a calculated gamble.

A final hurdle remained in relation to the problems of quarantine for the equestrian events. The IOC had decided that all events on the Summer Olympic Games program must be held in the same country. However, Hugh Weir, a member of the IOC in Australia, brashly proclaimed in the *Sydney Morning Herald* (May 16, 1965), "[T]here is nothing at this stage to indicate that the equestrian events will be on the same program for the 1972 Games." But it was unlikely that the IOC would agree to leave out equestrian events from the Olympic program. In addition to the problem of quarantine, the bid needed to secure support from both the state and federal governments before the mid-1966 submission deadline. The *Sydney Morning Herald*'s state political correspondent wrote under the headline "Games Campaign a Pipe Dream!": "The State Treasury is examining an estimate by Alderman Jensen that Sydney could stage the games for 15 million pounds, and will report to the Premier, Mr. Askin . . . But this proposal, in view of the political as well as the financial problems, looks to be moonshine" (October 7, 1965). And indeed it was.

Pride and euphoria abounded in Brisbane following the highly successful XII Commonwealth Games in 1982, so much so that within a month of the closing ceremony the lord mayor of Brisbane announced that the city would investigate the feasibility of hosting the 1992 Olympic Games. Some curious propositions were promulgated in Brisbane's favor. An "Olympics Down Under" would be held between July 25 and August 9, "when Brisbane enjoys idyllic dry weather," and when Northern Hemisphere athletes are "in-season." There was also, of course, the reminder that, since 1896, only one Olympic Games had been held in the Southern Hemisphere. "Surely to further the Olympic ideals in Oceania, and throughout the world, it is time to hold another," Murray Hedgcock (getting the seasons confused) wrote in the *Weekend Australian* (October 27–28, 1984): "It's difficult to know whether to applaud, laugh, or cry about Brisbane's belated campaign to grab the 1992 Summer Olympics. . . . The last thing they [the European countries] want . . . is to face a 1992 trek to the other side of the world and also be asked to compete out of season because Australia's summer is Europe's winter." Hedgcock concluded this article with an unkind yet prophetic reference to a shrewdly calculating IOC president: "He [Samaranch] can hardly be blamed for seeking to round off his term of office by persuading his fellows that Spain is ready."

Brisbane, Melbourne, and Sydney all submitted applications to the AOF to be Australia's bidding city for the 1996 Olympics. In November 1988 when the AOF gave Melbourne the nod for the 1996 games there were outcries about that city's inclement weather during the proposed dates of the games. The next day, November 19, 1988, Brisbane's *Courier Mail* cartoonist, Sean Leahy, depicted a frustrated torchbearer attempting to kindle the Olympic Flame in pouring rain; and the cartoonist for Sydney's *Daily Telegraph,* Paul Zanetti, drew a tongue-in-cheek cartoon of a Melbourne bid committee representative uttering, "Oh . . . we thought you meant the Winter Olympics" (depicted in the *Brisbane Sunday Mail,* November 20, 1988).

However, many of the IOC members and representatives from international sports federations who visited Melbourne were most encouraging in their comments. This was evident in their formal reports, in the media, and in personal communication with this author. David Miller, a most respected and internationally syndicated London-based sports journalist, argued Melbourne's case for hosting the Olympics in the London *Times* (reproduced in the *Weekend Australian,* October 18–19, 1989). He claimed they would be "clean, free, safe . . . and morally justified." Miller, who has also written a biography of Samaranch, has a powerful clout with Samaranch and in media circles, but his opinion did not win the day. In Tokyo in September 1990, the hopes of Melbourne's Olympic Flame being kindled in 1996 were doused (for the second time) when the IOC eliminated them in the third round of voting in favor of Atlanta, United States. One of the slogans used by the Melbourne Olympic Committee was that it was "Time for Another Continent." Not only had the Northern Hemisphere hosted all Summer Olympics apart from 1956, North America had hosted five.

Even before the day of Melbourne's defeat, its rival city Sydney showed its (some would say duplicitous) hand. Kevan Gosper stood down as president of the Australian Olympic Committee (AOC, formerly the AOF) and was replaced by John Coates, who had led Brisbane's 1992 Olympic bid and was clearly in favor of a Sydney bid. Coates invited all AOC board members to preview the proposed Olympic facilities at Homebush Bay and on November 16, 1990, put forward a notice of motion to the AOC that it should back a Sydney bid for the 2000 Olympic Games. Headlines of the *Telegraph Mirror* of November 17 ironically read, "Sydney Wins Games Battle."

Clearly, much had gone on behind the scenes even while Melbourne was preparing its candidacy for 1996, as can be ascertained from the comments of

Jean Walsh, a former director of communications for the Melbourne bid. Walsh's comments appeared in the *Sunday Age* of September 22, 1991: "[T]he decision for Sydney had been made well before Melbourne's loss a year ago. Flabbergasted by the democratic vote that gave Melbourne the nod in November 1988, the committed Sydney supporters with the Australian Olympic Committee moved to make sure the same 'mistake' didn't happen again. The pro-Melbourne members were challenged at the next committee election and enough of them lost their positions so that the Sydney push was able to dominate the committee." At the same time, a small group was formed to work on Sydney's Olympic prospects in hope and anticipation that rival city Melbourne would fail in its 1996 bid.

This intrigue shadowed the scene of the IOC meeting in Monte Carlo on September 23, 1993, the meeting which announced Sydney's victory for the 2000 games. And the sight of the then premier of New South Wales, John Fahey, leaping into the air when IOC president Samaranch pronounced "Syd-e-ney" as the host city for the 2000 Olympic Games remained etched into the memories of many Australians as they embraced the many ramifications and possibilities of the decision. The common and popular term "Sydney 2000" has engendered interesting responses and reactions throughout Australia and internationally since that announcement.

Olympic Sites

Homebush Bay was first promulgated as an Olympic site in the Bunning Report in 1973 and had already been developed as a State Sport Centre in 1984. The closure of the State Brickworks and State Abattoirs, along with the possible release of the federal government's Newington Armaments Depot, resulted in nearly seven hundred hectares of uncommitted land with waterfront owned by government. There were obvious environmental advantages in the New South Wales (NSW) government developing a former industrial site. But how could the Sydney Bid sell it as a location?

One big advantage was that most of the venues for the games would be located on the one site which was within twelve kilometers of the Sydney central business district. The housing of all the athletes in the one Olympic Village, within a travel time of a half hour to all venues, was also a big factor because in recent Olympics distances between village and venue had caused problems. Significantly, Homebush Bay provided an ideal solution to satisfy the post-Olympic problems of facilities becoming cost burdens—the venue would already have become the home of the Royal Agricultural Show and had the potential of attracting sports teams (including an Australian Football League club) and other international events. So, hosting the 2000 Olympics provided the opportunity for Sydney, which had been shown to rank last in the provision of sports facilities, to develop a site with international-standard sports facilities, especially for swimming and track and field.

However, none of this would have happened without support from the federal government. This occurred in February 1991 when it was announced that NSW could borrow $300 million over three years to allow an early start to construction to give Sydney's bid a greater chance of success. It is noteworthy that this "permission to borrow" was on top of a grant of $150 million if Sydney's bid was successful. The committee of the Sydney Olympics 2000 Bid Limited (Sydney Bid) was named fewer than twenty hours after the promise of the federal government loan, with Premier Nick Greiner as president, and John Coates as vice president.

One of the issues confronting the Sydney Bid was that the games had been held in Melbourne in 1956 and, at that time, only four countries and three cities had hosted (or would host) repeat Summer Olympics: the United States (Los Angeles in 1932 and 1984, St. Louis in 1904, and Atlanta in 1996), France (Paris in 1900 and 1924), Great Britain (London in 1908 and 1948); and Germany (Berlin in 1936 and Munich in 1972). However, a big plus was the argument that the Olympics had been held only once in the Southern Hemisphere—in 1956 in Melbourne. Clearly, this fact related to historian Geoffrey Blainey's concept of the Australian "tyranny of distance." The issue of the games being "Eurocentric" had been promulgated in the Brisbane and Melbourne campaigns. However, the consciousness and the conscience of some of the IOC members had been affected.

It was clear from previous Olympics, especially since Los Angeles in 1984, that revenue for the games organizers and the IOC, generated through the sale of television rights, especially to the wealthy American and European networks, was a significant consideration in the selection of a host city. The eastern Australia "time zone" problem was addressed aggressively by members of the Sydney Bid; one outcome was alluded to in an article published in the *Sydney Morning Herald* on September 23, 1992, entitled "Early Olympic Finals a Sop for US Networks": "[A] 2 P.M. track and field would be shown in prime time (8 P.M.) in Los Angeles and at 11 P.M. in New York. . . It is envisaged that swimming would retain its traditional pattern of morning heats and night finals, but there is a chance the finals may be moved back to finish at, say 10 P.M., for early morning viewers on the US East Coast." It was also envisaged that events that were of special interest to Europeans, such as soccer and European handball, would be scheduled at night so that they could be seen in the early afternoon in much of that continent. It was also proposed that there would, of course, be no viewing problems in the fast-growing Asian region, which has time zones closer to Sydney's.

Seven other cities had expressed an interest in bidding for 2000. London-based bookmakers, Ladbrokes, in what was believed to be the first odds quoted for the success of any Olympic host, posted thus: Manchester, 6 to 1; Berlin, 4 to 1; Tashkent, no odds given; Beijing, 9 to 4; Brasilia, 14 to 1; Milan, 10 to 1; Istanbul, 14 to 1; and Sydney, 2 to 1 (Mark Skelsey in the *Daily Telegraph Mirror,* April 21, 1992). Clearly, the odds were in favor of Beijing and Sydney; Brasilia, the only other city in the southern Hemisphere, was not considered a finals contender.

TABLE 17.1
World Time Zones

Algiers Paris Rome	Athens Cairo Capetown	Sydney	Seoul Tokyo	Los Angeles Seattle Vancouver	New York Lima Toronto
Midnight	1 A.M.	9 A.M.	8 A.M.	3 P.M.	6 P.M.
3 a.m.	4 A.M.	Noon	11 A.M.	6 P.M.	9 P.M.
6 a.m.	7 A.M.	3 P.M.	2 P.M.	9 P.M.	Midnight
9 a.m.	10 A.M.	6 P.M.	5 P.M.	Midnight	3 A.M.
Noon	1 P.M.	9 P.M.	8 P.M.	3 A.M.	6 A.M.

At the time Sydney's Olympic Games bid was delivered to Lausanne on April 16, 1991, IOC president Samaranch was told of the Australian government's commitment of a $300 million loan for the NSW government to build sports facilities to proceed with the bid. A significant coup of the Sydney Bid Committee was its foresight in lobbying for the hosting of the General Assembly of International Summer Sport Federations (GAISF). In October 1991 more than four hundred sports leaders from approximately forty countries visited Sydney for two weeks. Officially, under the bidding rules, none of the IOC members present could be "lobbied," but it was obvious that many were impressed early in the bidding campaign that the city of Sydney would have outstanding facilities in a compact location at Homebush Bay. The Sydney Bid chief executive, Rod McGeoch, was quoted in the Sydney press at that time: "Winning an Olympic Games involves winning it on an international stage." The GAISF congress two years prior to the election clearly provided that opportunity.

Immediately prior to the Barcelona Olympics in July 1992 the five finalists from the hundred entries for the building of the Olympic Village at Homebush Bay were announced; one was from the international environmental group Greenpeace. The village was planned as an "environmental showcase" which would, for example, include: solar-powered street lighting, water heating, and air-conditioning; insulation, refrigeration, and air-conditioning free of harmful gases; and the addressing of issues such as biodiversity (restoring natural flora and fauna), ozone depletion, air and water pollution, and global warming. Such promises were significant because IOC president Samaranch had intimated that the "ecological impact of the organisation . . . will be taken into account when the vote is held" (*Sydney Morning Herald*, December 22, 1992).

In the same month announcements pertaining to the eighty-thousand-spectator Olympic Stadium, the 12,500-seat Olympic Aquatic Centre, and the "supertrains" which would carry fifty thousand people every hour to Homebush Bay really encouraged Australians to "Share the Spirit."

Of course, visitations and lobbying took place soon after the bid documents were lodged, and the Sydney Bid throughout 1991 and 1992 was represented at all significant international sports events. One of the biggest coups of the entire bid campaign was pulled off at the Association of National Olympic Committees (ANOC) meeting in Acapulco in November 1992. Travel costs were not a major issue in the Euro-Asian bids, and Sydney's very impressive bid was constantly clouded by the issue of the time and cost involved in traveling. In a well-choreographed and spectacular fashion, the members of the Sydney Bid announced that all national Olympic committees would receive free air travel to and from the Olympics for all athletes, coaches, and officials. Immediately after that presentation each national Olympic committee received a letter outlining precisely the dollars they would receive for travel along with free board and accommodation in the Olympic Village. The positive reaction was encapsulated in the *Daily Telegraph Mirror* (November 7, 1992) by Australian journalist and Olympic specialist writer Michaelangelo Rucci, who reported, "Sydney's bid is now hailed as the best—even among the six other cities trying to win the 2000 Games." The predicted cost for such travel was $24.5 million.

Another significant feature of the Sydney Bid was that the ideals of the Olympic movement were promulgated through educational programs. One of these was the Schools Program, a joint initiative between the Sydney Bid Committee and the NSW Department of School Education, which included the "twinning," where all IOC members received correspondence and a scrapbook of students' work which outlined their studies of the Olympic movement. Evidence of the ongoing support from the schoolchildren of Australia is demonstrated in the Sign for Sydney program which resulted in more than 158,000 signatures being bound into seven volumes.

The IOC carefully considers community support within the city, state or province, and country for the staging of an Olympic Games. In every city polls are conducted and outcomes weighed competitively. Sydney's result was a huge 90 percent in favor in October 1992. Results of similar polls undertaken in other bidding cities at this time were Berlin, with 40 percent, and Beijing, with 94 percent. Sydney Bid was ecstatic—another hurdle overcome.

Ahead lay the candidature files, which had to be delivered to the IOC by February 1, 1993. Sydney's bid books comprised a three-volume, five-hundred-page file with five hundred thousand words in both English and French, more than eighty technical drawings, and fifteen hundred photographs of information about that city's plans to host the 2000 Olympics. The distribution of the limited print run of six hundred copies was to all IOC members, national Olympic committees, and international sports federations. For secrecy and safekeeping the bid books traveled from London to Sydney in the cockpit of a Qantas 747 and then on to Geneva via Swissair. Clearly, the bid books indicated that Sydney 2000 would be both Australia's Olympics and the "Athletes' Games."

The Share the Spirit campaign was aimed at promoting community support, which was essential to attain a high percentage of support by all Australians and to ensure that the many IOC visitors and international sports officials who visited Australia would be aware of the strong enthusiasm for the event. The very successful and innovative bid logo was the result of a competition and depicted the "sails" of the Sydney Opera House incorporating the use of Aboriginal Papunya art.

Another major obstacle was community relations at home. How would Australian organizations respond? The Sydney Bid's Community Relations Committee was established in November 1992, with Clean Up Australia program's Ian Kiernan as chair. Its aims were to educate target groups, such as ethnic and indigenous groups, schools, unions, service clubs, sports groups, local government, and service clubs and agencies. Much had been written and forecast about the relationship between the Sydney Olympics and key Aboriginal organizations. The bid committee was anxious for definite and positive support. Some magic words were forthcoming when, for example, the spokesperson for the NSW Aboriginal Land Council, which represents Aboriginal interest groups, feebly commented that "all sorts of good" could come from Sydney's hosting the games. Despite some dissenting voices in the Aboriginal community, the Sydney Bid had at least this statement to promulgate.

Australia holds a unique and infamous distinction in Olympic circles. The IOC was close to removing the 1956 games from Melbourne because they could not host the equestrian competition owing to strict quarantine regulations of the Australian government. For Sydney's bid there were more machinations behind the scenes, and eventually the Equestrian Quarantine Working Group deliberated an outcome which was more than satisfactory to international equestrian bodies and to the IOC.

There were some other issues that threatened to disrupt the race to win the bid. The IOC was beginning to see the Olympic and Paralympic Games as one sports festival. The initial problems between the Sydney Bid and Paralympic associations at the national and international levels sparked concerns, especially when in July 1993 it was reported that most other bidding cities, including Beijing, had offered government financial guarantees for the Paralympics. The Sydney Bid resolved the problem by ensuring cooperation and a close working relationship with the Paralympics organizers.

The biggest hurdle, and one of the most contentious, was how to win the hearts and minds of the ultimate decision makers, the omnipotent IOC members themselves, within the IOC rules of hospitality. The Sydney Bid solution was to establish a lobby team of the most influential and powerful members of Australian government, industry, and sports. There were also specialist consultants (former Australian prime ministers Malcolm Fraser and Gough Whitlam) for South America, the Arab countries, and the black African nations. Lobby team members attended most of the significant international sports meetings at which IOC members would be present. A most important outcome was the response to the formal invitations to all IOC members in mid-1992 to come to Sydney for a five-day (the maximum allowed under IOC rules) "package."

Anne Barbeliuk of Sydney's *Daily Telegraph Mirror,* wrote on Australia Day, January 26, 1993:

> Dr Indrapana, you are the first International Olympic Committee member to visit Sydney to assess our bid for the year 2000 games.
>
> During your stay, you will tour the jewel in our crown, our fabulous harbour, and visit planned Olympic sites and facilities. But as you tour our city it is not our scenery, our climate, our plans or constructions—spectacular though they are—that are our key to our bid for the games.
>
> The real spirit of our passion for the Olympics lies in the hearts of our people. People who will make you welcome to a city we believe is one of the greatest on earth. Already our $300 million stage one work on the sports facilities at Homebush Bay are on schedule and a massive campaign of public support is moving into high gear. Welcome, Dr Indrapana—and we look forward to seeing you again, in the year 2000.

On that Australia Day there were twelve IOC members in Sydney—all were welcomed to lunch at Darling Harbour where, as Barbeliuk wrote, "they were treated to chicken, veal, prawns and patriotism." In total, sixty-five IOC members visited Sydney in response to the "special invitation"; an additional five members, who were at the GAISF conference, did not make a second visit. Perhaps it will be some time before we will know the true impact of the contribution of this lobby team, and what "promises" were made.

Of course, there were many other initiatives which promoted Sydney as an ideal Olympic city for the millennium games. For example, the Ambassadors program utilized the services of twenty-five famous Australian athletes to assist in the promotion of sports tourism. When the Australian Chamber Orchestra toured twenty cities in the United States, they wore a Sydney Bid T-shirt when the occasion was suitable. The Friends of Sydney program enlisted the assistance of expatriates, especially in the entertainment industry (for example, Dame Edna Everage, Rolf Harris, Clive James, Kylie Minogue); there were approximately three hundred celebrities "on call" in the United Kingdom and nine hundred in the European Community.

Then there were the technical problems to be overcome. Again, Sydney came through with flying colors when the international governing bodies of all twenty-five Summer Olympic sports endorsed the proposed technical requirements for the Sydney 2000 games. For the first time in Olympic history the Sydney Bid included letters of approval from each international sports federation in the candidature file. This was a first in the history of Olympic bids. Added to that, in February 1993, the announcement that more than $8 million had been set aside for national Olympic committees to transport bulky sports equipment, such as yachts, canoes, and horses, to and from Australia was a further example of the Sydney Bid promoting the 2000 Olympics as "Athletes' Games."

The last test was the all-important visit in March 1993 of the IOC Inquiry Commission, which comprised five IOC members, three national Olympic committee members, and three delegates from the international sports federations.

The assessment was all the more significant because the previous four Summer Olympic Games were awarded to cities which had performed well in the eyes of the Inquiry Commission. Success! Their report revealed that Sydney was the best prepared of all six contending cities and actually stated that Sydney offered "conditions beyond what the IOC is asking for."

IOC supremo Samaranch's comments during his three-day visit in May 1993 also boosted Sydney Bid's morale when he said: "If you ask me my impression of this election . . . I have to say, that all six bidders are on the same starting line. But after the start, maybe one will be faster than the other, and I think the Sydney Bid could be, and will be, very, very fast."[1] By July 1993 there were only five cities contending for the 2000 games. Brasilia, Tashkent, and Milan had withdrawn their bids, leaving Berlin, Beijing, Istanbul, Manchester, and Sydney in the final run up to "decision day." On August 15, 1993, in an article entitled "The Spirit of Sydney," Greg Stolz of the *Gold Coast Bulletin* summarized fifteen reasons why Sydney believed it should get the 2000 Olympics:

1. With its harbour, beaches and forest, Sydney provides a "matchless setting."
2. Sydney's Games plan focuses on the athletes. Competitors will be housed a few minutes' walk from the 14 Olympic Park venues and no more than 30 minutes travel from any venue.
3. Our Olympic tradition is second to none. Australia is one of only two countries to have participated in every modern Olympics.
4. Australia is a stable democracy free from serious internal conflict and will stage a "safe, friendly Games."
5. Sydney's 2000 Olympic bid is environmentally friendly, prepared in collaboration with Greenpeace.
6. The Games would be staged in Sydney's spring, providing ideal climatic conditions for competitors.
7. The Olympics have been held in Oceania, symbolised by the fifth Olympic ring, only once in the past 100 years (Melbourne 1956).
8. Sydney is united in seeking the 2000 Games, with 90 per cent of Sydneysiders in favour of staging the event.
9. Professional security controlled by the NSW Police will ensure the safety of competitors, officials and spectators.
10. Round trip airfares for all athletes and officials, plus roundtrip transport costs for sporting equipment, will be footed by Qantas.
11. Sydney is a true multicultural city with 140 ethnic groups represented.
12. Sydney is well-placed to serve the growing Asian TV market as well a the lucrative US and European networks. Olympic events in Sydney would be beamed live in US prime time.
13. Australia would provide unsurpassed media coverage.
14. Sydney has ample hotel and motel accommodation with 80,000 hotel rooms and many more to be constructed before 2000.
15. Sydney's transportation will enable the city to move 300,000 people a day with safety, speed and reliability.

Decision Day

September 23, 1993, was decision day: the final opportunity to convince all the IOC members. Plans for the thirty-minute presentation had been kept secret but much was predictable. Accompanied by short video clips, prominent Australians would make the final pitch to ninety voting IOC members comprising thirty-eight from Europe, eighteen from the Americas, sixteen from Africa, fourteen from Asia, and only four from the Oceania region. Sydney was the second city to present, and Australian Olympian and IOC member Kevan Gosper began by responding to much of the rhetoric which abounded in Monte Carlo throughout the week: "At the end of the day, only the interests of the athletes and the Olympic Movement count. . . . Well, today, we promise the athletes of the world a superbly organised Games staged in a city which personifies friendship and the very essence of the Olympic Movement." Gosper was followed in turn by the premier of New South Wales and president of the bid committee; the president of the AOC; Kieran Perkins, gold medalist at the 1992 Barcelona Olympics; Tanya Blencowe, an eleven-year-old student; Paul Keating, Australia's prime minister; Annita Keating, wife of the prime minister (who mentioned she was one of the 25 percent of all Australians who were born overseas); and Rod McGeoch, chief executive of Sydney Olympics 2000 Bid Limited.

Meanwhile, tens of thousands of Sydneysiders gathered noisily and expectantly in the middle of the night at Circular Quay to await the announcement on the huge television screens. When the IOC president came to the podium at approximately 4:25 a.m., they fell silent as he fumbled with the envelope and announced, "The winner is . . . Syd-e-ney." The euphoria of the Sydney Bid members in Monte Carlo is clearly reflected in NSW premier John Fahey's request: "I just want to say to you back there in Sydney right now, turn to the person next to you, give them a kiss, give them a hug" (*Daily Telegraph Mirror,* September 25, 1993). Prime Minister Paul Keating said, "The feeling I have now is comparable to winning an election" (*Daily Telegraph Mirror,* September 25, 1993). The prime minister was later quoted in the press: "It's a defining decision that marks out the Australian nation as one that can carry the greatest international pageant of our time, the Olympics" (*Sydney Morning Herald,* September 25, 1993).

TABLE 17.2
The 2000 Bid Voting Tally

	Round of voting			
	1	2	3	4
Sydney	30	30	37	45
Beijing	32	37	40	43
Manchester	11	13	11	
Berlin	9	9		
Istanbul	7			

As can be ascertained from table 17.2, the Sydney winning margin was two votes ahead of Beijing. The financial cost of Sydney winning the bid for the 2000 games was just over $25 million dollars; corporations contributed by far the most ($16.8 million), with the federal and New South Wales government grants amounting to $5 million and $2.9 million, respectively.

The right to stage the 2000 Olympic Games came at a significant financial cost; there is also the responsibility to ensure that they are appropriately and successfully staged. We are now in the twenty-seventh Olympiad, the four-year period of activity, within the Olympic movement, which culminates in the celebration of the 2000 games in Sydney. At a dinner in Darling Harbour in November 1993 to celebrate Sydney's victory (and to raise funds for Australian athletes competing in the 1994 Winter Olympics in Lillehammer) the AOC president, John Coates, reiterated the promise "that if we won the Games, we would use them to promote the best ideals of the Olympic Movement and to advance the Olympic Spirit—not only in this city, but in the nation and throughout the world." Later in his speech Coates cited Article 6 of the Olympic Charter: "The goal of the Olympic Movement is to contribute to building a peaceful and better world by educating youth, through sport, practiced without discrimination of any kind and in the Olympic Spirit, which requires mutual understanding with a spirit of friendship, solidarity and fair-play." Coates continued: "I deeply believe that, in the final analysis, we won the Games for Sydney and for Australia because our Bid more closely meets this Olympic goal more than other[s]" (Coates 1993). It is to be hoped that in the years to come the Sydney Bid and the 2000 Olympic Games are, and remain, a reflection of all that is positive and glorious in the world of sports and human endeavor.

However, Coates's hope has been severely tested in the short-term. In December 1998 allegations of bribes paid by the Salt Lake City bid committee to help secure the 2002 Winter Olympics emerged in the press. Thirteen IOC members were requested to "explain" their association with receipt of "gifts" which were outside the IOC guidelines. In early 1999, additional IOC members, including Australian Phil Coles, a member of the SOCOG board and employed by the AOC as director of International Relations, were added to that list.

It was natural that inquiries would be made about whether similar practices occurred for the selection of the city to host the 2000 Summer Olympics. By the end of January 1999 Sydney Olympic officials were called upon to defend their bid practices. Although they used some clever strategies which fell *within* the bid guidelines, some clearly exceeded them. AOC president John Coates admitted that he had offered approximately U.S. $70,000 to Kenya and Uganda to develop their sports programs. He had also offered accommodations in a luxury London hotel to two IOC delegates while en route to casting their deciding votes. The senior IOC member in Australia, Kevan Gosper, in an effort to isolate Coates's behavior from the larger SOCOG establishment, initially refused to back his mate, stating, "[T]he perception will be quite damaging to Sydney, it's a very serious revelation . . . I can't rule out that some [IOC members] may call for the games not to proceed in Sydney" (SOCOG news release, September 23, 1998).

Coates defended his actions by claiming that Sydney would not have won the games solely on its world-renowned geographic features and the quality of its facilities. Following a visit by an IOC delegation to Sydney in February 1999, the practices of the Sydney Bid were cleared. Nonetheless, many of the excesses and corruption associated with Olympic bids were revealed by the investigations undertaken by the IOC and other agencies, especially the U.S. Senate Inquiry. Clearly, the Olympic movement has been harmed by allegations and revelations associated with a lack of accountability of the behavior of some of its members.

Throughout the history of the Summer Olympic Games most of the host cities have been in either North America or western Europe. The first, and only, games in the Southern Hemisphere were held in Melbourne in 1956; the only summer games held in Asia were hosted in Tokyo and Seoul in 1964 and 1988, respectively. For decades this author and other Olympic historians have discussed the need for changes in the method of selecting cities to host the Winter and Summer Olympics. The Olympic charter states that the Olympic symbol of five interlocking rings represents the union of five continents and the meeting of athletes from throughout the world at the Olympic Games. If the Olympic movement is truly a global event, it should promulgate a system which encourages and allows cities or regions from all continents to host the Olympics on a rotational basis over several decades (subject, of course, to some geographical and population density controls). Sydney, with the games of the next millennium, still has the opportunity to promote the high ideals of and philosophy behind the Olympic movement, despite demonstrations that the Olympic Games are subject to the foibles and frailties of humankind.

NOTE

1. This is from Max Howell's "The History of Sydney's Bid for the 2000 Olympic Games," 101, an unpublished internal SOCOG document, 1994.

CHAPTER 18

Sports for All?

The Politics of Funding,

Nationalism, and the

Quest for Gold

LYNN EMBREY

Excellence at the Olympic Games is recognized by the bestowing of medals on those who run the swiftest, soar the highest, and display strength barely imaginable to ordinary people. Almost since the inception of the modern Olympic Games, national medal tallies have proven to be a useful medium through which to convince ordinary citizens that their swiftest, highest, and strongest Olympic performers provide indisputable evidence of their nation's excellence in the eyes of the world, regardless of political, social, and economic pressures.

Australia, with an unbroken Olympics attendance record since 1896 and medals at all Summer Games except in 1904 (see table 18.1), has won a special place in Olympic history. For sports-loving Australians this tally provides solid evidence that the nation is in exceedingly good shape and is a worthy host for the millennium games. Such is Australia's passion for international competition

While our competitors at the Olympic Games epitomise the magnificent spirit of *citius, altius, fortius*, the growing demand for excellence now extends into administering Olympism in a way that is equal to the political, social and economic pressures that bear down on each one of us every day.

—*Juan Antonio Samaranch*

272

TABLE 18.1

Australia's Medal Tally
to the Summer Olympic Games

Year	Host City	Gold	Silver	Bronze	Total
1896	Athens	2	0	0	2
1900	Paris	3	0	4	7
1904	St. Louis	0	0	0	0
1906	Athens	0	0	3	3
1908	London	1	2	1	4
1912	Stockholm	2	2	2	6
1920	Antwerp	0	2	1	3
1924	Paris	3	1	2	6
1928	Amsterdam	1	2	1	4
1932	Los Angeles	3	1	1	5
1936	Berlin	0	0	1	1
1948	London	2	6	5	13
1952	Helsinki	6	2	3	11
1956	Melbourne	13	8	14	35
1960	Rome	8	8	6	22
1964	Tokyo	6	2	10	18
1968	Mexico City	5	7	5	17
1972	Munich	8	7	2	17
1976	Montreal	0	1	4	5
1980	Moscow	2	2	5	9
1984	Los Angeles	4	8	12	24
1988	Seoul	3	6	5	14
1992	Barcelona	7	9	11	27
1996	Atlanta	9	9	23	41
2000★	Sydney	20	20	20	60

★ Targets set by the Olympic Athlete Program (OAP)

that from the relatively small population of 18 million, the Australian Olympic team has been amongst the largest to have competed at recent Olympic Games. In 1996 with a record entry of over 10,000 athletes at the games, the Australian team comprised 425 athletes and 225 support staff, making it the third largest national contingent behind the host nation, the United States of America, and Germany.

Closer inspection of Australia's medal tally (see table 18.1) reveals the dramatic and much larger story. The Australian medal tally soared to its zenith in the 1956 games in Melbourne, then descended to the nadir of the national's 1976 performance in Montreal. This low point was the catalyst for the restructuring of Australian sports. In this case, failure rekindled the relationship between nationalism and sports prowess.

Australian Sports and Nationalism

The medal tally has served in a limited way as a de facto record of the high and low tide marks of Australian nationalism. The rises and falls in medals awarded have coincided with social, political, and economic changes reflecting the optimism of the 1950s and 1960s; political stumblings in the 1970s; and a surge of extreme optimism in the 1980s, when entrepreneurs raised expectations before a string of spectacular crashes hit the stock market in October 1987. In the good times sports reaffirmed Australia's self-confidence; in the bad times sports provided a momentary distraction—a bitter cue for what could be.

By and large the white colonials preferred the sports pastimes of Mother England and played vigorously to establish equality with, then superiority to, England in sports like cricket and tennis, fueling the belief that "Jack's as good as his master." As Bill Mandle (1985) noted in his discussion of the origins of Australian sports, with success came confidence and the emergence of a distinct style of playing and Australian-devised games, the most notable of which was Australian Rules Football. Sports prowess nevertheless was established to a large extent in sports such as cricket, tennis, and rugby, which are not central to the current Olympic program.[1]

During the 1950s postwar recovery had given most Australians and an influx of European immigrants the opportunity to enhance their lifestyles and put hardship behind them. In a nation with political stability and almost full employment it was time to reap the benefits of a predominantly Mediterranean climate. Local government provided basic recreation facilities. Armies of eager volunteers raised funds and maintained local sports facilities such as the "footy" and cricket ovals, lawn bowling greens, and tennis courts which dotted the abundant open spaces. The beaches were clean and free, as were the limited inland waterways. The white population, dwelling mostly around the coastal perimeter of the island continent, increasingly pursued aquatic leisure activities. Buoyed by the success of the elite swimmers and concerned about water safety, local government authorities underwrote the installation of open-air swimming pools, many of which were dedicated as war memorial pools or Olympic pools or both. State-based education systems, in partnership with the swimming associations, taught the nation to swim either in school time or during the long, hot summer vacations. Reclining on a towel either at the beach or pool darkened the suntan and sustained the mythology of the "bronzed Anzac."[2] A darker skin tone set Aussies apart from their English forebears and typified healthy outdoor living—despite most sun lovers' scorn for the darker pigmentation of the indigenous population. Through the 1950s and 1960s the sports Anzac enhanced his reputation around the world through international sports such as tennis, cricket, golf, and surfing while his "sheila" proved equally adept, claiming inaugural world championships in women's sports such as netball and softball.

Successive prime ministers capitalized on the nation's obsession with sports by attending most major events. During his two decades in office in the postwar era, Liberal prime minister Robert Menzies made substantial use of his passion for cricket. Through astute management he invoked it to affirm Australia's ties to the British Empire and to project empathy with the person in the street. Recent prime ministers regularly accept "number one" ticket holder status with leading clubs in Australian Rules Football in the southern states and rugby to the north. Increasingly, politicians (accompanied by larger and larger entourages) travel to international events, although they are not always accorded the welcome they expect. In Montreal in 1976 athletes snubbed Prime Minister Malcolm Fraser when he visited the Olympic Village, preferring to stay in their beds as a protest against his Liberal government's reduction in sports funding. His Labor successor, Bob Hawke, made the most of his office to pursue his unquenchable thirst for sports and attendant photo opportunities. While Fraser attempted to soften the blows of the country's economic hardships in the 1970s with his infamous proclamation, "Life wasn't meant to be easy," Hawke partied with the best of them as Australia celebrated victory in the America's Cup in 1983, and he appeared on television to uphold publicly the workers' right to be late for work the next day! In 1993 both Prime Minister Paul Keating and his Dutch-born wife, Annita, were key players in the Sydney team which bid to host the 2000 games.

The nadir of the medals tally for Australia in 1976 coincided with a period of political turmoil and rapid changes of leadership. After two decades of Liberal government, Labor took office in 1972 and embarked on an ambitious program of social and economic reform. After a series of financial disasters, Labor was sacked at the end of 1975. The Liberals were reelected and held office until 1983.

The nexus between sports, politics (especially foreign affairs), and money became transparent in 1980 when the Liberal government backed the boycott of the Moscow games instigated by the United States. The government vehemently opposed Australia participation and made it clear to the Australian Olympic Federation (as the AOC was then known) that the funds that had already been advanced were not to be used to send the team. Relationships between the government and the AOF became increasingly strained as the AOF opted to attend but allowed individual athletes and teams the right to make their own decision. In his comprehensive history of Australia and the Olympic Games, Harry Gordon (1994) explained that the AOF was able to send a team because it used funds generated from a very successful sponsorship drive. The government compensated the athletes and teams who supported the boycott with sums that were greater than those previously allocated for attendance at the games.

Labor resumed office in 1983, determined to push ahead with its social reform agenda. During the 1980s the Australian economy, under the spell of the entrepreneurs, grew vigorously. In the aftermath of the stock market crash of 1987 pessimism and cautiousness brought far more stringent accountability measures to all financial activities. In a more sombre society, unemployment, poverty, and crime became part of the daily reality, not just something on television. Sports, too, became accountable as economic restraints were applied to it by both government and the private sector. Where sports had once been a voluntary pastime in the 1980s, it was rapidly transformed into a business, then designated as an industry in the 1990s.

Australia's Olympic Record

The tally of medals resembles the moods of the ocean that surrounds the island continent which has a landmass equivalent to the continental United States. Generally calm prior to World War II, occasional surface ripples marked slight variations in performance as Australia's medal tally fluctuated between one (in 1936) and seven (in 1900). Immediately after the war a discernible swell occurred which crested in 1956 when, in front of a joyous home crowd, Australian athletes established a national record of thirty-five medals, comprising thirteen gold, eight silver, and fourteen bronze. Thirty-five medals became the benchmark for all subsequent Olympic performances. In particular, victories in the men's fifteen-hundred-meter freestyle and the women's one-hundred-meter freestyle (see table 18.2) signaled Australia's attempts to claim ownership of the pool. The men's race has been characterized by frequent success with six gold medals and multiple placings. Frank Beaurepaire, Andrew "Boy" Charlton, Murray Rose, John Konrads, and Kieren Perkins became household names in Australia. Another fifteen-hundred-meter swimmer, Stephen Holland, failed to win gold, but his bronze medal would have an enormous impact on sports funding in Australia.

Success in the women's race for medals has been less frequent, but two swimmers achieved success of a unique kind. Sarah "Fanny" Durack's victory in the first swimming event for women in 1912 was also the first medal won by an Australian woman. Dawn Fraser was the first woman to break the one-minute barrier for the one-hundred-meter freestyle and, until 1996, the only swimmer—male or female—to succeed at the same event in three consecutive Olympics. Intermittent success in the other swimming distances and disciplines perpetuated the sense of Australia's ownership and ease in the aquatic environment.

The tallies in Rome and Tokyo were disappointing but the country made allowances for the difficulties of competing overseas and out of season. Cautious expectations attended athletes at Mexico City where the rarefied air and high altitude exceeded all geographical features of "the wide, brown land." Here Australia's worst fears were confirmed when distance track star Ron Clarke collapsed a lap and half from the finish of the ten thousand meters. In the short events in the pool, the swimmers, led by Michael Wenden with two gold medals and Lyn McClements with one, secured almost half the total Australian tally.

TABLE 18.2

Achievements in the Men's 1,500-meter and Women's 100-meter Freestyle

Year	Men's 1,500 Meters	Medal	Women's 100 Meters	Medal
1908	Frank Beaurepaire	Bronze		
1912	Harold Hardwick	Bronze	Sarah "Fanny" Durack	Gold
			Wilhelmina "Mina" Wiley	Silver
1920	Frank Beaurepaire	Bronze		
1924	Andrew "Boy" Charlton	Gold		
	Frank Beaurepaire	Bronze		
1928	Andrew "Boy" Charlton	Silver		
1948	John Marshall	Silver		
1956	Murray Rose	Gold	Dawn Fraser	Gold
			Lorraine Crapp	Silver
1960	John Konrads	Gold	Dawn Fraser	Gold
	Murray Rose	Silver		
1964	Robert Windle	Gold	Dawn Fraser	Gold
	Allan Wood	Bronze		
1968	Greg Brough	Bronze		
1972	Graham Windeatt	Silver	Shane Gould	Bronze
1976	Stephen Holland	Bronze		
1980	Max Metzker	Bronze		
1992	Kieren Perkins	Gold		
	Glen Housman	Silver		
1996	Kieren Perkins	Gold		
	Daniel Kowalski	Silver		

Hopes soared for Munich. Swimming sensation Shane Gould, born one day after the opening of the Melbourne games in 1956, held the set of women's freestyle world records from one hundred to fifteen hundred meters. She was a clear favorite to reclaim the women's one-hundred-meter crown and the women's freestyle set, as well as the medley. She came away with three gold medals (all in world record time), a silver, and a bronze, the highest individual tally in the pool.

Munich was the country's high tide mark from which success rapidly receded. Four years later in Montreal, Australia was shocked as defeat after defeat revealed major deficiencies in the Australian Olympic program. Despite pre-games predictions of bountiful rewards, Australian athletes failed to win any gold medals. Five "lesser" medals—silver and bronze—in "minor" sports such as men's hockey, the equestrian events, and yachting failed to make amends. The brunt of the nation's displeasure was borne by reigning fifteen-hundred-meter freestyle world record holder and national hero Stephen Holland. Nicknamed "Super Fish," Holland managed only a single bronze medal. In response to the poor performances and the country's ire, John Daly, the head coach of the track-and-field team, defended the entire Australian team in a long letter to the national daily newspaper, the *Australian,* arguing that the athletes had not let Australia down but rather Australia had let the athletes down by expecting them to outperform those from nations with state sports systems incorporated in either their educational or military institutions.

True to the cliché "every cloud has a silver lining," five minor medals, and especially Holland's bronze, proved to be the catalyst needed to stimulate a serious examination into the government's role in sports. Slowly, Australia clawed its way back at the games, although the tallies for Moscow and Los Angeles will continue to be assessed with skepticism due to the boycotts which saw the United States and some of its allies withdraw in protest at the Russian invasion of Afghanistan, and Russia and the communist bloc retaliate in kind, on the basis of suspected threats to the safety of their athletes in the heart of capitalism.

By 1996 the total number of competitors at the Atlanta Olympics exceeded ten thousand. Australia's team had grown likewise, along with the pressure to produce more gold medals. The angst was clearly visible in the swimming pool. Prior to the final night of the program in Atlanta, gold had again proved elusive. Daniel Kowalski, with bronze medals in the men's two-hundred- and four-hundred-meter freestyle, was Australia's most successful swimmer. Quantity was, however, a poor substitute for color. Kowalski's self-criticism along with pleas from other swimmers to the Australian public not to be disappointed with their efforts, fueled negative press reports about the swimming team. Four days into the games, a cartoonist for the *Australian* captured the national sentiment by lambasting Australia for its tally of bronze medals. Former champion swimmer turned television broadcaster Neil Brooks blasted the team's poor technique. Head coach Don Talbot argued for more money for more international competition. So intense was the criticism that Kowalski's mother, Penny, felt compelled to come to the defense of her son, and indeed the whole swimming team, with a letter to the editor of the *Australian* expressing the enormous hurt felt by the family. An excerpt from the letter appeared on the front page under a photograph of a very forlorn Kowalski: "What should have been a wonderful week for us has been totally overshadowed. The pride we have in our son's achievements is something we will now share with only our close friends who do not consider them disappointing." The poignancy of the letter stood in stark contrast to the bluntness of the chef de mission and head of the Australian Olympic Committee (AOC), John Coates, who stated that the swimmers simply had to do better. They would be expected to contribute one third of the total tally—twenty medals—in Sydney in 2000. The statements from Penny Kowalski and John Coates highlighted the dramatic change in the way in the medal tally was interpreted by and to the Australian public. To the

FIGURE 18.1

"What? Not another bronze."

Courtesy of Peter Nicholson, *The Australian*, July 25, 1996.

former the medal represented tradition, a record of achievement. To the latter it was a measure of accountability for public spending.

Fortunately, swimming retrieved its pride when Susie O'Neill won the women's two-hundred-meter butterfly and Kieren Perkins, having qualified eighth fastest for the fifteen-hundred-meter freestyle, blitzed the field and secured back-to-back titles in Barcelona and Atlanta. By night's end the swimmers had contributed two gold, four silver, and six bronze medals—29 percent—to the national tally of forty-one medals, which finally exceeded the Melbourne haul. Perkins' victory, splashed across the front page of the daily newspapers, was cause for national celebration.

It was a victory celebrated only by Australians. As there were no Americans in that race with a chance of success, U.S. television chose not to broadcast it. In an odd twist to the display of nationalism at the games, American newspapers and television preferred to applaud the Australian women's softball team which had achieved the unthinkable feat of beating the American dream team. Australian softball achieved what Perkins could not—the front page of *USA Today* and major U.S. television coverage.

Officially, a points table is a violation of Principle 9 of the Olympic Charter, and the International Olympic Committee (IOC) does not sanction a medals table. As Allen Guttman (1992) explains in *The Olympics: A History of the Modern Games,* the IOC took its first stance against the publication of a points table as early as 1921 to deter chauvinism. This injunction, however, has not prevented outbreaks of nationalist propaganda to justify a particular ideology, as was the case in Helsinki in 1952 when athletes from the Soviet Union attended their first Olympic Games. The Russian athletes were housed separately from other athletes and, to emphasize their superiority and that of the socialist regime, a billboard in the compound displayed an unofficial points tally. Embarrassingly, the plot backfired on the Soviets as Americans overtook them on the last day of competition.

Such displays remain a standard item in the media reporting of the Olympic Games and any world championship in which there are multiple events such as swimming, track and field, cycling, and gymnastics. A debate rages today not about the keeping of the tally but about alternative methods of calculating success, taking into consideration total population, percentage of participants, size of respective Olympic teams, and the number of events contested by each nation. Another factor that needs to be taken into account is the number of participating nations, which has almost trebled from 67 in Melbourne in 1956 to 198 in Atlanta in 1996. The program has grown, too, with more sports—nineteen in Melbourne, twenty-eight in Atlanta—and consequently more events.

The accuracy of the tally has also come under closer scrutiny. Recent examination of the photo finish of the women's one-hundred-meter track race in Helsinki revealed that Australia's Shirley Strickland should have been awarded a bronze medal rather than the fourth place determined in the immediate post-trace hurly-burly. Graciously, Strickland declined to press her claims, accepting the decision made at the time. In another twist, the U.S. Olympic Committee identified in excess of fifty American athletes who could lay claims to the medals won by competitors from East Germany as prosecutions proceed against former coaches and doctors accused of administering performance-enhancing drugs to junior athletes. Some Australian swimmers and track athletes also came in behind East Germans, but in Australia there is an ambivalence about claiming secondhand, tarnished medals. [See chapter 13—eds.]

What the medal tally does not reveal and Australians seldom recognize is that Australian women have won proportionately more medals than their male teammates. Olympic historian Harry Gordon described Fanny Durack's 1912 victory as the start of a "whole glistening conga-line of champions: women like Clare Dennis, Shirley Strickland, Marjorie Jackson, Betty Cuthbert, Dawn Fraser, Shane Gould and Debbie Flintoff-King" (1994, 78). Since World War II women have comprised just under 20 percent of the Olympic team and yet, with fewer events to contest, have brought home 40 percent of the gold medals, including 75 percent of the track-and-field gold. Furthermore, with the addition of women's team games such as field hockey, basketball, and softball to the program, Australian women are showing consistency across all sports, including those requiring team work.

Finally, in determining a nation's overall ranking on the points table, gold medals take precedence, thus underscoring the inferior value of silver and bronze medals.

TABLE 18.3

Final medal table at the Atlanta Olympics

Country	Gold	Silver	Bronze	Total
United States	44	32	25	101
Russia	26	21	16	63
Germany	20	18	27	65
China	16	22	12	50
France	15	7	15	37
Italy	13	10	12	35
Australia	9	9	23	41
Cuba	9	8	8	25
Ukraine	9	2	12	23
South Korea	7	15	5	27

This is clearly evident in the final table from Atlanta. The United States, with 44 gold, 32 silver, and 25 bronze medals, for a total of 101, stood clearly on top. Russia ranked second with 26 gold out of a total of 63, while third-ranked Germany had a total of 65 but only 20 gold. China was fourth with 16 gold in a tally of 50. France and Italy, with 37 and 35 medals, respectively, had lower totals than Australia's 41, but France had 15 gold and Italy had 13. Australia, Cuba, and the Ukraine each had 9 gold, but Cuba and the Ukraine had 25 and 23 medals, respectively, in total (see table 18.3). Depending upon the target audience, Australian Olympic officials selectively emphasize either the country's fifth place on total medals or seventh (but never equal seventh) on gold medals.

Funding Australian Sports

Apart from some limited assistance to the 1956 Olympics and the 1938 and 1962 (British) Empire Games, federal government involvement in sports has been minimal. Australian athletes funded their own forays to international events, the hardships of which are poignantly revealed in Cynthia Nadalin's essay in this anthology. Many a sports team owed its success to raffling "chooks" (chickens) and selling that uniquely Australian cake, the lamington. With the modest successes that accumulated up to the 1970s, the funding model was, to all intents and purposes, a satisfactory arrangement. Sports controlled its own destiny but, as success became less frequent, unfavorable comparisons were drawn between Australia and the nations accumulating the highest medal tallies.

The first major funding challenge occurred in 1972 when Labor was elected to government. This election ended the separation of the state and sports. Labor deliberately undertook to ensure that all Australians had greater access to and participation in a range of leisure and cultural activities. Frank Stewart, the first federal minister for Tourism and Recreation, commissioned John Bloomfield of the University of Western Australia to prepare a report to serve as a framework for the new ministry into which money flowed generously: $1 million in the first year, $7.4 million by 1975. A subsequent report by Alan Coles of the University of Queensland recommended that a national institute of sports be established to oversee the preparation of the nation's elite athletes. When Labor was subsequently dismissed because of some controversial financial dealings, Coles's report seemed destined to become flotsam in a pool that was beginning to resemble the intermittent water holes of a drought-stricken river.

The reelected Liberal government gave priority to curbing the excesses of its predecessors. Sports funding was slashed by $2 million. Australian sports slid into a deep trough and was in danger of drowning. The sight of Stephen Holland symbolically towing the whole nation up and down the thirty laps of the fifteen-hundred-meter freestyle for a bronze was more than the citizens or Prime Minister Fraser cared to witness. "Bronze" was not a favored color. The international sports standard was gold and nothing less would do. When Prime Minister Fraser met with the small group of athletes who made the effort to get out of their beds after the final heats of the Montreal games, he attempted to console them. But the old platitudes valuing "taking part and how well you played the game" rang hollow. Fraser argued that the emphasis on medals defied the Olympic spirit. But the athletes knew their colleagues from the United States were on university scholarships and the communist bloc athletes held military ranks which allowed them hours each day to train. As the postmortems continued in the Australian press, Fraser relented and ordered an inquiry.

By 1976 sports were organized and had a collective national voice through the Confederation of Australian Sport (CAS). Staffed by former public servants, some of whom had experience in the Stewart Labor Ministry, CAS sought consensus from the burgeoning national sports organizations whose ranks now numbered over a hundred. With substantial evidence in its seminal publications, *The Financial Plight of Sport in Australia* and *Master Plan for Sport,* the CAS urged the government to formulate a national sports policy and set up the national sports institute for elite athletes.

Government funding not only was restored but began to increase, although the government-sponsored Moscow boycott seriously strained relations. Post-Moscow, the troubled waters between sports and the government were calmed by senior Liberal minister Bob Ellicott, who had since January 1980 steered discussions about the most suitable model for the national sports institute. National track coach and sports historian John Daly, in his authoritative text *Quest for Excellence,* described the institute as a form of reconciliation between sports and government. The Australian Institute of Sport (AIS) opened in Canberra in 1981 as a statutory body. From the outset it was dubbed the "gold medal factory" because it incorporated many of the features of eastern European elite sports academies. Times had changed irrevocably.

Seven sports took up residence in the first year. Five of them—athletics (track and field), basketball, gymnastics, swimming, and weight lifting—were Olympic sports. The other two were netball and tennis. Recognizing that Australia's sports agenda was more extensive than the Olympic program, noninstitute sports vied for inclusion. Claims and counterclaims about the advantages and disadvantages of a centralized institute further fueled protracted debates. To placate the protagonists and in recognition of regional strengths, other centers were established, for hockey in Perth, for cycling and cricket in Adelaide, and for squash and rowing in Brisbane. State and territory institutes were independently established. Almost a decade elapsed before they entered collaborative partnerships with the AIS. Funds and institutes do not, however, automatically produce medals. Those supporting a decentralized model used the lack of instant success to emphasize the need for athletes to be in familiar environments with their families.

When Labor resumed office in 1984 it rekindled its "good life" ideology. The Australian Sports Commission (ASC) was established that same year as a statutory body with three areas of responsibility: performance by the elite, participation by the masses, and fund-raising. Two statutory bodies with substantial budgets—the AIS and the ASC—quickly drew criticism, and in 1988 an inquiry was held into the funding and administration of sports in Australia. The inquiry was informed by the Darwinian pyramid model. The premise was that a wide base of participation allows all players the opportunity to apply their talent—with the best graduating to the elite level. The report's title, *Going for Gold,* openly supported medal tallies. It recommended that the government accept responsibility for "funding the pursuit of excellence by Australia's elite athletes" and increase funding.[3] The AIS and ASC became a single statutory body with the ASC as senior partner.

Faith in the Australian "system" was buoyed up by outstanding performances at the Commonwealth Games held between Olympic Games. Australia, as one of a handful of predominantly developed nations, was, however, a big fish in a small pond. Despite media coverage in Australia that rivaled that of the Olympics, it was easy to ignore the absence of the nations which were placed higher than Australia in the Olympic tally. So Australians marveled at massive hauls of medals— 162 in Auckland in 1990, 182 in Vancouver in 1994, and 198 in Kuala Lumpur in 1998.

For a while it seemed that sports and politics had reached a harmonious relationship. That dream was shattered in 1995. Labor floundered in very muddy waters when the minister for Sport and Recreation, Ros Kelly, was accused of bias toward marginal Labor electorates in the allocation of funds for sports facilities. She revealed (in a subsequent parliamentary inquiry into what became known as the Sports Rorts affair) that funding records were maintained on a white board in her office. This casual system was far less rigorous than the accountability measures introduced by the ministry on sports organizations. The Sports Rorts affair was one of many problems the electorate experienced with the federal Labor government. In 1996 the Liberals won the election with an overwhelming vote.

Funding the Olympic Team

Funding Australian Olympic athletes became a critical issue on September 24, 1993, when IOC supremo Juan Antonio Samaranch uttered the one word Australians had waited all night to hear, "Syd-n-ey." Consistently, AOC boss John Coates has stated his belief that the Australian public will only consider hosting the games a success if the athletes succeed, that is, if the number of gold medals is high. To that end, the AOC, together with the ASC, created an elite, well-endowed, financially secure Olympic Athlete Program (OAP). The initial budget for athlete preparation for the period from 1995 to 2000 was almost $200 million. A further sum of $231 million was set aside for the Sports Assistance Scheme to defray other expenses related to the Olympic and Paralympic sports. This would buy internationally acclaimed coaches, seed training scholarships of between $2,000 and $10,000 to over nine hundred world-ranked athletes, and establish a short-term Talent Identification Program (TIP) whereby schoolchildren could be screened for physical attributes, especially height and arm span. Altogether, 100,000 children were assessed, 1,315 of whom progressed to elite training programs in cycling, rowing, triathlon, water polo, and wrestling. The pyramid model of sports for all leading to limited elite development no longer applied. Rather, the inverted T model of the eastern bloc countries was adopted as a more efficient selection tool. In this model a large population sample is tested as early as possible to select children who meet specified anatomical, physiological, and genetic criteria. They then enter long years of training for excellence.

The apparent generosity of the OAP carries with it a large price tag. Olympic athletes must provide a return on the investment. At least sixty medals—twenty of each color—are required to move Australia from seventh on total medals in Atlanta to fifth in Sydney. Responsibility has been directed toward those sports with established Olympic records, such as swimming, field hockey, and equestrian events. Hence tallies for 2000 appear in Olympic tally tables like that of table 18.1—even though the Games have not begun! Officially, the sixty medals are "projections," not targets, in order not to violate the Olympic Charter.

The new Olympics initiatives were being implemented when the Liberals took office in 1996. In the lead-up to the election the party's sports policy, *Encouraging Players . . . Developing Champions,* clearly endorsed the existing elite sports programs of performance and participation. The rhetoric of the policy went further to advocate that all Australians should benefit from hosting the games. Essentially, hosting the games would inspire more people to participate in physical activity.

Funding sports was, however, a minnow in the minds of the new government. Within weeks of assuming office, the government declared that the nation faced a perilous financial situation and that severe measures would be implemented to eliminate the estimated $8 billion deficit. (Defense was the only government department spared.) The athletes preparing for Atlanta had increased pressure to perform. Winning was necessary in order to justify current spending and to ensure that funding was maintained at least up to 2000.

The first round of cuts targeted the non-Olympic sports, in particular those which had low participation bases (such as korfball) and organizations which service sports (such as sports medicine). The second round of cuts, technically termed "reallocation of funds," drew on the results of the post-Atlanta review. Those sports with few or no medals, such as track and field and gymnastics, had their budgets cut. Executing the funding decisions in two rounds promoted considerable debate in the sports community. For a population of just over 18 million, Australia probably has a more diverse array of sports and more national sports organizations than any other country. In Australia the Olympic sports are mainly "minor" sports, that is, they have fewer participants and draw small, if any, crowds. The "major" sports—the four football codes (Australian Rules, rugby league, rugby union, and soccer), cricket, netball, and lawn bowls—which have the highest participation rates and draw substantial crowds and media coverage, are non-Olympic sports. Cynics suggest that the definition of a minor sport is one which has more participants than spectators!

Active Australia

While the Sydney games and elite sports have taken the lion's share of funding and media attention, the government has not neglected mass participation. Overshadowed but developing in the same time frame has been another initiative, "Active Australia," which commenced with the Keating Labor government and has been continued by the Howard Liberal government. Philosophically, Active Australia builds on a strong tradition of mass participation of Australians in sports. One of the most successful public campaigns has been "Life. Be in It." With extensive television coverage, its central character, Norm, an overweight and unfit couch potato, urged Australians in the 1970s and 1980s to get out of their armchairs, move away from their television sets, and participate in the full range of sports and cultural activities available in the community. By the late 1980s "Life. Be in It" moved to the private sector; other Active Australia programs now run under the auspices of federal health authorities.

Active Australia has been acknowledged by many sports leaders and academics as conceptually sound, but until it has proven itself doubts will exist for its long-term viability. Cynics argue that Active Australia is not just a good idea but will "save face" for Australia when the television sets of the world are focused on Sydney in 2000.

Speculations

How would the Australian sports system have evolved if Stephen Holland had won a gold medal in Montreal? At what other point would sports have collided with the social, economic, and political pressures to produce one of the largest and best sports systems in the world? Arguably, the despised bronze medals have been better for the long-term development of the Australian sports system than the elusive gold medals. But gold produced legends which reinforced a belief in the quintessential Australian who relishes a "fair go."

How would the government have supported preparation of the 2000 Olympic team if Juan Antonio Samaranch had uttered "Beijing" on that eventful night in September 1993? And, what will the reality be in October 2000 when the euphoria begins to fade and Australia takes stock of its Olympic effort? Assuming that the athletes deliver on the investment in them, will sixty medals be sufficient sustenance for the sports industry? Will sixty medals satisfy what Samaranch has clearly identified as the "growing demand for excellence ... [in] administering Olympism"? What is the shelf life of sixty medals? Will Australians be inspired permanently to leave their television sets and become participants and so realize the vision of Active Australia? Will the government reverse its foreshadowed cuts and reward the athletes with adequate funds to win even more medals in Athens in 2004? Is there a critical mass at which the number of medalists precludes the emergence of individual Australian legends of the caliber of Dawn Fraser, Shane Gould, and Kieren Perkins? Or will the sheer quantity of medals generate a new definition of nationalism? And, what if the worst case scenario eventuates and less than sixty medals are added to the tally? What is certain is that sports in post-2000 Australia will be profoundly different in ways that have yet to be envisioned.

NOTES

1. Tennis attained Olympic status as a demonstration sport in 1988 and as a medal sport in 1992. Soccer is part of the Olympic program but only as an under-23 competition. Open competition in the World Cup is the preserve of FIFA.

2. "Anzac" denoted the badge of courage earned by Australian (and New Zealand) army corps on foreign soils.

3. House of Representatives Standing Committee on Finance and Public Administration, Parliament of the Commonwealth of Australia, 1989.

REFERENCES

Adams, P. 1998. Gamely to the Gallows. *Weekend Australian*. December 19–20, 32.

Alasuutari, P. Forthcoming. *The Inscribed Audience: The New Agenda of Media Reception and Audience Ethnography*. London: Sage.

Alkemeyer, T. 1996. *Körper, Kult und Politik*. Frankfurt: Campus.

Allgemeine Sport-Zeitung. 1903–1914.

Anderson, C. 1992. Olympic Row over Sex Testing. *Nature* 252: 784.

Ang, I. 1996. *Living Room Wars: Rethinking Audiences for a Postmodern World*. London: Routledge.

Arnaud, P., and T. Terret. 1993. *Le rêve blanc: Olympisme et sports d'hiver en France*. Bordeaux: Presses universitaires de Bordeaux.

Athletes of the Gay Games. 1998. *Advocate* 765–766 (August 18): 71–99.

Australian Society for Sports History. 1994. *The Oxford Companion to Australian Sport*. 2nd. ed. Melbourne: Oxford University Press.

Australian Sports Commission. 1996. *Annual Report*. Canberra: Australian Sports Commission.

Bale, J. 1991. *The Brain Drain: Foreign Student-Athletes in American Universities*. Urbana: University of Illinois Press.

Bamberger, M. 1996. Rowing. *Sports Illustrated Olympic Preview Issue,* July 22, 124–126.

Bandy, S. 1988. The Olympic Celebration of the Arts. In *The Olympic Games in Transition,* ed. J. Segrave and D. Chu. Champaign, Ill.: Human Kinetics Books.

Barham, S. B. 1985. The Phallus and the Man: An Analysis of Male Striptease. In *Australian Ways: Anthropological Studies of an Industrialized Society,* ed. L. Manderson, 51–65. Sydney: Allen and Unwin.

Baroni, D. 1994. Feminist: What *Is* It About That Word? *Cosmopolitan,* May, 196.

Batty, P. 1998. Saluting the Dot-Spangled Banner: Aboriginal Culture, National Identity, and the Australian Republic. *Australian Humanities Review,* 11. http://www.lib.latrobe.edu.au/AHR . . . e/Issue-September-1998/batty.html.

Bellear, S. 1993. Interview. *AM* Australian Broadcasting Corporation, Radio. Sydney: Australian Broadcasting Corporation.

Birrell, S., and C. L. Cole, eds. 1994. *Women, Sport, and Culture.* Champaign, Ill.: Human Kinetics Publishers.

Blair, T. 1998. Just Say Go. *Time,* July 27, 43.

Bohlen, F. 1979. *Die XI. Olympischen Spiele Berlin 1936.* Cologne: Pahl-Rugenstein.

Bomann-Larsen, T. 1993. *Den evige sne.* Oslo: Cappelens.

Booth, D., and C. Tatz. 1993–94. Sydney 2000—The Games People Play. *Current Affairs Bulletin* (December–January): 7.

———. 1994. Swimming with the Big Boys? The Politics of Sydney's 2000 Olympic Bid. *Sporting Traditions: Journal of the Australian Society for Sports History* 11, no. 1: 3–23.

Boulongne, Y. P. 1975. *La Vie et l'oeuvre pédagogique de Pierre de Coubertin.* Ottawa: LeMéac.

Bourdieu, P. 1990. *In Other Words: Essays Towards a Reflexive Sociology.* Cambridge: Polity Press.

Bringing Them Home: National Inquiry into the Separation of Aboriginal and Torres Strait Islander Children from Their Families. 1997. Sydney: Human Rights and Equal Opportunities Commission.

British Ski Year Book. 1905–1914, 1920–1932.

Brubach. H. 1996. The Athletic Esthetic. *New York Times Magazine,* June 23, 48–51.

Brundage, A. Collection. Lausanne: Comité International Olympique.

———. 1935. *Fair Play for American Athletes.* Chicago: American Olympic Committee.

———. 1968. *Speeches of Avery Brundage.* Lausanne: Comité International Olympique.

Budd, J. 1989. A Tall Poppy Who Refused to Bow. *Sunday Mail,* February 26, 1–2, 21.

Bunge, R. G. 1960. Sex and the Olympic Games. *Journal of the American Medical Association* 173, no. 12: 196.

Burchall, G. 1997. Olympic Events: The Festival of the Dreaming. Celebrating in a Big, Black Way. *The Age,* June 2, C-5.

Cahill, P. 1997. Pink Power's Diversity Carries Cash Clout. *Variety,* September 15–21, 34, 44.

Cahn, S. K. 1994. *Coming on Strong: Gender and Sexuality in Twentieth-Century Women's Sport.* Cambridge: Harvard University Press.

———. 1998. From the "Muscle Moll" to the "Butch" Ballplayer: Mannishness, Lesbianism, and Homophobia in US Women's Sports. *Feminist Studies* 19 (2): 343–368.

Carlson, A. 1991. When Is a Woman Not a Woman? *Women's Sports and Fitness,* March, 24–29.

Carmichael, G. S. 1992. So Many Children: Colonial and Post-colonial Demographic Patterns. In *Gender Relations in Australia: Domination and Negotiation,* ed. K. Saunders and R. Evans, 103–143. Sydney: Harcourt Brace Jovanovich.

Cashman, R. 1995. *Paradise of Sport: The Rise of Organised Sport in Australia.* Melbourne: Oxford University Press.

Charron, P., and T. Terret. 1998. *Une histoire de water-polo.* Paris: L'Harmattan.

Clark, J. 1994a. The End . . . of the Beginning. *Village Voice* 39, no. 27 (July 5): 140, 142.

———. 1994b. Let the Games Begin. *Village Voice* 39, no. 25 (June 21): 12.

Coakley, Jay J. 1998. *Sport in Society.* 6th ed. Boston: Irwin/McGraw-Hill.

Coates, J. 1993. Speech. Darling Harbour, Sydney. November.

Coe, R. M. 1986. *A Sense of Pride: The Story of Gay Games II.* San Francisco, Calif.: Pride Productions.

Cole, C. L. 1998. Addiction, Exercise, and Cyborgs: Technologies of Deviant Bodies. In *Sport and Postmodern Times,* ed. G. Rail, 261–276. Albany: SUNY Press.

Colebatch, D. 1998. Letter. *Sydney Morning Herald,* January 16, 18.

Confederation of Australian Sport. 1996. *Sport,* 16.

Connell, R. W. 1983. *Which Way Is Up? Essays on Sex, Class, and Culture.* Sydney: George Allen and Unwin.

Coplon, J., and C. Francis. 1991. *Speed Trap: Inside the Biggest Scandal in Olympic History.* London: Grafton Books.

Cruse, O. 1997. Welcoming Speech. Festival of the Dreaming. Sydney, Australia. September 14.

Daddario, G. 1997. Gendered Sports Programming: 1992 Summer Olympic Coverage and the Feminine Narrative Form. *Sociology of Sport Journal* 14, no. 2: 103–120.

Daly, J. 1991. *Quest for Excellence: The Australian Institute of Sport in Canberra.* Canberra: Australian Government Publishing Service.

de Coubertin, P. 1988. Why I Revived the Olympic Games. In *The Olympic Games in Transition,* ed. J. Segrave and D. Chu, 101–106. Champaign, Ill.: Human Kinetics Books.

de la Chappelle, A. 1986. The Use and Misuse of Sex Chromatin Screening for "Gender Identification" of Female Athletes. *Journal of the American Medical Association* 256, no. 14: 1920–1923.

de la Chappelle, A., and M. Genel. 1987. Gender Verification of Female Athletes. *Lancet* 11: 1265–1266.

de Moragas Spà, M., N. K. Rivenbaugh, and J. F. Larson. 1995. *Television in the Olympics.* London: John Libbey.

DeMeyer, T. A. 1996. Thorpe Family to Receive Medals at LCO. *Ojibwe Akiing (Wisc.),* December.

———. 1997. Medals Returned, Honor Restored. *Hayward (Wisc.) News from Indian Country,* mid March.

———. 1998. Jim Thorpe Named America's Greatest All-Around Athlete and Greatest Football Player of the Century. *Hayward (Wisc.) News from Indian Country,* late January.

———. 1998. Jim Thorpe Stamp Unveiled. *Hayward (Wisc.) News from Indian Country,* late February.

———. 1998. Soaring Eagles Honored. *Ojibwe Akiing (Wisc.),* March.

———. 1998. Thorpe's Medals Stolen, Returned. *Hayward (Wisc.) News from Indian Country,* late October.

Demo Derby. 1998. *Variety,* June 8–14, 24.

Der Winter. 1911–1914.

Desert, J. U. 1997. Queer Space. In *Queers in Space: Communities/Public Places/Sites of Resistance,* ed. Ingram, G., A. M. Bouthillette, and Y. Retter. Seattle, Wash.: Bay Press.

Dingeon, B. 1993. Gender Verification and the Next Olympic Games (Correspondence). *Journal of the American Medical Association* 269, no. 33: 357.

Dingeon, B., R. Hamon, M. Robert, et al. 1992. Sex Testing at the Olympics (Correspondence). *Nature* 358: 447.

Donohew, L., D. Helm, and J. Haas. 1989. Drugs and Len Bias on the Sports Page. In *Media, Sports and Society,* ed. Wenner, L. A. Newbury Park: Sage Publications.

Dorozynski, A. 1992. Olympic Committee Will Do Genetics Tests on Women Athletes. *British Medical Journal* 304, no. 6823: 3336.

Dorrance, A., with T. Nash. 1996. *Training Soccer Champions.* Apex, N.C.: JTC Sports.

Drane, R. 1997. The Dope Master. *Inside Sport,* November, 26–38.

Dreger, A. 1998. *Hermaphrodites and the Medical Invention of Sex.* Cambridge: Harvard University Press.

Du Bois, W.E.B. 1961. *The Souls of Black Folk.* New York: Fawcett.

Duncan, M. C. 1990. Sports Photographs and Sexual Difference: Images of Women and Men in the 1984 and 1988 Olympic Games. *Sociology of Sport Journal* 7: 22–43.

Dunn, K. 1997. Courney Love. *Rolling Stone,* November 13, 166.

Dusevic, T. 1993. Dangerous Games. *The Australian.* September 21.

Dyer, R. 1992. *Only Entertainment.* London: Routledge.

Dysart, D. 1997. Émigré Artists. *Art and Australia* 35, no. 2: 192–193.

Edwards, H. 1969. *The Revolt of the Black Athlete.* New York: Free Press.

———. 1980. *The Struggle That Must Be.* New York: Macmillan Publishing Company.

———. 1998. Race, Sports, and the American Dream. Keynote address presented at the Association of Black Sociologists, San Francisco, August 20.

Elliott, S. 1998a. Levi Strauss Begins a Far-reaching Marketing Campaign to Reach Gay Men and Lesbians. *New York Times,* October 26, C-1, 9.

———. 1998b. TV Sports Lose Some of Their Power to Reach America's Men. *New York Times,* October 26, C1, 9.

Faure, J. M. 1996. Forging a French Fighting Spirit: The Nation, Sport, Violence, and War. In *Tribal Identities: Nationalism, Europe and Sport,* ed. Mangan, J. A., 75–93. London: Frank Cass.

Fausto-Sterling, A. 1997. How to Build a Man. In *Science and Homosexualities,* ed. V. A. Rosario, 219–225. New York: Routledge.

Feder, A. 1994a. Kiss Me, Skate. *Village Voice* 39, no. 27 (July 5): 140.

———. 1994b. Au Pair Boys. *Village Voice* 39, no. 25 (June 21): 156–157.

Federation of Gay Games. 1997. The Gay Games. http://www.gaygames.org/games.htm.

———. 1998. The Gay Games. http://www.gaygames.org/milesto.htm.

Feminist Majority Women in the Olympics. 1997. Women Shine in 1996 Olympics: A Look Back at Atlanta. http://www.feminist.org/other/olympic/news1/html.

Ferguson-Smith, M. A., and E. A. Ferris. 1991. Gender Verification in Sport: The Need for Change? *British Journal of Sports Medicine* 25: 17–20.

Ferguson-Smith, M. A., A. Carlson, A. de la Chappelle, A. Ehrhardt, E. Ferris, A. Lingqvist, M. Genel, and J. L. Simpson. 1992. Olympic Row over Sex Testing (Correspondence). *Nature* 355 (January 2): 10.

Ferris, E. A. 1992. Gender Verification Testing in Sport. *British Medical Bulletin* 48, no. 3: 683–697.

Festle, M. J. 1996. *Playing Nice: Politics and Apologies in Women's Sports.* New York: Columbia University Press.

Findling, J., and K. Pelle, eds. 1996. *Historical Dictionary of the Modern Olympic Movement.* Westport, Conn.: Greenwood Press.

Fitzgerald, M. 1997. A Dream Beginning: Sydney's First Pre-Olympic Festival Offers the Myth, Craft, and Artistry of Aboriginal Culture. *Time,* September 29, 39.

Fox, C. 1989. Decade of the "New Man" Is Here. *Financial Review* 21 (January): 46.

Fox, J. S. 1993. Gender Verification: What Purpose? What Price? *British Journal of Sport Medicine* 27, no. 3: 148–149.

Freedland, J. 1998. *Sydney Morning Herald,* January 16, 15. Reprinted from the *Guardian.*

Glickman, M. 1996. *The Fastest Kid on the Block.* Syracuse: Syracuse University Press.

Goksøyr, M., et al. 1994. *Winter Games Warm Traditions.* Lillehammer: ISHPES.

Goldman, R. Oral History Interviews with Marty Glickman, Milton Green, Herman Goldberg, Margaret [Bergmann] Lambert. U.S. Holocaust Memorial Museum, Washington, D.C.

Gordon, H. 1994. *Australia and the Olympic Games.* St Lucia: University of Queensland Press.

Gottlieb, M. 1972. The American Controversy over the Olympic Games. *American Jewish Historical Quarterly* 61: 181–213.

Guttmann, A. 1984. *The Games Must Go On: Avery Brundage and the Olympic Movement.* New York: Columbia University Press.

———. 1992. *The Olympics: A History of the Modern Games.* Urbana: University of Chicago Press.

———. 1994. *Games and Empires: Modern Sports and Cultural Imperialism.* New York: Columbia University Press.

Hamermesh, C. S., and J. E. Biddle. 1994. Beauty and the Labor Market. *American Economic Review* 84, no. 5: 1174–1194.

Handler, A. 1985. *From the Ghetto to the Games: Jewish Athletes in Hungary.* New York: Columbia University Press.

Harari, F. 1993. The New Face of Beauty. *The Australian,* June 18, 15.

Hargreaves, J. 1984. Women and the Olympic Phenomenon. In *Five Ring Circus: Money, Power, and Politics at the Olympic Games,* ed. A. Tomlinson and G. Whannel, 53–70. London: Pluto Press.

———. 1994. *Sporting Females: Critical Issues in the History and Sociology of Women's Sports.* London: Routledge.

———. 1997. Muscles, Metaphors, and Myths: Examining Women's Sporting Bodies. Inaugural lecture, May 6, Roehampton Institute, London.

Hart-Davis, D. 1986. *Hitler's Game.* New York: Harper and Row.

Haworth, K. 1998. Lawsuit Accuses U. of North Carolina Women's Soccer Coach of Sexual Harassment. *Chronicle of Higher Education,* August 27.

Hay, E. 1972. Sex Determination in Putative Female Athletes. *Journal of the American Medical Association* 221, no. 9: 998–999.

———. 1974. Femininity Tests at the Olympic Games. *Olympic Review* (March–April): 76–77, 119–123.

———. 1977. Considerations of Women's Sport. *Olympic Review* (Nov.–Dec.): 121–122, 684–688.

Hecq, N. 1998. *Maurice Blitz 1891–1975 en Gérard Blitz 1901–1978.* Leuven: Katholieke Universiteit Leuven.

Herek, G. M. 1992. The Social Context of Hate Crimes: Notes on Cultural Heterosexism. In *Hate Crimes: Confronting Violence against Lesbians and Gay Men,* ed. G. M. Herek and K. T. Berrill. Newbury Park: Sage.

Heywood, L. 1998a. *Bodymakers: A Cultural Anatomy of Women's Bodybuilding.* New Brunswick: Rutgers University Press.

———. 1998b. *Pretty Good for a Girl.* New York: Free Press.

Higgs, C. T., and K. H. Weiller. 1994. Gender Bias and the 1992 Summer Olympic Games: An Analysis of Television Coverage. *Journal of Sport and Social Issues* 18, no. 3: 234–246.

Hipkin, L. J. 1991. Gender Verification in Sport (Correspondence). *British Journal of Sports Medicine* 25, no. 3: 171.

Home Box Office. 1996. *The Journey of the African American Athlete.* Time Warner, Home Box Office Special Documentary. Includes Ed Temple, Curt Flood, Wyomia Tyus, Harry Edwards, Ralph Boston, and Tommie Smith.

Hood-Williams, J. 1995. Sexing the Athletes. *Sociology of Sport Journal* 12: 290–305.

Horrocks, R. 1995. *Male Myths and Icons: Masculinity in Popular Culture.* New York: St. Martin's Press.

House of Aboriginality. http://www.mq.edu.au/hoa/.

Howell, M. 1994. Comments on Swimming with the Big Boys. *Sporting Traditions: Journal of the Australian Society for Sports History* 11, no. 1: 31–35.

———. 1997. The History of Sydney's Bid for the 2000 Games. Unpublished internal report for Sydney Organising Committee for the Olympic Games.

Ingram, G. B., A. M. Bouthillette, and Y. Retter. 1997. Strategies for Reconstructing Queer Communities. In *Queers in Space: Communities/Public Places/Sites of Resistance,* ed. G. Ingram, A. M. Bouthillette, and Y. Retter. Seattle, Wash.: Bay Press.

International Olympic Academy. 1987. *Report of the Twenty-Seventh Session, 1st–16th July 1987, Ancient Olympia.* Lausanne: International Olympic Committee and the Hellenic Olympic Committee.

International Olympic Committee. 1933. *Bulletin du C.I.O.* September 8 (24), 9

International Olympic Committee. 1934. *Bulletin du C.I.O.* October 9 (26), 8.

Jacques, B. 1998. Desperate Bid to Fill Financial Hole. *Bulletin,* December 15, 22.

Janke, T. 1997. *Our Culture, Our Future.* Canberra: Australian Institute for Aboriginal and Torres Strait Islander Studies. http://www.icip.lawnet.com.au.index.html.

Jennings, A. 1996. *The "New" Lords of the Rings: Olympic Corruption and How to Buy Gold Medals.* London: Pocket Books.

Jobling, I. 1994. Proposals and Bids by Australian Cities to Host the Olympic Games. *Sporting Traditions: Journal of the Australian Society for Sports History* 11, no. 1: 37–56.

Johnson, V. 1996. *Copyrites—Aboriginal Art in the Age of Reproductive Technologies.* Sydney: National Indigenous Arts Advocacy Association.

Karbo, K., and G. Reece. 1997. *Big Girl in the Middle.* New York: Crown.

Kessler, S. J. 1998. *Lessons from the Intersexed.* New Brunswick: Rutgers University Press.

Kidd, B. 1978. Canadian Opposition to the 1936 Olympics in Germany. *Canadian Journal of History of Sport and Physical Education* 9, no. 2: 20–40.

———. 1980. The Popular Front and the 1936 Olympics. *Canadian Journal of History of Sport and Physical Education* 11, no. 1: 1–18.

———. 1994. Comments on Swimming with the Big Boys. *Sporting Traditions: Journal of the Australian Society for Sports History* 11, no. 1: 25–30.

Knight, M. 1997. Welcoming Speech. Festival of the Dreaming, Sydney, September 14.

Krane, V. 1999. 'We Can Be Athletic and Be Feminine,' But Do We Want To? Femininity, Heterosexuality, and Women's Sport. Paper delivered at the University of Michigan, February 15.

Krane, V., and L. Romont. 1997. Female Athletes' Motives and Experiences at the Gay Games. *Journal of Gay, Lesbian, and Bisexual Identities* 2, no. 2: 123–138.

Kratz, C. A. 1994. *Affecting Performance: Meaning, Movement, and Experience in Okiek Women's Initiation.* Washington, D.C.: Smithsonian Institution Press.

Kristensen, P., ed. 1966. *De Olympiske.* Copenhagen: Danmarks Idraets-Forbund.

Krüger, A. 1972. *Die Olympischen Spiele 1936 und die Weltmeinung.* Berlin: Bartels and Wernitz.

L'Illustration. 1924.

La Montagne. 1908–1931.

Labrecque, L. 1994. *Unity: A Celebration of Gay Games IV and Stonewall.* San Francisco, Calif.: Labrecque Publishing.

Langton, M. 1995. *Diversity, the Arts, and the Way We See Ourselves: Representations and Indigenous Images.* Paper presented at the Global Diversity Conference, Sydney, Australia.

Lattas, A. 1990. Aborigines and Contemporary Australian Nationalism: Primordiality and the Cultural Politics of Otherness. In *Writing Australian Culture,* ed. Marcus, J. Special issue of *Social Analysis,* 27.

Leder, J. 1996. *Grace and Glory: A Century of Women in the Olympics.* Washington, D.C.: Multi-Media Partners Ltd.; Chicago: Ill.: Triumph Books.

Lehmann, J. 1998. Votes for Sale: The Olympic Meddlers. *Weekend Australian,* December 19–20, 13.

———. 1999. Playing Non-Political Games. *Australian,* January 4, 11.

Lemon, B. 1997. Male Beauty. *Advocate* 738 (July 22): 30–32.

Leonard, D. 1998. What Happened to the Revolt of the Black Athlete? A Look Back Thirty Years Later: An Interview with Harry Edwards. *Color Lines* 1: 1.

Levine, P. 1992. *From Ellis Island to Ebbets Field.* New York: Oxford University Press.

Life. 1996. July, photographs by Joe McNally.

Ljungqvist, A., J. L. Simpson. 1992. Medical Examination for Health of All Athletes Replacing the Need for Gender Verification in International Sports: The International Amateur Athletic Federation (IAAF) (Plan). *Journal of the American Medical Association* 267, no. 6: 850–852.

Longman, J. How the Women Won. *New York Times Magazine,* June 23, 24–26.

Lopiano, D. 1996. Don't Touch That Dial. *Women's Sports and Fitness,* July–August, 42.

Louganis, G., and E. Marcus. 1996. *Breaking the Surface.* New York: Plume/Penguin.

Lubin, F. J. Letter to Allen Guttman. January 3, 1998.

Lucas, J. A. 1992. *Future of the Olympic Games.* Champaign, Ill.: Human Kinetics Publishers.

Lunn, A. 1913. *Ski-ing.* London: Nash.

Luther, C. Archive, Deutscher Ski Verband, Planegg, Germany.

MacAloon, J. J. 1981. *This Great Symbol.* Chicago, Ill.: University of Chicago Press.

Mahoney, J. T. 1935. *Germany Has Violated the Olympic Code.* N.p.

Mandell, R. D. 1971. *The Nazi Olympics.* New York: Macmillan.

Mandle, B. 1985. Origins. In *Australian Sport: A Profile,* ed. Department of Sport, Recreation, and Tourism, 2–11. Canberra: Australian Government Publishing Service.

Mangan, J. A. 1996. Duty unto Death: English Masculinity and Militarism in the Age of the New Imperialism. In *Tribal Identities: Nationalism, Europe, and Sport,* ed. J. A. Mangan. 10–38. London: Frank Cass.

McGeoch, R., and G. Korporaal. 1994. *The Bid: How Australia Won the 2000 Games.* Port Melbourne: Reed Books Australia.

McKay, J. 1991. *No Pain, No Gain? Sport and Australian Culture.* New York: Prentice Hall

———. 1994. Embodying the "New" Sporting Woman. *Hecate* 20, no. 1: 68–83.

———. 1997. *Managing Gender: Affirmative Action and Organizational Power in Australian, Canadian, and New Zealand Sport.* Albany: State University of New York Press.

McLean, I. 1998. *White Aborigines: Identity Politics in Australian Art.* Melbourne: Cambridge University Press.

Mellor, L. 1998. Olympic Gold Comes at a $51.8m Cost. *Advertiser,* December 15, 7.

Michaels, E. 1994. *Bad Aboriginal Art.* Sydney: Allen and Unwin.

Miller, D. 1992. *Olympic Revolution: The Olympic Biography of Juan Antonio Samaranch.* London: Pavilion.

Moore, K. L. 1968. The Sexual Identity of Athletes (Editorial). *Journal of the American Medical Association* 205: 163–164.

Moore, M., and M. Evans. 1999. Olympics Face $700m Blowout. *Age,* January 15, 3.

Morton, J. 1996. Aboriginality, Mabo, and the Republic: Indigenising Australia. In *In the Age of Mabo,* ed. B. Attwood. Sydney: Allen and Unwin.

Mosaic in X & Y. 1967. *Time* 90 (Sept. 29): 70.

Murphy, G. N.d. Laurie Lawrence's All-Time Top 10. Australian Swimming and Fitness. http://www.magna.com.au/~iphala/sf_sweat.htm.

Murray, B. 1987. The French Workers' Sports Movement and the Victory of the Popular Front in 1936. *International Journal of the History of Sport* 4, no. 2: 203–230.

———. 1992. Berlin in 1936. *International Journal of the History of Sport* 9, no. 1: 29–49.

Nansen, F. 1890. *Paa Ski over Grønland*. Kristiania: Aschehoug.

Nationwide Realty National Convention. 1996. http://www.telstra.com.au/pres/event/nationw/html/howe/hilites/speakers/lawrence.html.

Nelson, M. B. 1998. *Embracing Victory: Life Lessons in Competition and Compassion*. New York: William Morrow.

———. 1994. *The Stonger Women Get, the More Men Love Football: Sexism and the American Culture of Sport*. New York, Avon.

New Scientist. 1996. December 7, 15.

New York Post. 1934. September 26.

Newsplanet Staff and J. McMullen. 1998. More Than Play at Gay Games. Newsplanet archive, August 4. http://www.planetout.com/newsplanet/article.html?1998/08/04/1.

Nixon, S. 1996. *Hard Looks: Masculinities, Spectatorship, and Contemporary Consumption*. New York: St. Martin's Press.

Norges Skiforbund. 1914, 1921. *Aarsberetning*.

Northrup, A. 1994. Athletics and Activism. *Out,* June.

O'Connor, J. J. 1997. Coming Out Party: The Closet Opens, Finally. *New York Times,* April 30, C-18.

O'Donoghue, L. 1998. Qtd. in O'Donoghue Holds Boycott Card, by D. Jopson. *Sydney Morning Herald,* September 25. http://www.smh.com.a . . . content/sydney2000/9809/oly20.html.

Official Site of the Sydney 2000 Olympic Games. 1998. 1997—The Festival of the Dreaming. *Sydney Organising Committee for the Olympic Games*. http://www.sydney.olympic.org/culture/dreaming.html.

Olympic Museum, Archives, Lausanne, Switzerland.

Osborne, R. 1995. Crime and the Media: From Media Studies to Postmodernism. In *Crime and the Media: The Postmodern Spectacle,* ed. D. Kidd-Hewitt and R. Osborne, 25–48. London: Pluto.

Outside Magazine. The Übergirl Cometh (fall 1996).

Page, S. 1997. Welcoming Speech. Festival of the Dreaming, Sydney, September 14.

Pallière, J. 1991. Les premiers jeux d'hiver de 1924: la grande bataille de Chamonix, *L'Histoire en Savoie* 103 (September): 1–80.

Paraschak, V. 1995. Aboriginal Inclusiveness in Canadian Sporting Culture: An Image without Substance? *Sport as Symbol, Symbols in Sport: Proceedings of the 3rd ISHPES Congress, Cape Town, South Africa,* 347–356.

Parliament of the Commonwealth of Australia. House of Representatives Standing Committee on Finance and Public Administration. 1989. *Going for Gold. The First Report into Sports Funding and Administration*. Canberra: Australian Government Publishing Service.

Paul, J. P., R. B. Hays, and T. J. Coates. 1995. The Impact of the HIV Epidemic on U.S. Gay Male Communities. In *Lesbian, Gay, and Bisexual Identities over the Lifetime: Psychological Perspectives,* ed. A. R. D'Augelli and C. J. Patterson, 347–397. New York: Oxford.

Peters, R. 1976. *Television Coverage of Sport*. Birmingham: Centre for Contemporary Cultural Studies.

Phillips, E. 1996. *The VIII Olympiad: Paris 1924, St. Moritz 1928*. Los Angeles: World Sport Research and Publications; New York: Firefly Books Ltd.

Phillips, S. 1998. Australian Women at the Olympics. Paper prepared for the Women and Sport Unit of the Australian Sports Commission.

Postel, B., J. Silver, and R. Silver. 1965. *Encyclopaedia of Jews in Sports.* New York: Bloch.

Pronger, B. 1990. *The Arena of Masculinity: Sports, Homosexuality, and the Meaning of Sex.* New York: St. Martin's Press.

Quindlen, A. 1996. And Now, Babe Feminism. In *Bad Girls/Good Girls: Women, Sex, and Power in the '90s,* ed. N. B. Maglin and D. Perry. New Brunswick: Rutgers University Press.

Rawlings, S. 1993. Luring the Big Boys. *B & T* 43 (February 12, 1923): 18–19.

Reece, G. 1997. Grace in Your Face. *Condé Nast Sports for Women,* December, 78.

Remnick, D. 1996. Inside-Out Olympics. *New Yorker* (August 5): 26–28.

———. 1998. American Hunger. *New Yorker,* October 12, 67.

Riess, S. A., ed. 1998. Introduction. *Sports and the American Jew.* Syracuse: Syracuse University Press.

Roberts, R. 1997. Welcome Speech. Festival of the Dreaming, Sydney, September 14.

———. 1998. Qtd. in Rhoda Roberts: Bridging a Cultural Gap, by K. Bourke. *Sydney Morning Herald,* March 14. http://www.smh.com.au/daily/conte . . . es/features/980314/features8.html.

Rowe, D. 1997. Big Defence: Sport and Hegemonic Masculinity. In *Gender, Sport, and Leisure: Continuities and Challenges,* ed. A. Tomlinson, 123–133. Aachen: Meyer and Meyer Verlag.

Rowe, D., and G. Lawrence. 1986. Saluting the State: Nationalism and the Olympics. In *Power Play: The Commercialisation of Australian Sport/Essays in the Sociology of Australian Sport,* ed. G. Lawrence and D. Rowe, 196–203. Sydney: Hale & Iremonger.

Royal Commission into Aboriginal Deaths in Custody. 1991. Canberra: Australian Government Publication Service.

Ryan, A. J. 1976. Sex and the Singles Player. *Physician and Sportsmedicine* 4 (October): 39–41.

Sargent, S. L., D. Zillman, and J. B. Weaver III. 1998. The Gender Gap in the Enjoyment of Televised Sports. *Journal of Sport and Social Issues* 22, no. 1: 46–64.

Segrave, J. O., and D. Chu, eds. 1988. *The Olympic Games in Transition.* Champaign, Ill.: Human Kinetics Books.

Shapiro, E. S. 1985. The World Labor Athletic Carnival of 1936. *American Jewish History* 74: 255–277.

Simpson, J., A. Ljungqvist, et al. 1993. In Reply (to Bernard Dingeon). *Journal of the American Medical Association* 269, no. 3: 357–358.

Ski Club Todtnau, Archives, Todtnau, Germany.

Smith, B. 1989. *European Vision and the South Pacific.* Sydney: Oxford University Press Australia.

Smith, W. 1996. Jealous Rivals Ruining Smith's Honeymoon. *Courier Mail,* July 24, 52.

Smith, Y. 1997. Socio-Historical Outcomes of African American Women in Sport. Paper presented at the North American Society for the Sociology of Sport, Toronto, November 6.

Solomon, A. 1994. Eight Days of Glory. *Village Voice* 39, no. 27 (July 5): 140.

Sontag, S. 1983. Fascinating Fascism. In *Under the Sign of Saturn,* 79–80. London: Writers and Readers.

Spence, S. N.d. http://www.allaustralian.com/stuartspence/duncanar.html.

Sport from the Settee. *Spectrum* 18 (summer 1995): 24.

Stancill, J. 1998. A Coach's Winning Ways. *News Observer,* November 22.

Stoddart, B. 1986. *Saturday Afternoon Fever: Sport in Australian Culture.* North Ryde, NSW: Angus and Robertson.

Swatling, D. 1998. Already a Winner. *Daily Friendship,* August 4, 4, 15.

Sydney Organizing Committee for the Olympic Games. 1993. Olympic Arts Festivals (Fact Sheets). Sydney: SOCOG.

Sydney Organizing Committee for the Olympic Games Web Site. 1996. Cultural Olympiad Facts, July. http://www.sydney.olympic.org/facts/atsi.htm.

Symer, D. S. 1996. Exclusion, Boycott, and Participation: Jewish Athletes and the 1936 Olympics. Unpublished conference paper, North American Society for Sport History.

Tachezy, R. 1969. Pseudohermaphroditism and Physical Efficiency. *Journal of Sports Medicine* 9: 119–122.

Tatz, C. 1993–94. Sydney 2000: The Games People Play. *Current Affairs Bulletin* (December–January): 7.

———. 1987. *Aborigines in Sport*. Adelaide: Australian Society for Sports History.

Teen People. 1998. October, 40.

This Is What They Said. 1998. *Inside Sport* (Australia) 82 (October): 7, 18.

Thorpe, G. F. 1981. The Thorpe Family: From Wisconsin to Indian Territory, Parts I and II. *Chronicles of Oklahoma*, 59.

———. 1996. Biography on Jim Thorpe. In *Encyclopedia of North American Indians*, ed. F. E. Hoxie, 627–629. New York: Houghton Mifflin.

Times (London). 1909–1913.

Tomlinson, A., and I. Yorganci. 1997. Male Coach/Female Athlete Relations: Gender and Power Relations in Competitive Sport. *Journal of Sport and Social Issues* 21, no. 2: 134–155.

Trask, H. 1993. Lovely Hula Hands: Corporate Tourism and the Prostitution of Hawaiian Culture. In *From a Native Daughter: Colonialism and Sovereignty in Hawai'i*, 179–200. Monroe: Common Courage Press.

Trujillo, N. 1991. Hegemonic Masculinity on the Mound: Media Representations of Nolan Ryan and American Sports Culture. *Critical Studies in Mass Communication*, 8.

Tulloch, J., D. Lupton, W. Blood, M. Tulloch, C. Jennett, and M. Enders, eds. 1998. *Fear of Crime*. 2 vols. Canberra: National Campaign against Violence and Crime Unit, Attorney General's Department.

Turnbull, A. 1988. Women Enough for the Games. *New Scientist,* September 15.

Uncle Donald's Castro Street. 1998. *A Brief History of the Gay Games*. http://www.backdoor.com/CASTRO/gaygames.html.

USA Today. 1998.

van Dam, R. 1998. The Proof That I Live. *Daily Friendship,* August 5, 4, 1.

van de Ven, A. 1993. Images of the Fifties: Design and Advertising. In *The Australian Dream: Design of the Fifties,* ed. J. O'Callaghan, 28–41. Sydney: Powerhouse Publishing.

Voss, N., and P. van Yperen. 1998. *Gay Games and Social Issues*. http://www.gaygames.nl/info/us/social.html.

Waddell, T. 1982. Welcome Speech, Gay Games I. August 28. http://www.backdoor.com/CASTRO/gaygamesI.html2.

———. 1986. Speech at Closing Ceremonies, Gay Games II. San Francisco. August 17.

Waddell, T., and D. Schaap. 1996. *Gay Olympian: Life and Death of Dr. Tom Waddell*. New York: Alfred A. Knopf.

Wallechinsky, D. 1996a. *The Complete Book of the Summer Olympics*. Boston: Little Brown.

———. 1996b. Vaults, Leaps, and Dashes: Women's Sports Go the Distance. *New York Times Magazine,* June 23, 47.

Ward, R. B. 1958. *The Australian Legend*. Oxford: Oxford University Press.

Wells, M. 1994. Slimmer Dooner Revs up McCann. *Advertising Age* 65, no. 43 (October 10): 50.

Wenner, L. A., and W. Gantz. 1998. Watching Sports on Television: Audience Experience, Gender, Fanship, and Marriage. In *Mediasport*, ed. L. A. Wenner, 233–251. London: Routledge.

Wheeler, R. 1979. *Jim Thorpe, World's Greatest Athlete*. Norman: University of Oklahoma Press (published in 1974 under the title *Pathway to Glory*).

White, R. 1993. The Shock of Affluence: The Fifties in Australia. In *The Australian Dream: Design of the Fifties*, ed. J. O'Callaghan, 11–25. Sydney: Powerhouse Publishing.

Who Goes There? 1967. *Newsweek* 70 (Sept. 25): 97.

Wiggins, D. K. 1997. *Glory Bound*. Syracuse: Syracuse University Press.

Wilson, J. D. 1992. Sex Testing in International Athletics: A Small Step Forward. *Journal of the American Medical Association* 267, no. 6: 853.

Wintersportmuseum, Mürzzuschlag, Austria.

Women in the Olympics. Celebrating 96 Years of Women in the Olympics. http://www.feminist.org/other/olympic/news1/html.

Wynne, B. 1996. May the Sheep Safely Graze? A Reflexive View of the Expert/Lay Knowledge Divide. In *Risk, Environment and Modernity*, ed. S. Lash, B. Szerszynski, and B. Wynne, 44–83. London: Sage.

Yanner, M. 1998. Qtd. in Black Ban Called for Olympics, by M. Robbins. *Australian*, December 1.

Young, A. 1996. In the Frame: Crime and the Limits of Representation. *Australian and New Zealand Journal of Criminology* 29, no. 2: 99–111.

Zdarsky Archives, Lilienfeld, Austria.

ABOUT THE CONTRIBUTORS

E. JOHN B. ALLEN is an emeritus professor of history at Plymouth State College, Plymouth, New Hampshire, and historian for the New England Ski Museum, Franconia, New Hampshire. He is the author of *From Skisport to Skiing: One Hundred Years of an American Sport, 1840–1940* and two other histories of ski teaching and skiing in New England as well as numerous articles in state, national, and international journals.

CHERYL L. COLE is associate professor of kinesiology, sociology, and women's studies at the University of Illinois at Urbana-Champaign. She is coeditor of *Women, Sport, and Culture* and *Exercising Power: The Making and Remaking of the Body*. She is currently completing a book on national popular culture and the construction of embodied deviance.

TRACE A. DeMEYER has spent most of the past five years writing for *News from Indian Country*, a national independent Native-owned newspaper, and has been editor of the regional newspaper *Ojibwe Akiing*, based on the Lac Courte Oreilles Reservation in Wisconsin. She holds a Bachelor of Fine Arts degree in theater from the University of Wisconsin-Superior. An award-winning writer and a member of the Native American Journalists Association, she received a NAJA award in the category of best news story for her interview with Leonard Peltier in 1998.

GEORGE EISEN, a professor of sociology and history at Amherst College, has degrees from universities in Hungary, Israel, and the United States. He is the recipient of many national and international awards for his scholarship, among them, Honorary Fellow of the European Committee for Sport History, 1997. He has authored or edited five books, over fifty articles, and numerous book reviews in refereed journals, including the prize-winning *Children and Play in Holocaust and Ethnicity* and *Sport in North American History and Culture* (edited with David K. Wiggins). His most recent publication is "Jewish History and the Ideology of Modern Sports," which will appear in the fall 1998 issue of the *Journal of Sport History*.

LYNN EMBREY is a senior lecturer in the School of Biomedical and Sports Science at Edith Cowan University, Western Australia. Her teaching responsibilities include coaching, sports science applications, and spot systems delivery as well as overseeing fieldwork for the sports science students. Lynn's research concentrates on gender and sports, and she has published on the sport of softball with special emphasis on its history in Australia. Embrey was national president of the Australian Council for Health, Physical Education, and Recreation and was the inaugural president of the Women's Sport Foundation of Western Australia.

DARREN J. GODWELL is a research fellow with the Centre for Indigenous Natural and Cultural Resource Management in Australia. Previously he was the national manager for a Royal Commission into Aboriginal Deaths in Custody initiative and director of the Indigenous Community Foundation. He also worked at the Australian Sports Commission and was manager of indigenous sport as an adviser and research officer in the Northern Territory Legislative Assembly. He has written a master's thesis on the experiences of Aboriginal rugby league players in professional football. In 1998, Godwell was made a member of the Australian Institute of Aboriginal and Torres Strait Islander Studies.

ALLEN GUTTMANN, who teaches at Amherst College, has written and/or translated a dozen books on the history of sports, two of which are devoted to Olympic history. Among his more recent titles are *Games and Empires* and *The Erotic in Sports*. He is working on a history of Japanese sports and is an editor of the forthcoming *International Encyclopedia of Women's Sports*.

C. KEITH HARRISON is a former student athlete and coach and teaches race relations and sports and social sports history at the University of Michigan. Harrison Harrison has published several articles and chapters on media images of African American athletes and is an assistant professor of kinesiology in the department of sports management and communication. He is also founder and director of the Paul Robeson Research Center for Academic and Athletic Prowess.

LESLIE HEYWOOD is associate professor of English and cultural studies at SUNY, Binghamton. She is the author of *Bodymakers: A Cultural Anatomy of Women's Bodybuilding* and the sports memoir *Pretty Good for a Girl*. Heywood is also a member of the Women's Sports Foundation's Advisory Board, a competitive power lifter, and a Special Olympics coach.

IAN JOBLING is an associate professor in sport and Olympic history in the department of human movement studies and director of the Centre for Physical Activity and Sport Education at the University of Queensland, Brisbane, Australia. He is currently a member of the International Steering Committee for the World Olympic Education Project being undertaken by the Greece-based Foundation of Olympic and Sport Education (FOSE), which has links with UNESCO and the IOC. Dr. Jobling was an inaugural member of the editorial review board of *Olympika: The International Journal of Olympic Studies,* a former president of the Australian Society for Sports History, and a current member of the editorial review board of that society's journal, *Sporting Traditions.* He is also the honorary regional director for Australia/Oceania of the International Council for Sports Science and Physical Education (ISP). One of the authors of *The Oxford Companion to Australian Sport* (now in its third edition), he is currently managing editor of the forthcoming *Oxford Companion to Australia and the Olympic Games.*

HEATHER KESTNER graduated from Amherst College, where she did research on Jews at the 1936 Olympics. Now she has begun graduate studies at the London School of Economics.

VIKKI KRANE is an associate professor in the School of Human Movement, Sport, and Leisure Studies at Bowling Green State University, Ohio. As a sports psychologist, she conducts research on the Gay Games, lesbians in sports, and issues related to body image and female athletes. She is a member of the editorial boards of the *Journal of Applied Sport Psychology* and the *Sport Psychologist.*

DONNA LOPIANO is currently executive director of the Women's Sports Foundation. The foundation, a national nonprofit educational organization, is among the top five grant-giving public women's funds in the United States, distributing over $1 million in grants to girls' and women's sports programs each year. She received her bachelor's degree from Southern Connecticut State University and her master's and doctoral degrees from the University of Southern California. She has been a college coach of men's and women's volleyball, and women's basketball and softball. As an athlete, Lopiano participated in twenty-six national championships in four sports and was a nine-time All-American at four different positions in softball, a sport in which she played on six national championship teams.

LISA MEEKISON is a doctoral candidate at the Institute of Social and Cultural Anthropology at Oxford University. She holds a Commonwealth Scholarship and a Social Sciences and Humanities Research Council of Canada doctoral fellowship. She completed her B.A. in drama and her M.A. in anthropology at the University of Alberta. She has worked as a consultant anthropologist and also in professional theater, cofounding The Free Will Players (now the River City Shakespeare Festival) in Edmonton, Alberta. She has written on the Sydney Olympics, the Bangarra Dance Theatre, and performance and ecological restoration; she also writes fiction.

TOBY MILLER teaches cinema studies at New York University. His books include *The Well-Tempered Self, Contemporary Australian Television* (with S. Cunningham), *The Avengers, Technologies of Truth,* and *Popular Culture and Everyday Life* (with A. McHoul), and he has coedited *SportCult* (with R. Martin), *Film and Theory: An Anthology* (with R. Stam), and *A Companion to Film Theory* (with R. Stam). He edits the *Journal of Sport and Social Issues* and coedits *Social Text.*

ANDREA MITCHELL is a postgraduate student in the department of English at the University of Queensland, Australia. Her thesis on the 1996 Olympic Games examines aspects of the media coverage in Britain and Australia. She teaches media studies part-time at Queensland University of Technology and the University of Queensland. An expatriate New Zealander, she is interested in the prominence placed on national sports achievements in Australasia, and the mediated connections between such success and national identity.

CYNTHIA NADALIN competed as a canoeist in the 1960 Rome Olympics. Two years later she began her tertiary level education, first at Los Angeles City College and then at Carleton University in Ottawa. She returned to Australia to complete her degree in Melbourne and worked as a teacher for many years. She is presently completing a master's degree in women's studies at La Trobe University in Melbourne. Nadalin is involved in political, community, and feminist activities. She remains deeply committed to the reform of elite sport in Australia and the Olympic movement itself.

KAY SCHAFFER is associate professor in the department of social inquiry at the University of Adelaide where she teaches in the areas of gender studies, cultural studies, and postcoloniality. She is the author of several books, including *Women and the Bush* (Cambridge, 1988) and *In the Wake of First Contact: The Eliza Fraser Stories* (Cambridge, 1995). Her latest publications include the edited anthologies *Indigenous Australian Voices: A Reader* (with Jennifer Sabbioni and Sidonie Smith), *Constructions of Colonialism* (with Ian McNiven and Lynette Russell). Kay Schaffer is also the president of the Cultural Studies Association of Australia.

SIDONIE SMITH is professor of English and women's studies and director of women's studies at the University of Michigan. Her books include *Subjectivity, Identity, and the Body: Women's Autobiographical Practices in the Twentieth Century; A Poetics of Women's Autobiography: Marginality and the Fictions of Self-Representation;* and *Where I'm Bound: Patterns of Slavery and Freedom in Black American Autobiography.* She has coedited the following volumes: *Women, Autobiography, Theory: A Reader* (with Julia Watson); *Indigenous Australian Voices: A Reader* (with Jennifer Sabbioni and Kay Schaffer); *Writing New Identities: Gender, Nation, and Immigration in Contemporary Europe* (with Gisela Brinker-Gabler); *Getting a Life: Everyday Uses of Autobiography* (with Julia Watson); and *De/Colonizing the Subject: Gender and the Politics of Women's Autobiography* (with Julia Watson). She has also written numerous essays in collections and journals. Her book on women's travel narratives, *Women on the Move: Twentieth-Century Travel Narratives and Technologies of Motion,* is forthcoming.

ALAN TOMLINSON is professor of sports and leisure studies, in sports and leisure cultures, Chelsea School Research Centre, University of Brighton, United Kingdom. He graduated in English and sociology for his B.A. at the University of Kent and studied at the University of Sussex for his master's and Ph.D. degrees in sociological studies. He is coeditor of *Five-Ring Circus: Money, Power and Politics at the Olympic*

Games; Off the Ball: The Football World Cup; Sport, Leisure and Social Relations; and *Hosts and Champions: Soccer Cultures, National Identities and the USA World Cup.* He edited *Consumption, Identity, and Style: Marketing, Meanings, and the Packaging of Pleasure.* With John Sugden, he coauthored *FIFA and the Contest for World Football—Who Rules the Peoples' Game?* He coauthored (with John Horne and Garry Whannel) *Understanding Sport: An Introduction to the Sociological and Cultural Analysis of Sport.* In 1999 he will publish *The Game's Up: Essays in the Cultural Analysis of Sport, Leisure, and Popular Culture* and *Sport and Leisure Cultures: Local, National, and Global Dimensions;* and, with John Sugden, *Great Balls of Fire: How Big Money Is Hijacking World Football.* Professor Tomlinson is the editor of the *International Review for the Sociology of Sport (2000–2004).*

JOHN TULLOCH is professor of media communication at Cardiff University, Wales. Previously he was professor of cultural studies and director of the Centre for Cultural Risk Research at Charles Sturt University, New South Wales, Australia. He is the author of twelve books in the areas of film, television, and theater analysis; and in recent years he has been involved in several projects in the area of risk and the media. A recent major consultancy on fear of crime in Australia is related to the chapter published here. Other aspects of risk publication include his book (with Deborah Lupton), *Television, AIDS, and Risk,* and his current Australian Research Council Large Grant (with Deborah Lupton), "A Risk Society? Australian Perceptions and Negotiations of Risk." He is also interested in the circulation of meaning via a wide variety of circuits of communication ranging from soap opera to Shakespeare and Chekhov, from everyday talk to mass-mediated forms.

JENNIFER J. WALDRON is a doctoral student in the department of kinesiology at Michigan State University. She received her B.A. in exercise science from the University of St. Thomas in St. Paul, Minnesota, and her M.Ed. in developmental kinesiology from Bowling Green State University, Ohio. Her research interests include the motivation of athletes, body image concerns in female athletes, and adolescents in sport.

HELEN YEATES teaches film, media, and feminist studies at Queensland University of Technology, Australia, where she is deputy director of the Centre for Media Policy and Practice and deputy head of the School of Media and Journalism. She has researched and published most recently in the areas of masculinities, sports, and the media; women, crime, and the media; the discourse of rape in film; Australian women filmmakers authoring the masculine; and sleuthing the aging masculine in the crime genre.

INDEX

    Olympics and, 52–53
American Olympic Committee, 1936
    Olympics and, 53
Amstutz, Walter, 81
androgyny, of swimming, 93–95
Anti-Defamation League, 53
Antill, John, 254
Apartheid, pressure against, 6
archery, women's, 10–11
Armstrong, Duncan, 94–95, 98
Ashe, Arthur, at Wimbledon, 66
Ashford, Evelyn, 68
Askew, Patricia Gladys, 48
Association for Intercollegiate Athletics
    for Women, 100
Association of National Olympic
    Committees, 265
Athens, 1896 Olympics in, 2
Athletes (*see also* Black athletes; Female
    athletes; Jewish athletes): afterlives of,
    221–223; commodification of, 95–98;
    diversity of, 9; in-fighting by, 22
Athleticism: female, 11; male, 8–14
Athletics: elite, 8–14 (*see also* Elite sports)
Atlanta: Olympics in, 13, 99–116, 172,
    175–178, 278; terrorist bombing at,
    225–226, 228, 236
ATSIC (*see* Aboriginal and Torres Strait
    Islander Commission)
Australia: code of silence in, 23–26;
    colonization of, 253–254; drug
    enhancement and, 211–212; indigenous
    people of, 7–8; Jewish athletes in, 57;
    kayaking and, 19–37; libel law in, 25;
    masculinity in, 92–93; medals of,
    273–274, 273*t*, 278–279, 281*t*; men's
    Olympic performances, 92; men's
    swimming and, 94; at Montreal
    Olympics, 277–278; nationalism and
    sports in, 272–281; Olympic record of,
    276–281, 277*t*, 281*t*; Olympic Team
    funding in, 284–285; political issues in,
    7; quarantine rules in, 260, 266; racial
    politics in, 220 (*see also* Aborigines);
    sport emphasis of, 5; sports funding in,
    281–283; sports stars in, 93; swimming
    medals of, 278–279; women's Olympic
    performances, 93
Australian Institute of Sports, 26
Australian Olympic Committee, 14;
    athlete selection by, 25; indigenous
    people excluded from, 14, 247
Australian Olympic Federation, 259;
    funding policy and, 21

Australian teams, weight-lifting and,
    24–25
Austria, sport emphasis of, 5
Awakening Ceremony, 182–189, 183*f*
    (*see also* Festival of the Dreaming);
    dancing in, 185–186, 191; exploitation
    of, 194; indigenous and nonindigenous
    agendas in, 182–183; purpose of,
    186–187; sociopolitical/corporate
    agendas and, 188–189

Baillet-Latour, Henri, 52, 53
Balck, Viktor, 74, 76
Balter, Mildred, 59
Balter, Sam, 59
Bangarra Dance Theatre, 185, 195n2, 248
Barbeliuk, Anne, 267
Barcelona, Olympics in, 9, 170–172, 264
Barr, Murray L., 143–144
Barr body procedure, 144
Baseball: free agency in, 66, 68; integra-
    tion of, 66; Thorpe's career in, 45–46
Bathurst, New South Wales, crime study
    in, 226–229
Batten, Kim, 99
Batty, Philip, 248
Beaurepaire, Frank, 258–259, 276, 277*t*
Bellear, Sol, 245
Bender, Jules, 56
Bennelong, 187; history of, 193
Bennelong Point, 193
Bennett, Harry, 47
Bergmann, Gretel, 55, 62
Berlin: 1916 Olympics in, 4, 76; 1936
    Olympics in, 9, 51–62, 174, 179
Bertram, Russ, 101
Black athletes: and 1968 boycott, 64–65;
    at 1936 Olympics, 9, 65–66; politics of,
    71
Black Panther Party, 66
Black Power Movement, 1968 Olympics
    and, 9
Black women athletes: exclusion of,
    66–67; stereotypes of, 67–68
Black Women's Sports Foundation, 68
Blair, Tim, 206
Blencowe, Tanya, 269
Blitz, Gerard, 58, 62
Bloomfield, John, 282
Blum, Léon, 55
bobsledding, Jamaican, 10
body(ies): celebrity, 222–223; commodifi-
    cation of, 95; diverse styles of, 9;
    female, 10–11; "lesbian," 11; normative
    heterosexual, 9

identity politics, of Aborigines, 245
indigenous culture, Festival of the
  Dreaming and, 190
indigenous people (*see also* Aborigines;
  Torres Strait Islanders): in Australia, 7;
  exploitation of, 14; stereotypes of, 250
individualism, in advertising campaigns,
  110–111
International Amateur Athletic
  Federation: gender verification and,
  134, 138–143; sex-testing by, 129
International Athletic Foundation, Work
  Group on Gender Verification of, 134,
  140–143
International Canoe Federation, rules of,
  33
International Federation of Skiing, 81–84
International Olympic Committee: art
  competitions and, 189; and control of
  drugs and gender verification, 134;
  controversy over 1936 Olympics,
  51–53; drug testing and, 199; gender
  verification and, 143–144 (*see also*
  Gender verification) ; host selection
  and, 216–217; medals tables and,
  279–280; skiing approved by, 76;
  Summer Olympic Games and, 260;
  Sydney Bid and, 266–268, 269–271;
  Winter Olympics and, 77, 82; women
  and, 91, 100; women's lobbying of, 11
International Skating Union, 154
International Ski Commission, 79
International Swimming Federation
  (*see* Fédération Internationale de
  Natation Amateur)
Internet, influence on women's sports,
  123–124
intersexual movement, 139
intersexuals: determining identity of, 145;
  eligibility of, 141–142
Ireland, drug enhancement by, 207–210
Israelis: kidnapping and murder of, 3, 15,
  224; at Munich Olympics, 225–226
Italy, medals at Atlanta Olympics, 281*t*

Jackson, Marjorie, 280
Jackson-Harmsworth polar expedition,
  73*f*
Jackson-Nelson, Marjorie, 253
Jacob, Mozes, 61
Jamaica, bobsledders from, 10
James, Clive, 267
Japan, 1948 Olympics and, 5
Japanese, racism against, 22–23, 34–37
Japanese Olympic Committee, 35

Jarlsberg, Wedel von, 74
Jewish athletes, 51–62; at 1936 Olympics,
  15, 53–60, 65; at 1980 Olympics, 220;
  dilemmas of, 55–56; Dutch, 61;
  exclusion from private clubs, 54;
  German exclusion of, 51; in Germany,
  55–56; in Hungary, 57, 61; killed
  during Holocaust, 60–62; restrictions
  on, 52; in U. S., 56–57, 58–60
Jewish Labor Committee, 54
Jim Thorpe Foundation, 40
Jobling, Ian, 2
John, Elton, 170
Johnson, Ben, 70, 206–210, 211
Johnson, Jimmie, 44
Johnson, Lyndon, 126
Johnson, Michael, 99, 101
Jordan, Michael, 70
Joyner, Florence Griffith, 11–12, 68, 218
Joyner-Kersee, Jackie, 68, 99, 101, 102
Julie, narrative of, 234–237
Junior Olympics, Thorpe's support of, 48
justice, women's sports and, 125

Kabos, Endre, 57, 61
Kantor, Roman, 58, 61
Karpati, Karoly, 57
kayaking: at 1960 Olympics, 7; women's,
  19–37
Keating, Anita, 269, 275
Keating, Frank, 49
Keating, Paul, 2, 13, 269, 275, 285
Kelly, Gene, 173
Kelly, Ros, 283
Kennedy, Bobby, 68
Kenya, sport emphasis of, 5
Keough, Donald R., 175
Kerrigan, Nancy, 3
Kestner, Heather, 6
Kiernan, Ian, 266
Kikila, Abebe, 3
King, Billie Jean, 125
King, Martin Luther, Jr., 68, 126, 177
Kirby, Gustavus T., 39, 52
Klammer, Hans, 3
Kleerekoper, Gerrit, 61
Klim, Michael, 197–198
Klobukowska, Ewa, 130*f*, 132*f*, 139;
  chromosomal screening of, 129–134;
  medals revoked, 129, 131
Knacke-Sommer, Christiane, 204, 205
Knight, Gladys, 178
Knight, Michael, 182, 186–187, 191, 194,
  196n7, 253
Konrads, John, 276, 277*t*